OPHB 93
PB= 60.80
B.O.D.

30 -
ES

Logic and Society

Logic and Society

Contradictions and Possible Worlds

Jon Elster
University of Oslo

JOHN WILEY & SONS
Chichester · New York · Brisbane · Toronto

Copyright © 1978, by John Wiley & Sons, Ltd.

Library of Congress Cataloging in Publication Data:

Elster, Jon, 1940-
  Logic and society.

  Includes bibliographical references and index.
  1. Social sciences—Methodology. 2. Economic
history. 3. Logic. I. Title.
H61.E43   300′.1′8   77-9550

ISBN 0 471 99549 5

Photosetting by Thomson Press (India) Ltd., New Delhi,
and printed in Great Britain by the Pitman Press Ltd., Bath

ACKNOWLEDGEMENTS

A number of friends and colleagues, over a number of years, have contributed to the ideas found in this book. First of all I would like to thank Raymond Aron, who taught me that sociology and economics are historical disciplines, and Per Schreiner and Dagfinn Føllesdal who conveyed to me, by example and by criticism, what intellectual honesty means and requires. I have also benefited from numerous discussions with Hans Fredrik Dahl, Gudmund Hernes, Knut Midgaard, and Francis Sejersted. Draft manuscripts to the present work were read by the following: Brian Barry, Gudmund Hernes, and Arthur Stinchcombe read the whole book and found the time to give me their detailed written comments; without their help the book would have been even more poorly organized and crammed with even more obscure digressions than is the case as it stands. Special thanks are due to Brian Barry for encouraging me to start work on a book-length manuscript in the first place. Amélie Rorty and Ludwig Siep read and commented upon Chapter 4; Raymond Boudon and Michael Taylor gave me their opinions of Chapter 5; and Dagfinn Føllesdal saved me from some nasty errors in Chapter 6. I have also had the invaluable help of Aanund Hylland, who pointed out a number of conceptual and mathematical errors in Chapters 1, 2, and 5. His positive contributions are acknowledged in the appropriate places.

J. E.

CONTENTS

viii

INTRODUCTION: LOGIC AND SOCIETY

> I dwell in Possibility—
> A fairer House than Prose—
> More numerous of Windows —
> Superior—for Doors—
> *Emily Dickinson*

Relations, numbers, probabilities, conflict, choice: this is the stuff societies are made of, this is what the social sciences are all about. In this book I try to bring out the abstract structure of these concepts by translating them into the more austere and more transparent language of formal logic. A brief outline of logical theory will be given in Chapter 1. In this introduction I shall not use this formal language, but rather try to give an intuitive motivation for what will be felt by some, perhaps, to be a rather strange endeavour. I do, indeed, stake out rather stronger claims for logical theory than what is usually done. Everyone will agree, I think, that logical analysis is a useful tool in constructing axiomatic theories, be it in the formal, the natural, or the social sciences. I want to take a further step, from the formal to the substantive level of theorizing.[1] I want to argue that logical theory can be applied not only in the formalization of knowledge already obtained by other means, but that logic can enter in the creative and constructive phase of scientific work. To take but one example which is explored in Chapters 4 and 5 below: most philosophers of science would argue that the notion of a *contradiction* has its place at the meta-level, that is, in the analysis of the logical form of scientific theories. I think it is possible to talk unambiguously about *real* contradictions, i.e. mental or social phenomena that—in a sense to be specified later—can be linked to the logical notion of a contradiction.

My general argument for regarding the language of logical theory as a vehicle for scientific research is the following. Science, in general, proceeds by way of abstraction, by *throwing away information* in order to focus upon some general feature of the object under study. In order to explain economic man and his behaviour in the market, we do not need to know (or so we assume) the colour of his hair or his place of birth. Probabilistic models of social mobility abstract from most features of the concrete man, except present and perhaps past class membership. The logical models used in this book carry this process of abstraction to what I think must be the ultimate limit. Instead of letting the number of individuals vary over the whole set of natural numbers, logic knows three degrees only: none, some, and all. Rather than quantifying probabilities along the continuum from 0 to 1, logic deals only with possibilities, impossibilities, and necessities. These two abstractions are at the root of quantified logic and modal logic, respectively. When performed simultaneously, they give us the full-blown structure of *quantified modal logic* which is the basic framework of this book. Just as important as the formal structure of quantified modal logic, is the interpretation of the concept of possibility. The crucial feature of the recent interpretations is that possible states are seen not as possible *tout court*, but as possible relatively to a given (actual) state. The affinity at this point with the social sciences hardly needs stressing.

I hope, of course, that this process of abstraction can be reversed; that insight into the abstract logic of social situations can lead the social scientist to ask new questions at a more concrete level. A typical example to show that logical theory can at least suggest new concepts is the following. In the study of social mobility an individual from a given class is sometimes described as having various transition probabilities to each of the several classes, including his own. In logical terms all the classes to which he has a non-zero probability of acceding are *possible* relatively to the initial class. The features, if any, that are common to all the possible classes, could then be called *necessary* features of the individual in his initial situation. It might — or it might not — turn out that these necessary features could serve as explanatory variables where the merely factual features of the individual did not. A more well-known example is the fact that abstract properties of relations — such as symmetry, transitivity, and reflexivity — are often useful in characterizing social relationships, e.g. power.

This book is primarily addressed to social scientists, and only secondarily to logicians. With the possible exception of some of the ideas in Chapter 6, the professional logician will not find much here of theoretical interest, even though I hope that parts of the material will prove useful for illustrative and pedagogical purposes. One sometimes gets the impression that logicians seek actively for examples either trivial or fanciful; I, for one, believe that the teaching of logic would benefit from more complex and realistic applications, much as physical examples are of great help in teaching mathematics. Perhaps this comparison could also be used to buttress a somewhat stronger claim. It was John von Neumann (I think) who said that mathematics out of touch with physical problems tends to become *baroque*, this term being used as a contrast to the *classical* style of thinking that is constantly revitalized by contact with the empirical sciences. As far as I can judge (but then I am no specialist in modal logic, so this may not be very far), there is a certain slant of the baroque — the somewhat futile embellishment of past glories — in some of the work done today by modal logicians. It is not to be excluded that a more extensive contact with the empirical sciences, and perhaps especially with the social sciences, could infuse a new life in the discipline. This has already been the case with temporal logic, which has drawn (even if not very extensively) upon problems in the philosophy of history.[2]

I would like to convey a feeling for some of the problems that made me write this book. The most important source of inspiration has been the long-standing controversy over Hegelian or dialectical versus formal logic. Proponents of the former have accused the latter of dealing with trivialities only; they have referred to a distinction between the lowly *understanding* that is at work in everyday life and in the sciences, and the elevated *reason* that is capable of metaphysical argument and dialectical insights. Analytical logicians have retorted by saying that dialectics overcomes triviality only at the cost of in-comprehensibility. In Chapters 3, 4, and 5 below I try to work out an inter-mediate position. I believe that dialectical thinkers have had a unique gift for singling out interesting and sometimes crucial *problems*, even if their attempts at a new *method* must be deemed a failure. As I see it, there is nothing of real importance in Hegel or Marx that cannot be formulated in ordinary language and formal logic.[3] If this statement is not to be a tautology, we clearly need some independent criterion for what *is* really important. My criterion is simply to take the analyses that are held up by the dialectical philosophers themselves as paradigmatic examples of dialectical reasoning, and show that they can be rendered into a straightforward logical argument.

Actually, as the reader will see for himself, the promises of the preceding paragraph are kept only for *some* of the dialectical notions. Towards the end of Chapter 3 I briefly indicate how the notion of *the negation of the negation* may be interpreted in terms of modal logic. The most important category which is subjected to translation from dialectical to formal logic is, however, the concept of a *contradiction*. We know what a logical contradiction is, but is it not a category mistake and an abuse of language to talk about 'real contradic-tions'? *A priori* I think one would like to impose the following conditions upon a workable concept of 'real contradiction' in the social sciences:

—It should be firmly linked to the concept of a logical contradiction,
—it should be linked to a theory of (individual or social) change,
—it should be fairly precise and operational,
—it should fit in with (at least some of) the writings of Hegel and Marx on the subject.

The first requirement is imposed for reasons of clarity of expression. The term 'contradiction' is basically a logical one, and should not be extended in a way that is totally divorced from the primary meaning. If by 'contradiction' we mean only opposition, conflict or struggle, then we should *say* opposition, conflict or struggle. We should firmly resist the temptation to play upon the logical connotation in order to make our opinions seem interesting, and then fall back upon the non-logical connotations in order to make them look plausible. The second requirement is reasonable in light of the link that from Heraclit onwards has been drawn between contradictions and change: 'Without

Contraries is no Progression' (William Blake). The third remark should not
need any justification, but a brief remark may be useful in order to bring out
the polemical intention behind this condition. A useful concept must be substantially less than all-embracing, which means that it is not very helpful to
say with Mao Tse-Tung that there are contradictions in all things. Upon my
definition of a real contradiction, there is a contradiction within the working
class, but no contradiction between the capitalist and the working class.
This restriction, far from being a disadvantage, is in my opinion a distinct asset
of the notion proposed below. In the later Marxist tradition, from Engels
onwards, there has been a tendency to use the term 'contradiction' in a manner
so elastic as to rob the notion of all analytical cutting edge; it would seem worth
while, therefore, if one could 'donner un sens plus pur aux mots de la tribu'.
The last requirement is the least important; its fulfilment should be seen more
as an extra bonus than as a desideratum in itself.

It is by no means obvious that these requirements can be simultaneously
fulfilled, and one might ask whether the intention to do so does not itself
constitute a contradiction in the sense of Chapter 4 below. I do think, however,
that they can be fulfilled, and in a manner that is not vulnerable to the standard
criticism by positivist or analytical philosophers of science. The general notion
of a 'real contradiction' is subdivided in two species: the individual contradictions and the social contradictions that form the subject of Chapters 4 and 5,
respectively. The notion of an individual or mental contradiction really is
very simple, as it is based only upon the idea that a person can very well entertain
self-contradictory opinions or desires, even if it is impossible that they could
be or become true. The notion of a social contradiction is slightly more complex.
It is tied up with the well-known *fallacy of composition*, which I interpret
(somewhat differently from the usual treatment in logic textbooks) in terms of
quantified modal logic. This fallacy can be used as a key to the understanding
of the two classes of social phenomena that I call *suboptimality* and *counterfinality*: the gap between the intention and the result, the gap between the possible
and the actual.

For both varieties of contradictions—individual as well as social—I also
try to show that they are indeed conducive to change. The link is only briefly
sketched for the individual contradictions, but rather more elaborated in the
case of social contradictions. In Chapter 5 the reader will indeed observe that
the substantive sociological discussion tends to assume equal importance with
the logical analysis. I do not apologize for this, even if it may throw some
readers off the track. It is important, I think, to see the concepts *at work* if
one is to be convinced of their fertility. Mere assertion will not make the reader
agree that the notion of a real contradiction can and should be the core of a
theory of social change. On the other hand it has not been possible, because of
lack of space, to present the theory in full detail, a task that I hope to undertake
elsewhere.

A second, and nearly as important source of inspiration for the ideas presented
here has been the problem of counterfactual statements in history. In Chapter 6,

especially, I deal at length with this question, tracing the history of the concept, discussing the connection with current logical analysis of counterfactuals, and commenting in some detail upon a number of examples of counterfactual constructions in recent historical work. It is fairly clear that counterfactual statements cry out for a treatment in the framework of modal logic, but among logicians there is no general agreement as to exactly how they should be analysed. My position is that in historical writings (and possibly in general) counterfactual statements should always be understood in the context of an implicit or explicit *theory*. This is often called the *meta-linguistic* approach to counterfactuals, in contradistinction to the *ontological* approach that has been more in vogue in recent years. A few words may be in order even at this introductory stage to clarify this distinction.

History, one used to say, is a seamless web. Everything that happened, had to happen; there are no joints where we can drive in a wedge and make the course of events a different one, not even as a *Gedankenexperiment*. Now at the level of universal determinism this may be true (disregarding the problems created by quantum mechanics), but science—the historical sciences included—is not content with this metaphysical assertion. We want to know not only *that* a given event has a cause, but also *which* cause. If we cannot specify the cause, it is as if the event were uncaused, for all that we know. This also means that we are free to conduct an imaginary experiment and assume that the event in question never took place, and to ask what would then have been the further course of history. Now the knowledge of causes must be related to a theory; the ignorance of the cause reflects the absence of a theory. This implies that if at a later stage in the development of sociological knowledge a theory is found that provides a cause for the event in question, the counterfactual experiment may no longer appear as legitimate. With each new theory much of counterfactual history must be rewritten or discarded, but so also must much of factual history. One important consequence of this meta-linguistic view should be mentioned, viz. the 'scissors' problem created by the twofold use of theory in counterfactual analysis. The reference to causal theories is crucial both for the delimitation of which counterfactual questions can legitimately be asked, and for our ability to answer them with a satisfactory degree of precision. Clearly there is a delicate balance to be struck here: a strong theory eliminates many possible questions as being meaningless, whereas a weaker theory may not enable us to answer the questions it allows.

The examples given in Chapter 6 are, I believe, of substantial interest in their own right. The controversy over the standard of living during the Industrial Revolution in England is often characterized in terms of 'optimist' versus 'pessimist' views, but actually this is a confusion of two distinct issues. There is the largely (but not wholly) factual issue of pessimism versus non-pessimism: did things get worse or not? There is also the counterfactual issue of optimism versus non-optimism: could things have been better? The last issue has the unique feature of being a search for the *optimal counterfactual*, the best of all possible pasts. In other historical examples the actual course of development is not contrasted with all other possible courses, but rather with one alternative sequence of events: the United States economy without the railroad, the Southern ante-bellum economy without slavery. These examples are drawn from the work of Robert Fogel (done jointly with Stanley Engerman in the second case); if in my discussion I focus largely upon what I see as the defects of his analyses, this should not overshadow the immensely stimulating effect of his work.

Among the pioneers in the methodology of counterfactual history I mention Max Weber, who linked our interest in alternative pasts to our freedom of choice between alternative futures. If we feel that we have a real choice *ex ante*, it would seem legitimate to explore *ex post* what would have happened if some other option had been chosen. (I do not imply that this is the only way in which counterfactual exercises can be justified.) In Chapter 3 I explore the general logic of such possibilities before the fact, with political possibility as my main example. This analysis can be intuitively motivated from several points of view. Firstly, we all have some intuitive notion that not all abstractly or even technically possible courses of action are possible *hic et nunc*, relatively to the given state of affairs. Take the following comment by Steven Lukes (*Sunday Times*, 9 November 1975) on what was then the political situation in Portugal: 'In these conditions, a number of options must probably be ruled out. ... Nor is an East-European People's Democracy, whose spectre haunted the country until recently, a real possibility in Portugal. ... The possible scenarios appear to be few.' Turns of speech like these clearly imply that there is a set of logically possible outcomes, some of which are judged to be politically possible. It is then a natural step to ask some further questions relating to these politically possible subsets: When is political change irreversible? When is it possible to skip a step in a political development? Is *status quo* always a feasible option? Or in formal terms: Is the relation 'politically possible relatively to' symmetric, transitive, reflexive? I shall also argue that such examples allow us to explore in full the potentialities of *quantified* modal logic for sociological or historical analysis.

Secondly, the notion of political possibility is interesting from the formal point of view; the point of view, to be precise, that pertains to the semantics of modal logic. As briefly mentioned above, the revolutionary breakthrough in modal logic came with the relativization of the notion of possibility, which enabled logicians to make sense of much that had previously been obscure in the axiomatic systems of modal logic. Still, it turned out that when one should exemplify the notion of relative possibility (often called the relation of *accessibility*), the interpretations were either trivial or not strictly modal. Some attempts were trivial, in the sense that they amounted to a reintroduction of the absolute (i.e. non-relativized) concept of possibility, so that one lost all the ground gained. Other attempts were highly interesting and non-trivial, such as the interpretation in terms of deontic, epistemic, or temporal logic, but on the other hand these seemed rather distantly related to the substantive notion of possibility. The political interpretation of accessibility has the formal feature, therefore, of offering an interpretation that is both non-trivial and strictly modal. This is no theoretical breakthrough, but the idea may have some heuristic value for the logic teacher who is asked by his students how it can be that the revolution in modal *logic* has no implication for *modal* logic.

Thirdly, I believe that the notion of political possibility may be studied as a limiting case of the notion of political *power*. Power is usually conceptualized in terms of the probability of an actor getting his way or realizing some desired state of affairs; by going from probabilities to pure possibility we get the basic idea of Chapter 3. It also turns out that the analyses of power and of political possibility encounter some of the same problems, notably the difficulty of entangling the causal from the intentional aspect. Power is neither the production of desired results nor the production of intended results, but the intelligent production of intended results; similarly political possibility is here circumscribed so as to emphasize the intentional and rational aspects of politics.

To many readers of the present work a surprising and no doubt puzzling feature will be the constant emphasis upon possible worlds. For the social scientist, at any rate, it may be hard to overcome the idea that his object of study is the actual world, whereas possibilities may be safely left to the novelist. To this query I think it possible to give two distinct answers, by indicating two avenues that lead to the realm of the possible. In the first place possible worlds are a hidden and implicit aspect of all model-building and of all theorizing. A theory that covers the actual world and only the actual world, is not a theory but a description. A theory must have implications for possible worlds by specifying the set of jointly realizable values of the relevant variables. This is spelled out in detail in Chapter 6 below. In the second place we may refer to possible worlds in order to characterize the actual world. An analogy may bring out the idea behind this statement. In system dynamics the explanatory ideal is to predict the values of all variables at time $t + 1$ (or the rates of change at time t) given the values at time t only. In some cases, however, it turns out that the analysis is more easily carried out if we admit past values of the variables.[4] We know on general metaphysical grounds that the past cannot really have a causal influence upon the present over and above the influence that is mediated by the traces left by the past in the present, but nevertheless it may be convenient (and in a few cases even necessary) to speak *as if* past values of the variables exert an independent effect. In a similar manner it may be convenient to admit possible values of some variables in order to predict future developments of the system under consideration, even if we know quite well that these could *in principle* be replaced by other variables taking actual values only.

The last remarks should amply indicate that I do not advocate an Aristotelian conception of potentialities. Possibilities are not shadowy entities that hover between existence and non-existence and exercise some kind of causal influence upon the actual, no more than infinitesimals are entities that somehow manage to be different from zero and still smaller than any magnitude you can name. Possible worlds, like infinitesimals, are just a *façon de parler* that can always in principle be dispensed with. You cannot get more out of them than you have put into them yourself; they are not out there awaiting further inspection and promising further discoveries. This point will be further emphasized in Chapters 3 and 6 below.

Whereas Chapters 3 to 6 attempt to break some new ground, Chapter 2 is essentially a reminder for the social scientist that unlike M. Jourdain he has really been talking poetry all the time without knowing it. I attempt to show, that is, that in many well-known analyses from the social sciences possibilistic reasoning has a prominent place. Thus the step from the matrix of transition probabilities to the so-called 'adjacency matrix' in the study of social mobility really is a step from probability to possibility. An example of a possibilistic notion (grammaticality) that can *not* be defined as a non-zero probability is taken from linguistic theory, which seems to be *the* field where pure possibility really comes into its own. A discussion then follows of French structuralist thought, where I argue that the obsession of this school with the possible is linked to its search for *finite* structures. The human mind is finite, we rejoice in the finite that we can understand. If the set of possible cases is infinite, we cannot encompass them all. We can characterize the feasible set by aggregate features, such as convexity or compactness, or we can single out the best member of the set according to some criterion of optimality, but we cannot really grasp the fine grain of the possible. For feasible sets of finite cardinality we can know all there is to know, once and for all. The last two cases discussed in Chapter 2 are, I believe, of great philosophical interest as well as being outstanding examples of imaginative reasoning in the social sciences. The work of Paul Samuelson and Amartya K. Sen shows that the apparently simple notion of real national income hides a chasm of counterfactual implications, whereas the seminal work of C. C. von Weiszäcker on endogenous change of tastes opens up a vista of the human mind as creating, predicting and reacting upon its own possibilities. These two cases are also further used in later chapters.

I would like to close this introduction by a few remarks on the kind of book the reader is embarking upon. If like most readers (including myself) he prefers to read books that defend a thesis or offer him some hard-won information, he will be deceived by this one. On the other hand, even if a scientific community where everyone did empirical work and no one did philosophy of science is certainly to be preferred to a community where it was exactly the other way around (and the reader will perhaps be able to think of actual communities that approach these extremes), most people will agree that the selection against philosophy of science should not be so strong as to eliminate it altogether. Take, however, the following argument. Mediocre science has its proper place in the cumulative research process,[5] but mediocre philosophy of science is at best harmless and will often create more confusion than it dispels. On the other hand, if someone is talented enough to be a good philosopher of science, he should exercise his gift on science proper. The Norwegian economist Ragnar Frisch is said to have warned his future biographers in roughly the following terms: if someone were to write an intellectual biography of myself, he would have to be so good that he should not waste his time doing *that*. I prefer to think that there are different criteria of excellence. Science is advanced by people with a single-minded obsession with one or two ideas which they defend in the face of common sense and of the organized scepticism of the profession. Other people are better at having good ideas than at pursuing them to their conclusion; their reasoning is tentative and hypothetical rather than assertive and categorical. From the history of philosophy Descartes and Leibniz are good examples of the two types. Most people will agree that Descartes was the more important thinker; personally I have a penchant for Leibniz.

Notes

1. I do not claim to be the first to do this. For other attempts in the same direction, see Kanger and Kanger (1966), Pörn (1970), or Körner (1976). These authors, however, write mostly for philosophers and suffer (in my view) from a poverty of good examples and concrete material that could persuade the social scientist that their work *makes a difference.*
2. Cf. for example Rescher and Urquhart (1971).
3. This implies a rejection of all attempts to formalize the Hegelian dialectics in a language that is different from standard logical theory, such as Günther (1959) or Dubarle (1970).
4. Cf. Elster (1976a) for a further analysis of some cases where hysteresis (i.e. past values of variables) has been integrated in social-science explanations.
5. But see Cole and Cole (1973, Chapter 8) for an argument to the contrary.

1

FORMAL LOGIC—AN INFORMAL EXPOSITION

The language of quantified modal logic is used throughout this book. For the reader who is not familiar with these concepts, the present chapter offers, with a minimum of technical apparatus, the necessary prerequisites.[1] The aims of the exposition are, firstly, to familiarize the reader with the logical notions and their interrelations and, secondly, to sketch some of their interpretations. I leave completely aside all matters pertaining to the axiomatization of logical systems, such as provability, decidability, completeness, etc. With an analogy from linguistics I am concerned with surface structure only, the generative rules that constitute the deep structure being hardly relevant for the purposes of this book. Logic is a language, and like any other language it can be learned for use or for study. This is an attempt to give the non-logician a new tool, and not a tool-making manual. This, of course, does not exclude the possibility that there may come a point where further proficiency in tool-using presupposes an understanding of how the tools are made.

Three separate sets of concepts are involved in formal logic, belonging respectively to the propositional calculus, the quantificational calculus and the logic of the modalities. The second is built upon the first, whereas the third may build either upon the second or directly upon the first. I shall here deal mainly with the full three-tiered structure of *quantified modal logic*. This structure may be studied from two distinct points of view, the relation between which is the central problem of metalogical enquiry: that of proof theory and that of model theory (or semantics). In proof theory we enquire about the set of formulae that can be deduced (given certain inference rules) from the axioms of the system. In model theory we are concerned with the set of formulae that come out as true under all possible interpretations. (What 'interpretation' means here is explained below.) As already stated, the proof-theoretic aspect of logic has no part in the present study, whereas the model-theoretic aspect is important.

In *propositional logic* we deal with relations between atom-like propositions, the internal structure of which is irrelevant. We bring out the atom-like character of the propositions by indicating them by single letters 'p', 'q', 'r', etc. Thus 'p' is a *dummy* for a proposition such as 'it rains', whereas ' "p" ' is a name for 'p'. I shall indiscriminately use dummies as if they were the real thing, but try not to confound propositions and their names. From the atoms we may build up molecular sentences using the *negation operator* and the *sentence connectives* 'and', 'or', 'if-then', 'if and only if'. We say that the molecular sentences are *truth functions* of their constituents, meaning that the truth value of the compound depends only upon (i) the truth value of the components and (ii) the manner in which the components are combined in the molecular proposition. Assume, for example, that we have a molecular proposition 'S_1', one of whose components is the atomic proposition 'p'. Replacing 'p' with 'q' everywhere (and supposing that 'q' does not already occur in 'S_1') we get a new molecular proposition 'S_2'. The requirement that the molecular sentence be a truth function of its components then implies that if 'p' and 'q' have the same truth value, then so shall 'S_1' and 'S_2'. In propositional logic we do not want to know whether a given statement is about Richard Nixon or about CO_2, only whether it is true or false. As an example of a complex proposition that is *not* a truth-function of its component parts, we may take 'I believe that it rains'. We may assume that this proposition ('S_1') is true and that the component part 'it rains' ('p') is also true. Nevertheless, it does not follow that the proposition 'I believe that there is no greatest prime number' ('S_2') is true, even if the truth value of the component part 'there is no greatest prime number' ('q') is the same as the truth value of 'it rains'. An important philosophical problem is whether such non-truth-functional complexes can be reduced to or translated into equivalent truth-functional complexes (of different component parts).

The negation operator and the sentence connectives are defined as truth functions by giving, for all possible combinations of truth values of their constituents, the truth value of the compound. Briefly this is done in the following manner:

Negation: '$\bar{p}$' ('not–p') is true if and only if 'p' is false.
Conjunction: '$p \& q$' ('p and q') is true if and only if 'p' and 'q' are both true.
Disjunction: '$p \vee q$' ('p or q') is true if and only if either 'p' or 'q' or both are true.
Conditional: '$p \supset q$' ('if p, then q') is true if and only if 'p' is false or 'q' is true.
Biconditional: '$p \equiv q$' is true if and only if 'p' and 'q' have the same truth value.

The only definition that requires some brief comments is the conditional, 'if p then q'. The definition implies that if the *antecedent* 'p' is false, then the conditional as a whole is always true, regardless of the truth value of the *consequent* 'q'. To many people this seems counter to our intuitive notions about truth, as we then have to admit the truth of all conditionals with false or even absurd antecedents. One feels vaguely that this may be acceptable in some cases, such as 'If all humans are rational and four-legged, then all humans are rational', because here there is a link between the antecedent and the consequent. The idea seems less acceptable in cases where no such link is present, such as 'If all humans are goats, then $2 + 2 = 5$'. I shall argue in a moment that the logical link between antecedent and consequent in the first example is better dealt with under another heading. Here I shall only state that for most purposes no harm comes from treating as vacuously true statements like the second example, much as we accept as vacuously true the statement that 'All A are B' even if there does not actually exist anything which is A.

The main case where the definition of the conditional *does* create serious problems, concerns the counterfactuals (also called 'contrary-to-fact conditionals') such as 'If Hitler had never been born, then the Second World War would never have taken place'. If this statement is acceptable, as it may very well be, it is certainly not in the trivial sense of being vacuously true. If we try to assess the truth value of such counterfactuals on the assumption that it is a conditional whose truth value is a truth function of the constituent truth values, then we shall have to accept as true both the preceding statement and the statement 'If Hitler had never been born, the Second World War would have taken place all the same', as both these conditionals have the same false antecedent. Given this absurd consequence, one might try either to define a different truth function for the counterfactual or accept that the relation between antecedent and consequent in this case is not a truth-functional one. It is clear that only the second option is really open; for a further analysis the reader is referred to Chapter 6 below.

At this point it is useful to distinguish between *truth* and *validity*. A complex statement is true relatively to *one* (not necessarily unique) assignment of truth values to the constituents; it is valid if true under *all* possible assignments. As an example we may quote Quine's dictum that 'Implication is validity of the conditional'. If 'S_1' and 'S_2' are two molecular propositions, we say that 'S_1' implies 'S_2' if '$S_1 \supset S_2$' comes out true under all possible assignments of truth values to the constituent atoms. The reason why we felt that 'If all humans are rational and four-legged, then all humans are rational' was acceptable, even if having a false antecedent, is that it exemplifies a valid conditional of the form '$(p \,\&\, q) \supset q$'. In most methodological discussions it is indeed the case that our interest is in the conditionals where there is some *link* between the false conditional and the consequent, either in the sense of a logical link that makes for the validity of the conditional or in the sense of a causal link that makes us see the relevance of the conditional ('If all humans are goats, they must eat leaves'). Nevertheless it is useful and harmless to admit the truth of conditionals with false antecedents, even when such links are lacking. In the strict definition the conditional is only an assertion of the co-tenability of certain statements, and does not at all imply any formal or substantial links between statements. On the other hand, if the conditional is false, with a true antecedent and a false consequent, then no logical or causal link can be present.

An *interpretation* of a complex proposition means the assignment of truth values to all constituents. For a given interpretation, a complex proposition is either true or false. (The logic of truth is two-valued.) With respect to the set of all *possible* interpretations, it is either valid (or tautological), consistent or contradictory. (The logic of validity is three-valued, a feature which it shares with modal logic.) When later we come to deal with *fallacies*, we refer to conditionals that are set forward with a pretension of validity, but are not really valid. The non-validity of a conditional does not mean, however, that it cannot be true under some interpretation; it may even be true in the non-vacuous sense of having a true antecedent and a true consequent. This concludes our account of propositional logic.

In quantificational logic we split the atom in order to take account of its internal structure. We are now able to talk about individual objects and their properties; about the relations between such objects; about the number of objects satisfying certain conditions. Individuals can be referred to in two ways: through constants and through variables. *Individual constants* '*a*', '*b*', '*c*' ... refer to fixed objects in the universe of discourse, whereas *individual variables* '*x*', '*y*', '*z*' ... range over all objects in the universe. *Predicates* '*F*', '*G*', '*H*' ... are attached either to individual constants or to individual variables, so that for example '*Fa*' means that the object *a* is *F*. *Dyadic relations* '*R*', '*S*', '*T*' ... connect with each other two individual constants, two individual variables or one individual constant and one individual variable, so that for example '*Rxa*' means that '*x* has *R* to *a*'. *N-adic relations* do the same for *n* constants or variables. In the present work all predicates and relations are taken as constants; for example there are no variables ranging over the set of all properties. In higher-order systems of logic it may be possible to formalize statements such as 'Every object has at least one property', but in the framework used here this cannot be done; nor shall we have any need to do so.

The crucial notions in quantificational logic are the *quantifiers*. The *universal quantifier* '$(\forall x)$ $(...x...)$' says that it is true of all *x* that ... *x* ..., where the dots should be filled in with some predicate or a more complex expression. The *existential quantifier* '$(\exists x)$ $(...x...)$' says that there exists at least one *x* in the universe of discourse such that ... *x* ... The individual variables that stand within the scope of a quantifier are said to be *bound*, and sentences whose variables are all bound are said to be *closed*. In the present work we deal with closed sentences only. In logical theory, then, we refer either to specific individuals (named by individual constants) or to individuals in general through one of the concepts 'none', 'some', or 'all'. It is possible to express more fine-grained numerical distinctions in logical language, but from the point of view explained in the Introduction the restriction to three degrees is an asset rather than a drawback. In order to get out some basic structures of the reasoning in the social sciences we do not want to be encumbered with the whole set of natural or real numbers.

These arid definitions will now be worked out in a number of examples. Let us first introduce the notion of *relationally defined predicates*, which is discussed more fully for the interested reader in an appendix to the present chapter. The sentence 'Peter is unconquered' reads superficially as '*Fa*', but on a deeper level it comes out as '$(\forall x)$ $(\overline{Rxa})$', where '*Rxa*' is the relation '*x* conquers *a*'. In words, there is no *x* such that *x* conquers *a*. In attributing this property to Peter, we say nothing about his relation to anyone else in particular, but indirectly the proposition relates him to all the individuals in the universe of discourse. As a more complex example, take the relational predicate

$$(\forall x)(\exists y)(Rayx) \& (\forall x)(\exists y)(Ryax).$$

Reading '$Rxyz$' as 'x is better than y at z', we see that this relationally defined expression unravels the monadic predicate 'a jack of all trades and a master of none', or at least an important component of that predicate.

The use of nested quantifiers (quantifiers that stand within the scope of each other) in the last example is an essential feature of quantificational logic.[2] As many of the distinctions in the present work turn upon the *order* in which nested quantifiers (and other operators) occur in the sentence, several examples will be given to familiarize the reader with this problem. As a simple example that shows how crucial is the order of the quantifiers we may take a classical proof of the existence of God, which rests upon the fallacious confusion between

$(\forall x)(\exists y)(Rxy$—everything has a cause,
$(\exists y)(\forall x)(Rxy)$—there is something that is the cause of everything.

Donald Davidson has argued that the same confusion is present when we conclude from materialism and determinism to reductionism. 'If a certain psychological concept applies to one event and not to another, there must be a difference describable in physical terms. But it does not follow that there is a single physically describable difference that distinguishes any two events that differ in a given psychological respect.'[3] That is, writing 'Rxy' for 'x falls under description y', 'Fy' for 'y is a psychological description' and 'Gy' for 'is a physical description', Davidson warns us against confusing

$$(\forall v)(\forall x)(\forall z)(\exists w)((Rxy \& \overline{Rzy} \& Fy) \supset (Rxw \& \overline{Rzw} \& Gw))$$

with

$$(\forall y)(\exists w)(\forall x)(\forall z)((Rxy \& \overline{Rzy} \& Fy) \supset (Rxw \& \overline{Rzw} \& Gw)).$$

From the social sciences a similar example is the distinction between the personal and the functional division of labour, i.e. between the distribution of persons over jobs and the system of jobs itself. Letting '$Rxyt$' stand for 'the person x occupies position y at time t', two distinct societies may be described respectively by

$$(\forall x)(\exists y)(\forall t)(Rxyt), \qquad (\forall x)(\forall t)(\exists y)(Rxyt).$$

The first society is very different from the second, even if at any given moment they are indistinguishable. Only a longitudinal view that sees the job turnover rate as a part of the social structure is able to capture this distinction. In *The German Ideology* Marx seems to commit the fallacy of affirming that a society with functional division of labour must also have a frozen personal (i.e. lifelong) division of labour,[4] but in *Capital* the distinction between the two—between manufacture and industry—is fundamental.[5]

A last example is the interpretation of Lincoln's famous impossibility theorem. Setting 'Rxt' for 'you can fool person x at time t', the theorem can be understood in four distinct ways:

$$(\forall x)(\exists t)(Rxt) \ \& \ (\exists x)(\forall t)(Rxt) \ \& \ \overline{(\forall x)(\forall t)(Rxt)},$$
$$(\exists t)(\forall x)(Rxt) \ \& \ (\exists x)(\forall t)(Rxt) \ \& \ \overline{(\forall x)(\forall t)(Rxt)},$$
$$(\forall x)(\exists t)(Rxt) \ \& \ (\forall t)(\exists x)(Rxt) \ \& \ \overline{(\forall x)(\forall t)(Rxt)},$$
$$(\exists t)(\forall x)(Rxt) \ \& \ (\forall t)(\exists x)(Rxt) \ \& \ \overline{(\forall x)(\forall t)(Rxt)}.$$

When in modal logic we also introduce the modal operators, the fallacies arising from quantifier/operator shifts are added to the fallacy list. These fallacies, and especially *the fallacy of composition*, are a central topic of the present work, in particular of Chapter 5. It is important, however, that the reader has a secure grasp of the fallacies created by the simpler quantifier shifts. With a universal quantifier preceding the existential, a rather weak claim is made that for each object of one kind (the kind bound by the universal quantifier) some object of another kind (the kind bound by the existential quantifier) can be found which satisfies certain relations. With the order of the quantifiers reversed, the claim is very much strengthened, for now we assert that one object of the second kind will do the job for all objects of the first kind.[6]

The notions of interpretation and validity in quantificational logic are rather more complex than in the propositional case. An interpretation requires, firstly, a specification of the universe of discourse, i.e. the set of objects over which the variables are to range. In the second place we must give extensional interpretations of the predicates and the relations; i.e. we must specify for each predicate and each object whether the predicate can be truly asserted about that object, and for each n-adic relation and each ordered n-tuple of objects whether the relation holds between these objects. Validity is then defined as truth under all possible interpretations, which means all possible specifications in all possible universes of discourse. (Actually one can show that only the *number* of objects in the universe is relevant, so that a valid formula is one which comes out true under all possible extensional specifications in universes of all possible cardinalities.) This concludes the account of quantificational logic.

In modal logic we introduce two additional operators, 'M' and 'N', whose standard interpretations are possibility and necessity, respectively. The operators are attached to whole statements, be these molecules or atoms of the propositional calculus or structured wholes of the quantificational calculus. Thus a sentence '$N(p \vee q)$' is to be read 'It is necessarily true that either p or q be the case', and '$M(\exists x)(Rax)$' as 'It is possible that there exists an x such that a has R to x'. (The non-standard readings of the operators are left for later discussion.) The syntax and semantics of modal logic are, however, more opaque than in the cases previously discussed. On the syntactical side, it is difficult to lay down the axioms that will govern the so-called *mixed and iterated modalities*, such as '$MNMp$' or 'NNp'. Several postulates have been discussed from 1912 onwards, one of them stating that there can be no simplification of mixed and iterated modalities; another (S-4) that iterated modalities are to be reduced to simple modalities (MM being equivalent to M, NNN to N, etc.); a third (S-5) that *any* string (mixed or iterated) of modalities is equivalent to the rightmost operator ($MNNMN$ being equivalent to N, etc.).[7]

The reason why no firm choice was made between these axiomatic systems was the equally uncertain state on the semantical side. The only well-established interpretation of possibility and necessity was the one proposed by Leibniz: possibility is truth in some possible world, necessity is truth in all possible worlds. These notions coincide with the notions of consistency and validity as defined above. The difficulty with this interpretation, however, is that it makes all mixed and iterated modalities collapse into simple modalities, so that we are left only with the rather trivial system S-5. Perhaps the underlying problem can be formulated in the following terms: in order to obtain interesting formal structures the logicians wanted to make sense of mixed and/or iterated modalities, but the only plausible interpretation available had the consequence of collapsing these into simple modalities.

The revolution in modal logic occurred during the late 1950s when several authors independently proposed a *relativization of the notion of possible worlds*. Instead of saying that a world is possible *tout court*, we now say that a world is possible relatively to another world. As a synonym for relative possibility we also use the more suggestive term 'accessibility'. 'Np' is then taken to mean that 'p' is true in all worlds that are possible relatively to the actual world. 'NNp' receives a natural interpretation to the effect that 'p' is true in any world that is possible relatively to any world that is possible relatively to the actual one. In words, 'p' is necessarily necessarily true (in our world) if it is true in all worlds that are accessible in two steps from the actual one. Similarly, a mixed modality such as 'MNp' now means that there exists at least one world x that is possible relatively to the actual one such that p is true in all worlds that are possible relatively to x. The various axiomatic systems previously proposed could now be classified according to the logical conditions they impose upon the accessibility relation. With a reflexive, transitive and non-symmetric relation of relative possibility we get the system S-4; with a reflexive, transitive, and symmetric relation S-5. Numerous other possible systems now emerged in a natural way; indeed systems could be tailor-made for the most varied purposes.[8]

From the viewpoint of model theory it was satisfactory indeed to be able to give semantic sense to the various systems other than S-5 and to construct new and previously unthought of systems. Still, the idea of relative possibility is nothing but a convenient algebraic device until we have specified in concrete cases what such a relative possibility could mean. Systems of modal logic are interpreted by the means of so-called model systems, or sets of sets of sentences satisfying various conditions. In the statement of some of these conditions the notion of relative possibility enters crucially, but only as a relation between sets of sentences; no concrete specification of possibility is implied. The attempts to provide such a specification have resulted in the following rather paradoxical situation. Either the specification proposed brings us back to S-5 and to Leibniz, so that all mixed and iterated modalities collapse and we lose all the ground apparently gained; or the specification can only metaphorically be called *modal* concepts in the classical sense. I shall briefly review the first kind of interpretation, and then dwell at greater length on the second.

The most natural specification would be to say that a world is possible relatively to ours if it obeys the same logical or causal laws. In this case, however, the essential use of the word 'same' in the definition makes the accessibility relation into an equivalence relation, i.e. a relation that is reflexive, symmetrical, and transitive. The resulting system is, of course, S-5. It is not quite correct to say that necessity comes out as truth in all possible worlds, as was the case in the original Leibnizian analysis. Rather, a statement is necessarily true if and only if it is true in all the worlds in the equivalence class to which our world belongs under the equivalence relation. Thus, neither logical necessity nor physical necessity are plausible candidates for the kind of structure—modal and non-trivial that we have in mind. They are modal, but trivial.

For non-trivial and non-modal candidates we may look to deontic, epistemic or temporal logic, which are all 'non-standard' interpretations of the axiomatic systems of modal logic. Epistemic logic is discussed in some detail in Chapter 4. Here we may only note that it comes in two versions, one in which the operator 'N' is interpreted as knowledge and one in which it is understood as belief. In temporal logic we may interpret 'Np' as 'It is true at all (past, present and future) times that p', and 'Mp' as 'It is true at some (past, present or future) time that p'. Another version takes 'Np' as 'It is and will always be the case that p' and 'Mp' as 'It is or will be the case that p'. The first version just gives S-5, whereas the second leaves us with S-4 because 'MNp' does not collapse into 'Np'. Even if from some future date onwards it will always be true that p, this does not imply that p is the case now. Still further versions of temporal logic have been worked out, many of them by the late A. N. Prior.[9]

In deontic logic there is an obvious analogy (going back to Leibniz) between necessity and obligation, and between possibility and permissibility.[10] Here it is easily seen that neither S-4 nor S-5 will catch our intuitive notions, and as a matter of fact a rather complicated system must be worked out if we are not to get into counterintuitive situations. Among the more interesting properties of the system we may note that the accessibility relation is not reflexive. The actual world is not necessarily an ethical alternative to itself, though it is an alternative to itself if there exists another world to which it is an alternative—a property to which I return in Chapter 3 below under the heading 'limited reflexivity'. In addition to the 'pure' systems of deontic, temporal, or epistemic logic, one might imagine 'mixed' systems for the formalization of phrases such as 'I believe that it will be the case that p' or 'It is obligatory to know that p'; even further extensions might try to render 'I desire that p' or 'I hope that p'. Little work has been done on these problems, and we shall not try to deal with them here.

In the present work two non-trivial specifications of the modal operators are spelled out. In Chapter 4 extensive use is made of epistemic logic, while

Chapter 3 introduces the operator of political possibility. The latter has the mildly interesting formal feature of being both non-trivial and strictly modal. To say that the relation of political possibility is reflexive, symmetrical, and transitive, would imply that the *status quo* is always a feasible option, that political change is always reversible and that what can be done in two steps can always be done in one, which are controversial assumptions indeed. I do not argue that there exists one correct system of political possibility, but I think that politics as an S-5 system is a very uninteresting notion that can be ruled out of court without further discussion, so that the system really is a non-trivial one.

As regards interpretation and validity, the situation is vastly more complex than in the preceding cases. In modal logic there is no general notion of validity that encompasses all possible interpretations. Rather, there is one notion of validity for each interpretation, specified by indicating (i) the formal properties of the accessibility relation, (ii) the relative sizes of the populations in the various possible worlds, and (iii) the way in which we decide to assign truth-values to assertions and denials concerning non-existent objects. Instead of entering into the details of these problems, which soon become forbiddingly complex,[11] I shall give a well-known example of a formula whose validity depends crucially upon the way in which we specify the various aspects mentioned above. (In Chapter 3 below, other examples are given.) This is the so-called Barcan formula, which may be written in two alternative and equivalent forms:

$$(\forall x)(N(Fx)) \supset N(\forall x)(Fx), \qquad M(\exists x)(Fx) \supset (\exists x)(M(Fx)).$$

Before we look at the interpretation of these formulae, it may be useful for the untrained reader to see exactly in which sense they are equivalent to each other. (The reader may skip the rest of this paragraph if he feels sufficiently familiar with the manipulation of logical concepts.) Firstly we observe that the two quantifiers are definable in terms of each other, as are also the two modal operators: $(\exists x)(Fx) \equiv (\forall x)(\overline{Fx})$ and $Mp \equiv \overline{N\bar{p}}$. In the second place a well-known (and intuitively obvious) theorem of the propositional calculus states that $(p \supset q) \equiv (\bar{q} \supset \bar{p})$. This means that (setting 'Gx' for '$\overline{Fx}$') the following are all equivalent to each other:

$$(\forall x)(N(Fx)) \supset N(\forall x)(Fx),$$
$$\overline{N(\forall x)(Fx)} \supset \overline{(\forall x)(N(Fx))},$$
$$M\overline{(\forall x)(Fx)} \supset (\exists x)\overline{(N(Fx))},$$
$$M(\exists x)(\overline{Fx}) \supset (\exists x)(M(\overline{Fx})),$$
$$M(\exists x)(Gx) \supset (\exists x)(M(Gx)).$$

Thus if the first of these inferences is valid, then so is the last, and vice versa. The first states that if all objects in the actual world have the property F in all the worlds that are possible relatively to the actual one, then all the objects in all the worlds that are possible relatively to the actual one have the property F. A sufficient condition for this to be true is clearly that a given world and all the worlds that are accessible from it contain exactly the same objects.

If one of the accessible worlds contains an object that is not part of the actual world, the Barcan formula breaks down if that object is not F. Another difficulty that often arises when interpreting modal formulas is a problem first stated by Bertrand Russell: How are we to analyse a statement such as 'The present king of France is not bald'?[12] Does it deny the existence of a bald king or affirm the existence of a non-bald king? On the first reading it is true, on the second false. I return to this problem in Chapter 3 below.

The second (and more common) version of the Barcan formula is often discussed in terms of a distinction between modalities *de re* and modalities *de dicto*. I may be quite prepared to admit the possibility (*de dicto*) of a surviving dodo with a game leg, but I do not thereby feel committed to accept the existence of a dodo that possibly (*de re*) has a game leg. In order to be able to make this distinction, we shall have to reject the Barcan formula. This means that in the interpretations where we want to have the Barcan formula come out as non-valid, care must be taken to specify the rules governing accessibility, individuals, and non-existence so as to obtain this result. For an example from epistemic logic, which is further discussed in Chapter 4 below, we may take the inference from 'Everything which is a dragon is believed to be green' to 'It is believed that all dragons are green'. Even if we limit ourselves to the case of *rational* belief, the conclusion clearly does not follow, as it would require the added premise that it is believed that those, say, 12 dragons are all the dragons there are.[13]

Another example of the fallacious inference from modality *de dicto* to modality *de re* is *the fallacy of composition*, which is discussed at length in Chapters 3 and 5. As the Barcan formula, this fallacious inference exists in two alternative and equivalent variants:

$$N(\exists x)(Fx) \supset (\exists x)(N(Fx)), \qquad (\forall x)(M(Fx)) \supset M(\forall x)(Fx).$$

A counterexample that disproves the first operator/quantifier shift is the following: in a republic there is necessarily someone who is president, but there is no one who is necessarily a president. This and other political modalities are examined in Chapter 3 below. For a counterexample to the second, take the inference from the possibility of overproduction in any single sector of a (non-monetary) economy to the possibility of simultaneous overproduction in all sectors. This and numerous other examples are discussed in Chapter 5. Once again it is easy to find examples from non-standard interpretations. From 'I believe you are thinking about something' it cannot be inferred that there is some specific object such that I believe that you are thinking about *it*. It may often be obligatory to choose *some* course of action, even when the choice between the possible courses is morally arbitrary; this, indeed, is often said to constitute the essence of military decision. Such examples suggest that the inference in question comes out as invalid in *all* interpretations of modal logic, and this can indeed be shown to be the case.[14]

Concerning individuals and their properties in the possible worlds where they exist, recent philosophical discussion has raised a number of profound questions that are related to ancient problems about essentialism. Some of these issues are discussed in the Appendix to the present chapter, while others enter importantly in the analyses of Chapters 3 and 6. Here we shall only state without argument the need for a *genetic* theory of individuation. A necessary and sufficient condition for some individual in some possible world to be the same person as a given individual in the actual world, is that they have the same ancestors in the actual world. This solution to the problem of 'transworld identity' has distinct advantages over the main alternative, which is to loosen the criteria of identity so as to permit a given individual to have *several* 'counterparts' in a given possible world.

APPENDIX TO CHAPTER 1

Relational logic and social relations

Take two images of society: Marxist class theory and the theory of social stratification. The first uses a single (economic) criterion for the definition of the basic social units, the second uses multiple criteria (income, education, status, power). The first strives to explain the distribution of attributes other than class as a function of class differences, both at the structural and the individual level.[15] The second starts out with a set of rankings and then goes on to search for correlations between the various dimensions. The first theory sees social inequality as the main cause of change, and is thus led to see 'status inconsistency' or 'rank disequilibrium' as an obstacle to change, The second tends to see social inequality as a universal and inevitable fact that *per se* has no potential for change, so that social unrest is explained by the persistence of status inconsistencies, on the assumption that people tend to act so as to equalize their positions in the various dimensions of stratification. The first theory has a realist position on the question of class existence, whereas for the second, classes exist only in the eye of the beholder. The first theory looks at class *interaction*, the second at class *differences*.

In this appendix I shall explore some logical problems related to the last of the above propositions. I shall discuss the thesis[16] that Marxist and 'bourgeois' theories of class differ in fundamental logical respects, the first being a theory of internal class relations and the second postulating external relations only between classes. I shall argue that the interaction–comparison difference can indeed be analysed in terms of relational logic, but that it does not quite coincide with the internal–external distinction. Before coming to the details of the analysis, however, I would like to propose a redefinition of the oppositions sketched in the preceding paragraph. On the one hand I group all the theories that use interactional concepts in the definition of the basic social units, on the other hand I place together all the theories that use differential concepts. Within the economic sphere this is a distinction between the theory of exploitation and the theory of income groups. The exploiting and the exploited classes are related to each other by interaction; they do not only 'stand in a relationship to each other, but they actively relate to each other'.[17] The income groups, by contrast, are related to each other only by the relationships of having larger or smaller incomes, which is a relation of difference or comparison rather than of interaction. It is well known that Marx rejected this quantitative conception of class.[18]

Within the political dimension the same distinction can be used to classify the various theories of power that have been proposed in recent years. On the one hand there is the interactional approach that sees power basically as 'power over someone', a conception that implies a qualitative distinction between the tenants of power and the objects of that power. On the other hand there is the differential approach that attributes to each person or group a certain *amount* of power and then goes on to distinguish (quantitatively) between groups on this basis. In the latter case power is not power over someone, no more than money is money over someone. The differential notion of power is rather like purchasing power, an all-round capacity to get what one wants. The interactional notion is analogous to exploitation, in that it implies the existence of a polar individual or group that is the object of power. It is my contention that in the typologization of theories of class or stratification, the distinction between economic and political criteria of class is less important than the distinction between unidimensional and multidimensional criteria, and also less important than the distinction between interactional and differential theories. Dahrendorf is closer than is Wright Mills to the Marxist tradition, even if Wright Mills is certainly closer to that tradition than is Parsons.

Implicit in what has been said above is a distinction between the following relational statements:

$$a \text{ exploits } b, \tag{1}$$
$$a \text{ has more money than } b, \tag{2}$$
$$a \text{ has power over } b, \tag{3}$$
$$a \text{ has more power than } b. \tag{4}$$

We may also add

$$a \text{ ranks himself higher than } b, \tag{5}$$
$$a \text{ has more prestige than } b, \tag{6}$$

Of these (1), (3), and (5) stand for interactions, whereas (2), (4), and (6) stand for comparisons. The task of this appendix is to account for this difference in logical terms. The idea of distinguishing between two kinds of relations goes back at least to Leibniz, who wrote that 'relations either are relations of comparison or of connection'.[19] The terminology of internal and external relations is more recent, but the meaning of the terms is far from being well established.[20] Equally ill-stated are the theses that various philosophers have tried to work out by means of these concepts. As far as I can see it is possible to distinguish three main assertions that have been put forward: all relations are internal; all relations are external; in inanimate nature all relations are external, whereas in society all relations are internal. I shall mainly discuss the second half of the third assertion. On my analysis of the notions of external and internal relations, this half-assertion comes out true, even though the first half of the assertion does not seem to be correct.

I shall mention, mostly for later reference, the traditional approach to external and internal relations.[21] In most philosophical discussions the distinction has generally been seen as similar to the distinction between accidental and essential properties: internal relations are the relations without which one or both of the relata would not have been what they are, whereas external relations are such that we may abstract from them in thought without the relata losing their identity. If we want to say, on intuitive grounds, that the relation 'being taller than' is an external relation, this seems permitted on this approach. If, on the other hand, our linguistic intuitions (for what they are worth[22]) tell us that 'being in love with' is an internal relation, it is not obvious that this can be made good by equating internal relations to essential relations. My being in love may be what makes me into the individual I am, but it may also be what makes me into a different person:

> Now thou hast loved me one whole day,
> Tomorrow when thou leav'st, what wilt thou say?
> Wilt thou when antedate some new made vow?
> Or say that now
> We are not just those persons which we were?[23]

As pointed out by G. E. Moore in a classical contribution to the problem,[24] it is trivial to say that if *a* has the relation *R* to something, then anything that does not have that relation to this something cannot be *a*. The real problem is a counterfactual one, whether anyone that did not have that relation to anything could not have been *a*. We know that all persons that do not have John F. Kennedy for a brother are not Edward Kennedy, but still we might want to know whether Edward Kennedy could not have been Edward Kennedy without having John F. Kennedy for a brother. In order to answer the latter question we should have to define identity criteria for things being what they are, a difficult question indeed. We can easily define the properties or relations that are necessary for a chair to be a chair, but not what is required for a chair to be *that* particular chair. The very fact that it comes so easily to us to italicize 'that' in order to convey the meaning of individuality is evidence of the deeply felt need we have of referring to particulars in a manner that is independent of any specific properties or relations. As argued by Hegel in the first chapter of the *Phenomenology of Mind*, any object can be 'that' object, so that the expression we use for the identification of particulars really is the most universal of all expressions. Bare particulars would be indistinguishable and thus identical.

In Chapters 3 and 6 below we shall look at the solution to this problem that has recently been proposed by Saul Kripke and Michael Dummett. Here, however, I shall simply avoid the problem by using a different and purely formal approach to the distinction between external and internal relations, according to which there is no need at all to appeal to the purported distinction between essential and accidental relations. If someone should feel that by doing so I make an arbitrary break with the philosophical tradition, I can only answer (i) that the definition proposed here has the advantage of being tolerably precise, and (ii) that it seems adequate with respect to at least some of our linguistic intuitions (for what they are worth, once again). My starting point will be some recent philosophical work on the theory of relations in the philosophy of Leibniz.[25]

A main problem in the interpretation of Leibniz is that he seems to hold two distinct and incompatible theories about the relations between monads. On the one hand he seems to argue that all relational statements can be reduced to or inferred from non-relational statements,[26] but on the other hand he has some rather explicit statements to the effect that all monadic predicates on further analysis turn out to have a relational structure.[27] The solution (proposed by Hintikka) that makes it possible to reconcile the two theses, will also help us in the analysis of external and internal relations in the social sciences. Let us start out with a tentative definition of external relations:

Tentative definition: Rab is an external relation if there exist predicates (not necessarily unique) $F_1 \ldots F_n$ and $G_1 \ldots G_m$ such that 'Rab' can be inferred from a truth function of 'F_1a', 'F_2a', $\ldots$ 'F_na', and 'G_1b', 'G_2b' $\ldots$ 'G_mb'.

On this definition 'a is richer than b' expresses an external relation because it is implied by 'a has 10 dollars and b has 5 dollars'. On the other hand, 'the particle a is attracted by the particle b' expresses an internal relation, a conclusion which does not conflict violently with our intuitions. These two examples apparently show that the imputation of internal relations only to the social sciences and of external relations only to the natural sciences cannot be correct. The matter, however, is not that simple. Leibniz, for example, would argue that in the second example he can prove by general metaphysical reasoning that the relation of attraction can be reduced in the manner indicated by the definition. For the present purposes, however, I think we can avoid this problem and just say that as long as the reduction has not been *effectively* accomplished, the relation of attraction must be regarded as an internal one. Objections—of a more serious nature—can also be raised to the interpretation of 'a is richer than b' as an external relation. Consider for example the following statements:

$$a \text{ has more power than } b, \qquad (4)$$
$$a \text{ is taller than } b. \qquad (7)$$

According to the tentative definition these are both external relations, but the reducing predicates F and G are quite different in the two cases. The predicate 'n centimetres tall' is a reducing predicate that is itself irreducible, i.e. that contains no hidden relational components. On other hand 'having n degrees of power' *is* an implicitly relational predicate that cannot be defined without referring to other persons or to objects or to both. This can be done in different ways in different models of power,[28] but a purely monadic concept of power would surely be an absurdity. If we now go back to Leibniz, he can be interpreted as having held the following thesis: even if a relational statement '*Rab*' is reduced so that it can be inferred from, say, '*Fa & Gb*', this does not exclude that the reducing predicates '*F*' and '*G*' themselves may have a relational structure, such as 'being everybody's master' or 'being nobody's slave'.[29] Actually Leibniz held an even stronger thesis, viz. that *all* statements '*Rab*' can be reduced to statements containing monadic predicates only and that *all* monadic predicates have a hidden relational structure. I do not accept these views, but nevertheless I find that the double reduction can fruitfully be used in a revised definition of external relations:

Revised definition: Rab is an external relation if (i) it is an external relation according to the tentative definition above, and *either* (ii) the reducing predicates F_i, G_j have no hidden relational components *or* (iii) no F_i with a hidden relational structure contains a bound variable among whose possible values is b, and no G_j with a hidden relational structure contains a bound variable among whose possible values is a.

Conversely *Rab* is internal in one of the two cases: either the relation cannot be reduced, or the reduction is such that we implicitly refer to b in some statement '$F_i a$' or to a in some statement '$G_j b$'. Note the difference between referring to another individual directly, as in the statement '*Rab*', and referring indirectly to the same individual, as in the statement '$(\exists x)(Rax)$', where the reference to b can occur through the fact that b is a member of the class of individuals from which the values of the bound variable x may be drawn. I think it intuitively reasonable to say that the reference to b is an internal one in both cases. This means, for example, that not only the relation 'power over someone', but also the relation 'more power than' are internal relations according to the revised definition. In one simple model, for example, the amount of power is derived from the number of persons over which one exercises one-step or two-step control.[30] (Here control means the same thing as 'power over someone'.) This means that the analysis of the statement '*a* has more power than *b*' goes as follows. Firstly we single out some reducing predicates, for example '*a* has two degrees of power' and '*b* has one degree of power'. Then we observe that these can be further analysed as

'$(\exists x)(\exists y)(x \neq y \, \& \, Dax \, \& \, (Dxy \vee Day) \, \& \, (\forall z)((Daz \vee Dxz \vee (Day \, \& \, Dyz))$
$\supset (z = x \vee z = y)))$'

and

$(\exists x)(Dbx \, \& \, (\forall y)(Dby \supset y = x))$',

respectively, where 'Dxy' means 'x has control over y'. If we assume that b is among the individuals over which range variables x and y in the first expression and a among the individuals over which ranges variable x in the second, then clearly '*a* has more power than *b*' has been shown to be an internal relation on the revised definition. It is of course possible that individuals in disjoint social systems are being compared, as in the statement 'The pre-Colombian Aztec kings had more power than their European homologues', in which case the relation is an external one on both definitions. I submit, however, that in most cases where comparisons of amounts of power would seem relevant, we are dealing with comparisons between individuals belonging to the same social network.

Substantially the same analysis is valid for the relation between (1) and (2) or between (5) and (6). It is not necessarily the case that the reducing predicate 'having n degrees of money' is itself reducible to the exploitation relation (as the relation 'having n degrees of power' in the above example was reducible to the relation 'power over someone'), but it must surely be reducible to *some* relational statement involving bound variables that range over individuals and their resources. To think that the possession of money is a natural property of the individual on a par with his age or height, would be a case of fetichism similar to the 'commodity fetichism' of attributing to a product the property of being a commodity as if it were a natural and inherent feature. People are rich because other people accept their money; products are commodities because they are treated as commodities in exchange with other commodities. The empiricist fallacy, if any, would not be the use of external relations in the analysis of class, but rather the neglect of the implicitly relational character of the attributes used for the comparisons. You cannot start out by describing isolated individuals and then go on to define the (comparative) relations between them that constitute society, because the (interactional) relations must be implicitly present from the very beginning.

Possession of prestige or status is more obviously, perhaps, a socially defined attribute. In order to determine the objective prestige hierarchy of a society, one usually first collects the subjective rankings of a sufficiently large sample and then goes on to aggregate them in some manner to an overall ranking list. In most cases 'sufficiently large' means, among other things, that all the categories (e.g. occupations) that are being ranked will themselves be represented among the respondents, so that it will be possible also to study the image of self in a systematic manner. It may turn out, for example, that no one places his own occupation at the bottom of the list and still there will be some occupation that is at the bottom of the aggregate ranking list, so that in some cases (5) will be true and (6) false. Again it would be incorrect, on our revised definition, to say that (6) represents an external relation, if b is one of the individuals whose subjective ranking enters into the construction of the aggregate scale on the basis of which we ascribe to a a certain amount of prestige.

Notes

1. A good introduction to propositional and quantificational logic at the elementary level is Quine (1959). A more advanced treatment is Church (1956). Good introductions to modal logic are Snyder (1971) and Hughes and Cresswell (1972).
2. As noted by Dummett (1973, pp. 8–9), nested quantifiers are inextricably bound up

with the use of relations, in the sense that every sentence containing one-place predicates only is equivalent to some sentence where no quantifier stands within the scope of any other quantifiers.

3. Davidson (1973, p. 717).
4. Marx (1845–46, p. 33).
5. Marx (1867, pp. 484 ff).
6. Formulae with nested quantifiers can be interpreted in an instructive and amusing way, first proposed by Jaakko Hintikka. Exploiting the fact (for which see Church (1956, pp. 209 ff.) that any quantificational sentence can be converted into 'prenex normal form' (an initial string of quantifiers followed by a matrix which does not contain any quantifiers) Hintikka (1973, p. 63) goes on to compare the sentence to a game with Nature: 'My end in the game is to make a substitution-instance of the matrix true. My Opponent's (nature's) aim is to make the outcome of the game to be a false substitution-instance of the matrix. Each existential quantifier marks my move: I choose (produce, find) an individual whose name is to be substituted for the corresponding bound variable. Each universal quantifier marks a move by my opponent: he is free to produce an individual whose name is to be substituted for the variables bound to the universal quantifier. The order of the moves corresponds to the order of the quantifiers. ... For a sentence to be true it is necessary and sufficient that I have (as a matter of fact) a winning strategy in the correlated game, in the sense of game theory.'
7. The names 'S-4' and 'S-5' for these systems derive from Lewis and Langford (1932). The systems are extensively studied in the literature; see Snyder (1971) for further details.
8. As an afterthought to his analysis of deontic logic, Snyder (1972, p. 197) remarks: 'This excursion into building a system of modal logic to meet a particular need should indicate that while it is not the case that a formal system be constructed having *whatever* combination of properties we can dream up, there is obviously great flexibility in the machinery available, and formal systems *can* be developed which meet rather specialized conditions.'
9. Cf. especially Prior (1967).
10. For the analogy between alethic and deontic modalities, see Leibniz (1948, p. 606). In addition to this formal analogy Leibniz also postulated a substantial connection between the two sets of notions, in defining obligatory actions as what is necessary for a good man (Leibniz, 1948, p. 606).
11. Cf. Snyder (1971, Chapter V) for a quite full discussion.
12. Russell (1905).
13. Example taken (with modifications) from Snyder (1971, p. 204).
14. Hughes and Cresswell (1972, pp. 197–198) argue that it is possible to define a system in which the formula '$N(\exists x) (Fx) \subset (\exists x) (N(Fx))$' comes out as valid, by letting the variable range over *intensional* objects, i.e. over individual concepts rather than over individuals. Intensional objects differ from ordinary objects by the criteria of identity: as ordinary objects Walter Scott and The Author of *Waverley* are identical, but as intensional objects they are distinct. In this sense there is an intensional object of whom it is true that he is necessarily president of the republic, viz. the object The President of the Republic. Even disregarding the general problems that arise as soon as we admit intensional objects, the interest of this interpretation is severely curtailed by the fact that it makes not only the above formula as a whole, but even the consequent, taken by itself, come out as valid.
15. By this opaque phrase one could for example mean the following. Suppose that a population is distributed along the economic and, say, the political dimension according to the distributions f and g. At the structural level Marxist theory could be interpreted as saying that there exists a functional F such that $g = F(f)$. At the individual level, knowledge of a person's position on the economic dimension should give the

probability distribution of his position on the other dimension.

16. For this thesis, see especially Ollman (1976). I am indebted to Hayward Alker, Jr. for drawing my attention to Ollman's work.
17. Marx (1879–80, p. 362).
18. Marx (1847, p. 349).
19. Leibniz (1903, p. 355).
20. Cf. for example Russell (1910, p. 374): 'I maintain that there are such facts as that x has the relation R to y, and that such facts are not in general reducible to, or inferable from, a fact about x only and a fact about y only: they do not imply that x and y have any complexity, or any intrinsic property distinguishing them from a z and a w which do not have the relation R. This is what I mean when I say that relations are external.' This characterization of external relations would for me be part of the definition of internal relations.
21. Cf. Rorty (1967) for a good exposition.
22. This rider refers to the possibility that our linguistic intuitions may themselves change as a result of the conceptual analysis, until we arrive at what Rawls (1971, pp. 20 ff.) has called a 'reflective equilibrium'.
23. Donne, *Woman's Constancy*. These lines should be read in the light of *The Broken Heart* and *The Paradox*, both of which are touched upon in Chapter 4 below. For a similar view in another authority on love, cf. the following remark upon the choice of confidant: 'Perhaps the wisest thing is to confide in oneself. Using borrowed names, but including all the relevant details, write down tonight what took place between you and your mistress, and the problems with which you are faced. In a week's time, if you are suffering from passionate love (*si vous avez l'amour-passion*), you will be someone else entirely, and then, on reading your case-history, you will be able to give yourself good advice.' (Stendhal, *De l'Amour*, Chapter 34.) Who is advising whom here?
24. Moore (1922).
25. Mates (1968); Ishiguro (1972a, 1972b); Hintikka (1972).
26. He actually tries to operate such reductions in the relational statements 'Peter is like Paul', 'Titius is wiser than Caius' and 'Paris loves Helen'; see Mates (1968) and Hintikka (1972) for details. Contrary to the definitions proposed here, Leibniz admits non-truth-functional sentence connectives in his reductions.
27. He says, for example, that 'there is no term so absolute or so detached that it does not contain relations, and whose perfect analysis does not lead to other things and even to all other things' (Leibniz, 1875–90, vol. V, p. 211).
28. One simple model is that proposed by Kemeny *et al.* (1966, p. 384), in which 'power over someone' is the basic notion, absolute amounts of power a derived notion and 'more power than' derived at one further remove. A more complex model is that given by Coleman (1973a), where the basic notions are the actors' control over resources and interests in resources, from which may be derived, firstly, the relation 'power over someone' and absolute amounts of power, and, secondly, the relation 'more power than'.
29. Hintikka (1972).
30. This is the model given by Kemeny *et al.* (1966).

2

POSSIBILISTIC REASONING IN THE SOCIAL SCIENCES

In this chapter I shall examine a number of models from the social sciences that in various manners exhibit 'possibilistic features', i.e. models where pure possibilities (as distinct from quantified probabilities) have an important theoretical function. In some cases I shall try to speculate upon eventual links between these models and the modal concepts set forth in Chapter 1. In other cases the link is indirect at most. The function of the present chapter is not so much to offer specific applications of modal logic (this is the task of the later chapters), as to convince the sceptical reader that the general notion of possible worlds already has a place in the social sciences. The models presented are the following:

—social mobility,
—finite state grammars,
—kinship systems,
—evaluation of real national income,
—endogenous change of tastes.

Social mobility

The simplest model for the study of social mobility is the Markov chain approach. Assuming that we have n classes, the approach postulates that for each pair i, j of classes, there is a number p_{ij} that uniquely characterizes the probability of an individual in class i at time t being in class j at time $t + 1$, this number being independent (i) of the past history of mobility of the individual, (ii) of other present characteristics than class membership, and (iii) of events in calendar time. In principle the same conceptualization can also be used for the study of mobility between generations.[1] In many cases a transition matrix of these p_{ij}'s will contain some zeros, that is, for some pairs of classes there is zero probability of (one-step) mobility. This, of course, does not mean that it is impossible for (the descendants of) a member of the first class to belong ultimately to the second. It may be possible to make the transition in several steps, each of which is represented by a non-zero entry in the transition matrix.

In order to study this problem we may replace the probability matrix p_{ij} with the possibilistic matrix d_{ij}, where $d_{ij} = p_{ij}$ if $p_{ij} = 0$ and $d_{ij} = 1$ otherwise. The matrix d_{ij} we call the *adjacency matrix*.[2] It expresses in a simplified form the essence of short-term mobility possibilities. It is quite possible that for some purposes this simplified matrix is more analytically fertile than the full probabilistic structure. It might be the case, for example, that *perceived* possibilities of mobility have this simple Yes–No form rather than the gradual character of the p_{ij} matrix. The unique Negro that becomes a high court judge or the woman who becomes the president of a large corporation, may have a qualitative impact that is largely independent of the underlying numerical realities.[3]

Having constructed the adjacency matrix, we may go on to define the *reachability* matrix, whose entries give the possibility of going from class i to class j in any number of steps.[4] If the reachability matrix has some zero entries, this means that the social structure in certain respects resembles a caste system, some positions being inaccessible for members that start out in certain other positions. Both the short-term adjacency relation and the long-term reachability relation may be interpreted in terms of modal logic. For a given state of the world, i.e. a given distribution of individuals over classes, the accessible states are the states which are possible according to either the short-term or the long-term matrix. The modal concepts of possibility and necessity then immediately follow. In particular we may note that it now becomes possible to speak of *necessary features* of an individual, viz. the features that characterize all the individuals in all the classes to which he may accede in one step (or in a number of steps). Some individuals may be contingently F, i.e. they may have immediate or ultimate access to non-F classes, whereas others may be necessarily F. This distinction might conceivably be correlated with other properties of the individuals. I do not say that they ever are, only that this modal interpretation of mobility immediately produces this notion of a necessary feature. If one believes, as I do, that it is a good thing to have as many and as varied concept-generating structures as possible, this is at least a prima facie argument for the study of these logical ideas being worth while.

Necessary features, it may be observed, are not the same thing as *constraints*: the former is the wider concept. In order to explore this distinction we may digress briefly from the theme of this section, and consider the notion of a feasible set in economic theory, such a set being defined by a number of constraints. Given some initial economic state, for example, various conditions may be imposed that limit the set of states that may follow the initial state. In addition to technological constraints, consumption may not be allowed to fall below some limit, whereas investment must be kept above some minimal level. It may turn out that all ways of satisfying simultaneously these (and perhaps additional) constraints involve the use of heavily polluting technology, which then becomes a necessary feature without being an explicit constraint. A quite different kind of example might be the following. Let us suppose that in a conflict over school reforms both teachers and parents have some last-ditch demands that serve as constraints on the Board of Education. Teachers demand shorter teaching hours, and parents more mathematics and science, from which it follows that all feasible outcomes include a reduction of languages and history. This feature, while necessary, is not imposed as a constraint by anyone and may actually be against the (mild) preferences of everyone. The distinction between constraints and necessary features may also be compared to the distinction between axioms and theorems in a formalized system. Every axiom may be seen as a theorem with the particular feature that it is derived from one axiom only, viz. itself; the other theorems are all derived from several axioms taken together. Taken singly, the axioms are constraints; taken jointly, they generate the necessary features.

Returning now to the study of social mobility, it has turned out that the Markov process is not really adequate for this purpose.[5] The main empirical finding that invalidated the approach was the fact that the proportion of individuals that stay in their class from time t to time $t + 2$ is much greater than what would be expected on the Markov assumption.[6] The longer an individual has been observed as a member of a given class, the greater are the chances that he will remain there for the next period. As always in such cases, this empirical regularity may be interpreted theoretically in two distinct ways. Either we are dealing with a sampling effect, so that the individual reveals himself as being (and as always having been) a typical 'stayer' rather than a 'mover', or we are dealing with a genuine after-effect where the individual himself is changed by prolonged class membership.[7] The last notion—the hypothesis of cumulative inertia, as it has been called—is especially interesting in this context. This notion implies that the 'halo of possibilities' that surround the actual may change by the very fact that time goes on, without any change in the actual state. This is an idea to be explored again in Chapter 3. Here it will only be pointed out that of course I am not implying the absurd idea that the mobility possibilities may change without *any* changes in the actual world. The point is simply that the transition probabilities (and possibilities) may change without any change in the individual *as defined*, i.e. without any change in the actual class membership variable. Other things will certainly have changed, such as aspiration level, relative or absolute income, etc.

More formally: given the empirical observation that the value of variable x at time $t + 1$ cannot be predicted from the value of x at t, we may extend the model in one of two distinct ways. Either we may introduce the value at t of some new variables y, z ... or we may introduce the value at $t - 1$, $t - 2$ ... of x. From the metaphysical point of view the last approach is not very satisfactory, as it seems to imply that the past can somehow exercise a causal influence upon the present, over and above the influence that is mediated by the traces left by the past in the present.[8] On the other hand it may be more convenient to use past values of the same variable rather than to introduce new variables. There may be a trade-off here between explanatory elegance and metaphysical realism.[9]

Finite-state grammars

The relation between a probabilistic Markov model and the corresponding possibilistic structure may also be used to throw some light upon our understanding of linguistic processes. We want to answer the following question: What are the rules that govern sentence formation in a given language? More precisely, this question may be understood in two distinct ways: as an empirical query about the sentences actually uttered by native speakers in the ordinary course of life, and as a theoretical enquiry into the sentences that are judged to be grammatical by native speakers. Starting with the first question, it is clear enough (i) that words are uttered with different frequencies and (ii) that a given word is followed by other words with varying frequencies, the frequency being zero for many or most of the possible successors. A first attempt at an understanding of sentence formation would then be the following hypothesis: the probability p that a sentence '$a_1 \ldots a_n s$' is uttered, where the a_i are single words and 's' represents 'end of sentence', is the product of the probabilities

$$p_1 \cdot p_{1,2} \cdot p_{2,3} \cdots p_{n-1,n} \cdot p_{n,s},$$

where p_1 is the frequency of a_1 and $p_{i,j}$ is the probability of a_j occurring immediately after a_i. A moment's reflection, however, shows that this is not a very plausible model. The probability of a_j occurring after a_i depends heavily upon the words preceding a_i in the sequence; a succession of pairwise compatible words may give an incomprehensible whole, as in the following example: 'The head and in frontal attack on an English writer that the character of this point is therefore another method for the letters that the time of who ever told the problem for an unexpected.'[10]

Taking past history into account, by letting the probability of a word occurring depend upon, say, the four words preceding it in the sequence, does not guarantee probable or even possible utterances. Using word quintuplets with word frequency representative of English, a well-known study[11] generated the following: 'Road in the country was insane especially in dreary rooms where they have some books to buy for studying Greek.' In principle one might try to overcome this difficulty by making the probability of a word occurring depend upon an even larger number of preceding words, but the required number of transition probabilities would soon become impossibly large. In addition there is a problem concerning the relation between probability of utterance and grammaticality of a sentence. If one starts out with a higher-order Markov model (i.e. a Markov model capable of taking past history into account) for the probabilistic study of sentence utterance, then it would be nice if the possibilistic version of this model generated exactly the set of all grammatical sentences. 'Grammatical' would then simply mean 'having non-zero probability of being uttered by a native speaker'.[12] It can be shown, however (and I shall do so in a moment), that no kind of Markovian model is capable of generating all the sentences that a native speaker would accept as grammatical and only those sentences. One may also advance the stronger claim that some grammatical sentences have zero probability of being uttered, if for example the time required for their utterance exceeds the duration of the physical universe. There certainly is a need for a probabilistic model of sentence utterance, but it can never serve as a foundation for a possibilistic model of sentence grammaticality. On this point there is a sharp contrast to the model discussed in the previous section, where possibility was defined directly as non-zero probability.

The argument against a Markovian model of grammaticality[13] uses the notion of a *finite state machine*, special cases of which are the various models described above. The machine has n states $s_1 \ldots s_n$, s_1 being the initial state. When the machine is in state s_i, there is a well-defined set S_i of states into which it can pass from s_i. When the machine goes from s_i to $s_j \varepsilon S_i$, it may write down any word from a set S_{ij} of words. A grammatical sentence is a string of words that may be the result of the machine's going from the initial state via other states and back to the initial state. For the generation of strings longer than n (containing more than n words), the machine must obviously go through a sequence of states in which at least one state, s_k say, occurs twice. Between the two occurrences of s_k there must be a sequence $s_{n_1} s_{n_2} \ldots s_{n_p}$ of states, with a corresponding substring being written down. But if $s_k s_{n_1} \ldots s_{n_p} s_k$ is a possible sequence of states, then so also is

$$s_k s_{n_1} \ldots s_{n_p} s_k s_{n_1} \ldots s_{n_p} s_k,$$

with the substring of words repeated. This also means that the sentence in question must contain a substring that can be repeated (by extension of the same argument) indefinitely, any number of times, without violation of grammaticality. To put the matter briefly: if the language is to be generated by a finite state grammar, any sufficiently long sentence must contain a substring that can be repeated any number of times without breach of grammaticality.

We shall now show that this is not the case for sentences of the form

$$A_k : \text{If}^k \text{ it rains (then it blows)}^k, \qquad k = 1, 2 \ldots,$$

where the exponentiation signifies repetition. Clearly all A_k are perfectly grammatical. It is also clear that for any proposed finite-state grammar with n states, we can find a k such that the length of A_k exceeds n. This means that for sufficiently large k, A_k must contain a substring that can be repeated indefinitely. However, it is an easy matter to check that this cannot be the case for any of the possible substrings of an A_k. This means that we have found a sentence that (i) on intuitive grounds must be accepted as grammatical, and (ii) cannot be generated by the finite state grammar in question. Since such counterexamples can be found for any finite state grammar (even if there is no counterexample that will serve against all such grammars), these are inadequate in principle for the analysis of natural languages. (In an appendix to the present chapter a similar theorem is proved for a wider class of grammars.) At the root of this possibilistic analysis is a basic postulate of modern linguistics, the idea that what we study is competence rather than performance—the possible rather than the actual.

Kinship systems and structuralist thought

There is one school of thought whose object of study *par excellence* is the possible rather than the actual, viz. the French school of structuralism. There is no general agreement as to the essence, or even the existence, of this group; some of its presumed members vehemently deny any such affiliation. Nevertheless I think we are on safe grounds if we single out Claude Levi-Strauss as a main exponent of structuralist thinking. His general approach may be briefly describ-ed as finitistic, combinatorial and possibilistic. Similar features characterize the work of such thinkers as Roland Barthes, Jacques Lacan, and Louis Althus-ser (before he made his autocritique). I shall refer quite briefly to the Althusser school of Marxism, but otherwise I shall limit myself to Levi-Strauss.

It is possible to trace several stages in Levi-Strauss's methodological reflec-tions. A first important distinction was proposed in 1958 between mechanical and statistical models.[14] These concepts are carefully left undefined, and there is no general consensus as to their meaning.[15] One important aspect, however, seems fairly clear: a mechanical model describes society by a set of rules in a way that makes it appear as one of many possible sets, whereas a statistical model is nothing but an empirical resume of the actual society. This aspect is further spelled out in a distinction introduced in a 1964 essay on the difference between the human sciences and the social sciences.[16] The former include such disciplines as linguistics (*the* human science *par excellence*), textual criti-cism, psychology, and social anthropology (*a la* Levi-Strauss), whereas the latter comprehend economics, sociology, and political science. The social sciences are closely linked to a given society, for which they perform technical and perhaps ideological functions; they are essentially limited and practical. The human sciences, on the other hand, are general and theoretical, being in this respect much closer to the natural and exact sciences which are clearly the methodological ideal of Levi-Strauss.[17] The object of the human sciences is society as such or man as such;[18] the range of variation of all possible objects of a given kind;[19] the common features of all possible objects of a given kind;[20] the possible and the necessary, never just the actual.

Omnipresent in Levi-Strauss' work is the analogy with linguistics and especially with phonology, which is used to justify his own combinatorial approach to anthropology. It is, of course, a very common practice in the social (and the human) sciences to work with dichotomized variables, the combina-tions of which permit us to construct a rough but hopefully fertile classification. In phonology (and especially in the work of Roman Jakobson), however, the binary oppositions are seen as features of reality rather than as heuristic devices. It is claimed that the analysis of phonemes in terms of the absence or presence of some 12 distinctive features is not just one possible description among many other, but that it corresponds to the mental structure of the speaker.[21] If this claim is accepted, the use of combinatorial analysis to generate all possible sounds, so to speak, is clearly justified. If it is rejected, the outcome of the combi-natorics will have no particular interest or significance, because any of the other equally valid conceptualizations could be used to generate a different set of possibles. It is not necessary to discuss here whether the claim is justified in linguistics. What seems to me fairly certain is that the corresponding claims made by Lévi-Strauss when analysing cooking into 'gustemes'[22] or myths in 'mythemes'[23] cannot be made good. It is certainly amusing to read a description of the difference between French and English cooking in terms of three binary oppositions, but no evidence at all is given that these oppositions have any existence at all outside the mind of Lévi-Strauss. In my opinion his later work on classification schemes and mythology has degenerated into an arbitrary and gratuitous exercise of misplaced ingenuity, totally lacking in intersubjective validity.

Nevertheless this work is taken seriously by many, a fact that calls for explanation. One reason may be the prestige derived from his earlier work on kinship systems, where the combinatorial analysis actually seems to have offered crucial insights. Even in this case I believe that some of his analyses are seriously flawed by arbitrary reasoning, such as his use of the 'atom of kinship' consisting of the relations between brother and sister, husband and wife, father and son, maternal uncle and nephew. The general thesis set forward[24] was that of these four relations, two would always be negative and two be positive. To the obvious criticism that human relations are typically ambivalent, being at the same time (but in different aspects) positive and negative, Lévi-Strauss offers an answer[25] that, as far as I understand it, amounts to saying that any *difference* can serve as an *opposition*. This, however, would seem to leave the anthropologist complete liberty of choice as to which relations shall be called positive and which negative, making the theory so flexible as to be impossible to falsify.

The most influential of Lévi-Strauss' kinship analyses is certainly *Les Structures Elémentaires de la Parenté*, where he showed (jointly with the mathematician André Weil) that given certain structural requirements concerning marriage and descent, there are but a finite (and small) number of kinship systems that are possible. Later writers have offered more elaborate analyses.[26] In the present exposition I shall define a *kinship system* as any partition of the society into 'types' such that (i) only individuals from the same type can marry each other, (ii) the type of an individual depends only upon the individual's sex and the type of his parents, and (iii) two boys (or two girls) having parents of different types will themselves be of different types. The third requirement implies that the change of type from parent to son will be a permutation of the set of types, and similarly for the change of type from parent to daughter. With n types there are $n!$ permutations for each sex, and thus $(n!)^2$ different kinship systems. This number increases so rapidly with n that with only a moderate number of types there are too many kinship systems for us to be able to survey them all. Thus four types imply 576 kinship systems; of these a great number will be isomorphic with each other, but even so very many remain. By imposing some further requirements, however, it is possible to reduce drastically the number of kinship systems. Let us call *permissible kinship systems* the systems that, in addition to (i), (ii), and (iii) above, satisfy (iv) the rule that whether a man is allowed to marry a female relative of a given kind depends only on the kind of relationship; (v) in particular no man is allowed to marry his sister and (vi) for any two individuals it is possible for some of their descendants to intermarry. Using matrix and group theoretic reasoning it is not hard to prove that there are rather few permissible kinship systems; thus with four types there are just six non-isomorphic ways of satisfying (i) – (vi).

What are the implications of these results? In the present context I would emphasize the fact that they permit us to place a given kinship structure in the field of all possible kinship structures of the same dimension (i.e. with the same number of types). Even more important is the fact that this field is not only of finite cardinality, but that it will typically be very small, so that it is possible to see whether any of the other possible structures in the field are realized. Among the six permissible systems in the field of dimension 4 only two turn out to be realized in actual societies: an obvious question then is to ask what are the features of the other systems that explain their absence. The answer to this question would also, of course, provide a valuable insight into the nature of the systems that *are* realized in actual societies. Here, then, we have another (metaphorical) sense in which the halo of possibilities that surround the actual should be explored for a full understanding of the actual itself.[27]

I have no quarrel with this analysis; on the contrary it appears (to my limited competence) an exemplary piece of reasoning. I would like to insist, however, upon the dangers inherent in—and the obstacles to—the transfer of these methods to other fields. The binary nature of the kinship relations (marriage and descent) is part of the order of things and not an analytical artifact. The same cannot be said of, say, the relation between the forces of production and the relations of production in Marxist theory. To analyse this relation in terms of binary oppositions and then go on to generate all possible modes of production, is a completely arbitrary procedure, based on a fallacious and pernicious reasoning by analogy.[28] Like the gustemes of Levi-Strauss, the periodical table of modes of production is pseudo-science of the same order as, say, the biologically inspired sociology of the 1890s.

The evaluation of real national income

The title of this section is taken from an important paper by Paul Samuelson, where among other things he explored the following question: Why should economists want to include such wasteful outputs as war goods in their calculation of national income? His answer is that 'presumably they serve as some kind of index of the useful things that might be produced in better times',[29] i.e. a clearly possibilistic or counterfactual answer. Another question—the central problem of the paper—pertains to the difficulties of comparing the welfare levels of two different states of the economy. I shall first discuss this problem within Samuelson's frame of reference, where it is supposed that the two states include exactly the same set of (unchanged) individuals. Then I shall add some remarks on the manner in which A. K. Sen has recently extended this analysis to deal with comparisons between the welfare levels of different groups of people.

Given, then, two states involving exactly the same individuals, the simplest method for comparing welfare levels is by the criterion of *Pareto-superiority*: state A is better than state B if the welfare levels of all persons are at least as great in A as in B, and the level of at least one person strictly greater in A than in B. This criterion is open to the obvious comment that even if we accept that it is correct when applicable (which is controversial, as shown below), it is applicable only to a very small subset of the total number of pairs of economic states. The ordering that results from Pareto-superiority is partial indeed, and it is no wonder that economists have sought to extend it somewhat. The story of these unsuccessful extensions has been often told, and I shall be very brief in my statement of them. The *Kaldor criterion* or *compensation test* implies that state A is better than state B if, by a redistribution of income (a compensation scheme) in A, it is possible to make A Pareto-superior to B. T. Scitovsky showed, however, that the Kaldor criterion did not have the desired property of anti-symmetry: on this criterion A could be better than B and B also better than A.[30] He then proposed the *Scitovsky criterion*, according to which A is better than B if A can be made Pareto-superior to B by redistribution but not vice versa; this criterion, however, turns out to lack the desired property of transitivity.[31]

Samuelson's article must be seen on the background of these failures to extend the Pareto-criterion. He strives to make explicit the possibilistic ideas behind both the Kaldor and the Scitovsky criteria, and the result is a wholesale counterfactualization of the actual economies. I shall briefly sketch his main ideas for a two-person, two-good world. We assume that the actual distribution of goods A and B between individuals I and II is in amounts A_I, B_I, A_{II}, B_{II}, leading to ordinal utility levels u_I and u_{II} respectively. A first concept introduced by Samuelson is the *utility possibility curve*: the Pareto-optimal frontier of the set of points (u'_I, u'_{II}) that can be realized by a redistribution of the total amounts $(A_I + A_{II}, B_I + B_{II})$ of goods A and B between I and II. Arguing on this assumption of constant total amounts of both goods, Samuelson postulates that the only case where one situation can unambiguously be said to be better than another is when the utility possibility curve of the first lies wholly outside the utility possibility curve of the second (if we plot u_I and u_{II} along the two axes). That is, even when A is Pareto-superior to B, we cannot unambiguously say that A is better than B, for if the utility possibility curves going through A and B intersect, simultaneous redistributions in both states can make B come out Pareto-superior to A.

Samuelson's next step is to introduce production and technology into the picture, so that we can no longer assume that A and B are present in constant total amounts. Knowledge of the production function will tell us which possible combinations (A', B') could have been produced instead of $(A_I + A_{II}, B_I + B_{II})$, given the existing factor endowments. For each such combination it is then of course the case that it might have been distributed between I and II in a large number of ways. This double counterfactualization enables us to define a more rigorous notion of the utility possibility curve, by the following procedure. First we use our knowledge of the production possibilities to determine all the possible combinations of A and B that could have been produced. For each such combination we construct a utility possibility curve in the sense defined above. Finally we define the *inclusive utility possibility curve* as the outer envelope of all the particular functions constructed in this manner. A state is then unambiguously better than another (and its real national income larger) if and only if the inclusive utility possibility curve of the first lies wholly outside that of the second, i.e. if all states attainable from the second, through redirection of the productive activities and redistribution of income, are also attainable from the first, but not vice versa. According to this definition we are allowed to say that an economy producing large amounts of war goods while starving the consumer has a larger national income than an economy where all consumers are thriving.

I gather that Samuelson's main point is the following. *Either* we compare national income and welfare levels in terms of *actual* want satisfaction, and then only the Pareto-criterion can serve. *Or* we may feel that the *potentiality* for want satisfaction is also relevant, but then we have to go the whole way and counterfactualize everything, distribution as well as production, in both states. Halfway houses, such as counterfactualization of one situation only, or counterfactualization of distribution and not of production, have no theoretical justification. These are not obviously true assertions. On the production side, the redirection of productive activities is neither instantaneous nor frictionless. If we affirm that society 'could' have produced (A', B') today instead of (A, B), we have to add a rider such as 'if certain crucial choices in the past had been different'. It is not obvious that counterfactualization of the (perhaps rather distant) past is relevant when comparing *today's* national incomes. On the consumption side, Samuelson himself stresses that not all redistribution schemes may be politically feasible. The problem is that the only redistribution technique that does not have an impact upon work incentives (and thus upon the total that is to be redistributed) is the so-called 'lump-sum tax', which is virtually impossible to operate in practice.[32] The techniques that *are* feasible, such as progressive taxation or rationing, will, on the other hand, lead to a reduction in efficiency and to a smaller total being available for redistribution. For this reason Samuelson suggests that we may have to narrow down the inclusive utility possibility curve so as to comprehend only the positions that are attainable through *politically feasible* means of income redistribution. This notion of political possibility forms the subject of Chapter 3.

According to Kenneth Arrow and Tibor Scitovsky, Samuelson's 'purist approach was not fully accepted by the profession',[33] presumably because of the dizziness generated by the counterfactuals required. On this count, however, Samuelson's analysis is sobriety itself when compared to the recent analysis by Amartya K. Sen of the logic of comparisons involving different sets of individuals.[34] Sen starts out by observing that even in the case of a comparison between states A and B involving the *same* set of individuals, there is an important difference between

(1) the group is better off with A than it would have been with B; and
(2) the group is better off with A than it was with B,

because the ordinal or cardinal structure of the social preference relation may change over time. A similar distinction is useful for comparing the welfare levels of two different groups or communities of individuals. Supposing for simplicity that the communities have the same number of members,[35] we should distinguish between

(3) community I is better off with A than it would have been with B; and
(4) community I is better off with A than community II is with B.

Statement (4) is what we want to discuss, but a direct analysis is clearly impossible if we accept the non-additivity of individual utilities. As a proxy we must confine ourselves to the counterfactual statement (3), but then we must first resolve two problems. Firstly we must decide which persons in community I shall be given which consumption baskets from community II. Sen mentions several ways of tackling this difficulty, the two most attractive of which are the following. Either we try to single out some privileged one-to-one correspondence between persons in I and baskets in II, and say that (3) is true if and only if I is socially preferred to II under this correspondence. We might for example require that the basket of the individual at place i in the income hierarchy of II should be given to the individual in the same place in the hierarchy of I. Or we might impose the much stronger requirement that statement (3) is true if and only if I is socially preferred to II for *all* of the $n!$ possible correlations between persons and baskets. Secondly we must decide what is meant by 'socially preferred'. This, of course, brings us back to the questions discussed in the first paragraphs of this section. I shall not discuss Sen's solution, except to note that he does not confront the problem of counterfactual production and distribution that is crucial to Samuelson's paper. It seems that on the 'purist' approach a comparison between the welfare levels of two distinct communities should involve (i) a counterfactualization of production, (ii) a counterfactualization of distribution, and (iii) for each pair of successive counterfactualizations of production and distribution, a counterfactual imputation (or a set of imputations) of baskets to persons.

In Chapter 6 below we shall see that these problems arise in a quite natural way in the analysis of historical problems, such as the impact of the slavery system in the ante-bellum South upon the non-slaveholding free. To compare the actual community I in A with the actual community II in B by asking how well off the individuals in I would have been in B, is logically similar to (even if simpler than) comparing the actual community in A with a hypothetical community in a hypothetical state B by asking how well off the actual individuals would have been in that hypothetical state.

Endogenous change of tastes

Some of my readers may have had the same childhood fantasy as myself: a walk in a landscape where from any point you could come to any other point without ever having to go uphill, because the landscape contours were changing all the time as a function of your path. A modified fantasy, still rather extravagant, might be the following. From any given point in the landscape you may move effortlessly to any point situated at a lower level, regardless of any hills that might lie between. Also suppose that as you go from one point to a lower-level point, the landscape changes so that some of the points formerly situated at a higher level now become lower-level points. An intriguing question would then be to ask *which* points are attainable in this way from a given initial point a_1. Obviously a point b would be accessible if and only if there is a sequence $a_1 a_2 \ldots a_n b$ such that a_2 is downhill from a_1, a_3 downhill from $a_2 \ldots$, and b downhill from a_n. This, however, is not very helpful unless we also specify how, as a result from the step from a_i to a_{i+1}, the set of points downhill from a_{i+1} and the set of points downhill from any other point as well, are changing. In modal terms, we have to specify how the possibly possible changes when we realize one of the possibles. In the modal systems of Chapter 1 the set of worlds that are accessible from a given world is not, of course, subject to change. In our fantasy, however, we are not bound by this rigid conception of the possible. Possibilities are constantly appearing and disappearing; some may be lost for ever, others may turn up again; some may be permanently acquired, others are transient only.

Moral education can be understood by this parable. The uphill points are the states to which the present state is preferred, the lower-level points represent an improvement over the present state. As we strive for short-term improvement, however, we are ourselves changed so that our notion of what *is* an improvement may not remain the same. It may turn out, for example, that from situation a_1 we go to a_2, subjectively seen as an improvement; and from a_2 to a_3, likewise seen as an improvement; even if in a_1 the step to a_3 was seen as a change for the worse. Ourselves, or our guardians, may exploit such facts in order to bring us painlessly and effortlessly on to our long-run optimum positions by a succession of short steps, each of which is seen as a short-term improvement. As Aristotle tells us,[36] our actions flow from our character and our character is formed by our actions. In the words of the economist, 'choice depends on tastes and tastes on past choices'.[37] This holds up a promise of improvement and a danger of inconstancy; a tool for self-education and for manipulation alike. The crucial feature of this approach to human action is that it brings together two aspects often thought to be incompatible: intentionality and causality. Choice according to consistent preferences is an important part of what we mean by intentionality, whereas the laws governing the endogenous change of preferences are purely causal, operating 'behind the back' of the actor concerned. The actor may, of course, try to anticipate the impact of present behaviour upon future preferences and make his present choice in the light of his evaluation of these consequences; indeed, this is what Aristotle tells us to do.[38] This, however, gives rise to the same problem at one further remove, for even if in this manner we can choose our preferences, the possibility remains of an endogenous change of meta-preferences, and so on. I return to this problem in Appendix 2 to Chapter 5 below.

The economic analysis of endogenous change of tastes goes back to 1944, when Trygve Haavelmo opened up wholly new vistas with some brief and perceptive remarks in his doctoral dissertation.[39] Important later developments are linked to the names of Nicholas Georgescu-Roegen, C. C. von Weiszäcker and Robert Pollak.[40] Here I shall sketch some of the ideas in von Weiszäcker's seminal paper. For simplicity he assumes (i) that present preferences depend only upon consumption in the immediately preceding period, and (ii) that the income of the consumer is to be allocated over two goods only. It has been shown recently[41] that the second assumption is crucial for the results obtained by von Weiszäcker, so that they do not easily generalize to the n-commodity case. I shall disregard this problem, as I think there are philosophically important questions to be discussed even in the rather special cases where the results *are* valid. The first assumption is rather disturbing, as it excludes the possibility of cumulative character formation. (Indeed, parts of von Weiszäcker's own discussion are in flagrant contradiction with this assumption.[42]) Nevertheless it is clear that the introduction of the whole consumption history as a variable would complicate the analysis so as to make it virtually unmanageable, and that at the present stage of research the strategy chosen by von Weiszäcker probably is the right one.

Economists, when studying the consumer's choice, use, more or less interchangeably, three distinct concepts: preferences, utility functions, and demand functions. Given various conditions, which we shall assume to be fulfilled, any two of these concepts can be deduced or constructed from the third.[43] Let us suppose that the consumer at time t has a preference structure P_t, represented by a utility function u_t, from which we can derive a demand function f_t that to each set of prices and income correlates a certain (two-component) commodity vector chosen by the consumer: $q_t = f_t(p, y)$. We now assume that present demand is a function of demand and consumption in the immediately preceding period: $f_t = F(f_{t-1}, q_{t-1})$, where F is some functional that represents the constant character traits underlying the changing preferences. More specifically, we assume that F is such that there exists a g such that $q_t = g(p, y_1 q_{t-1})$. This latter form only is used by von Weiszäcker. Now successive applications of the function g generate a sequence q_i of commodity bundles, which under certain conditions (whose economic interpretation is not obvious) is shown to converge to a point $q = h(p, y)$ that is independent of the initial bundle. (This result shows that the danger of inconstancy and of endlessly changing preferences is avoidable in at least some cases.) The relation h may be formally interpreted as a demand function, as to each set of prices and income it correlates a certain commodity bundle. To this demand function there also corresponds (given certain crucial and controversial assumptions) an 'as-if' utility function U, in the sense that we can deduce the bundle $\mathbf{q} = h(\mathbf{p}, y)$ if we assume that the consumer is maximizing U, given $\mathbf{p}$ and y. Alternatively, we may construct the 'long-term preference structure' P, with the property that $\mathbf{x} P \mathbf{y}$ if and only if $U(\mathbf{x}) > U(\mathbf{y})$.

Let us now return to the 'instantaneous' preferences P_t. There really is no need to index these by *time*, because the only relevant difference between P_{t_1} and P_{t_2} is the consumption in the immediately preceding periods $t_1 - 1$ and $t_2 - 1$; if consumption in these periods was the same, then the instantaneous preferences in the following periods will also be the same. We may therefore more usefully index preferences by consumption in the preceding period, writing '$\mathbf{x} P(\mathbf{z}) \mathbf{y}$' for '$\mathbf{x}$ is preferred to $\mathbf{y}$, given that consumption in the immediately preceding period was $\mathbf{z}$'. Von Weiszäcker now proves the following theorem, valid under certain conditions that verbally may be expressed as inertia or conservatism of the consumer:

Given two commodity vectors $\mathbf{x}$ *and* $\mathbf{y}$, *then* $\mathbf{x} P \mathbf{y}$ *if and only if there exists a sequence of vectors* $\mathbf{r}_1 \ldots \mathbf{r}_n = \mathbf{x}$ *such that* $\mathbf{r}_1 P(\mathbf{y})\mathbf{y}, \mathbf{r}_2 P(\mathbf{r}_1)\mathbf{r}_1, \mathbf{r}_3 P(\mathbf{r}_2)\mathbf{r}_2 \ldots \mathbf{r}_n P(\mathbf{r}_{n-1}) \mathbf{r}_{n-1}$.

The theorem says, in other words, that $\mathbf{x}$ is better than $\mathbf{y}$ according to my long-run preferences if and only if there exists a path from $\mathbf{y}$ to $\mathbf{x}$ such that each step in the path is an improvement according to the instantaneous preferences at the beginning of that step. Two observations should be made at this point. Firstly, it may very well be the case that $\mathbf{y} P(\mathbf{y})\mathbf{x}$, which implies a conflict between my short-term and my long-term preferences. The theorem then states that such a conflict may be overcome by the use of indirect strategies: it is the childhood fantasy (in the modified version) come true. Secondly, it may be the case that although both $\mathbf{x}$ and $\mathbf{y}$ are within the feasible set of the consumer, some of the vectors $\mathbf{r}$ may be unattainable at the given prices and income. In this case the consumer cannot educate himself to realize his long-term preferences, or rather, his education must be an uphill battle rather than a downhill stroll. The government or some other guardian may, however, subsidize his self-improvement by bringing the intermediate steps within his feasible set. Von Weiszäcker gives as an example the problem of regional mobility, where the government may exploit its knowledge about the endogenous change of preferences in order to subsidize a painless transfer from the countryside to the city.

It would seem that, according to von Weiszäcker, this kind of manipulation through subsidies is always ethically acceptable; he also seems to think that the individual could have no grounds for opposing the manipulation. Imagine, however, the following situation.[44] I am a non-smoker, and I do not like the cheap tobacco that is within my budget possibilities. If, however, someone were to subsidize my buying finer tobacco, my craving for nicotine would become so great that after some time I would gladly accept the cheap tobacco which formerly I rejected. Would it be ethically justifiable for someone, a tobacco producer, say, to offer me such subsidies; and should I have no qualms in accepting them? Both of these questions should presumably be answered in the negative (if you are not convinced of this, substitute heroin for tobacco), which shows that my 'long-run' preferences are not necessarily my 'real' preferences. To seduce someone into doing something that is against his real interest, is not more justifiable than to coerce him into doing it. (Between the pure seduction case, where each step is perceived as an improvement, and the pure coercion case, where the behaviour in question can only be maintained by permanent violence, there is the interesting intermediate case of a coercive act that is quickly habit-forming and thus makes itself superfluous. This, perhaps, would correspond to what moralists and novelists have had in mind when discussing seduction, as in *Les Liaisons Dangéreuses*.)

The cases of possibilistic reasoning discussed in this chapter have virtually nothing in common, except that in one way or another pure potentialities have an important role to play. In the context of the present work as a whole, these cases fulfil a double function. Firstly, they serve to remind the reader that the social sciences already 'dwell in Possibility'; that a number of well-known theories crucially turn upon the relation between what individuals and groups actually do and what they can do (or could have done). Secondly, some of the specific examples will be used in later discussions. In particular the analysis of real national income will concern us again in Chapter 6, whereas the problem of endogenous change of tastes is touched upon both in Chapter 4 and in Appendix 2 to Chapter 5 below.

APPENDIX TO CHAPTER 2

An impossibility result for context-free grammars

In the section on finite state grammars we proved that these are inadequate in principle for the generation of natural languages. A similar argument may be used to prove the inadequacy of what Chomsky[45] calls Type 2 grammars, or context-free grammars. To my knowledge this inadequacy has never been proved in the literature, claims to the contrary notwithstanding.[46] As an introduction to the proof we must explain the difference between finite state grammars and context-free grammars. Let us suppose that a phrase $w_1 w_2 w_3 w_4 w_5$ has been generated by a finite state grammar passing through the following sequence of states: $s_1-s_2-s_3-s_4-s_5-s_1$. This may also be expressed by saying that the sentence has been generated by applying successively the following *rewriting rules*:

$$s_1 \rightarrow w_1 s_2,$$
$$s_2 \rightarrow w_2 s_3,$$
$$s_3 \rightarrow w_3 s_4$$
$$s_4 \rightarrow w_4 s_5,$$
$$s_5 \rightarrow w_5.$$

These rules have the formal feature that on the left we see a single abstract symbol, which is then transformed either into a word or into a word followed by an abstract symbol. This, indeed, gives an independent characterization of the class of finite state grammars. A context-free grammar permits more complex rules: on the left we still have a single abstract symbol, but this may be transformed into any concatenation of abstract symbols and words. (More complex still are the context-sensitive grammars that allow for rules of the kind $ABC \rightarrow ADC$, where B is a single abstract symbol and A, C, D may be any concatenation of abstract symbols and words. No proof exists for the inadequacy of such grammars.) For these context-free grammars Bar-Hillel et al.[47] have proved the following theorem:

Let A be a context-free grammar and $L(A)$ the set of sentences generated by A. Then there exists a number p such that for any z in $L(A)$ longer than p, there exist x, u, w, v, y such that
  (i) $z = xuwvy$,
  (ii) $xu^m wv^m y \; \varepsilon \; L(A)$ for all m;
  (iii) u and v are not both empty.

More briefly the theorem states that in a language generated by a context-free grammar any sufficiently long sentence can be extended by indefinite repetition of *two* subparts without violation of grammaticality, just as we know that in languages generated by a finite state grammar any sufficiently long sentence can be extended by indefinite repetition of one subpart. In order to prove the inadequacy of context-free grammars for natural languages, we must come up with a counterexample of a grammatical sentence that cannot be extended in this way. The counter-examples of the form 'If^k it blows, (then it rains)^{k}' will not do for this purpose, for these sentences *can* be indefinitely extended by repetition of the two exponential blocks. Now let us look at the following sentences:

B_1: The first two million numbers in the decimal expansion of π are $a_1 a_2 \ldots$
       $a_{2000000}$.
B_2: The first two million million numbers in the decimal expansion of π are
       $a_1 a_2 \ldots a_{2000000000000}$.
       .
       .
       .
B_k: The first two (million)^k numbers in the decimal expansion of π are $a_1 a_2 \ldots$
       $a_{2 \cdot 10^{6k}}$.
       .
       .
       .

Given a context-free grammar and the number p of the above theorem, it is easy to find a k such that B_k is longer than p. Such a B_k must then permit a double extension as stated in the theorem. It is not difficult to see that these extensions must occur within the blocks 'million^k' and '$a_1 \ldots a_{2 \cdot 10^{6k}}$' if the result is not to be obviously ungrammatical. Suppose, then, that u in the theorem has the form 'million^q' and v the form '$a_r \ldots a_t$'. Choosing $m = 2$ in the theorem, it then states that the following sentence must be a grammatical one if we assume that the context-free grammar in question is adequate for English:

C: The two million^{k+q} first numbers in the decimal expansion of π are $a_1 \ldots$
$a_t a_r \ldots a_t \ldots a_{2 \cdot 10^{6k}}$

I shall show that C is not a grammatical sentence in English. If C is grammatical, then the number 'two million^{k+q}' must be the same as the number '$2.10^{6k} + t - r + 1$', i.e. the same as the number of numbers in the decimal expansion. Note that this is a requirement not of mathematics, but of linguistics, just as the lack of grammaticality of the sentence,

D: the two largest animals in the zoo are a mouse,

is a matter of linguistics, and not of mathematics (or of zoology). But as $q \geqslant 1$ and $t - r + 1 \leqslant 2.10^{6k}$, we have

$$2.10^{6k} + t - r + 1 \leqslant 4.10^{6k} < 2.10^{6k+1} < 2.10^{6(k+q)},$$

whereas the grammaticality of C would require $2.10^{6k} + t - r + 1 = 2 \cdot 10^{6(k+q)}$.

Apart from the intrinsic interest of the impossibility result just proved, it has the advantage of bringing out (even more clearly than the counterexample to finite state grammars) the purely possibilistic nature of linguistic reasoning. We have clearly intuitive notions concerning the grammaticality of sentences with zero probability of being uttered, and even a grammar that could generate exactly the set of sentences with a non-zero probability of being uttered must be rejected if it fails to generate a single grammatical sentence such as B_k.

Notes

1. But see the caveats of Duncan (1966).
2. See Fararo (1973, pp. 142 ff.).
3. This was the view of Sombart, as quoted by Lipset and Bendix (1959, p. 12).
4. See Fararo (1973, pp. 147 ff., 277 ff.). If D is the adjacency matrix, the reachability matrix is $D + D^2 \ldots D^{n-1} + D^n$.
5. Cf. McFarland (1970) for an elegant survey.
6. See Coleman (1973a), Boudon (1973), and Fararo (1973) for various expositions.
7. See Feller (1968, p. 122). He uses the example of automobilists having had one accident being more likely to have more accidents, which may be interpreted either in terms of 'naturally bad drivers' or in terms of initially indistinguishable drivers being selectively shocked into bad driving through their first accident. Another example might be unemployment: given the empirical finding that the probability of finding a job decreases with the duration of unemployment (Cripps and Tarling, 1974), this may be understood either as a result of some individuals being 'by nature' less eager or less capable than others, or on the hypothesis that people are changed (for the worse) through unemployment even if initially they lost their job through a purely random mechanism. Such irreversible creation of differences through random choices in an initially homogeneous population may turn out to be a major mechanism for the explanation of social change.

8. Cf. McFarland (1970) for a perceptive remark on Markov processes as the stochastic analogue to deterministic processes.
9. Cf. Elster (1976a) for a fuller discussion.
10. Chomsky and Miller (1963, p. 429).
11. Chomsky and Miller (1963, p. 429).
12. Cf. Hockett (1955, p. 10), as quoted by Chomsky (1957, p. 17): we should replace 'zero probability, and all extremely low probabilities, by *impossible*, and all higher probabilities by *possible*'. This would mean that possibilities are defined as *truncated probabilities*.
13. The following proof is taken from Rabin and Scott (1959).
14. Lévi-Strauss (1958, pp. 311 ff.).
15. For two divergent readings see Nutini (1970) and Barnes (1971), of which the latter is close to my own reading of Lévi-Strauss.
16. Lévi-Strauss (1973, pp. 351 ff.).
17. 'The social sciences stand in a client relationship to the exact and natural sciences, whereas the human sciences aspire to a disciple relationship' (Lévi-Strauss, 1973, p. 362).
18. 'The human sciences are those which situate themselves outside each particular society; either because they adopt the perspective of society in general (*une société quelconque*) or of an individual in general in society in general (*un individu quelconque au sein de n'importe quelle société*), or because they are grasping for an immanent human reality and thus situate themselves in a perspective that is prior both to the individual and to the society '(Lévi-Strauss, 1973, p. 360).
19. 'In this way one could obtain a source capable of generating a periodical table of linguistic structures, similar to the periodical table of the elements which modern chemistry owes to Mendeleieff. We would then only have to locate the languages already studied in this table, to note the position and the relation to other languages for those which remain insufficiently known theoretically, and to discover the location of still other languages—past, future or simply possible' (Lévi-Strauss, 1958, p. 66).
20. Lévi-Strauss (1967, p. 98).
21. Jakobson and Halle (1963, pp. 145 ff.).
22. Lévi-Strauss (1958, p. 99).
23. Lévi-Strauss (1958, p. 233); cf. also Lévi-Strauss (1964–71).
24. Lévi-Strauss (1958, Chapter II).
25. Lévi-Strauss (1973, p. 107). For a different and rather incompatible answer to this objection, see Needham (1962, p. 35).
26. See Kemeny *et al.* (1966, pp. 424 ff), and Fararo (1973, Chapter 18).
27. See also Bourdieu *et al.* (1968, p. 80): 'One should treat the ideal type not as an autonomous object (*non* en lui-même et pour lui-même), but as a member of a transformation group and in its relationship to all the other members of the family of which it is a privileged member.'
28. For this example, see Balibar (1966, p. 211).
29. Samuelson (1950), quoted from the reprint in Arrow and Scitovsky (1969, p. 418).
30. For a numerical example exhibiting the possibility of this situation, see Quirk and Saposnik (1968, p. 121).
31. For a numerical example, see Quirk and Saposnik (1968, p. 122).
32. Cf. Graaff (1971, pp. 77 ff.), for an exposition of this issue. The difficulty, roughly, is the following: for the lump-sum solution to work, people must have no incentive to hide their real abilities, which presupposes a solidarity that would have prevented the problem to which the tax is a solution from arising in the first place. Cf. also Sen (1973, Chapter, 4).
33. Arrow and Scitovsky (1969, p. 385).
34. Sen (1976).
35. Sen (1976) extends the analysis to the case of communities of different size.

36. *The Nicomachean Ethics*, 1113–1114. Following Kenny (1963) we may explain Aristotle's theory of moral education in the following terms. A character is something that is acquired through actions; Aristotle refers to this character as a *hexis*, something you 'have'. The actions which establish this *hexis* fall under the headings of *kinesis* or *poiesis*, at least (I think) when they are done in order to set up this *hexis*. The actions that stem from the *hexis*, come in the category of *energeia* or *praxis*; they are not means towards an end, but have their end in themselves. The good man *becomes* good by performing good actions (*kinesis*); when he *is* good, these actions (*energeia*) flow unstrainedly from his being. Becoming good is an uphill battle, being good is like water seeking its natural downhill course. For a simple model of the relation between *kinesis*, *hexis* and *energeia*, we may take the relation between learning to speak French, knowing French and speaking French.

37. Gorman (1967, p. 218).

38. 'Therefore only an utterly senseless person can fail to know that our characters are the result of our conduct; but if a man knowingly acts in a way that will result in his becoming unjust, he must be said to be voluntarily unjust' (Aristotle, *loc. cit.*). There is a serious ambiguity here, for even if I know (in a general manner) *that* my present actions will have an impact upon my future character, I may be unable to tell *how* they will change my preferences. In Chapter 4 below I argue that this is an inescapable feature of *la condition humanie*; that although we often know that our actions will have important consequences, we are unable to say which consequences; that although we know for sure that at a later time we shall regret some of our present actions, we do not know which actions; that although we can state in the preface of a book that it contains errors, we are unable to point to them. The impossibility of having specific knowledge about the impact of present behaviour upon future character traits does not stem from uncertainty about the environment, nor from practical difficulties in establishing the relevant causal connections. We are dealing with an absolute impossibility, for the reason that the causal link between our actions and our first-order character traits is itself a second-order character trait that can be modified by actions, and so on in an ever-ascending sequence. It is impossible in principle to have specific knowledge about all the levels in this infinite hierarchy, although we can have general knowledge about the existence of a hierarchy and specific knowledge about some of its levels. Cf. also Appendix 2 to Chapter 5 below and Elster (1976d).

39. Haavelmo (1944, pp. 17 ff.).

40. Georgescu-Roegen (1950); von Weiszäcker (1971a); Pollak (1976a).

41. By Pollak (1976a).

42. In Section 5 of his paper von Weiszäcker (1971a) asks why 'the long-run demand behaviour should differ from the short-run demand behaviour', and answers that the change is due to the consumer's undergoing a learning process. He may start out being rather ignorant of the various consumption possibilities and easily changing his mind, in the sense of the *ex-post* evaluations differing from the *ex-ante* ones. After some time, however, he will have run through large regions of the commodity space and will have formed stable preferences that reflect his past experience. This is certainly a very important idea, that could be incorporated into a theory of endogenous social change (cf. Elster, 1976a, for a sketch of how this can be done). It is incompatible, however, with the very short memory postulated elsewhere in the paper. If the consumer follows a sequence of consumption vectors $q_1 \ q_2 \ q_3 \ q_4 \ q_5 \ q_1 \ q_2$, the state of mind of the consumer when arriving at q_2 the second time does not reflect the experience of $q_3 \ q_4 \ q_5$ if we postulate $q_t = g\,(\mathbf{p},\, y,\, q_{t-1})$.

43. Cf. for example Georgescu-Roegen (1968) for an exposition.

44. This counterexample was independently given by Pollak (1976a, pp. 294–295). El-Safty (1976, p. 300), offers the following example: 'Johnny was asked why he didn't eat spinach. He replied, "I don't like spinach." To this an adult responded, "Try it, you'll like it." "I know", Johnny replied, "but I don't want to like it."' For

this example to be convincing, we have to assume that what Johnny really does not want is the side-effects of spinach-eating, such as acquiring the strength of Pop-Eye that would make him liable to more domestic chores or whatever.

45. Chomsky (1959).
46. Postal (1964, especially pp. 145 ff.) claims to have proved that context-free grammars cannot generate the Mohawk language. He first refers to the proof by Chomsky (1959) of the following theorem:

Let K be an alphabet with at least two symbols and let A be the set of all words over K. Then the diagonal set D_{A^2} (i.e. the set of all strings XX where X is a member of A) cannot be generated by a context-free grammar.

Postal then states in a footnote (note 27) that this result can be generalized to the following theorem:

Let K be an alphabet with at least two symbols and let A be any infinite set of words over K. Then the diagonal set D_{A^2} cannot be generated by a context-free grammar.

This, however, is wrong. For a counterexample, take $K = (a, b)$ and $A = ((ab), (ab)^2 \ldots (ab)^n \ldots)$. Then $D_{A^2} = ((abab) \ldots (abab)^n \ldots)$, which is generated by $S \to abab$, $S. \to ababS$, a context-free grammar. For his argument to go through, Postal requires the generalized version of the theorem, or at the very least he would have to show that the theorem is valid for the particular set A in Mohawk singled out for discussion. (I owe the substance of this note to suggestions from Aanund Hylland.)

47. Bar-Hillel, *et al.* (1964).

3

POLITICAL POSSIBILITY

Modal logic is the science of the possible, politics is the art of the possible, and never the twain have met. In this chapter I attempt a partial synthesis of the two fields, through a political interpretation of the basic notions of modal logic. I do not think this exercise can provide new and substantial insights into the nature of politics, nor that we can pull any empirical rabbits out of the logical hat. The justification for what I shall do is, firstly, that the slight formalization attempted below can throw into relief some connections between notions that at first glance would seem unrelated and, secondly, that the modal notions may lead us to put some new questions that would not otherwise have arisen in a natural way. Modal logic, here as elsewhere, is at most a machine for generating questions, not a short cut to the answers. In addition to the relevance of the approach to political scientists, I believe, with some diffidence, that this use of logical theory may be of some interest to the logician in search for illustrative material—and perhaps even be an incentive to conceptual development.

The basic postulate of the approach is that in any given state of society there exists a set of states that are politically possible with respect to that state. I shall use the abbreviation 'PP w.r.t.' for the relation of political accessibility. Instead of talking about the states themselves, it is perhaps more appropriate to talk about the states as described in a certain way, e.g. by a certain set of variables. For any given state—as an ontological entity—there presumably is at most *one* state that is PP w.r.t. that state (we shall see below why it would not be correct to say exactly one state), but for the state as described in a certain manner the set of states that are PP w.r.t. it may have more than one member. This under-determination of the future arises from the under-specification of the present which is an inevitable feature of any finite description. If the reader keeps in mind this distinction between the state and the state description, he will not be surprised by such prima facie strange statements as that the set of political possibilities in a given state may change even when the state itself remains the same. In a similar manner hysteresis, or temporal action at a distance, is impossible at the ontological level, but may appear at the epistemological level as a feature of our theories about certain processes.ᶠ

The approach presented is actor-oriented, in the sense that I am only referring to the states that can be *brought about* deliberately, while excluding the states that can only *come about* causally. Any given state must be succeeded by some other state (or by itself), so if political possibility was defined in the purely causal sense, the set of states that are PP w.r.t. a given state could never be empty. I shall argue, however, that there may be states presenting the peculiar feature that purposive political action is bound to fail, so that there are no possibilities in the intentional sense of the term.

At this point we may usefully invoke an analogy to the study of power. In general we do not want to say that power is just production of results, a behaviour that has the consequence of making people behave differently from what they would have done otherwise.[2] Rather we want to say with Bertrand Russell[3] that power is the production of *intended* results, or perhaps the capacity to produce such results. In this definition both the causal and the intentional aspects of power enter essentially. The reason why the causal aspect is essential is well brought out by Alvin Goldman: 'To say that S is powerful is not to say that he usually gets what he in fact wants, but that whatever he wanted he would get, no matter what he might happen to want.'[4] Without the last clause of this definition, we might have to ascribe extreme power to the chameleon, i.e. to the person that always changes his preferences so as to be on the winning side. In Chapter 6 below I shall argue that the counterfactual aspect of power creates problems that for the moment appear to me as insoluble, but I agree with Goldman that neglect of this aspect also leads us to counterintuitive imputations of power to powerless persons. Now in the case of the chameleon the intentional aspect is present and the causal aspect is lacking. Conversely a person may be crucially placed from the causal point of view, in the sense that what he does will be decisive for the outcome of the situation, and still be incapable of bringing about the desired result. This may be exemplified in the small by the captain of a ship lost at sea without possibilities of navigation, and in the large by a government contemplating various measures against, say, inflation. If anyone has power to curb inflation, it surely is the government; it is in the driver's seat. If, however, it lacks the knowledge about ends–means relationships that is required, the 'if anyone...' clause is vacuously fulfilled; the intentional element is lacking even if the causal element is present.

It is possible to go a step further in the analysis and affirm that even causal production of intended results is not always an exercise of power, viz. if the results come about by a different mechanism from what the actor had in mind. Just as knowledge is not only true belief, but *justified* true belief, so power is not only causal production of intended results, but *intelligent* causal production of intended results. The government may intend to curb inflation by means of measures $X_1 \ldots X_n$ and at the same time try to realize various other ends by means of measures $Y_1 \ldots Y_m$. If inflation is actually reduced because *either* $(X_1 \ldots X_n Y_1 \ldots Y_m)$ is a sufficient cause while $(X_1 \ldots X_n)$ is not, *or* because $(Y_1 \ldots Y_m)$ alone is a sufficient cause, while $(X_1 \ldots X_n)$ is not, then we should hesitate to say that the government has exercised its power to curb inflation. (If the government thinks that this is what it has done and acts accordingly the next time inflation occurs, we would be dealing with a case of 'superstitious learning'.[5])

For reasons analogous to those just given for the notion of power, the notion of political possibility is also dependent upon the intentional and intelligent production of desired states. In this sense, as stated, the approach is actor-oriented. On the other hand it is not actor-oriented in the sense of restricting itself to what is seen *ex ante* as PP by the actors themselves. This is a crucial point that must be examined at some length. Let us first observe that there is indeed within political life an aspect of routine struggles for power within limits accepted and understood by all. Inside the limits are the possible outcomes for which it is worth while engaging in a fight; outside are the political impossibilities that no one in his senses could want to turn into an issue. In Spinozistic terms this routine behaviour is *politicized politics*, as opposed to the *politicizing politics* where the routines are created. (We shall have more to say about this distinction in Chapter 5 below.) In the former the fight, by common agreement, takes place within the borders of the possible; in the latter the fight concerns how these borders should be drawn. In linguistics there is a similar distinction between 'rule-governed creativity' and 'rule-changing creativity';[6] both deal with possibilities, but only the former with the possibilities that have been made amenable to scientific study. Sartre, writing that consciousness '*est été*',[7] certainly violated French grammar, but in so doing he also created a new grammatical possibility that was added to the stock of the language. Political grammar similarly may be violated and reconstructed by the invention of new political institutions, such as the multinational firm; by new forms of action, such as guerrilla warfare; by new political concepts, such as the negative income tax.

To the extent that a theory of political possibility were to be actor-oriented in the sense now under discussion, it could only be a theory of routine politics. That is, to confine oneself to the set of states that are recognized by all *ex ante* to be PP w.r.t. the given state would exclude the creative process where the possible is *conquered* rather than just realized. An example from Marxist revolutionary theory may help to bring out this point. In that theory an important role is attributed to the 'analysis of the situation', i.e. to the assessment of the revolutionary potential of a given situation. This analysis is intended not only to reflect or describe the situation for the usage of the revolutionary leaders, but to be a weapon in the transformation of the situation itself, through the impact it has—when published—on the political actors. By saying that the situation *is* revolutionary one may cause it to *become* revolutionary, by a kind of self-fulfilling prophecy. In the general case, of course, we know that saying does not make it so and that only exceptionally will it be possible to achieve political goals through wishful thinking.[8] And even when it *is* possible to place the revolution on the map by saying that it is there, this possibility can never be delineated in advance. For let us suppose that it were possible to specify the features of a situation that would permit the leader to transform it from a situation where revolution by universal consent is impossible to a situation where it is recognized as a real possibility, by the simple expedient of affirming this possibility. We may call such a situation a pre-revolutionary one, implying some kind of latent or partly crystallized unrest that only needs the right word at the right time in order to emerge in recognizable form. In that case the leaders would naturally seek for the features of a situation that would permit them to make it into a pre-revolutionary one simply by affirming that it is pre-revolutionary, and so on in an infinite regress that shows the elusive character of *ex-ante* political possibilities. Between what is unambiguously possible and what is unambiguously impossible there is a limbo where only *action* can decide. The social scientist, on the other hand, may draw the dividing line with precision, but only at the condition that he remains apart from the event he studies.[9]

On the 'ought implies can' principle it would seem natural to require that for a given state to be PP w.r.t. a given state, it must also be economically feasible relatively to that state. In Chapter 2 I referred to Paul Samuelson's notion of the politically feasible income distributions, where it was taken as a matter of course that these form a subset of the economically feasible states. Here I shall also impose this requirement, but we may pause to point out an alternative conceptualization, where the states that are PP w.r.t. a given state are the states that may be *accepted* as political goals even if they cannot be brought about. Until quite recently no political party in Western Europe could state openly that full employment, economic growth, and stable prices were ends that could not be realized simultaneously within the framework of a modern capitalist economy. All political parties, therefore, had to state economic impossibilities as political possibilities; indeed they were political *necessities* (in the sense now under discussion) since they were common to all parties. (The Kalecki–Lindbeck–Nordhaus analysis of the 'political business cycle'[10] could presumably be extended to cover such cases, by endogenizing political goals.) Similar problems face the newly liberated countries where political development is more advanced than the state of the economy; here, too, it may be a political necessity to proclaim rates of growth or to promise levels of consumption that are plainly impossible at that stage. A variant of this quandary is the case where the planners find it useful, and perhaps necessary, to set infeasible targets for the plan so as to ensure that the economy operates at full stretch and to create an incentive to improved performance.[11] It may even be politically necessary (or at least possible) to set up as goals states that are *logically* contradictory, as when the Chinese planners instruct local leaders to give priority to industry, but not at the expense of agriculture, in the hope that this contradictory injunction shall set up a creative tension and mobilize the masses.[12] (In actual fact, the contradictory instructions more often than not seem to have had the destructive effect of a double bind, of which more in Chapter 4.) The machinery of modal logic might no doubt be used to explore the logic of politically acceptable proposals, but in what follows I always assume that the proposals are also economically feasible. If no proposals satisfy both requirements, then the set of politically possible states is empty.

Having offered these remarks on the general interpretation of the model,

I now proceed to specifics. Let us start with the political modalities applied to the propositional calculus. 'It is PP that p' means that there is a politically possible state where p obtains, and 'It is politically necessary that p' means that p obtains in *all* states that are PP w.r.t. the given state. It is only by the introduction of the necessity operator that we can get some mileage out of the approach, as possibility in itself does not bring us very far. As observed in Chapter 2, necessity usually enters into a model in the form of constraints on the set of feasible states, but using the modal approach we have seen that there may be necessary features that are not explicit constraints. Typically there are three steps in the construction of a modal interpretation of social facts: the specification of the constraints, the definition of the feasible states that satisfy simultaneously all the constraints, and the identification of the features that are common to all the feasible states. Politically necessary features may take the form of constraints; it is, for example, virtually axiomatic that in modern capitalist societies income redistribution can never take place by an explicit reduction of the nominal before-tax wages of any income groups; a more equal distribution can only come about through economic growth, inflation, or taxation. On the other hand, political necessities may also emerge as the third step in the above construction, as the indirect result of the constraints. In Chapter 2 I gave two examples of such indirectly necessary features, one involving the implications for technology of simultaneous constraints on consumption and investment, and the other the implications for school curricula of demands from parents and teachers that constrain the political authorities. It is clear here how new concepts may emerge when the work of economists and of logicians are confronted with each other. For economists the constraints are the basic elements and the set of possible states a derived notion; for the logician the set of alternative worlds to a given world is taken as given and the necessary features derived from this set. By merging the two two-step constructions into a three-step model, the distinction between the two kinds of necessity immediately follows.

From the primitive notions of possibility and necessity we may go on to iterated and mixed modalities. 'It is PP that it is PP that p' means that there are states of affairs x and y such that x is PP w.r.t. the given state, y is PP w.r.t. x, and p obtains in y. As we shall discuss below, this does not necessarily imply that p is PP w.r.t. the given state. Iterated necessity is interpreted in the obvious manner. A typical problem in political affairs is the following: given that it is politically necessary that $\bar{p}$, is it PP that it is PP that p, or is it rather the case that it is politically necessary that it is politically necessary that $\bar{p}$? In words: if a given proposal is politically impossible, is it possible to bring it about by first advancing another proposal, or are all such two-step operations politically impossible as well? As to mixed modalities, 'It is PP that it is politically necessary that p' means that there is a state x that is PP w.r.t. the given state such that p obtains in all states that are PP w.r.t. x. Even when it is politically impossible to bring about p, it may be politically possible to bring about a state from which all roads lead to p. Creating precedents, using irreversible investments to commit future generations, exploiting hidden complementarities or unforeseen consequences may all be relevant mechanisms for this purpose, as participants in the budgeting process know quite well.[13] Similarly, 'It is politically necessary that it is PP that p' means that there is no way of getting p out of your system; whatever you do, p remains possible. Right-wing regimes seem incapable of rooting out the revolutionary potential, social democrats of eliminating the possibility of Poujadism.

The mixed and iterated modalities acutely pose the problem of how the states are to be situated in *time*. For obvious reasons a continuous-time approach cannot serve here, so that we must think in terms of discrete states. The simplest case is one of periodic elections, but a more general analysis must take account of the fact that much of politics does not have this regular rhythm. (A fascinating problem is to think out the implications for political possibility if one were to realize the idea—due to Assar Lindbeck[14]—of having randomly distributed elections.) An 'analysis of the situation' that concludes by stating that a revolution is possible, does not and cannot set any definite time limit. On the other hand the revolution will not remain possible for an indefinite period, even supposing that no change of state (as defined by a finite set of variables kept constant throughout the analysis) occurs. *In politics it may be an event that nothing happens.* This kind of consideration suggests an extension of the notion of state. Define a *situation* as the actual state plus the possible states that go with it; then a change in the situation may take place even when the state remains the same. Some possibilities, so to speak, have a short life. This again implies that political time is punctuated not only by the changes of state, but also by change in the situation generally. In Chapter 2 we observed that in social mobility research a notion of *cumulative inertia* has been found useful; a similar notion—and perhaps even more the idea of a cumulative loss of inertia—may serve in the study of political processes. Again I emphasize the methodological point that these notions are not essential, even though they may be useful. By redefining the state, e.g. by the addition of new variables, the notion of a situation may always be rendered superfluous so that only the state remains (as a state variable).

A full-blown logic of politics clearly must go beyond sentence variables and also introduce quantification. As an example of a statement that easily lends itself to analysis in terms of political modal logic with quantification we may take the 'impossibility theorem' discussed in Chapter 1 above: You can fool some of the people all the time and all the people some of the time, but not all the people all the time. Actually the opposite problem is more important in modern societies, viz. the impossibility of doing something to some individuals (e.g. conscription) without doing it to everyone. The technically optimal solution, such as imposing a long military service on some individuals rather than a short service on everyone, may be politically impossible because of the universalistic tendencies inherent in modern societies. (A frequently used solution to this problem is randomizing, which reintroduces universality at the level of possibilities.) In some cases it may be technically or economically impossible to confer a given benefit on everyone at once, whereas it is politically impossible to confer it on some units only, in which case universalism may be an obstacle to progress (unless it is neutralized by Hirschman's 'tunnel effect'[15]). A similar problem arises in dividing the benefits from cooperation if every feasible arrangement is likely to imply an unequal division. If all social groups benefit from stability, whereas each possible set of stable rules would bring an additional benefit to some particular group, it is quite possible that no stable arrangement will emerge at all. (Note that this is not the same as the free-rider problem in the Prisoner's Dilemma. The relation between these two obstacles to cooperation is discussed briefly in Chapter 5 below.)

For a more detailed insight into quantified political logic we may consider the following propositions:

(1) *In a monarchy it is necessary that* $(\exists x)$ $(x$ *is a monarch*).
(2) *In a monarchy* $(\exists x)$ $(x$ *is necessarily a monarch*).
(3) *In a republic it is necessary that* $(\exists x)$ $(x$ *is president*).
(4) *In a republic* $(\exists x)$ $(x$ *is necessarily president*).
(5) *It is politically necessary that* $(\exists x)$ $(x$ *is a monarch*).
(6) $(\exists x)$ $(it$ *is politically necessary that x is a monarch*).
(7) *It is politically necessary that* $(\exists x)$ $(x$ *is president*).
(8) $(\exists x)$ $(it$ *is politically necessary that x is president*).

We saw in Chapter 1 above that the deduction of (2) from (1) is an invalid inference (equivalent, in fact, to the fallacy of composition), and similarly for the three other pairs of propositions. Thus in 1936 (5) was true in England, but (6) was false. The truth value of propositions (5)–(8) will depend upon the specific circumstances to which they are applied, and I shall not say more about them here, except to state that it is important to distinguish them from propositions (1)–(4) that rely on a quite different notion of necessity. If we are dealing with logical possibility and necessity, then (1) and (3) are true, whereas (2) and (4) are false. On the other hand there seems to be a sense, if only we could get at it, in which (2) differs essentially from (4). Kings are kings by some kind of necessity, and not everyone can become a king; presidents are presidents more or less by accident, and almost everyone can become one. Let me propose a tentative (and slightly frivolous) exploration of these issues.

One way of bringing out the difference between (2) and (4) has recently been proposed by Saul Kripke and further refined by Michael Dummett.[16] Defending a *genetic* approach to necessity, Kripke argued that the metaphysically necessary properties of an object are those that are linked to the way it came into being or to the stuff out of which it is made. One of his examples is related to (2) above, viz. his discussion of whether it would be true to say that Queen Elizabeth might not have been born of royal blood. He answers this question in the affirmative, as a negative answer would have to demonstrate the necessity of the Queen's parents being the royal family, and this according to Kripke is a contingent fact, presumably because of the possibility of baby-switching, etc. What *is* answered in the negative, however, is the question whether Queen Elizabeth might have been born of other parents than her actual parents. The fact of having her actual parents for parents is a necessary property (on the genetic criterion) of Queen Elizabeth, whereas the fact of having John F. Kennedy for a brother would not (on the same criterion) be a necessary feature of Edward Kennedy.

Using this genetic criterion of necessity, the possibilities of baby-switching or of elected kings clearly make proposition (2) come out as false. Nevertheless, it may be argued that these are perverse or marginal cases that could not become typical without the very notion of kinghood being dissolved. By 'typical' here I mean 'as a principle' and not just 'frequent'. Nothing excludes the possibility of an intertemporal conspiracy of midwives for royal baby-switching, but still this would not be part of the concept of a king. If things always happened as they typically happen, we must conclude that (2) would come out true. On the other hand (4) would not be true under any such clause; it makes no difference to the truth value of this proposition if we rule out the possibility of an impostor taking the place of the elected president, etc.

Before accepting the truth of proposition (2) in the standard case, we should take a closer look at the restrictions imposed upon individuals and upon the truth value of propositions that ascribe properties to non-existent objects. If all the possible worlds have exactly the same individuals as members, then Queen Elizabeth is Queen in them all and therefore necessarily Queen in ours. If, however, there exists a world where Queen Elizabeth has an elder brother and sister, then she is not Queen in that world and therefore not necessarily Queen in ours. If, finally, there exists a world where Queen Elizabeth is not around at all, but no world where she has an elder brother or sister, then we must turn to the interpretation of propositions about non-existent objects, of which something was already said in Chapter 1 above. If all propositions about non-existent individuals are taken as true, then it is true that Queen Elizabeth is Queen in the worlds where she does not exist and she is therefore necessarily Queen in our world. If, on the other hand, we ascribe falsity to statements about non-entities, then Queen Elizabeth is not Queen in the worlds where she does not exist and therefore not necessarily Queen in ours. Kinghood or queenhood may look like essential properties, because of their link to the essential property of having one's parents for parents, but on closer inspection they turn out to be accidental because it is not essential for the parents to have their children as children. The genetic criterion of necessity works backwards in time only. Even when we abstract from baby-switching in the actual world, baby-switching between worlds destroys the necessity of queenhood. What is preserved, however, is the necessity of royalty, i.e. the property of belonging to the royal family, at least if we assume that ascription of this property to Queen Elizabeth is true also in the worlds in which she does not exist.

From these facetious remarks I now turn to somewhat more substantial matters, the logical properties that we may attribute to the PP relation between worlds. In Chapter 1 above it was mentioned that various systems of modal logic (such as S-4 or S-5) may be classified according to the properties they ascribe to this relation. I shall argue that systems of political philosophy, or at least parts of them, may also be formulated in terms of such properties. There are an indefinite number of properties that might be singled out for inspection, but for convenience I shall limit myself to the seven properties discussed in a recent textbook.[17]

(1) *Existence*: $(\forall x)(\exists y)(y$ is PP w.r.t. $x)$
I have already touched upon some of the reasons why this is not a trivially satisfied property. The set of politically possible states may be empty because all economically feasible states are politically unacceptable. Even if a given state is politically acceptable and actually becomes realized, this does not prove it to have been politically possible *ex ante*, because it may have been realized by accident rather than by deliberate and intelligent action. (Cf. the comments on the proper definition of power earlier in this chapter.) In a society where changes in political structure and personnel depended upon some chance mechanism with an unknown probability distribution, as in Borges's short story *The Lottery*, nothing could be brought about by the actors themselves, even though every state would be succeeded by some other state. Less fancifully, non-existence may be a result of counterfinality (in the sense to be defined in Chapter 5 below). If actors $a_1, a_2 \ldots a_n$ propose to bring about states $s_1, s_2 \ldots s_n$ respectively, and if for each i it is the case that s_i can be realized only on the condition that for at least one $j \neq i, s_j$ is not proposed, then none of the states will be realized. This situation might arise if there are several minority groups with different interests in each of the (abstractly possible) states. China at the end of the Han dynasty provides an example of this chaotic structure, where the lack of a common political framework, the intensity of conflict and the multiplicity of interests made successful political action—in the sense of bringing about a result defined in advance—virtually impossible.[18] Some of the actors will achieve what they wanted, in the sense of getting the power, but the uses to which this power may be harnessed will be radically different from what they had in mind.

(2) *Limited reflexivity*: $(\forall x)((\exists y)(x$ is PP w.r.t. $y) \supset (x$ is PP w.r.t. $x))$
If a given state is itself PP w.r.t. some state, then it is also PP w.r.t. itself. Or: if a state can be brought about, then it can also be maintained. Or again: if conservation of the *status quo* is not politically possible, then this state cannot be *brought about* from any state (even if it may *come about* in a non-intentional or non-intelligent manner, as explained above). This property certainly does not hold universally. In modern industrial societies political immobility is impossible, and nevertheless any given state (whose maintenance is impossible) often results from the deliberate realization of *ex-ante* possibilities. This modern preoccupation with change was admirably expressed by Leibniz: 'We regress if we do not progress, for it is impossible to stand still.'[19] We may pause here to observe that in the notion of limited reflexivity there is implicit an idea of *inherently inaccessible states*, which form the polar concept, so to speak, of the states whose set of politically possible states is empty. Independently of the question whether limited reflexivity obtains, we may ask whether there are

political states that can be realized, if at all, only in a non-intentional or non-intelligent manner, just as there may be states that can only be left in this manner. We may ask, for example, whether there could be *self-defeating proposals*, i.e. goals whose very enunciation is incompatible with their being realized. A candidate for such goals could be the proposal to realize a state of innocence; compare also the discussion of symmetry below.

(3) *Reflexivity*: $(\forall x)$ (x is PP w.r.t. x)

A fortiori, this fails to hold when one of the preceding two properties fails to hold.

(4) *Transitivity*: $(\forall x)$ $(\forall y)$ $(\forall z)$ ((y is PP w.r.t. x and z is PP w.r.t. y) $\supset$ (z is PP w.r.t. x))

What is PP w.r.t. a state that is PP w.r.t. the actual state, is itself PP w.r.t. the actual state. This is a most controversial proposition, acceptance of which may be said to be the essence of Utopian approaches to politics. Utopianism says that what can be done in two steps can also be done in one step. I restrict myself here to the political aspects of Utopianism. Most people will accept that in matters concerning capital accumulation and economic growth it is often impossible to take short cuts, but it is less obvious that similar restrictions may obtain for political development.

Refutation of the Utopian approach may take place on two distinct grounds. Firstly, one may argue on the analogy of a spatial horizon: in order to see what is behind the next hill, you have to get there first. The intransitivity and asymmetry of seeing have in fact been exploited in the construction of semantic models for modal logic.[20] More profoundly, Ernst Bloch has used the idea of a horizon to express the concept of a *relative Utopia*.[21] More profoundly still, we can appeal here to Husserlian phenomenology with its distinction between full and empty intentions. From my present point of view I have a full awareness of the front of all the objects in my visual field, but only a formal and empty awareness of the side that is hidden from my view. I know, that is, that they must have a backside, but I do not know how it appears in specific detail. Also from my present point of view I know that if I were to deplace myself to some other point in the field, new objects would become visible to me, even if I do not know which objects. The same holds for my awareness of the future, which is given in formal and empty 'protentions' which, together with my present impressions and my retentions of the past, constitute the network of inner subjective time. The formal structure of this network, for example, imposes on every present experience the indelible stamp that it is also something that 'will have been'.[22]

In a similar manner I may ignore which states are PP w.r.t. the states that are PP w.r.t. the present, but I do know—in an empty and general manner—that any state that comes to be realized will also have its horizon of political possibilities. And if one cannot know which states are possible at two removes, then *a fortiori* one cannot strive to realize them either, so that transitivity of the PP relation breaks down. The notion of ignorance of future possibilities may be taken in a weak and a strong sense here. Either it may be taken to mean that I do not know which of the states in a given and constant spectrum of abstractly possible states will appear as PP w.r.t. the states that are PP w.r.t. the present, or to imply that for all I know some qualitatively new states may be added to the spectrum. The last interpretation is in my opinion the most interesting. It is also, I think, at the root of Marx's critique of Utopianism in a well-known passage from *The Civil War in France*:

> The working class did not expect miracles from the Commune. They have no ready-made utopias to introduce *par décret du peuple*. They know that in order to work out their own emancipation, and along with it that higher form to which present society is irresistibly tending by its own economical agencies, they will have to pass through a series of historic processes, transforming circumstances and men. They have no ideals to realize, but to set free the elements of the new society with which old collapsing bourgeois society itself is pregnant.[23]

Secondly, one may argue at a more tactical level that even if the political leaders have full knowledge of what will be PP w.r.t. the states that are PP w.r.t. the present, their followers may lack the political maturity to skip the intermediate step. This argument is actually most plausible if used in combination with the first, on the basis of a distinction between pioneers and latecomers in the political development. For the country that is the first to develop, say, democratic institutions or working-class organizations, each new advance takes place on unknown territory and adds new possibilities to the spectrum. Here the argument of the preceding paragraphs suffices to refute Utopianism. For the latecomers, however, the pioneer example demonstrates the states that will be possible at two or more removes, and for these countries there will a permanent temptation to skip the intermediate step; to go directly, say, from feudalism to communism or to import democratic institutions in fully developed form. Against this some will argue that abstract knowledge is not sufficient to create the conditions for the more advanced forms, which can only be viable if rooted in the concrete experience that must be acquired gradually. To Marx's phrase, 'The country that is more developed industrially only shows, to the less developed, the image of its own future',[24] we may oppose Trotsky's acid comment that, 'For such pedants, the history of one capitalist nation repeats the history of another, with, of course, certain more or less important divergences'.[25]

For the political leaders that have acquired an understanding of what will be possible at two or more removes, there arises a peculiar paradox that is incarnated in *the theory of the necessary failure*.[26] On this view the political leaders should propose goals which they know to be politically impossible, for only through the harsh defeat in the struggle for these goals will the revolutionary class acquire the maturity and the organization that are required for their ultimate realization. This might be called an indirectly self-fulfilling prophecy, in contrast to the immediately self-fulfilling prophecies discussed earlier in this chapter. It should be emphasized that the theory of the necessary failure is much more acceptable, from a moral point of view, if seen as an explanation after the event than if made the foundation of an analysis before the fact. Marx did indeed say *in 1850* that

> With the exception of a few short chapters, every important part of the annals of the revolution of 1848 to 1849 carries the heading: Defeat of the revolution! But what succumbed in these defeats was not the revolution. It was the pre-revolutionary traditional appendages, results of social relationships, which had not yet come to the point of sharp class antagonisms—persons, illusions, conceptions, projects, from which the revolutionary party before the February Revolution was not free, from which it could be freed not by the victory of February, but only by a series of defeats.[27]

In his writings *before* 1848, however, Marx never stressed this idea, as far as I know. The manipulative idea that the working class can advance only by fighting for goals that the leaders have deliberately chosen because they are just out of reach, is proper to Rosa Luxemburg.[28] It is clearly impossible to say to the workers that they shall revolt in order to be defeated and by defeat acquire the class consciousness required for a mature revolutionary class, for workers ready to accept this argument would already be in possession of that consciousness. The alternatives for the leaders are *either* to abdicate from leadership for the benefit of less experienced members who can make their *own* mistakes, *or* to present victory as a real possibility for the rank and file although they know that defeat is certain. The first option hardly needs commenting upon; the second, I submit, is manipulation, though not of the Leninist variety. As far as I know, Lenin never stressed the dialectic where failure becomes success and falsity truth; failure may have been for him, as it was for Rosa Luxemburg, the result of a lack of class consciousness, but not—as it was for her—the prerequisite of class consciousness. (It is easily seen that many of these comments are also valid for the relationship between teacher and pupil, between parents and children, or between psychotherapist and patient; compare for example the use of paradoxical instructions in behaviour therapy. On the other hand there are important differences between the collective case and the individual case, notably that the latter has far greater room for strategic self-education)

(5) *Limited symmetry*: $(\forall x)\,(\forall y)((x$ is PP w.r.t. $x) \supset ((y$ is PP w.r.t. $x) \supset (x$ is PP w.r.t. $y))$

If a given state is PP w.r.t. itself, then if an alternative y is PP w.r.t. that state, the state is also PP w.r.t. y. Or: if the *status quo* is PP, then every change is reversible. This is a proposition that seems neither obviously true nor obviously false, so that one would have to look at the empirical evidence to circumscribe the kind of situations where it is likely to hold.

(6) *Symmetry*: $(\forall x)(\forall y)((y$ is PP w.r.t. $x) \supset (x$ is PP w.r.t. $y))$
Every state is PP w.r.t. the states that are PP w.r.t. itself. Or: every political change is reversible. This is certainly not correct. The verbal symmetry, for example, of the concepts of revolution and counter-revolution is only an apparent one, for the goal of the counter-revolutionaries certainly is not to bring about a situation where revolution remains on the order of the day. The present (December 1976) situation in Chile is a reversal *beyond* and not *to* the pre-Allende situation, as Eduard Frei found out too late. For an explicit expression of this idea we can do no better than cite the following statement of Valery Giscard d'Estaing: 'Il n'est certainement pas question de revenir à la situation d'avant 1968, et d'abord parce que la situation avant 1968 comportait les conditions qui ont créé 1968.'[29] Political irreversibility may also arise from the impossibility of cutting your losses even when it is the rational thing to do; the Concorde project and the Vietnam War are but two examples of enterprises that should never have been set up and that became virtually irreversible for reasons of prestige. Experience once acquired may be hard to undo, so that one might conjecture that traditionally neutral countries such as Sweden or Switzerland would not return to neutrality if one day they got mixed up in a war. We may note, in connection with this last source of asymmetry, that the problem of irreversibility may turn upon the way in which the states are defined. Thus if B is PP w.r.t. A and if having a past without B is part of the description of A, then A cannot be PP w.r.t. B. If, on the other hand, states are described in terms of state variables only, then irreversibility cannot be affirmed on these purely logical grounds. If innocence is defined as a state that has never known doubt, then innocence, once lost, can never be regained. If, on the other hand, innocence is defined as a certain mode of behaviour, the question of irreversibility is an empirical rather than a purely conceptual one.

I shall take the last remarks as my starting point for some comments upon the Hegelian and Marxist notion of *the negation of the negation*. I do not subscribe to any 'law' of the negation of the negation as postulated by Engels, if by this it is implied that *all* processes of change in nature, consciousness or society proceed according to this pattern. On the other hand I do not quite agree with the critics of Marxism who say that 'the main difficulty about the law of the negation is that it can be made to fit almost anything by carefully choosing what is to count as the negating terms'.[30] It is no doubt true that many instances of the 'law' are mere verbal juggling, where the hand rarely is quick enough to deceive even the most credulous eye. Nevertheless I think that many of the examples traditionally subsumed under the heading of the 'negation of the negation' do exhibit a common pattern that can be defined with some precision and that is capable of applications in many contexts.

A simple example of the kind of pattern I have in mind is given by Husserl in his discussion of *doubt* as a mode of consciousness.[31] Here he notes that doubt can be seen as the negation of the naive belief, and that even after restoration of the belief the doubt has irreversibly left its mark on the consciousness. The step from unthinking belief to doubt can be seen as some kind of 'negation', as can also the step from doubt to mature belief; quite obviously the end result of these two operations is not the same state as the starting point. The step from the *Songs of Innocence* to the *Songs of Experience* can be seen as a negation, and the step from the latter to the state of mind capable of writing them both as a second negation. Donne tells us that ' 'Tis less grief to be foul, than to have been fair', and at any rate we can agree that these two states are wholly different. A perfectly explicit statement of this idea is given by Emily Dickinson:

> None can experience stint
> Who Bounty—have not known—
> The fact of Famine—could not be
> Except for Fact of Corn—
>
> Want—is a meagre Art
> Acquired by Reverse—
> The Poverty that was not Wealth—
> Cannot be Indigence.[32]

Underlying all these cases, to which the reader can no doubt add a number of his own, is the following structure. Given an actual sequence $p-q-r$, we say that it exemplifies the pattern of the negation of the negation if (i) p, q, and r are *contraries*, in the sense that no two of them can be jointly realized; (ii) the sequence $p-q-p$ is impossible; (iii) the sequence $p-r$ is impossible. The first condition gives a (rather weak) meaning to the notion of a negation. It has the effect of excluding purely organic and cumulative growth, where each stage directly includes the preceding one, as in (say) the process of learning a foreign language. The second condition imposes antisymmetry, meaning that the experience of going through q irreversibly changes the subject of the process. The third condition imposes antitransitivity, implying that the passage through q is indispensable for arriving at r. I submit that the processes satisfying (i)–(iii) form an important subclass of changing structures in general; I also think it corresponds fairly well to some of the examples offered by Hegel and Marx. In particular the sequence feudalism–capitalism–communism[33] exhibits all the features specified above. In this important example the impossibility in question is partly economic in that capitalism is required for the development of the forces of production and partly political, in that the alienation of capitalist society is a prerequisite for the fully developed liberty under communism. For purely political examples of the negation of the negation the development over the last few years of Portugal and Chile might well serve; in contradistinction to what happened in Greece where the passage through the regime of the colonels does not seem to have made a great difference. These concepts, I freely admit, are not rigorous, but I find them suggestive.

(7) *Quasi-equivalence*: $(\forall x)(\forall y)(\forall z)((y \text{ and } z \text{ are PP w.r.t. } x) \supset (y \text{ is PP w.r.t. } z \text{ and } z \text{ is PP w.r.t. } y))$

All states that are PP w.r.t. a given state are PP w.r.t. each other. This might be included in the definition of a parliamentary regime, because in the absence of quasi-equivalence the losing party in an election might just have to go out of business, which is, of course, what the losing side in a revolution often has to do. We may note that if conservatism is PP, then quasi-equivalence implies symmetry.

I shall not set up for discussion further properties of the PP relation,[34] but conclude the chapter with some further observations upon the general argument I have presented. In the first place I would like to re-emphasize the modest aims of the approach. I believe this to be necessary because of the obviously trendy aspect of the idea of applying modal logic to political affairs; if I am not to end up in someone's Pseud's Corner, I must repeat that I aim to be useful rather than profound. Possible worlds, to repeat, are just a manner of speaking, and in principle nothing can be said with modal concepts that could not also have been said without them. Still, for some purposes the language of possible worlds may be more convenient and less cumbersome than alternative modes of expression. I have several times made use of an analogy that seems to bring out the point quite well, viz. the comparison with hysteresis. We know on general principles that the past cannot have a causal impact upon the present (over and above the influence mediated by the traces left by the past in the present), but nevertheless we may find it convenient to speak as if the past does exert some kind of direct influence. In a similar manner we also know *a priori* that a possibility is not the kind of thing that can exercise a causal influence, or that two states cannot differ *only* in their haloes of possibilities. These elementary truths notwithstanding, we may sometimes find it useful to describe a situation as a state with its adjoined possibilities rather than as something which is actual through and through. Past or possible values of the variables may sometimes serve as proxies for the present and actual values.

In the second place the reader may have wondered exactly which *are* the uses to which the political modalities may be put. From what has been said above, two main applications seem to emerge. The first is that we may be able to classify political regimes in terms of the properties they impose upon the relation of political possibility; this holds both for actual regimes and for the possible regimes that can be generated by combination of the various properties such as the seven mentioned above. The reader may observe that this implies that politically possible transitions can occur only within regimes, never between regimes. To the extent that this approach is chosen, we are in a sense dealing with the more routine aspects of politics, even though it does not imply that we should restrict ourselves to the actors' notion of what is and what is not possible. The second application is in the analysis of theories of political development, where the logic and the coherence of a conceptual scheme may be tested by bringing it out in the form sketched in the chapter. The analysis of the negation of the negation provides one example of how this may elucidate notoriously elusive notions. The interrelations between political concepts may also be well brought out in this way; if, for example, an author affirms existence, transitivity, and symmetry, but denies reflexivity of the PP relation, then he is in trouble.

Notes

1. Elster (1976a); also Davidson (1973), as quoted in Chapter 1 above.
2. See Simon (1953) for a good statement of the 'power as causality' approach.
3. Russell (1938).
4. Goldman (1972, p. 223).
5. See Lave and March (1975), p. 294–305.
6. Chomsky (1964, p. 59). For a similar (and explicitly Spinozistic) distinction between 'la parole parlée' and 'la parole parlante', see Merleau-Ponty (1945, p. 229).
7. Sartre (1943, p. 58).
8. It may be worth while to spell out why this is so. Assume that a political leader (or a social scientist) thinks that the outcome of a situation is a function of variables x_1, $x_2 \ldots x_n$ and of his own prediction (y) of the outcome: $z = f(y, x_1, x_2 \ldots x_n)$. In that case he may either seek for a fixed point $\bar{z}$ such that $\bar{z} = f(\bar{z}, x_1, x_2 \ldots x_n)$ or he may seek for the value $\underline{z}$ that maximizes some function $g(z)$ of the outcome, but normally he cannot do both without the system becoming overdetermined (Haavelmo, (1971, p. 46)). The National Economic Bureau cannot both seek to predict prices correctly in a manner that takes account of the impact of the prediction on the economic agents *and* choose the prediction so as to maximize employment for next year. The revolutionary leader may seek the prediction that, say, has a maximal impact upon the combativity of the revolutionary class, but in that case the chances are good that he will be proved wrong; or he may want his analysis of the situation to be incorporated as one of the elements of the situation that is being analysed, but in that case there is no reason to think that his cause will be furthered.
9. See also note 43 to Chapter 5 below.
10. See Kalecki (1943), Nordhaus (1975), and Lindbeck (1976) for an exploration of this concept.
11. Heal (1973, p. 20).
12. See Schurmann (1967, pp. 76 ff.) and Eckstein (1968, p. 713) for the use of contradictory directives in Chinese politics. For discussion of the fluctuations generated by this political style, see Skinner and Winckler (1969), Suttmeier (1974), Nathan (1976), and Winckler (1976).
13. Wildavsky (1964, p. 111).
14. Lindbeck (1976, p. 18, n. 8).
15. Hirschman (1973, p. 545) describes the effect in these terms: 'An individual's welfare depends on his present state of contentment (or, as a proxy, income), as well as on his expected future contentment (or income). Suppose that the individual has very little information about his future income, but at some point a few of his relatives, neighbors, or acquaintances improve their economic or social position. Now he has something to go on: expecting that his turn will come in due course, he will draw gratification from the advances of others—for a while.'
16. Kripke (1972) and Dummett (1973, pp. 130–131).
17. Snyder (1971, p. 210). The properties are singled out by Snyder because of their importance for the systems he studies, and there is no reason why they should be especially relevant for the political modalities. They are examined here simply in order to illustrate the expressive power of the modal language; in addition properties like existence, reflectivity, transitivity, and symmetry have a simplicity that make them obvious candidates for analysis.
18. Balacz (1968, pp. 71–138).
19. 'Regredimur nisi progrediamur, quia stari on potest' (Leibniz, 1948, p. 94). I believe that this proposition expresses in an admirable manner one specific difference that separates the modern world from the traditional. Leibniz probably intended it to cover many levels, from the universe as a whole and down to the experience of the individual consciousness, passing through the evolution of society and the state.

For the interested reader I mention here some problems that arise if we interpret the proposition as being about individual pleasure cf. especially Leibniz (1875–90), vol. V, pp. 175,182). If we assume that utility is a continuous function of the level of consumption and of the rate of change of consumption, so that $u(t) = f(c(t), dc/dt)$, then Leibniz can be interpreted as stating (i) that no utility is derived from a constant consumption, i.e. that $f(c,o) = 0$ for all c and (ii) that no stream of consumption can give a constant stream of utility, so that the differential equation $f((c(t), dc/dt) = k$ has no solution for positive k. Aanund Hylland has shown (in a note to the author) that if f is a non-decreasing function of the first argument and an increasing function of the second, then the differential equation always has a solution, and that if it is non-decreasing in both arguments it has a solution in the sense that there exists an almost everywhere differentiable function which satisfies the differential equation almost everywhere. If we permit utility to be a decreasing function of consumption, we may find a function f such that the ensuing differential equation has no solution, but would Leibniz have accepted this condition?

20. Hughes and Cresswell (1972, pp. 63 ff.).
21. Bloch (1954).
22. Cf. Husserl (1966) for the problem of temporality.
23. Marx (1871, pp. 96–97).
24. Marx (1867, pp. 8–9).
25. Trotsky (1972, p. 50).
26. I take this phrase from Avineri (1969, p. 239), who seems, however, to use it in the sense of an *inevitable* failure (given the prevailing causes), whereas I use it in the sense of an *indispensable* failure (given the goal to be achieved).
27. Marx (1820, p. 33).
28. Luxemburg (1899, pp. 404–405); Luxemburg (1906, pp. 133, 141 ff.).
29. Interview in *Le Monde*, 8 January 1975.
30. Acton (1967).
31. Husserl (1967, pp. 33 ff.).
32. *Complete Poems*, No. 771; cf. also No. 1197, No. 1515. The line from Donne is in his elegy *The Anagram*. The same distinction, but the opposite conclusion, is expressed by 'It is better to have loved and lost than never to have loved at all'.
33. Marx (1867, p. 763), Cf. also Marx (1862–63, vol. 2, p. 111; vo. 3, p. 41).
34. In addition to limited reflexivity, we might examine the following property: $(\forall x)$ $((\exists y)(y$ is PP w.r.t. $x) \supset (x$ is PP w.r.t. $x))$. Writing 'PP(x)' for the set of states that are PP w.r.t. a state x, we might ask whether the PP relation is complete in PP(x), which would be a less strict form for quasi-equivalence. Or we might ask whether the set PP(x) contains any (and if so, how many) subsets such that the accessibility relation is an equivalence relation when restricted to a given subset; the existence and number of such sets of states might throw some light upon the regime in question. Quite possibly, results from the theory of graphs could also be invoked here. It is a matter for further reflection to decide whether these or other questions have any substantial interest.

4

CONTRADICTIONS OF THE MIND

This chapter and the following have a common goal, which may be described as 'the vindication of dialectics'. I hasten to add that I do not want to vindicate all modes of reasoning that have been called 'dialectical' by friend or foe. On the contrary, I believe that the treatises on dialectics written by Hegel, Engels, or Mao Tse-Tung hardly offer a single interesting idea. What is comprehensible, is trivial; what seems profound, is opaque, not only on a first reading but on the tenth or the hundredth reading. Instead of trying to make sense of what these and other writers have been saying *about* dialectics, I shall attempt to make explicit the logical structure (which one could call dialectical) of the non-methodological writings of Hegel and Marx. In particular I shall focus upon the idea of a contradiction. I am just as unable as Karl Popper to understand what Hegel says about contradictions in his *Logic*, but I do think it possible to make sense of his use of the term 'contradiction' in the *Phenomenology of Mind*, which is to me without comparison Hegel's greatest work. I also believe that the most important occurrences of the term[1] in the writings of Marx lend themselves to an interpretation in terms of ordinary everyday logic. I shall finally argue that these concepts are not only perfectly clear, but extremely fertile as well.

I do not abide, that is, by any distinction between the understanding (*Verstand*) that is limited to the sterile reasoning of formal logic and the reason (*Vernunft*) that proceeds by the creative dialectical method. Nor am I prepared to accept that my refusal of this distinction merely shows how valid it is. I do not believe that the relation between the dialectical and the analytical thinker is comparable to the relation between the sane and the insane, where the first member of each couple can understand the second, but not vice versa. Nor can I accept that the superiority of the dialectical thinker shows itself in that he is capable of solving problems that do not even exist as problems for the analytical bent of mind. Finally, I believe that if one is right, then it should be possible to convince others by *argument* rather than demanding a spiritual *conversion*.[2] On the other hand it is difficult to refute someone who insists that every one of your objections is just another sign that you have not understood what is it all about. Whence the necessity of an indirect strategy: as the dialectical thinkers themselves agree that such analyses as Hegel's master–slave dialectic or Marx's theory of the falling rate of profit are summits of dialectical reasoning, a rendering of these into ordinary analytical language would give a prima facie reason for thinking that the gap is not that large.

In the present chapter I shall first give a brief exposition of Hegel's *theory* of contradictions (as distinct from his *use* of the concept), drawing attention to its main sources and commenting upon the standard analytical criticism of the theory. I shall endeavour to show that this criticism, while valid, is rather superficial and that it is possible to define a notion of 'contradiction' that is not open to these objections. This notion is then further explored in two main variants: the contradictions of the mind that will occupy us in the remainder of this chapter, and the contradictions of society that are the object of Chapter 5.[3] The mental structures that are said to be contradictory are further subdivided in two main classes: contradictory beliefs and contradictory desires.[4] It may be useful for the reader to know how these phenomena compare to the 'forms' studied by Hegel in the *Phenomenology of Mind*. The first three chapters of that work are all concerned with theoretical or epistemic contradictions, at the level of the individual consciousness; to be precise, Hegel follows the successive contradictions that arise in the philosophical attempts to make sense of the external world. Chapter IV of the *Phenomenology* goes on to explore the mental contradictions that arise at the practical level of desires and conduct; here the master–slave dialectic is a crucial moment. In Chapter V (or rather in the second and third subsections of that chapter) Hegel makes the transition to social contradictions.

In this very general sense the chapters on contradictions in the present work correspond to what Hegel is talking about in the *Phenomenology of Mind*. Nevertheless Hegelian scholars will see at once that I am offering neither exegesis nor paraphrase of that work. Even when my explicit starting point is the Hegelian text, as in the discussion of the master–slave dialectic, I endeavour to interest the non-Hegelian reader rather than to remain faithful to the intentions of the original. I might have tried to do both, but I have not. Also my level of ambition is lower than Hegel's, especially in the sense that I am not presenting a theory of the *relation* between the various classes of contradictions. For Hegel the *order* in which the various contradictions is presented is a crucial feature of the exposition, as are also the transitions from one kind of contradiction to the following. In the present analysis, on the other hand, no such systematic intention is at work. I offer the reader a bunch of rather unconnected notions, not a philosophical system. The coherence of the approach, if any, must be sought at the methodological rather than at the theoretical level. That is, I believe that *the link between logical contradictions and the study of change* is an important and fertile one, that can be studied in several variants even if these variants are not linked up with each other in a substantive theory.

If the Hegelian scholar is likely to go unsatisfied from a reading of these chapters, social scientists may also have some problems in understanding exactly what they are being offered. Even for each variety or subvariety of contradictions, no precise theory is presented, at most some kind of explanatory framework or 'perspective', to use a term that may cover many sins. In the last section of Chapter 5 an attempt is made to specify some of the mediating notions between social contradictions and social change, but even here the empirically oriented reader (for whom I am primarily writing) will feel that it is all very sketchy; a feeling that will be overwhelmingly strong, perhaps, in the present chapter where next to nothing is said about the precise mechanism for change. For all this I offer no apology. Or rather, I willingly apologize if it turns out that the present work is a bad book of its kind, but I do not feel apologetic for having written a book of that kind. If no social scientists are tempted into filling in some of the holes in my outline sketches, this will indeed be an indictment, but I would still plead not guilty to the accusation that drawing outline sketches is a waste of time anyway.

Hegel's theory of contradictions

I shall not try to present Hegel's view of contradictions as it is set forth in the *Science of Logic*, with the whole set of conceptual paraphernalia, because I think Hegel's basic intuition is vastly more simple than one could think from this exposition. Fundamentally he does little more than iterate the Eleatic paradoxes, with a somewhat different conclusion. The most important of these paradoxes, from Hegel's point of view, certainly is the Arrow Paradox.[5] This purports to prove that a flying arrow both is and is not at rest at each moment of its flight. *It is at rest*, for by definition an object cannot move during an instant. Movement requires duration; it is impossible to get from one place to another in an interval of length zero. *It is not at rest*, for if it were it would be impossible for it ever to get anywhere. The last argument may be spelled out in two distinct ways. Firstly we may observe that if at *any* instant during its flight the arrow did not move, i.e. were at rest,[6] then it would be at rest at all succeeding instants, because it would have lost its state of motion. Secondly, and less anachronistically, we may argue that if the arrow were at rest at *all* instants during its flight then it would never leave the bow and never traverse any distance at all, as a compounding of immobilities can only give immobility as a result. The first argument appeals to Newton's first law, the second to the intuitive idea that adding up zeros, however many, can never bring us beyond zero.[7]

The reader would be wrong to dismiss this out of hand as mere sophistry. Zeno's paradoxes, the Arrow not least among them, point to deep and difficult problems in the conceptual analysis of space and time. It would be perverse to say that they constitute a solid foundation for the Hegelian dialectic, but nevertheless it must be admitted that the Hegelian theory of contradictions was intended as a solution to what is far from being a pseudo-problem. Schematically three distinct elements enter into the Arrow Paradox: the possibility of a real movement, the possibility of real contradictions, and the validity of the paradox itself. The modern view is that since movement is possible and since real contradictions are impossible, there must be something wrong with the argument behind the paradox, even if there is no general consensus as to exactly where it goes wrong. The Eleatic view was that since real contradictions are impossible and since the argument is valid, we have a *reductio ad absurdum* proof against the possibility of movement. Hegel's position was even more radical: arguing that movement is real and that the argument is valid, he concluded to the existence of real contradictions.[8] It is highly significant that this admission of 'real contradictions' is linked to the analysis of change. How, Hegel seems to ask, can a thing change if it just is what it is? How, so to speak, can it ever get out of its skin if it does not in its very nature contain its opposite? It is also important to note that Hegel never discusses the paradox that by some authors[9] have been compared with the Arrow, viz. the paradox of the millet seed: as a single seed does not make a sound in falling, 1000 seeds falling simultaneously should make no sound either, because zero multiplied by 1000 remains zero. In this paradox there is no question of change, only a comparison between successive cases of seeds in varying amounts falling to the ground. Hegel never says that we both do and do not hear a single seed falling.

Given Hegel's comments upon the Arrow Paradox and, more generally, the section on contradictions in the *Science of Logic*, I think one can reasonably impute to him the following two assertions:

First thesis: There are contradictions in reality.
Second thesis: An adequate description of reality must contain self-contradictory propositions.

Similar assertions may be found in later writers,[10] though perhaps not with the same inscrutable depth of intention. I now turn to what I take to be the standard analytical criticism of the two theses, a criticism exemplified in Karl Popper's well-known article, 'What is dialectic'.[11] He argues, in outline, that the first thesis is either meaningless or trivial, while the second is false. If by 'contradiction' we really *mean* contradiction, the first thesis is meaningless and rests upon a category mistake similar to, say, the error of asking what in reality corresponds to the negation sign. One could also say that the idea of 'real contradictions' in this literal sense is a case of the pathetic fallacy, ascribing to reality features that characterize our thinking about reality or our attitude towards it. J. Pen[12] has justly remarked that it is wrong to say that a situation with bilateral monopoly is 'indeterminate': the *situation* is perfectly determinate in the sense that all variables must have some value at each moment of time, but our *theory* may be indeterminate in the sense of being unable to predict these values. And just as reality has no blank spaces, it has no doubly filled spaces either: from the fact that a theory ascribes contradictory features to the real world, we may draw some conclusions about the theory but not about reality.

If, on the other hand, by 'contradictions' we merely mean conflict, divergence, opposition, or struggle, the first thesis becomes completely general and trivial. No one could possibly deny the facts, say, of class conflicts or of the struggle for survival. The first thesis might perhaps be strengthened to say that there are contradictions *everywhere* in reality, i.e. that *all* phenomena in nature, society, or thought contains struggles or oppositions. In that case we would have to ask for an exact definition of the feature that is said to be omnipresent. Either the concept is precisely defined so that the first thesis becomes susceptible to empirical analysis and to falsification, or the meaning is left so vague that after the fact one can always point to some feature of a given process that is 'contradictory' in *some* sense. A proponent of the first thesis (in the reading in which it states that all phenomena contain struggles or oppositions) might perhaps retort that the quest for a precise definition is misplaced, and that the notion of contradiction is more like the notion of a game, there being no set of features that are common to all contradictions, but only a family resemblance.[13] Such an answer might be understood in two ways: as a description of how the word 'contradiction' is actually used in everyday language, or as a way of making the concept scientifically useful. In the first interpretation the observation implied in the answer is correct enough, but does not help us very much in our present task. In the second interpretation, the answer must be understood as a proposal that the concept of a contradiction be defined disjunctively: anything is contradictory which satisfies at least k out of n given criteria. Such disjunctive definitions may indeed be useful in science,[14] on the condition that a list of criteria is also forthcoming. As the advocates of dialectical reasoning never tell us what criteria they have in mind, it is hard to take them seriously. As a matter of fact I suspect that the disjunctive definition governing their use of the term would rather be the following: anything may be called contradictory which has at least one feature in common with at least one of the phenomena that have already been classified as contradictory. It is not surprising that this imperialist and expansionist concept ends up by swallowing the whole of reality; less surprising, at any rate, than the fact that a third of humanity has to adopt this nonsense as its canon of thought.

As for the second thesis, that correct descriptions of the world may contain self-contradictory statements, it clearly requires the meaningless reading of the first thesis and might therefore be dismissed without further ado. Popper, however, also gives a separate argument against the thesis, referring to the logical truth that from a set of propositions from which two contradictory statements can be derived, any proposition whatsoever also follows. Dialectical reasoning is indeed fertile, but it is not the kind of fertility that is a desideratum of a scientific theory; rather the fertility Poincaré had in mind when he made a famous crack about the fertility of formal logic being proved by the antinomies it generated. Popper's point, I take it, is that it is not possible to be selectively self-contradictory: the smallest fissure in a theory will make it crumble altogether.[15] He adds a remark that is related to a point made below, to the effect that contradictions may have some real utility in that they will induce us to change the theory when its inner inconsistencies come to light. Here, then, we already glimpse the possibility of another and less obscure link between contradictions and change: instead of arguing that change is contradictory and must be described by self-contradictory statements, we can more plausibly say that the discovery that a theory contains contradictions will generate a change of theory.

Even if I accept Popper's criticism without reservations, I do feel that it is in a sense somewhat trivial. It is true that Hegel seems to have held the absurd view refuted by Popper, but there is more to Hegel than this. The sense in which I think it possible to talk without obscurity about real contradictions is given by the following thesis:

Third thesis: There are situations in reality that can only be described by means of the concept of a logical contradiction.

Someone who accepted the first and the second theses would certainly also accept the third, but I shall show that the converse is not true. Furthermore, I shall argue that the 'real contradictions' in this sense—i.e. the situations covered by the third thesis—are closely linked to processes of change; partly because they are themselves a variety of change and partly because they generate a movement of change in the direction of consistency. Also, examples will be given in this chapter and in Chapter 5 to substantiate the claim that at least some of the writings of Hegel and Marx can be analysed in terms of this thesis. A final statement of intention may perhaps be in order. My first wish is that the analysis be found to be of interest in its own right, also by that majority of readers whose interest in formal logic will be limited and who could not care less about Hegel or dialectics. In the second place the analyses should function within the book as a whole, i.e. as examples of the use of logical analysis in the social sciences. If, in the third place, I can offer something to that small but passionate minority who care deeply about Hegel and dialectics, this will not be an unwelcome result. Of course, I do not think that I have found *the* correct use of the term 'real contradiction' or that I have unravelled the hidden secret of dialectics; there are no such animals to be found or unravelled. Nor do I claim that my analysis exhausts all that is of interest in Hegel or Marx. I *do* hope, however, that the analysis will make up in precision for what it lacks in scope and in exegetical fidelity, so that the critic will be enabled—and obliged—to tell me *exactly* what is wrong with my account of the contradictions.

Contradictory desires: master and slave

The contradictions of the mind to which I referred above have a very simple structure. Basically it is this. Let us assume that the set of statements $(p, q, r, s \ldots)$ together imply a contradiction. Either of the two following situations will then fall under the heading of the third thesis above:

Contradictory desires: A wants (hopes, strives for) $p, q, r, s \ldots$ to be true simultaneously.[16]
Contradictory beliefs: A believes that $p, q, r, s \ldots$ are true.

In the first two sections I shall deal with contradictory desires, reserving the contradictory beliefs for the last sections. Some general remarks that are valid for both the affective and the cognitive contradictions may be made at the outset. Firstly, note the difference between the following situations:

(1) A believes/wants $(p, q, r, s ...)$. From $(p, q, r, s ...)$ a contradiction can be deduced.
(2) A believes/wants $(p, q, r, s ...)$ w is the case. From $(p, q, r, s, w ...)$ a contradiction can be deduced.

Taken literally the third thesis above covers both of these situations, but I shall here limit my attention to the first. We certainly have many *false* beliefs and entertain desires that *as a matter of fact* cannot be realized, but these phenomena are too general to be of much interest. Instead I shall try to show the importance of *contradictory* beliefs and of desires that *as a matter of logic* must remain unrealized.[17] Examples will be given below to show that this distinction is perhaps not a hard-and-fast one, but for the present purpose I believe that the reality of the distinction in the standard cases is more important than its possible collapse in the situations envisaged by Quine and others.[18] As a second general remark we may distinguish between 'degrees of contradictoriness'. Compare, for example, the following cases:

(3) A believes/wants p; A believes/wants $(p \supset \bar{q})$; A believes/wants q.
(4) A believes/wants p; A believes/wants $\bar{p}$.
(5) A believes/wants $(p \, \& \, \bar{p})$.

The last case may presumably be called pathological; only schizophrenics and Hegelians can have the contradictory as an explicit object of belief or desire. Situations like (3), on the other hand, probably are fairly common. A mathematician might for example entertain simultaneously several ideas which are later proved to be logically incompatible. I suspect that situations like (4) are more common than one might believe. It may be possible to believe p as a part of one field of experience and $\bar{p}$ as a part of a quite different field, the contradiction remaining undiscovered because the fields do not interact.

To have one's cake and eat it, is a feat sometimes impossible to achieve, but always possible to undertake. The main example that will be used to bring out this point is Hegel's master–slave dialectic from the *Phenomenology of Mind*, together with a number of earlier and later statements of what is basically the same insight. Let it first be said that the 'moving force' of Hegel's work is the emergence and then the overcoming of contradictions in situations of types (1) and (3) above. Hegel is very insistent that *he* is not trying to refute the consciousness whose Odyssey he is following. He is not applying external standards of truth nor adducing facts that are not given to the consciousness itself; rather he is trying to show how the subject itself discovers the inconsistency of its current 'form' (*Gestalt*) when comparing its own mental structure with its own criteria of adequacy.[19] The 'surfacing' of the contradiction to an explicit object of consciousness induces a change in the form of the consciousness, but the new form always turns out to harbour a contradiction of its own, and so on until the level of absolute knowledge has been reached. In Chapter 5 I return to the logic of this hierarchical learning process, and suggest that Hegel strikingly anticipated later analyses of inherently unsuccessful learning. Here, however, I shall deal only with one specific mental contradiction, the master–slave relationship.

In order to avoid a common misunderstanding, let us start out by observing that according to Hegel there is no contradiction *between* the master and the slave, only a contradiction *within* the mind of the master. (There is also a contradiction inherent in the consciousness of the slave, but I shall not explore this aspect of the dialectic here.) The point of departure, however, is a *struggle between* two consciousnesses, a fight for recognition where one ends up by yielding, preferring a life in subjection to death in combat. As the slave he has identified himself with brute matter, whereas the master–wagering his life in the fight–has transcended natural existence and demonstrated his absolute liberty. The issue is that the master is doubly powerful. Through the slave he has power over the material objects of consumption, which he can enjoy without having to work for them. Through the material objects the master enjoys power over the slave, for by the arbitrary and conspicuous consumption of these objects he demonstrates his power over the being that has produced them. Nevertheless, the master is caught in a trap, for he can get no real satisfaction from his power over a being that he treats like a thing, an *instrumentum vocale* as the Romans called their slaves. Indeed, the central idea of this section is that the notion of a *unilateral recognition*, which is what the master wants from the slave, is contradictory; this can be seen even more easily, perhaps, by thinking through the farcical notion of a nation seeking diplomatic recognition from one of its own colonies. You cannot force someone to respect you, even though you can try to do so. The master would like to have both the satisfaction deriving from the recognition accorded to him by the slave *and* the satisfaction deriving from his absolute power over the slave. This, however, really is like trying to have your cake and eat it; the master disappears from the history as a blind alley and the slave becomes (for a while) the carrier of the further development.[20]

In the remainder of this section we shall explore some variants of this dialectic, drawing upon poetry and fiction as much as upon psychology or philosophy. Hegel's work has been called a metaphysical novel,[21] and conversely the metaphysical poets such as Donne (or Emily Dickinson) know as much about the contradictions of the mind as Sartre or Bateson. To the writers cited in the preceding sentence we must add the name of Eugene Genovese, who has analysed the psychology of American Negro slavery in terms of the master–slave relationship. Among the many ideas worked out by Genovese is that through that relationship the masters somehow became the slaves of their slaves: 'The masters desperately needed the gratitude of their slaves in order to define themselves as moral human beings. The slaves, by withholding it, drove a dagger into their masters' self-image.'[22] This paradoxical insight certainly was not original with Hegel. It has found a perfect expression in Donne's verse:

> Take heed of hating me,
> Or too much triumph in the victory
>   Not that I shall be mine own officer,
> And hate with hate again retaliate;
>   But thou wilt lose the style of conqueror,
> If I, thy conquest, perish by thy hate.
>   Then, lest my being nothing lessens thee,
> If thou hate me, take heed of hating me.[23]

Rousseau pregnantly had said that 'Quiconque est maître ne peut être libre', and indeed this idea seems to have been a commonplace paradox of the late 18th century.[24] From another point of view Hegel's notion may be compared with the idea that the most efficacious power is exerted invisibly, through internalized norms rather than by overt sanctions, and that the use of power is an act of consumption rather than an act of investment.[25] Such precedents notwithstanding, Hegel should certainly be credited for bringing into focus the contradictory and inherently unrealizable nature of the master's desire, and for having seen this contradiction as but one of the many tangles in which we ensnare ourselves in our attempt to find a *durable satisfaction* (which would be a *contradictio in adjecto* according to Leibniz).[26]

The reader may have asked himself in exactly which sense the master's desire is *contradictory*. Do we really have a situation of type (1) above, or do we have to add—as in type (2) situations—some additional factual premise in order to generate a contradiction? It is certain that from the idea of unilateral recognition we cannot immediately deduce anything like 'p & $\bar{p}$'. We are dealing with some kind of *conceptual impossibility* here; a case where the spelling out of the implicit content and presuppositions of the concept generates a contradiction, even if the overt form is consistent. In the present case this spelling out may be done roughly as follows. The concept of recognition differs from such related notions as acknowledgement or appreciation in that what is recognized is not the existence or some aesthetic aspect of the person, but his moral worth. By seeking recognition one implicitly recognizes the moral worth of the person from whom recognition is forthcoming, but in seeking appreciation one does not implicitly appreciate the aesthetic value of the person by whom one is to be appreciated. This is so because moral competence *is* moral worth. To recognize someone as morally competent—as I implicitly do when seeking his recognition of my moral worth—is to recognize him as morally worthy as well. Aesthetic competence, on the other hand, does not in any way imply that the competent person also has aesthetic value.

For these reasons unilateral appreciation is a consistent notion, while unilateral recognition is not. By taking into consideration the implicit presuppositions of a concept it may be possible to generate a logical contradiction that does not follow from the manifest form of the concept. The problem, obviously, is how to distinguish these 'implicit presuppositions' from the purely factual premises that enter into situations of type (2) above. Is it an *empirical* (even if very important) fact about human beings that moral competence is inseparable from moral worth, or should we say that this link is as constitutive of humanity as the fact that we are mortal? Such questions show what I had in mind when I stated above that the distinction between logical impossibility and empirical falsity may not be a hard-and-fast one. Again we may turn to Donne for illumination and illustration. In *The Paradox* we read the enigmatic lines

> I cannot say I loved, for who can say
> He was killed yesterday?

Turning to *The Broken Heart*, the paradox is set forth in more easily understood terms:

> He is stark mad, who ever says,
> That he hath been in love an hour,
> Yet not that love so soon decays,
> But that it can ten in less space devour;
> Who will believe me, if I swear
> That I have had the plague a year?
> Who would not laugh at me, if I should say
> I saw a flask of powder burn a day?

The point is that some verbs cannot be used in the first person singular and in the past tense without giving rise to what Jaakko Hintikka[27] has called an *existential inconsistency*. To say 'I was killed yesterday' is certainly inconsistent for purely logical reasons; to say 'I saw a flask of powder burn a day' is inconsistent only if we add some factual permise as to the likelihood of surviving this event if one is near enough to observe it; to say 'I loved' is existentially inconsistent if we add the premise that love so transforms a person as to make him into another individual, but what kind of premise is this?

After this digression into the ambiguities of the notion of a mental contradiction, let us return to the substance of the problem. The brief reference above to Eugene Genovese's work was not intended as an exhaustive discussion of his version of the master–slave dialectic. Much remains to be said about the way in which he transforms metaphysical assumptions into empirical problems, thus making the issue of 'dialectical versus positivist' interpretations of slavery a matter amenable to factual study. In Chapter 6 below I return to one such confrontation, related to the meaning of 'irrationality' in planter behaviour. Here I shall discuss a problem that is more directly related to what was said above concerning the immanent contradictions of the master's consciousness. In a recent study of the treatment of American slaves G. Canarella and J. Tomaske[28] distinguish between sadistic and paternalistic masters, the first having their utility increased by a reduction in slave welfare and the second drawing positive utility from slave welfare. This may be contrasted with Genovese's picture of the typical planter: 'They were tough, proud, and arrogant; liberal-spirited in all that did not touch their honor; gracious and courteous; generous and kind; quick to anger and extraordinarily cruel; attentive to duty and careless of any time and effort that did not control their direct interests.'[29] On the Hegelian lines sketched above and further elaborated by Genovese, the relevant distinction would not be between two kinds of masters, but between two behavioural stances for each master, oscillating between kindness and cruelty as one or the other side of the contradiction gets the upper hand. In admittedly very loose, but hopefully suggestive, terms, we could say that the 'positivist' view assumes that individuals are (i) consistent and (ii) different from each other, whereas a 'dialectical' interpretation insists that each individual is *different from himself* and thus inconsistent. The merit of Genovese is to have shown that this opposition is not to be resolved at the *a-priori* level of metaphysical reasoning, but that on the contrary it should be perfectly accessible as a research problem in social psychology.[30]

Jean-Paul Sartre's *Being and Nothingness* is in many aspects one large variation upon these Hegelian themes. Indeed Sartre asserts that man has 'a certain capacity for forming contradictory concepts;'[31] even if it is always tempting to apply the epithet 'contradictory' to the vertiginous analyses offered by Sartre himself, I think that many of them make excellent sense once we understand that he is subscribing not to the second, but to the third of the three theses on contradictions discussed above. As a typical example of the kind of reasoning to be found in Sartre's work, we may take his discussion of love. The lover does not want the total subjection of the beloved person, nor a free and voluntary engagement; he wants the impossible, 'to possess a liberty'.[32] Sartre faithfully reflects the new psychological analysis that has been with us from Stendhal onwards. To an often-cited question from Racine's *Andromaque* 'Je t'aimais inconstant, qu'aurais-je fait fidele? (I loved you while you were inconstant, what would I not have done had you been faithful?)' Stendhal, Proust, and Sartre all give the opposite answer of what was implied by Racine: reciprocation is the death of love—and the object of love. Love is an impossible project, 'une passion inutile' to use the expression that according to Sartre sums up the human conditions as a whole.[33] Love requires the 'impossible synthesis of the assimilation and the maintained integrity of the assimilated object'.[34] (For those interested in national differences of intellectual style, we may observe that this is French for 'To have your cake and eat it'.) In a more general manner, man's existence, according to Sartre, is defined by the contradictory desire to be simultaneously a thing (*en soi*) and a consciousness (*pour soi*); to be as solid and as positive as a white dwarf where no room is left between the atoms *and* to know this. It would not, I think, be far off the mark if one said that for Sartre man's predicament is to be haunted by the wish to listen to his own funeral oration. If like Tom Sawyer and Huck Finn we could be secretly present at our own funeral, then we could both hear the final summing-up of our essence ('tel qu'en lui-même enfin l'éternité le change') *and* retain the consciousness that is necessary to enjoy it; both rest in ourselves in complete freedom from freedom *and* keep the distance from ourselves that is the mark of consciousness. No prolonged explanation is needed to see why it is existentially inconsistent, in Hintikka's sense, to affirm that one has been present at one's own funeral, and why the desire to be so present is inherently contradictory.

The impact of these ideas upon modern psychology has (to my knowledge) been relatively slight, but some parallel developments may be traced. Using the *Gesamtregister* to the Collected Works of Sigmund Freud,[35] it is easy to survey what Freud had to say about negation and contradiction. Essentially two ideas stand out. Firstly, the unconscious does not contain negations or contradictions: in it each element is full, positive, and unrelated to all others.[36] Secondly, the therapist knows that during the analysis negation is just another mode of confirmation; to deny something is just another way of affirming it. This last idea could perhaps be said to contain a germ of the double bind theory proposed by Gregory Bateson.[37] The richness of Bateson's thought is equalled only by its elusiveness; I shall refrain, therefore, from exposition or exegesis and only state that to my mind Bateson is much closer to Hegel and Sartre than to cybernetics, Russell's theory of types, von Neumann's theory of games and the modern theory of evolution, all of which are abundantly and not very convincingly quoted in his work. Essentially Bateson has rediscovered, along with Joseph Heller and others, a paradoxical insight with very ancient roots, as we have seen. In order to see that it is really the same insight, we may consider a simple example of the setting up of a double bind, a mother saying to her child: 'Remember that you are not even to think about this forbidden thing.' Here the implicit presupposition of the injunction—in order to fulfil it the child must remember (i.e. think) of the forbidden object—contradicts the overt content. Indeed.

> The Heart cannot forget
> Unless it contemplate
> What it declines[38]

It is inherently impossible to realize a *decision to forget*; except, perhaps, by the use of complicated and indirect strategies such as those envisaged by Pascal in his instructions about how to realize the equally paradoxical decision to believe.[39] We might distinguish here between active and passive negation, between denial and indifference, and state as an axiom that the latter can never be the state that results from the former. This, again, is a recurring idea in Hegel's *Phenomenology*. The mind is forever tainted with what it rejects; the rebel with the society he wants to abolish; the disappointed rebel with the God that failed. The link to the concept of the negation of the negation, as spelled out at the end of Chapter 3, should be obvious.

Contradictory desires: the economics of irrationality

We tend to think that a person exhibiting contradictory attitudes is 'irrational' in some sense of that term. To what extent is the converse also true? That is, when an economist talks about irrational behaviour, does he refer to something that lends itself to analysis in terms of a logical contradiction? In this section I shall try to answer this question for some of the varieties of behaviour that have been called 'irrational' by economists. The primary and 'standard' sense of irrationality in the economist's parlance is that of an intransitive set of preferences, i.e. an individual preferring a to b, b to c and c to a. Now from this intransitivity no contradiction can be deduced, unless we also add that the person has a meta-preference for transitive preference structures over intransitive structures. Several empirical studies have shown that people sometimes exhibit intransitive preferences and that, when this is pointed out to them, they usually modify their preferences in the direction of consistency. This change, presumably, may be said to reveal their meta-preference for transitivity. We have to add, however, that the meta-preference for transitivity must be hierarchically superior to all other preferences, for otherwise a person caught in flagrant intransitivity might reply something like the following: 'Yes, I agree that transitivity is a good thing, but not at all costs. Here as elsewhere trade-offs apply, and if I feel sufficiently strongly about a given set of alternatives I am quite prepared to give up transitivity.'

There is, I think, no logical contradiction involved in the concept of such a person, but for reasons spelled out in the next paragraph the idea is not very plausible. It becomes less far-fetched, however, if we look to decision-makers that are collective rather than individual actors, be they firms, organizations, or states. From the theory of social choice the following two propositions are well known. (a) If social choice is by majority voting, there exist constellations of individual preferences that induce intransitive social preferences. (b) If a moderate consensus—far from unanimity—is imposed upon the individual preferences, then intransitivity of social preferences cannot arise.[40] In this case, however, it makes quite good sense for the community in question to say that transitivity should not be an overriding desideratum; that it is more important to respect the individual opinions than to avoid the paradoxes. We expect an individual to change his preferences when they are seen to be intransitive, but the paradoxes of majority voting do not give a compelling reason for streamlining opinions. A community might very well choose to make Whitman's words its own: 'Do I contradict myself? Very well, I do. I am large, I contain multitudes.'

There is an amusing and instructive way[41] to bring out the irrationality of intransitivity. A person preferring a to b, b to c, and c to a could be bled to death in the following manner. As he prefers a to b, he must be willing to pay *some* amount, even if perhaps very small, in order to exchange b for a; likewise he must be prepared to pay some money in order to exchange a for c, and, of course, a further amount in order to exchange c for b. By the end of this process he is left with *b* as in the beginning, but short of some money. By repetition of this process the individual could *improve himself to death* (unless the preferences were such that the successive amounts of money given up form a series converging to a sum less than the amount of money he had at the outset). I suggest that this notion of ruining yourself through a series of steps, each of which is seen as an improvement, can be generalized.[42] This paradoxical process may arise from inconsistency, as in the example just given, or from inconstancy, as in the case of endogenous change of preferences. If the reader will refer back to the account in Chapter 2 of von Weiszäcker's analysis of such change, he will recall that the notation '$x P(y)z$' means that the individual in question prefers x to z, given that his consumption in the immediately preceding period was y. Von Weiszäcker has proved that given certain conditions, that may be interpreted as a tendency[43] to downgrade the *status quo*, we may construct a sequence q_i such that $q_{i+1} P(q_i)q_i$ for all i, where nevertheless the q_i converge to zero in each component. A two-component example might be the sequence $(1/2, 3/2,)(3/4, 1/2), (1/4, 3/4), (3/8, 1/4)\ldots$, where each step is accepted because it implies an increase in the smallest component. This is a case of improving yourself to death, as the result of a myopic preference for change.

In itself, this case of endogenously changing preferences would not qualify to the epithet 'contradictory'. It is no doubt tragic that a person may be driven to his death by causal forces that act in him without his knowledge or understanding, but as will be argued in Appendix 2 to Chapter 5, subintentional causality is a fact from which we can none of us escape. It is natural, however, to ask if we should not talk of a contradiction when the individual is *aware of* the global implications of his actions (i.e. is not only the passive vehicle of the changing preferences) and nevertheless acts according to the instantaneous preferences. When the question is put in this manner, it is clear that it is but a special (and somewhat artificial) case of the more general problem of pure time preferences. For a variety of reasons[44] persons may prefer the present or the near future to the distant future. (They may also, as the miser, prefer the future to the present, but I shall abstract from this in what follows.) This preference has been dubbed 'irrational' on general grounds: a year is a year is a year, and there is nothing but lack of will or imagination that can induce a preference for one year over another. This is too simplistic. For an individual, the fact that he is mortal makes it rational indeed to attach greater weight to the present than to a future in which he may no longer be around. For a society that wants to allocate resources between the present and the future within an infinite planning horizon, attaching equal weight to all generations may give the paradoxical result that each generation should allocate everything to investment and nothing to consumption (above subsistence).[45] If, however, we restrict ourselves to the individual case and abstract from considerations of mortality, which is justified by the fact that time preferences often are much stronger than what the statistics of mortality tables should imply, we are left with a behaviour which may perhaps be called 'irrational'. Should it also be called 'contradictory'?

I shall distinguish between the general problem of time preferences and the special problem of *inconsistent time preferences*.[46] The special problem is implicit in Augustine's prayer: 'Give me chastity and continence, only not yet',[47] which I interpret in the following manner. Starting tomorrow I shall be 'chaste and continent', which implies, among other things, that I shall not attach undue weight to the present. Today, however, I would like to indulge in my several vices, one of which is a preference for the present. I am intelligent enough, on the other hand, to see that when tomorrow comes along, I shall still feel the same way. For this reason I ask of Thee to grant me the virtues that I lack — starting tomorrow. My situation is similar to a person who has inherited a fortune, which he would like to dispose of in the following manner. In the first year he would like to go on an enormous binge, spending half of his inheritance, and then he would like to spread the rest evenly over his lifetime. If he is sufficiently clear-headed he will see, however, that when the second year arrives, he will want to spend half (or at least a disproportionate amount) of what then remains in the second year, leaving the rest to be distributed evenly over the following years, and so on. One counter-strategy would be to buy an annuity with the half that he does not intend to spend in the first year; this would be equivalent to asking God to grant me chastity instead of relying upon my own will power. Another counter-strategy is what R. H. Strotz calls *the strategy of consistent planning*, which roughly amounts to choosing the best of all consumption sequences that satisfy the budget constraint and the inconsistent preferences.[48]

Rather than entering into the detail of these counter-strategies, let us take a closer look at the inconsistency to which they are solutions. Writing $f_i(j)$ for the discounted value at time i for one unit of utility experienced at time j, we can impose two requirements upon the time preferences:

Constant time preferences: $f_i(i):f_i(i+1)=f_j(j):f_j(j+1)$
Consistent time preferences: $f_i(j):f_i(j+1)=f_j(j):f_j(j+1)$

From this we at once get the condition of

Exponential time preferences: $f_i(i):f_i(i+1)=f_i(j):f_i(j)+1)$

The assumption of constant time preferences may of course be questioned. In the discussion above of endogenously changing preferences, I explicitly assumed that what changed was the preferences over the set of commodity vectors *at any given moment*. Not only was there no question of endogenously changing time preferences, but I even appealed to constant time preferences for an explanation of the 'irrational' tendency to seek the short-term gain. I do not know of any discussion in the literature of endogenously changing time preferences, but there might be at least two possible sources for such a phenomenon. In the first place, time preferences stemming from the analysis of mortality tables will necessarily change as we move on in age without dying; in the second place the possession of inconsistent time preferences in the sense under discussion might in itself induce a tendency to change, in conformity with my general thesis that contradictions induce change. As for the assumption of consistent time preferences, I have tried to capture the idea that a consistent person should not have to constantly revise his plans, or rather: the internal structure of his plans should not be such that they will *necessarily* have to be revised even without any 'real change' in the character of the person. There are degrees of rationality here. It is certainly not irrational to change your plans because you become convinced by experience, persuasion, or argument that your former preferences were immoral or superficial. Nor is it formally irrational, even if potentially disastrous, to revise your plans because of endogenously changing preferences. It would seem unambiguously irrational, however, to have plans that are inherently unrealizable. A necessary and sufficient condition for the plan to be realizable is that the relative weight of any two given years in the future does not change as time moves on, for on that condition the planned allocation of consumption between the two years will in fact be realized.

To form plans that are 'inherently unrealizable' would seem to imply that a contradiction is present somewhere, but the logical form of the contradiction in this case is not immediately clear. I shall postpone further discussion of this form to Chapter 5, because I believe that the inconsistent time preferences have a structure that is more similar to the contradictions of society than to the contradictions of the mind. Let it only be briefly stated that each of the successive incarnations of the individuals wants to be free to bind its successors while not feeling bound by the decisions of its predecessors. While any single incarnation may be able to realize this desire, we commit the fallacy of composition if we conclude that all incarnations may be so able. I also postpone to the next chapter a further discussion of the way in which non-exponential time preferences may arise.

I now pass to the general problem of time preferences, which I propose to subsume under the even more general heading of *akrasia* or weakness of will. In the main I follow the analysis proposed by Donald Davidson.[49] It has long been recognized that weakness of the will somehow has something to do with contradictions, not in the sense of the third thesis above, but rather in that of the first. It has been asked, that is, not whether the mental structure of the *akrates* rests upon contradictory attitudes or beliefs, but whether the very concept of such a person is at all meaningful. Is it at all (logically) possible for a person to act against his better judgement, to know the good and nevertheless do the evil? Is not the very fact that one does the evil sufficient proof that one does not know the good, or does not think it good? Davidson's way of resolving the problem—and of proving the possibility of *akrasia*—is based upon his general theory that reasons are causes.[50] Imagine that you have a free choice between x and y. On the basis of the set of reasons s you prefer x to y, but on the basis of reasons r (which include s) you prefer y to x. Nevertheless you do x, for the reasons s. You act freely and intentionally (for you have a reason for acting as you do), but you do not take into account all the relevant reasons. How can you override the additional reasons that enter into r? According to Davidson

There is no paradox in supposing a person sometimes holds that all he believes and values support a certain course of action, when at the same time those same beliefs and values cause him to reject the course of action. If r is someone's reason for holding that p, then his holding that r must be, I think, a cause of his holding that p. But, and this is what is crucial here, his holding that r may cause his holding that p without being his reason; indeed the agent may even think that r is a reason to reject p.[51]

If we use the term 'motivation' for the relation between a reason and an action for which it is the reason, then the reason r may motivate me to do y rather than x *and* cause me to do x rather than y, in which case my reason for doing x is also a part-cause of my doing x, since s is included in r. This is but one of the many intriguing ways in which the causal and the intentional lives of the mind may play havoc with each other. Some further remarks on this difficult topic are offered in Appendix 2 to Chapter 5. A preliminary summing-up might be the following. We should distinguish between contradictory intentions on the one hand and conflicts between intentional and causal processes on the other hand. Inconsistent time preferences and (with some additional assumptions) intransitive preferences are clear cases of contradictory desires, or inherently unrealizable intentions. Consistent time preferences, or more generally weakness of will, should rather be seen as intentional *surdity*, in Davidson's term; here the actor is in the grip of causal forces that elude him and make all his plans come to nought. The phenomenon of endogenously changing preferences has a similar character.

Contradictory beliefs: Hintikka

Having argued that Hegelianism and the economic theory of rational behaviour are two main sources for the analysis of contradictory attitudes, I now go on to contradictory cognitions. The logical analysis of what should be *meant* by the term 'cognitive contradiction' draws extensively upon Jaakko Hintikka's work in epistemic logic, whereas the analysis of what *happens* when people entertain contradictory beliefs mainly refers to Leon Festinger's theory of cognitive dissonance. It is not obvious to all writers that contradictory belief systems *can* occur at all. Take, for example, the following passage from an influential article by Alasdair MacIntyre:

Calvin was committed to the following propositions: 1. God commands good works; 2. It is of the highest importance possible to do what God commands; 3. Good works are irrelevant to what is of most importance to you, your salvation or damnation. It is a requirement of logic, not of psychological pressures, that one of these propositions be modified; the alternative is contradiction.[52]

Even granted the questionable characterization of these three propositions as contradictory, there is no reason for excluding their co-tenability *qua* objects of belief, even if it is probably true that this would set up psychological pressures. To conclude from the impossibility of certain beliefs being true simultaneously to the impossibility of anyone entertaining them simultaneously is bad logic indeed,[53] unless one explicitly adopts the psychological interpretation of the law of contradiction.[54] But I do not think MacIntyre would do this.

I shall follow quite closely Hintikka's discussion in Chapter 2 of *Knowledge and Belief* where he discusses 'criteria of consistency' for his epistemic logic. Now this logic intends to deal both with knowing and believing, and the criteria of consistency will be quite different for these two 'propositional attitudes'. In ordinary parlance it would be contradictory to say of someone that 'He knows that p and that not-p'; such a person would not have a contradictory mental structure, he just could not exist. (This is the distinction between the first and the third theses on contradictions.) On the other hand it is not contradictory, as argued above, to say of someone that 'He believes that p and that not-p'. Hintikka, however, does not want to admit statements of the latter kind as consistent. He wants to explore, that is, what one could call *rational belief*, or in his own terms: *defensible beliefs*. A defensible system of beliefs has 'immunity to certain kinds of criticism', so that it cannot be refuted on purely logical grounds. (To sketch a link to Festinger's theory, we may observe that a defensible system of beliefs should not be a source of cognitive dissonance, unless the individual wrongly thinks that a contradiction may be deduced from what he believes or unless psychological criteria of consistency are added to the logical ones.)

In Hintikka's work the modal operators 'M' and 'N' are given two sets of interpretations, corresponding to knowledge and belief. In the analysis of knowing '$K_a p$' (corresponding to necessity) means that 'a knows that p', whereas '$P_a p$' (corresponding to possibility) means that 'It is possible, for all that a knows, that p'. For belief, '$B_a p$' means 'a believes p' and '$C_a p$' that 'p is compatible with everything that a believes'. In his analysis of knowledge, Hintikka discusses a number of criteria of consistency, of which the most important is the following:

A_K: If a set L of sentences is consistent and if '$K_a p_1$', '$K_a p_2$' ... '$K_a p_n$' and '$P_a q$' are all members of L, then the set ('$K_a p_1$', '$K_a p_2$', ... '$K_a p_n$', q) is also consistent.

In other words, 'If it is consistent of me to say that it is possible, for all that I know, that q is the case, then it must be possible for q to turn out to be the case without invalidating any of my claims to knowledge'.[55] The important word here is *claim* to knowledge. If we only required that q could turn out to be the case without invalidating what I know, then the following and weaker criterion would be in order:

B_K: If a set L of sentences is consistent and if '$K_a p_1$', '$K_a p_2$' ... '$K_a p_n$' and '$P_a q$' are all members of q, then the set ($p_1, p_2 ... p_n, q$) is also consistent.

The difference between A_K and B_K is that the first is a criterion for knowledge as *justified* true belief and the second for knowledge as true belief only. If, namely, it turned out that q, if true, would undermine my claim to know, say, p_1, e.g. by demonstrating the unreliability of the evidence on which I base my claim to know that p, then the cognitive system implied in the antecedents of the criteria would be inconsistent if knowledge is taken as justified true belief, but not if it is taken as true belief. As a further criterion Hintikka proposes the following and quite obvious one:

C_K: If the set L of sentences is consistent and if '$K_a p$' is a member of L, then the set $L + (p)$ is also consistent.

From A_K and C_K we at once get:

D_K: If the set L of sentences is consistent and if '$K_a p_1$', '$K_a p_2$' ... '$K_a p_n$' and '$P_a q$' are all members of L, then the set $(p_1, p_2 ... p_n, 'K_a p_1', 'K_a p_2' ... 'K_a p_n', q)$ is also consistent.

When we go from knowledge to belief, we obtain criteria A_B, B_B, C_B and D_B by replacing everywhere '$K_a p$' by '$B_a p$' and '$P_a q$' by '$C_a q$'. Of these criteria C_B clearly is not valid, for we certainly want to permit false beliefs. Criteria A_B and B_B are valid if D_B is, so that we may concentrate upon Hintikka's argument for the need for imposing consistency criterion D_B, which can thus be verbally expressed: 'If something is compatible with everything you believe, then it must be possible for this something to turn out to be the case together with everything you believe without making it necessary for you to give up any of your beliefs.'[56] Hintikka gives a striking and ingenious example to show the need for, and the implications of this criterion. Take the following sentences:

The Laputans believe that they will be attacked by the Ruritanians.

The Laputans believe that the Ruritanians will attack them only if the attack comes as a surprise,

where the second sentence is to be read as

The Laputans believe that the Ruritanians will attack them only if they do not believe that they will be attacked.

This means that we have a pair of sentences of the form $(B_a p, B_a(p \supset \overline{B_a p}))$. According to Hintikka this belief system is such that it must intuitively be characterized as inconsistent, and it is hard not to agree. For a criterion that makes this pair come out as inconsistent we need D_B; both A_B and B_B are too weak. On criterion D_B it is easy to see that the set $(B_a \bar{p}, B_a(\overline{B_a p} \supset p))$ also comes out as inconsistent, while the following systems are both consistent: $(B_a p, B_a (\overline{B_a p} \supset p))$ and $(B_a \bar{p}, B_a(p \supset \overline{B_a p}))$. All this is well in line with our intuition. An interesting implication also follows, viz. that the single belief $B_a (\overline{B_a p} \equiv p)$ is inconsistent on criterion D_B. For if $B_a (\overline{B_a p} \equiv p)$, then one of the following must hold, either

$$(B_a(\overline{B_ap} \equiv p), B_ap) \quad \text{or} \quad (B_a(\overline{B_ap} \equiv p), \overline{B_ap}).$$

The first of these sets is inconsistent because the set $(B_a(p \supset \overline{B_ap}), B_ap)$ is inconsistent, as just shown. The second set can be rewritten as $(B_a(\overline{B_ap} \equiv p), C_a\bar{p})$. If this is consistent, then according to D_B the following must also be: $(B_a(\overline{B_ap} \equiv p),$ $\overline{B_ap} \equiv p, \bar{p})$; but from the latter we at once deduce $(B_a(\overline{B_ap} \equiv p), B_ap)$, which is just the first inconsistent set again. The Laputans cannot consistently believe that they will be attacked if and only if they do not believe that they will be attacked. They can, however, consistently entertain the following belief system: $(B_a(B_ap \supset \bar{p}), B_a(B_a\bar{p} \supset p))$, for this, while being incompatible both with B_ap and with $B_a\bar{p}$, is compatible with $\overline{B_ap}$, i.e. with $C_a\bar{p}$. If we believe that the enemy will do the opposite of what we believe, if we believe anything at all, then we are on safe ground only if we do not believe anything.

The last remarks remind us of the fact that the logic of belief, like that of the other modalities, is three-valued. We may believe that p, we may believe that $\bar{p}$, or we may just have no beliefs at all concerning p. That we can deny K_ap without affirming $K_a\bar{p}$ is not hard to accept, but I suggest that to many people there is a psychological compulsion to believe either p or $\bar{p}$ once the question of p has been raised. An important source of confusion here may be that the logic of action is often two-valued, even if the logic of the beliefs on which action is based is three-valued. I may believe that there is going to rain, I may believe that the sun will shine, or I may have no ideas whatsoever concerning the weather, not even a subjective probability distribution. On the other hand the choice between taking an umbrella and not taking an umbrella is perfectly clear cut, leaving no third option. It is perfectly consistent to believe that if I take an umbrella, there will be sunshine and that there will be rain if I leave it at home; that the need for the umbrella will arise if and only if I do not take an umbrella. On the other hand it is inconsistent to believe that there will be rain if and only if I do not believe that there will be rain.

A person may take his umbrella, or leave it at home, without any ideas whatsoever concerning the weather, acting instead on general principles such as maximin or maximax reasoning, i.e. acting as if the worst or the best is certain to happen. He may also take or leave the umbrella because of some specific belief concerning the weather. These two cases may be considered together under the heading of *revealed belief* (on an analogy to revealed preference), i.e. acting as if one believes that p. Writing 'RB_ap' for 'a acts as if he believes that p', there is no inconsistency in the belief $B_a(\overline{RB_ap} \equiv p)$, nor, I suppose, in the revealed belief $RB_a(\overline{RB_ap} \equiv p)$, though it is not clear to me how it would be to act as if one believes that the need for an umbrella will arise if and only if one does not take one. Also there is no inconsistency in $(RB_ap, RB_a\bar{p})$. Someone may be totally ignorant and non-believing as regards the weather, and yet take his umbrella (acting as if he believes that it will rain) and also lower the sunshade (acting as if he believes that the sun will shine during his absence). There is no inconsistency in taking precautions against two mutually exclusive events, even if one cannot consistently believe that they will both occur. (In the next section I briefly return to the role of revealed belief in scientific research.)

A more elaborate example may be useful at this point, the so-called *Newcomb's problem* stated by Robert Nozick.[57] Here a person is given the following instructions:

> On the table before you are two boxes A and B. Box B contains 100 dollars. Box A contains either 0 dollars or 1000 dollars. You have the choice between either opening A and take as your reward what is inside, and opening both A and B and take as your reward what is inside both. The money is placed inside box A *before* you make your choice, by a Being who in the past has had an uninterrupted run of one million correct guesses as to which choice would be made by other subjects (given these very same instructions) subsequent to the placing of the money, and he has consistently placed the money so that everyone who has opened A has got 1000 dollars and everyone who has opened both boxes has got 100 dollars only. In other words, when the Being foresees that someone is going to open both boxes, he places nothing inside box A, otherwise he places 1000 dollars inside box A, and he has always been successful in his anticipations so far. Now make your choice.

In this way of stating the instructions (and in any other way I can conceive of) there is an obvious inconsistency, in that the million persons preceding you in the situation cannot all have been told truthfully that the Being has made an uninterrupted run of one million correct guesses. There is no problem in the notion of a Being who can predict the choices of people that are told just the payoffs without being told the story of the omniscient Being: he will predict (correctly) that they will open both boxes. The notion of a Being predicting the choice of persons who believe in such a Being is, however, more problematic, for how did these people come to believe in the existence of such a Being in the first place? Not, surely, by noting his successful predictions in the case of people who did not believe in his existence? Let us, however, ignore this complication and just assume that we are dealing with an individual who believes in the existence of such a Being, even if his grounds for doing so may be less than adequate.

The dilemma of such an individual is obvious. On the one hand he knows that the money is already inside box A, so that he has nothing to lose by opening both boxes. On the other hand the successful predictions of the Being indicate that he is somehow able to foresee the choice. Since the individual believes in the story of the Being, he would be willing to bet money on anyone else in the same position getting only 100 dollars if he were to open both boxes, so why should he not apply the same reasoning to himself? Now let 'p' be the statement 'There are 1000 dollars in box A' and 'q' the statement 'Individual a opens both boxes'. Let us also make a series of assumptions. Firstly, we assume that the individual wants to have a consistent belief system. Secondly we assume that he is rational, so that $B_a p \supset q$. Thirdly, we assume—not very extravagantly—that he believes himself to be rational, so that $B_a(B_a p \supset q)$. Lastly we have assumed that he believes the story of the omniscient Being, so that $B_a(q \supset \bar{p})$. The last two beliefs imply $B_a(B_a p \supset \bar{p})$, which was shown above to be incompatible with $B_a p$. Given, then, the rather reasonable second and third assumptions the person cannot consistently believe both that the story of the Being is true and that there is money in box A. On the other hand, to open box A only would not make sense unless he believed that p. It follows that—under the stated assumptions—he should open both boxes.

For the reader who wants his confusion compound rather than simple, we may comment briefly upon the following reasoning by Anatol Rapoport: 'Knowing the Being's great accuracy in predicting my choice, I engender a belief that with high probability I shall make the correct decision. What is in the box, is not under my control, but what I believe to be there is. I shall act so as to engender a belief that I have an excellent change of getting 1000 dollars.'[58] Now in the first place (as remarked in passing above) you cannot *decide to believe* something in order to obtain an end. You believe something because you have reasons to do so, not in order to achieve something, though you can of course feign belief for a purpose. In the second place, this *a fortiori* also holds for the doubly impossible feat of deciding to have an inconsistent belief system. The only way out, perhaps, would be to follow Pascal and set up a series of actions whose (predictable) end result is my believing the impossible. In the third place, however, even Pascal did not say that the belief induced by acting as if I believe is the religion of 'I believe because it is absurd', which is what Rapoport would have us accept. And, in the fourth place, should not the desire to transform oneself into the kind of person capable of having inconsistent beliefs be characterized as a contradictory desire?

Contradictory beliefs: Festinger

The most important study of what happens when people have inconsistent belief systems is no doubt Leon Festinger's work on cognitive dissonance. In the formal definition of that notion. Festinger states that '[cognitive elements] x and y are dissonant if not-x follows from y'.[59] This definition, however, turns out to be less closely related to epistemic inconsistency than the wording would indicate. The 'cognitive elements' are not really (or not only) cognitive in the strict sense. According to Festinger, even an action can be a cognitive element, as when there is said to be cognitive dissonance when a person goes on smoking even when he knows that smoking is dangerous. A want or a preference may also function as a cognitive element, as when a person goes to a concert and then finds that he really wanted to go to a movie. Festinger's justification for the term 'cognitive' in such cases is that if a person does something, he presumably also knows and *a fortiori* believes that he does it; and similarly that 'a wants p' implies 'a knows and *a fortiori* believes that he wants p'. This, while correct, does not suffice to turn cognitive dissonance in Festinger's sense into inconsistent beliefs in Hintikka's sense. No formal contradiction can be derived from the set of statements ('a believes that he smokes', 'a believes that he should not smoke'). Rather we should talk about practical dissonance in such cases, or about weakness of will. It is also clear that the phrase 'follows from' in the definition is not to be interpreted as logical implication, but rather as some kind of 'psycho-logical' implication. The knowledge that you have chosen car A over car B is dissonant with the knowledge (acquired after the purchase) that car B is in crucial respects better than car A: here there are no contradictory beliefs nor any practical dissonance, only a feeling of regret.

Nevertheless, inconsistent belief systems (in Hintikka's sense) is one species of the vaguely defined family of cognitively dissonant systems, and at least some of the notions, problems, and theories that have evolved have some relevance for our discussion. The general thesis of the Festinger school is the following: 'The existence of dissonance gives rise to pressures to reduce the dissonance and to avoid increases in dissonance.'[60] I shall comment upon some aspects of this thesis, in so far as it relates to contradictory belief systems. As a first observation I shall elaborate upon what was said above in the discussion of Popper's criticism of dialectics: the discovery of logical contradictions in a theory certainly is a powerful impetus to a change of theory. In logic and mathematics this happens all the time; being contradictory is indeed the main (though not the only) way in which a mathematical theory can be false. In the empirical sciences logically inconsistent hypotheses would seem to be the exception rather than the rule. The ergodic hypothesis—a very attractive idea from Descartes to Maxwell[61]—turned out to be contradictory, but I do not know of many other substantial examples. According to some critics both psychoanalysis and Marxism are inconsistent because they imply their own falsity, but I do not think this is a valid objection. (It would be valid only if one could impute to these theories the ideas that any theory that can be causally explained is false and that all theories can be so explained, but I do not think either of these imputations can be sustained.) Empirical theories are usually proved false for empirical reasons.

We may observe here, for later reference, that in historical work inconsistent revealed beliefs may have a genuine role to play. Let us assume that I want to defend the thesis that the importance of event x (e.g. the invention of the railroad) for phenomenon y (e.g. American economic growth) was rather small. In order to prove this contention I assume that x did not take place and go on to calculate the hypothetical value of y. For this calculation I may need the value of some other variable z which (i) is causally affected by the absence of x, and (ii) is causally relevant for y. Let us further assume that z is relevant for y in two distinct ways: we may suppose, for example, that the larger is v and the larger is w, the larger is y, and that the larger is z the larger is v and the *smaller* is w. Finally, we assume that we are unable to find the exact hypothetical value of z, but that we are confident that it must lie in the interval (z_1, z_2). In that case I shall behave as if $z = z_1$ when calculating w and as if $z = z_2$ when calculating v;

if nevertheless the value of y does not differ much from the actual value, the hypothesis is corroborated. The Devil's Advocate in scientific work may have inconsistent beliefs.[62]

If we are dealing with genuine belief rather than with revealed belief, the idea that inconsistency induces change may seem too obvious or trivial to merit further comment. Yet on the large and vague definition of dissonance as any kind of logical or emotional incompability or 'lack of fit' it has been argued that people may actually strive for dissonance, because they find total consistency unpleasant. Anthony Kenny[63] quotes Bertrand Russell as saying that 'to be without some of the things you want is an indispensable part of happiness', and adds the comment that 'In so far as Russell wants to be happy, he must, in conformity with his dictum, want to be without some of the things he wants'. I do not think Kenny is right when he sees an inconsistency here. Given my non-possession of things $a_1, a_2 \ldots a_n$ (let us call this non-possession ϕ) I may prefer a_i to ϕ for all i and yet either prefer ϕ to $(a_1, a_2 \ldots a_n)$—i.e. to the simultaneous possession of all these things—or at least prefer $(a_1, a_2 \ldots a_{i-1} a_{i+1} \ldots a_n)$ to $(a_1, a_2 \ldots a_n)$ for all i or for some i. (What is involved here is the fallacy of composition, of which more in Chapter 5.) Nevertheless I believe he is right when he says that the corresponding epistemic attitude is contradictory. It is definitely inconsistent on Hintikka's criteria to believe that some of the things I believe are false. I also think Kenny is right in arguing that modesty should prevent me from claiming infallibility, which is exactly what I would be claiming if I believed that, say, all the statements in this book are true. I do believe that they are true individually, but collectively I believe that there are some false statements among them. Individually I may also believe that each of my present actions is morally right, and also believe that I shall find later that some of them were (i.e. are) wrong—I only wish I knew which. If this is inconsistency (and it is), then let us beware of consistency.

A rather similar problem crops up in Festinger's discussion of the possible strategies people can employ to reduce dissonance. One of these strategies—perhaps the most controversial[64]—is the selective exposure to information. In the first version of the theory of cognitive dissonance Festinger stated that, 'If a person is led, for one reason or another, to expect an information source will produce cognitions which will increase consonance, he will expose himself to the information source. If the expectation is that the cognition acquired through this source would increase dissonance, he will avoid it.'[65] Now there is a glaring paradox latent in this formulation, for if a person already has grounds for believing that a given source of information will contain information dissonant with his mental state, then he already *has* information dissonant with his mental state and therefore should have no compelling incentive to avoid the source. Information about information dissonant with X *is* information dissonant with X. As Kenneth Arrow has repeatedly emphasized, information as a commodity has some peculiar features in that 'its value for the purchaser is not known until he has the information, but then he has in effect acquired it without cost'.[66] In the present case the value is negative, but the problem is a similar one. To say 'I believe that p, and I also believe that in book A there is information incompatible with p, although I do not know what that information is' is inconsistent in much the same manner as the admission of fallibility was inconsistent. In both cases I believe that in some general and unspecified way I entertain false beliefs, even though I am unable to pinpoint the contradiction.

We shall see that in his later work Festinger recognized that his earlier statement was erroneous, but first we may comment upon an ingenious way in which the difficulty was tackled in one of the studies on which Festinger based his first book. If one could find some privileged source of information where the person involved could expect to find dissonance-reducing or dissonance-increasing information without the expectation itself being dissonance-reducing or dissonance-increasing, the problem would be solved. Such a source is obviously advertising, where the one thing to be sure of is that 'it always boosts the product which is being advertised';[67] one might also consider the 'information' disseminated by political parties. Thus if I want to be confirmed in my purchase of car A rather than car B, I know *a priori* that I shall achieve this goal by reading advertisements for A while shunning those for B, without this knowledge being equivalent (in its effects) to the actual reading. Now I do not deny the existence of persons who hire other persons to tell them what they want to hear, but I would like to question their rationality. The avid reader of advertisements for products in his own possession is like Wittgenstein's example of a man who buys several copies of the morning paper in order to assure himself that what it said was true;[68] we might also invoke an analogy used above, by imagining a nation trying to obtain diplomatic recognition from its own colony. In all these cases an actor is trying to derive genuine pleasure from what he receives with the left hand, while strenuously trying to forget that the donor was no one but his own right hand. For a rational person, both recognition and information must be derived from some independent source if they are to reduce dissonance.

In his later work Festinger recognized that 'once the person has been told that the information exists that does not support his decision, additional information has already been introduced—in a sense it is impossible for him to avoid it since he knows it exists'.[69] When a person is in the possession of such general and unspecified knowledge, two opposing tendencies will be simultaneously at work. On the one hand 'there might well be a tendency to avoid discovering the concrete details of the information that is dissonant with the decision', but on the other hand 'without knowing the concrete details it is very difficult to counterargue, reinterpret and reduce the dissonance'.[70] In the experiments reported by Festinger both tendencies were present in varying proportions, making the net result rather ambiguous. Here I would only like to add some general arguments for the importance of the first tendency. The impact of statements and beliefs seems in many cases to be reduced if they are couched in rather general terms. My second-order belief that some of my first-order beliefs are false does not enter squarely into conflict with these first-order beliefs, because it belongs to a different level of generality. To say of someone 'If I spoke my true opinion of him, I would be subject to the laws of defamation of character' is not to make oneself subject to the laws of defamation of character. The Watergate tapes showed that 'I do not want to know the details' was a recurring expression in the ramblings of the principal actor. I may believe that torture, illegal detention, blackmail, etc. do not take place in government agencies, while also knowing that some of the things I want done (and that get done) can only be accomplished by such means. So long as I do not know exactly *which* of these means is employed, the inconsistency is more supportable than if I had knowledge at the concrete level.

Before going on to the discussion of social contradictions in Chapter 5, I briefly recall to the reader the underlying purposes of the present analysis. I have tried to show, firstly, that one can give a precise meaning to the term 'real contradiction' in a manner that is not open to standard analytical objections. Secondly, I argue that this notion can not only be made precise (after all, there is much irrelevant precision around), but that it is extremely fertile as well. This is so especially because of the link between contradictions and change. Indeed I believe that the contradictions of the mind represent one of the two prime movers of endogenous psychic change, the other being the perversion of intentionality by causality. The need for focusing upon *endogenous* change should be clear, for the approach to change through exogenous influence is just another case of passing the buck. Sometimes someone must say, 'The buck stops here.'

Notes

1. I am referring to the term *Widerspruch*, not to be confused with *Gegensatz* (opposition). To my knowledge, for example, Marx never refers to a *Widerspruch* between labour and capital; nevertheless both Louis Althusser (1965, p. 104) and Maurice Godelier (1966) use the term 'contradiction' about this relationship.
2. The statements against which I argue in the last three sentences are found in Merleau-Ponty (1945, p. 31). See also Taylor (1971, p. 47).
3. A similar distinction between intrapersonal and interpersonal contradictions is proposed by Pörn (1970, p. 34 ff.). In his discussion of the rational or consistent exercise of power, Pörn lays down three criteria of consistency, the first of which is internal to the power-holder and the last two deal with the relations between several power-holders and between several power-subjects.
4. A similar distinction between practical and theoretical contradictions is proposed by Körner (1976, Chapter 16). Like Hegel, and unlike the present chapter, Körner also tries to work out the relations of interdependence and priority of the two forms of consistency. His results do not easily carry over to the present approach, but the interested reader certainly should consult what he has to say about the problem.
5. For an exposition see especially Lee (1936), who gives the full Greek texts with translation and commentary.
6. This 'i.e.' is open to controversy. Thus G. Vlastos (1967) argues that it is a category mistake to assume that the arrow must be either in movement or at rest at each

moment, just as it is a category mistake to assume that a point must be either straight or curved.

7. Once again, these are controversial matters. See for example the distinction between rest and immobility in Koyré (1971, p. 33).

8. A quote may be in order at this point: 'Something moves, not because it is here at one point of time and there at another, but because at one and the same point of time it is here and not here, and in this here both is and not is. We must grant the old dialecticians the contradictions which they prove in motion; but what follows is not that there is no motion, but rather that motion is existent Contradiction itself'. (Hegel, 1961, vol. II, p. 67).

9. See for example Whitrow (1961, p. 141): 'Logically, a non-zero magnitude cannot be generated by combining a *finite* number of zero magnitudes: *ex nihilo nihil fit*. If, therefore, an audible sound can be produced by the combined effect of a *finite* number of "inaudible sounds", then "something" has been produced by a finite set of "nothings", and so we are faced with a contradiction between reason and experience. The analogy with the argument that motion cannot be compounded by a set of immobilities is obvious'. Whitrow's use of the term 'finite' (italicized here) shows, however, that the analogy is very far from complete, for there is an infinite number of instants in the arrow's flight, and according to one writer 'elementary calculus taught us that the product of zero by infinity can be equal to any finite value' (Capek, 1972, p. 336). Now elementary calculus certainly taught us nothing of the kind, but it remains true that there is an essential difference between the finite and the infinite cases.

10. Thus J. Laplanche (1970, p. 6) explains the occurrence of contradictory statements in the writings of Freud by the fact that he was dealing with a contradictory object, the human mind. Cf. also the following discussion of a possible source of cognitive dissonance: 'Third, the fault may lie in the stars and not in ourselves. The notion of a society free of inherent contradictions is going out of fashion. Cognitions that reflect an inconsistent social world... must be internally contradictory' (McGuire, 1966). In Chapter 5 I show that the last statement is wrong: the conjuction of belief systems that are individually consistent may give an inconsistent whole; it may be possible for any single individual to have his cake and eat it, but not for all individuals simultaneously.

11. Popper (1940).

12. Pen (1959, p. 91 ff.).

13. Wittgenstein (1953, pp. 32 ff.).

14. See Hull (1965) for a discussion of disjunctive definitions in biology.

15. As Dag Prawitz has pointed out to me, this would not be true on a system such as the 'minimal calculus' of Johansson (1936).

16. This definition of contradictory desires may be compared to the discussion in Körner (1976) of various kinds of practical contradictions. In his account (especially Körner, 1976, pp. 96 ff.) there are three such varieties: opposition, discordance, and incongruence between practical attitudes. Opposition is rather similar to what is here defined as a contradictory desire, whereas discordance is related to what is discussed in the text as weakness of will. Incongruence is defined as a set of second-level attitudes directed towards an opposed pair of first-level attitudes. To this trichotomy Körner adds another, viz. a distinction between logical, empirical, and practical impossibility. This would seem to give a very rich array of contradictory stances, but the lack of non-trivial examples in Körner's discussion makes it difficult to see how much one can get out of the approach.

17. For this distinction, see also Sen (1970, p. 61): 'A man who judges that "consumption today should be maximized" and "consumption a year hence should also be maximized" is not involved in ... a logical conflict, since the two judgments conflict

only under specific (though plausible) circumstances. ...in contrast, the kindly man who wishes everyone an income higher than the national average seems to have an analytical problem of some magnitude.'

18. For doubts about the usefulness of the analytic–synthetic distinction, see Quine (1953, Chapter II) and Quine (1960).

19. For this method of 'immanent refutation' see the Introduction to the *Phenomenology of Mind.*

20. Actually the master–slave relationship forms the matrix of the following forms as well. *Stoicism* is the slave as master; *scepticism* the slave as slave; *the unhappy consciousness* contains both master and slave within itself, in a relationship that has been compared to the between superego and ego.

21. Hegel was inspired especially by the French *roman de culture*, such as Marivaux's *La Vie de Marianne*. The best comparison would seem to be with *A la Recherche du Temps Perdu*, which like Hegel's work is circular in structure and concerned with the *genesis of genetic thinking*. The process that enables the mind to understand its own history is identical with that history.

22. Genovese (1974, p. 146).

23. *The Prohibition*. Observe that Donne, as Hegel after him, takes the view that the master's purpose is self-defeating, so that there is no need for the slave to be his 'own officer'. It is appropriate to reproduce here the first stanza of the poem:

> Take heed of loving me.
> At least remember, I forbade it thee;
> Not that I shall repair my unthrifty waste
> Of breath and blood, upon thy sighs, and tears,
> By being to thee then what to me thou wast;.
> But, so great joy, our life at once outwears,
> Then, lest thy love, by my death, frustrate be,
> If thou love me, take heed of loving me.

This is a much more conventional idea: if you love me too much I shall die of joy and bereave you of the object of your love. In the comment in the text upon Sartre, Stendhal, and Proust, I argue that on a modern view love is best by the same paradox that Donne applies to hate; indeed the two can hardly be separated.

24. I owe this observation to Jens Arup Seip; see Seip (1958, pp. 34–35), who attributes the quote from Rousseau to his *Lettres de la Montagne*.

25. Cf. Elster (1975a, pp. 171 ff.) for a discussion of this problem in the writings of Leibniz.

26. Cf. footnote 19 to Chapter 3 above.

27. Hintikka (1967).

28. Canarella and Tomaske (1975).

29. Genovese (1974, p. 96).

30. Cf. for example Milgram (1974, pp. 132 ff.), who argues that we should not distinguish between obedient and autonomous *persons*, but rather between an obedient and an autonomous *state* of a given person. The analogy is not complete, for in what Milgram calls the 'agentic shift' from the autonomous to the obedient mode the triggering factor lies outside the individual himself, whereas the cyclically changing moods of the master do not depend upon changes in the environment. There is no *contradiction* involved in Milgram's analysis, because the frame of reference is causal rather than intentional.

31. Sartre (1943, p. 95).

32. Sartre (1943, p. 434).

33. Sartre (1943, p. 708).

34. Sartre (1943, p. 668).

35. Freud (1968).

36. Cf. also Hyppolite (1966) and Lacan (1966) for comments upon the text where Freud denies reality to the negation in the unconscious.
37. See especially Bateson (1956); also Watzlawick *et al.* (1967).
38. Emily Dickinson. *Complete Poems* No. 1560. The poem as a whole reads like this:

> To be forgot by thee
> Surpasses Memory
> Of other minds
> The Heart cannot forget
> Unless it contemplate
> What it declines
> I was regarded then
> Raised from oblivion
> A single time
> To be remembered what—
> worthy to be forgot
> Is my renown

It might be said, perhaps, that in this setting the three lines quoted in the text acquire a different meaning; I think, however, it could be said with equal justice that the reading offered here of these lines permits a new and somewhat ironic interpretation of the setting. 'If thou will forget me, take heed of forgetting me.' Cf. also Elster (1976d).
39. Cf. especially his *Pensée* 233, commented in Elster (1976d).
40. The Condorcet paradox assumes that a community of three individuals shall make a choice between alternatives (a, b, c) by majority voting. If the first person prefers a to b and b to c, the second b to c and c to a, and the third c to a and a to b, it is immediately seen that there is a majority for a over b, for b over c and for c over a. A sufficient condition that prevents this cycle from arising is the following: for any three alternatives (a, b, c) there is some alternative, say a, such that all the concerned individuals agree that it is not best, or all agree that it is not worst, or all agree that it is not medium. For details, see Sen (1970) or Riker and Ordeshook (1973).
41. Due to Raiffa (1968, p. 78).
42. Actually the notion of an improvement to death forges a link between the contradictions of the mind and the contradictions of society discussed in Chapter 5. In the latter, a crucial point is that what may be good for each person taken individually may be disastrous for everyone taken collectively; in the improvement to death the point is that what may be good at each moment taken individually is sometimes disastrous for all moments taken collectively. In other words, there is something like the fallacy of composition behind these mental contradictions.
43. Von Weiszäcker (1971a, p. 356) uses the term 'preference' for this tendency, but this is clearly inadequate if taken literally. It is very important here to distinguish between the intentional language of preferences and the causal language of tendencies; cf. also Appendix 2 to Chapter 5.
44. For which see Strotz (1955–56), Ainslie (1975), and Elster (1976d).
45. Actually matters are more complex. Without time preferences, and given certain technical conditions, there may be no optimal plan at all; for every plan involving a positive amount of consumption (above subsistence) another and better plan involving less consumption may be found, but the plan involving no consumption is inferior to them all. The point is that the set of all feasible plans is open and does not contain one of its accumulation points, viz. the zero consumption plan. See Heal (1973) and Hammond and Mirrlees (1973) for further discussion.
46. See Strotz (1955–56) for a path-breaking analysis of this problem.
47. Augustine, *Confessiones*, VIII, vii.

48. Unfortunately Strotz's analysis of consistent planning was mathematically incorrect, as shown by Pollak (1968). Within Pollak's framework a simple example is the following. We assume that we are dealing with a three-year period and with an amount K of consumption goods to be allocated over the period. We set C_1, C_2, and C_3 for the amounts consumed in the three years; we also let U_1 (C_1, C_2, C_3) be the utility function at the beginning of the first year and U_2 (C_2, C_3) the utility function at the beginning of the second. If the time preferences are consistent, then the allocation made at the beginning of the first year according to U_1 will be such that the couple (C_2, C_3) included in this allocation will also maximize U_2 (C_2, C_3), subject to $C_2 + C_3 = K - C_1$. If, however, the time preferences are not consistent, three possibilities present themselves. The individual can act naively and change his plans at the beginning of the second year; he can bind himself (e.g. through an annuity) to the allocation that is best according to U_1; finally—if the first option is undesirable (because the individual is too sophisticated) and the second impossible (for institutional reasons) he can choose the strategy of consistent planning, on the basis of the following argument. He knows that when he has chosen C_1 (no matter how), he will have in his possession $K - C_1$ at the beginning of the second year. He also knows that this amount will be allocated over the last two years according to U_2. Given U_2 and $K - C_1$, he can determine C_2 and C_3; we set $C_2 = g(K - C_1)$ and $C_3 = K - C_1 - g(K - C_1)$. He knows, that is, that being the kind of person he is, only consumption sequences of the form $(C_1, g(K - C_1), K - C_1 - g(K - C_1))$ can simultaneously satisfy the budget restraint and his sophisticated insight into his own inconsistent preferences. Among all the possible sequences of this form he then chooses the one that is best according to his preferences at the beginning of the first year; in other words he chooses C_1 so as to maximize U_1 $(C_1, g(K - C_1), K - C_1 - g(K - C_1))$. This strategy satisfies both reason and passion; reason because the choice is sophisticated rather than naive, passion because the instantaneous preferences determine the choices. For some doubts about this ingenious strategy, see Elster (1976d).
49. Davidson (1969); see also the papers collected in Mortimore (1971).
50. See for example Davidson (1963; 1970).
51. Davidson (1969, p. 111).
52. MacIntyre (1962).
53. Cf. Singer (1963, pp. 58–59) for a similar criticism of B. Mayo.
54. See Husserl (1913, paragraph 25) for an exposition and criticism of this interpretation.
55. Hintikka (1961, p. 17).
56. Hintikka (1961, p. 24).
57. Nozick (1969).
58. Rapoport (1975, p. 619), slightly modified.
59. Festinger (1957, p. 13).
60. Festinger (1957, p. 31).
61. According to Descartes 'matter must take successively all the forms of which it is capable' (*Œuvres*, ed. Adam et Tannery, vol. IX-2, p. 216 = *Principes de la Philosophie*, vol. III p. 47), where 'capacity' probably refers to the requirement of constant 'force' (erroneously thought by Descartes to be a requirement of constant mv scalarly interpreted). The corresponding statement by Maxwell is 'that the system, if left to itself in its actual state of motion, will, sooner or later pass through every phase which is consistent with the equation of energy' (quoted after Farquhar (1964, p. 75)). The underlying problem that gives rise to the contradiction here is that a continuous curve that does not intersect itself cannot fill out a multidimensional space.
62. Of course if the value of y did turn out to be very different, one might try a more sophisticated approach, by looking for the value of z in the interval that maximizes Δy when inserted both in the calculation of v and in the calculation of w. This, however, may be impracticable and time-consuming compared with the method discussed in the text.

63. Kenny (1965–66). For statements of the need for dissonance, see also Singer (1966, p. 55) and Leibniz (1875–90, vol. V, p. 175): 'L'inquiétude est essentielle à la félicité des créatures.' Cf. also note 19 to Chapter 3 above.
64. See Freedman and Sears (1965).
65. Festinger (1957, p. 128), quoted from the slightly expanded version in Festinger (1964, p. 96).
66. Arrow (1971a, p. 152).
67. Festinger (1957, p. 49).
68. Wittgenstein (1953, p. 94).
69. Festinger (1964, p. 82).
70. Festinger (1964, p. 82).

5

CONTRADICTIONS OF SOCIETY

The progression of the *Phenomenology of Mind* goes from the intrapersonal to the interpersonal mode of contradiction. Similarly Jean-Paul Sartre's intellectual itinerary goes from the analysis of psychological contradictions in *Being and Nothingness* to the analysis of social contradictions in the *Critique of Dialectical Reasoning*. For Hegel the transition from one kind of contradiction to the following was an essential part of his philosophy; in the case of Sartre the link is much less obvious. Indeed many have wondered whether the later analyses of Sartre's work supersede or supplement the earlier. My view is that the two are compatible, but that neither implies or presupposes the other. A similar relation holds between the present chapter and the preceding one. I think it might be possible ultimately to work out a theory that linked the psychological contradictions to the social ones in a coherent framework, just as it should be possible to give an integrated exposition of contradictory desires and contradictory beliefs. I have not felt up to this, however, and in that sense the present analyses should be seen as building-blocks or stepping-stones to an ulterior synthesis. A tentative step in that direction is taken in Appendix 2 below.

The strategy of the present chapter is the following. In a first section I discuss at some length the fallacy of composition, whose importance for the social sciences has often been casually acknowledged, but never—as far as I know— been the object of a systematic analysis. In the second section I then define a main variety of social contradictions which—following Sartre—I call *counter-finality*: the unintended consequences that stem from uncoordinated actions. Closely linked to counterfinality is the other main variant, that forms the object of the third section. This I call *suboptimality*, as exhibited for example in the Prisoner's Dilemma. In a fourth and last section I then try to bring together these notions in a *theory of social change*, arguing that there are intimate— even if rather complex—links between the two varieties of contradictions on the one hand and economic and political change on the other. To this are added two appendices. In the first I give a thumbnail sketch of game theory for the reader without previous acquaintance with strategic thinking; in the second I sketch some implications of the two chapters on contradictions for the theory of rational behaviour.

To give the reader a preliminary notion of what this is all about, I will state at the outset a transparently simple example, taken from Keynesian economics. As it has been said by one of Keynes's radical pupils, an 'essential paradox of capitalism' is that each capitalist wants low wages for his own workers (this makes for high profits) and high wages for the workers of all other capitalists (this makes for high demand).[1] Now it *is* possible for any capitalist taken individually to have his cake and eat it, but all capitalists cannot simultaneously be in this happy position. To conclude from the individual to the collective case would be to commit the fallacy of composition. The paradox of capitalism is also at the root of the Keynesian theory of crises and counterfinality. Given an exogenously induced reduction of demand and thus of profits, each capitalist tries to counteract this fall by reducing the wages of his workers. From the point of view of the individual actor this is a rational measure, but when they all take it simultaneously the collective result is a further reduction of the workers' buying power and therefore of profits, contrary to the intended result. Now the capitalists may end up by understanding this (and understanding that all understand it, etc.), in which case the situation is transformed into a game. The solution of the game, however, gives exactly the same behaviour as before: now each capitalist will reduce wages out of fear from being the only one not to do so, whereas before he did so out of hope to be the only one to do so. The suboptimality of the situation makes for paradox and tension; it is hard to accept misery when everyone could better their lot if everyone behaved differently. The outcome, given certain structural conditions, is a pressure towards organization, collective action, or government intervention: a case of *contradictions inducing change*.

Before coming to grips with the detail of these notions, let me also state how I see their relevance for Marxism. I shall argue that the most important occurrences of the term 'contradiction' in the corpus of Marx's writings all fit in quite well with my analysis. As to criteria for what is important, I suggest that on commonsensical grounds it will be accepted (a) that an occurrence is more important than another if it is found more frequently in the corpus, and (b) that an occurrence in the title of a chapter or a subsection of a chapter is more important than an occurrence in the running text, both criteria being subject to a *ceteris-paribus* clause. Using these criteria three occurrences stand out: the 'contradiction in the general formula of capital' discussed in Chapter 5 (of the English edition) of the first volume of *Capital*; the 'contradiction of the law of the falling rate of profit' that is the subject of Chapter 15 of the third volume; the 'contradiction between the forces of production and the relations of production' referred to in numerous texts, especially in the *German Ideology* and in the writings from the period 1857–61. These occurrences will be examined in, respectively, the first, second and third sections below.

The fallacy of composition

The philosophical and sociological literature on valid inference contains many references to this fallacy. Here I will first give an overview of several fallacious inferences that seem substantively related to each other, some of which have actually been called 'the fallacy of composition'. I then single out one of these fallacies and propose that it be called *the* fallacy of composition. There are, unfortunately, several reasons that count against this proposal. In the first place the fallacy I have in mind has never to my knowledge been referred to as the fallacy of composition. In the second place to the fallacy in question there corresponds no fallacy of division, the traditional converse of the fallacy of composition. The converse of the fallacy that I call the fallacy of composition is in fact a valid inference, and there is no other obvious candidate. Nevertheless I believe that the structure of the fallacy corresponds better to the term 'fallacy of composition' than is the case for any of the other fallacies in question; also the intrinsic importance of the fallacy makes it useful to have a name for it; finally the lack of agreement upon the proper definition takes out some of the bite of the first counter-argument above. Now these are moot points, and I do not invite to a quarrel about words. If the reader does not like my terminology, I hope he will focus instead upon the substance of what I am saying. Let us now look at some examples of fallacies that in some sense can be said to involve composition.

(1) The most common interpretation in the philosophical literature is the deduction of 'This group of individuals is F' from 'Each member of this group is F'; the fallacy of division is then taken as the converse deduction. In many cases the fallacy hinges upon the ambiguity of the property-name 'F'. 'Strong' clearly does not mean the same when applied to an army and when applied to the individuals that constitute the army; thus the upward or downward inference of one kind of strength from the other would be instances of the fallacies of composition and division, respectively. In other cases the fallacy arises even when no ambiguity is found. The word 'indecisive' presumably means the same when applied to individuals and when applied to groups, i.e. 'unable to come to a decision'. Yet an indecisive jury most probably is not composed of indecisive jurors; rather the contrary.[2] It may be possible to give some independent characterization of the properties that do permit one or both of these inferences, but I shall not dwell upon this here.

(2) Instead of the member-set opposition, the fallacy of composition is sometimes defined through the part–whole distinction, as when we infer that the chair is light from the fact that every one of its parts is light. Here again the fallacy is due to an ambiguity in the word 'light'. This term, according to recent analyses, should be spelled out as 'lighter than most objects of its class'. As each conceivable objects belongs to infinitely many classes, there is an inherent ambiguity here that makes the field wide open for fallacious inferences. If, for example, each part of a chair is situated in the class of objects of the same volume, whereas each chair is situated in the class of chairs, all the parts may be light and not the whole, and vice versa. I have not been able to find any examples where the part-whole fallacy rests upon non-ambiguous terms, and I suspect that in this case the ambiguity is a necessary condition for the inference

to be invalid. This conjecture, if true, could be related to the fact that a member, and the set of which it is a member, belong to different levels, whereas part and whole belong to the same level.

(3) The ecological fallacy and its nameless converse might also be plausible candidates to the titles of the fallacies of division and of composition, respectively. The ecological fallacy is the inference from a correlation at the community level to a similar correlation at the individual level, as when from the fact that a high proportion of Negroes in a community goes together with high crime rates we conclude that Negroes commit more crimes than whites. This, of course, is invalid because the community-level correlation may also be due to Negroes being more often *victims* of crimes. An even more striking example[3] is the following: from the fact that juvenile delinquency and senile dementia are correlated at the community level, we can hardly conclude that they are often found in the same individuals. The converse fallacy is not often discussed, presumably because data on individual correlations are so hard to come by and must be inferred from other data rather than serve as a basis for inference; also when data on individual correlations do exist they usually permit a direct inspection at the community level. As an example of the converse of the ecological fallacy we may reverse the Negro-crime problem. If we knew that on a nationwide scale Negroes commit more crimes than whites, we should not be justified in concluding that communities with higher proportions of Negroes also have higher crime rates, for the Negroes in these communities might feel more secure and therefore commit fewer crimes or the Whites in these communities might be more afraid and therefore commit fewer crimes. Once again, the data underlying the nationwide generalization will often have been assembled at the community level, so that the community-level correlation may be inspected directly without using the nationwide individual correlation.

(4) In Chapter 1 above I stated that the fallacy of composition is the inference '$(\forall x)\,(M\,(Fx))\supset M\,(\forall x)\,(Fx)$': what is possible for any single individual must be possible for them all simultaneously. This, then, is the inference I propose to call the fallacy of composition. It has not been much discussed in the literature,[4] but I shall argue that it is of crucial importance for an understanding of the social sciences. Now for this inference to be a fallacy, it must be possible to exhibit cases where the antecedent is true and the consequent false. To say that the consequent is false, amounts to saying that '$(\forall x)\,(Fx)$' is impossible. In which sense can the attribution of a property to all members of a class be contradictory? We exclude at once the case (discussed in Chapter 4) where 'Fx' is contradictory by itself, for this would also falsify the antecedent. The property F must be in some sense *non-universalizable*, for reasons that may roughly be classified into logical, conceptual, and causal.

The notion of non-universalizable properties is a very important one in many contexts. It is also a very ambiguous notion. In addition to the universalizability asserted in the fallacy of composition, we have the universalizability asserted in the following inference: $(\exists x)(M(Fx)) \supset (\forall x)(M(Fx))$: what is possible for some individual is possible for any individual. In ethical theory, where necessity and possibility are interpreted as obligation and permission respectively, this inference is crucial: if something is permitted to someone, it must be permitted to everyone. Even more important, perhaps, is the following kind of ethical universalizability: what is obligatory for someone, is also obligatory for everyone; or $(\exists x)N(Fx)) \supset (\forall x)N(Fx)$. Edna Ullman-Margalit has recently shown[5] that in the so-called *generalization argument*[6] in ethical theory this inference and the fallacy of composition both enter essentially. Let us write 'U' for the operator 'it is undesirable that', 'O' for the denotic operator 'it is obligatory that' and let 'Fx' stand for 'x does F'. The generalization argument then is deduced in the following manner:

$$GC: \ U(\forall x)(Fx) \supset (\exists x)(O(\overline{Fx}))$$
$$GP: \ (\exists x)(O(\overline{Fx})) \supset (\forall x)(O(\overline{Fx}))$$

$$GA: \ U(\forall x(Fx) \supset (\forall x)(O(\overline{Fx}))$$

The premise GC states that if the consequences of everyone doing F would be undesirable, then someone ought to do non-F (or not to do F). The premise GP is the universalizability argument just given: if it is obligatory for someone to do non-F, then it is obligatory for everyone to do non-F. The conclusion is the generalization argument (very closely related to the categorical imperative in Kant's philosophy): no one ought to commit an action which would have disastrous consequences if committed by everyone. Ullman-Margalit argues convincingly that even though the deduction is valid, the premise GC is unacceptable. Rather it should be replaced by

$$AGC': U(\forall x)(Fx) \supset O(\exists x)\overline{Fx}$$

The difference between the consequents of GC and AGC' is the difference between modality *de re* and modality *de dicto*. GC asserts that there is someone (Jones, say) who ought to refrain from F, whereas AGC' only says that it ought to be the case that some (unspecified) person refrain from F. If it would be disastrous if everyone did F, then surely it ought to be the case that not everyone did F, but more than this we cannot say. To single out some particular individual and say that *he* ought not do F, would be arbitrary. If someone accepts AGC' and from the consequent of AGC' deduces the consequent of GC he will of course get GC, but this deduction is exactly the fallacy of composition in its alternative ·and equivalent form $N(\exists x)(Fx) \supset (\exists x)(N(Fx))$.

Returning now to the notion of universalizability asserted in the fallacy of composition, we must explore the grounds on which a property is said to be non-universalizable. I shall deal mainly with the properties that are non-universalizable for purely logical reasons. Such properties must be relationally defined: i.e. 'Fa' must be defined by an expression involving a, together with bound variables x, y, z... and some relation. Simple predicates such as having red hair or six toes must be ascribable to everyone simultaneously if they can be ascribed to anyone; contradictions can arise only if we ascribe to everyone a property that is defined by a reference to other persons. An important special case is the following property:

$$Fa \equiv (Ga \,\&\, (\forall x)((x \neq a) \supset \overline{Gx})) \equiv (\forall x)((x = a) \equiv Gx),$$

which is the property of being the only individual to have property G. All individuals may simultaneously be G, any individual may be F, but all cannot simultaneously be F. Setting 'Gx' for 'the workers employed by x have low wages' we recognize the Keynesian example stated at the beginning of the chapter.

Before going on to give more examples of the fallacy of composition in the social sciences, I will offer some remarks on the cases where the property in question is non-universalizable for causal or conceptual reasons. The distinction between causal and logical impossibility may be illustrated by the following example: it is logically impossible for all particles in a gas to have a velocity above the average, and causally impossible (but logically possible) for all particles to have exactly the average velocity, even if any given particle may be assumed to have the average velocity without getting into trouble with the laws of physics. Krönig, in fact, deduced Boyle's law on the assumption that all particles had the average velocity.[7] If this assumption was self-contradictory the deduction would automatically be valid, as any statement can be deduced from a contradiction. This, however, is not the case: the assumption is just a simplification from which can be deduced a theorem that turns out to hold also in the more general case. Physical impossibility is also involved in an example given by Peter Geach:[8] from 'Every one of these books it is possible to read in less than half an hour', we should not conclude that 'It is possible to read every one of these books in less than half an hour'. The impossibility in this case is not due to any intrinsic relations between the books, for in order to understand what it is to read a book we do not have to refer to other books. Rather the impossibility stems from the common relation of the books to the temporal container 'half an hour' and from certain physical limitations of that relation. A similar problem is involved in the relation between 'It is possible to bring local broadcasting to any region of Norway before 1980' and 'It is possible to bring local broadcasting to all regions of Norway before 1980'. Physical, technological, and economic constraints make it impossible to conclude from the former to the latter, to which we may add that for *political* reasons the falsity of the latter brings about the falsity of the former. As observed in Chapter 3 above, in politics it is often the case that non-universalizable properties cannot even be realized in individual cases. A last example of the causal fallacy of composition is the notion of an average man.[9]

The conceptual-impossibility version of the fallacy of composition is more interesting, but also harder to analyse. Peter Winch[10] has drawn attention to a very explicit affirmation by Hume of the validity of the inference:

In vain do you pretend to have learned the nature of bodies from past experience. Their secret nature, and consequently their effects and influence may change, without any change in their sensible qualities. This happens sometimes, and with regard to some objects: Why may it not happen always and with regard to all objects? What logic, what process of argument secures you against this supposition?[11]

Against this we may set an equally explicit statement by Wittgenstein:

'What sometimes happens might always happen.' What kind of proposition is that? It is like the following: If '*Fa*' makes sense '$(\forall x)(Fx)$' makes sense. 'If it is possible for someone to make a false move in some game, then it might be possible for everybody to make nothing but false moves in every game.'—Thus we are under a temptation to misunderstand the logic of our expressions here, to give an incorrect account of the use of our words. Orders are sometimes not obeyed. But what would it be like if no orders were *ever* obeyed? The concept 'order' would have lost its purpose.[12]

Typical examples of the impossibility affirmed by Wittgenstein (and by Winch) would be moral cases such as everyone always breaking promises, epistemological cases such as our senses or our memory always deceiving us, and physical cases such as all objects constantly breaking down and disintegrating before our eyes. These are not cases of straightforward logical impossibility, nor do I think these authors would argue that they are due to causal impossibility of some sort. What are they then? In my opinion only the moral cases are genuine examples of that elusive notion, conceptual impossibility. The problem of universal promise-breaking may be seen in the light of the categorical imperative, that states that one should not act on a maxim if one 'cannot will' that it should be made into a general law. Kant gives several examples to explain this requirement of universalizability. Of these examples one— the refusal to help others—is non-universalizable only in the weak sense that if everyone did that, the consequences would be disastrous; the situation is in fact a Prisoner's Dilemma. (The reader will recall Ullman-Margalit's argument to the effect that these disastrous consequences do not give an argument for everyone always helping others.) We are perfectly able to imagine a situation of universal distrust, egoism, and suspicion; such a world would be unpleasant, but there is no contradiction in the concept.[13] Another of Kant's examples is the non-repayment of loans, which is identical in structure to the breaking of promises. Non-repayment of loans is non-universalizable in the strong sense that we cannot even imagine—and *a fortiori* not rationally wish for—a society where loans were never repaid. In such a society the institution and the concept of a loan would be absent: the repayment of loans is embedded in the very notion of a loan as distinct from a gift. This idea may be generalized to many other cases of meaningful behaviour. Take the case of letters that do not arrive at their destination. This fate may conceivably befall any given letter, but it could not possibly befall all letters, for in that case letters would not be letters, but only pieces of papers that for mysterious (perhaps ritual) reasons are dropped into boxes at street corners. To anticipate a point made in the next paragraph, not only would the inhabitants of such a world not have the concept of a letter, but *we* would not say that they were posting letters either.

As to the physical examples, I submit that Hume is right. We know what it is for one object to disintegrate before our eyes, and we also know what it would be like for all objects constantly to break down before our eyes. Winch argues that in this case we should not speak of *objects* at all, but this conclusion seems valid at most for the inhabitants of the world in question. In a world where objects are constantly being formed and constantly disintegrating, we should have, so to speak, nothing on which to peg the notion of an object. This, in my opinion, is a question of psychology rather than of conceptual analysis or of logic. At any rate nothing should exclude the inhabitants of one world (ours, say) to speak about disintegrating objects in another world (Mars, say). If we can meaningfully speak about some objects disappearing in the actual world, we can also meaningfully speak about all objects disappearing in one of the many possible worlds (but in *no* world could it be the case that letters never arrive at their destination). We may, perhaps, interpret the purported impossibility of constantly disintegrating objects as a *causal* impossibility, involving a reference not to the laws of physics but to the laws of psychology. We may define, that is, a world as accessible to our world (in the technical sense of modal logic) if our world is conceivable from that world.[14] A world with constantly disintegrating objects could not (as a matter of psychological fact) form the concept of an object; thus our world would not be conceivable from that world, which would *ipso facto* not be accessible from ours. This again implies that any proposition asserting the possibility of all objects always disintegrating would be false (in our world). A similar argument holds for the purported cases of epistemological impossibility.

I now proceed to give a number of examples of the fallacy of composition in the cases where the relevant property is non-universalizable for purely logical reasons.

(a) From the fact that in any given society a given institution or technique may have arisen (for all that we know) by import or loan, the anthropological theory known as diffusionism concludes fallaciously that this may explain innovation in all societies.

(b) From the fact that anyone may put all their money in the bank and draw interest on it, it is sometimes concluded that everyone might do so simultaneously.

(c) From the fact that anyone may retire his deposit from the bank when he wants to, it is tempting (but fallacious and disastrous) to conclude that everyone might do so simultaneously.

(d) From the fact that in a society of commodity owners any single owner may make profit by buying cheap and selling dear, some early economists concluded that all commodity owners might profit simultaneously by cheating each other. This is the 'contradiction in the general formula of capital' referred to by Marx. He quotes Destutt de Tracy to the effect that 'industrial capitalists make profits because "they all sell for more than it has cost to produce. And to whom do they sell? In the first instance to one another"', and then goes on to comment that 'The capitalist class, as a whole, in any country, cannot over-reach themselves'.[15]

(e) From the fact that overproduction may occur in any single sector of the economy, some early critics of capitalism (especially Sismondi) concluded that overproduction can occur in all sectors of the economy simultaneously.[16] Note that this is a fallacy only if we abstract from Keynesian arguments about liquidity preference.

(f) Several examples may be taken from the logic of marginal analysis, where it is always tempting to think that everyone could be at the margin. A familiar example will be the way in which we tend to calculate the real cost of tax-deductible items, using for all such items the marginal tax rate that really applies to one item only. A second example may be taken from James Coleman's analysis of power. The problem is how much power we shall ascribe to an individual taking part in a jointly controlled operation such as a vote. As noted by Coleman, the question should not be answered by using the individual's probability of casting the decisive vote on the assumption that the others are equally likely to vote Yes or No. In a three-person model this would ascribe to each person relative power of $\frac{1}{2}$, getting a total control of $\frac{3}{2}$, which is contradictory. The difficulty here is that, 'Each actor is assuming in effect that he casts the final vote; that the environment, consisting of the others, acts, and then he acts. But this assumption obviously is not valid, for *each of the three cannot be the last*.'[17] A third example was discussed in Chapter 4, where we saw that Anthony Kenny fallaciously argued that it is contradictory to want to be without some of the things you want. A fourth example is the following:

[Plants] in the United States that produce components for assembly overseas have tended to charge the assembling subsidiary the full wholesale price for 'completely knocked down' kits of components. This practice, by itself, has not generally been thought of as exploitative. But when any item has been deleted from a complete kit before shipment, such as a bumper or a headlight, the price of the kit has generally been reduced only by the marginal cost of the deleted item. It has sometimes been remarked, not altogether facetiously, that on this pricing basis the cost of the shipping container, with all contents deleted, would generally exceed 1000 dollars.[18]

From the wording of this passage it would seem that the author does think of the last-mentioned practice as exploitative. The notion of *exploitation of labour* shall indeed be my last and most important example under this heading. In the theory of income distribution we may distinguish, firstly, between the (minority of) economists who think that the worker should in some sense 'gets what he produces' (to each according to his work), and those who think this principle much too narrow (what about invalids?). Secondly, there is a distinction within the first school between those who hold that the worker should get the equivalent of his *average* product and those who would rather have him paid according to his *marginal* product.[19] Now I would like to suggest that there are two institutional facts about capitalism that make the marginal-product interpretation of a just income distribution look plausible. In the first place, the existence of a class of capital owners seems to justify the notion of aggregate capital as a 'factor of production' on a par with labour, and with the same 'right to reward' as labour.[20] Using Euler's theorem for first-order homogeneous production functions, we then know that when both factors are paid according to their marginal product, total factor rewards exactly exhaust the total product. Indeed, given a continuous and differentiable function $f(K,L)$ of capital and labour, such that $f(tK,tL) = t(f(K,L)$ for all t, Euler's theorem states that $f(K,L) = f_K(K,L).K + f_L(K,L).L$, where f_K and f_L are the partial derivatives of f with respect to capital and labour. This beautiful expression of class harmony in mathematical language would seem to justify the marginal interpretation, for if both factors were to be paid according to their *average* product the total product would be exhausted twice over. In the second place, and this is the more relevant notion from the present point of view, individual wage negotiations make the marginal theory seem irresistible, for each worker can be treated as if *he* is the marginal worker. To each worker the employer can say, with apparent justification: 'Without you total production will be reduced by an amount x; therefore I can at most pay you the equivalent of x in order to afford keeping you employed.' This, while correct for any single worker, cannot be true for all workers simultaneously, for between them they gobble up the whole product and not just the marginal product multiplied by number of workers.

The two reasons adduced for the apparent plausibility of the neo-classical notion of just income as the equivalent of marginal product, also point to the obstacles that must be overcome by the working class if it is to claim the whole product as its own. The step from individual to collective bargaining alone does not suffice, for in addition the workers must overcome the alienation that makes present capital goods appear as the property of present capitalists rather than as the product of past workers. (Indeed, I believe that this use of *end-result principles* could be used as a definition of alienation.[21]) This twofold solidarity—between all workers at each instant of time, between workers of successive generations—is a necessary and sufficient condition for the illusion of marginalist theories of income distribution to be dispelled. I have dealt in some detail with this example, because it seems to me exemplary in the way it shows up the *practical* importance of the fallacy of composition. *Divide et impera*; if you can treat each man as if he were the marginal man, the class confronting you is reduced to a dust of individuals.

The reader may have observed that in example (b) and (c) above, some clause such as 'being the only one to . . .' must be implicitly presupposed if these are to come out as *logical* rather than causal fallacies. These two examples also have obvious implications for action. If everyone did simultaneously deposit their money in a bank, the economy would come to an immediate standstill and no one would get any interest;[22] a run on the banks also has the contrary effect of the expected effect that motivates the individuals to action. Indeed, many situations that can be described through the fallacy of composition also give rise to the unintended consequences that I subsume under the heading of counterfinality and which form the subject of the next section. Counterfinality per definition (see below) involves the fallacy of composition, but many instances of the fallacy have nothing to do with counterfinality.

Counterfinality

By this term I shall understand *the unintended consequences that arise when each individual in a group acts upon an assumption about his relations to others that, when generalized, yields the contradiction in the consequent of the fallacy of composition, the antecedent of that fallacy being true.* It is clear that counterfinality thus defined is a species of real contradictions in the sense of the third thesis on contradictions asserted in Chapter 4. The requirement that the antecedent of the inference be true, i.e. that there be nothing contradictory in the individual assumption taken separately, guarantees individual rationality. The collective irrationality arises only from the incompatibility of the belief systems. (Presumably the study of incompatible belief systems might use the same machinery of epistemic logic as was applied in the preceding chapter to the analysis of a single contradictory belief system, but I shall not attempt this here.[23]) In the examples given below, the assumption giving rise to the contradiction will always be of the form 'being the only one (the first one, the best one, etc.) to do x'. This, of course, is shorthand for 'being among the few (or the first, the best, etc.) to do x.' Before spelling out these examples, however, I believe it may be useful with some introductory remarks about the history and logic of the concept.[24]

The notion of counterfinality has many ancestors in the history of ideas—the invisible hand, the ruse of reason, alienation. Among the main contributors to the notion I believe we must name Bossuet, Mandeville, Vico, Adam Smith, Hegel, and Marx. From recent discussions the names of Oskar Morgenstern, Jean-Paul Sartre, Robert Nozick, and Trygve Haavelmo[25] may be singled out, a bit arbitrarily perhaps. In Bossuet's and Vico's philosophies of history[26] the notion of unintended consequences is certainly crucial, but to some extent— more so in Bossuet than in Vico—counterfinality is seen as a tool for the divine finality, so that their idea of social causality does not really define an immanent process. If we accept Robert Nozick's definition of *invisible-hand explanations* as an account that 'explains what looks to be the product of someone's intentional design, as not being brought about by anyone's intentions',[27] Bossuet and Vico place too much emphasis upon the guiding hand of God in history to be subsumed under this category. Nevertheless both works contain passages that taken in isolation read like Hegel or Marx, stressing both the free choice of the actors and the sometimes unforeseen results of their actions.

Sandwiched in time between Bossuet and Vivo is Bernard Mandeville, whose importance for the history of the social sciences can hardly be exaggerated. If you want to find the origin of the notion of latent functions, go to Mandeville–not to Merton; for the concept of the invisible hand, go to Mandeville–not to Adam Smith. In his criticism of the fallacy of composition he is a pioneer again, as seen in the praise bestowed upon him by Keynes.[28] His influence has in part been subterranean, because his logic was too rigorous and his conclusions too cynical; he was probably much more read than quoted. His slogan 'Private Vices, Public Benefits' is made more precise in the following passages:

> The short-sighted vulgar in the chain of causes seldom can see further than one link; but those who can enlarge their view, and will give themselves the leisure of gazing on the prospect of concatenated events, may, in a hundred places, see *Good* spring up and pullulate from *Evil*, as naturally as chickens do from eggs.[29]

> I flatter myself to have demonstrated that, neither the friendly qualities and kind affections that are natural to man, nor the real virtues he is capable of acquiring by reason and self-denial, are the foundations of society, but that what we call evil in this world, moral as well as natural, is the grand principle that makes us sociable creatures, the solid basis, the life and support of all trades and employment without exception: that there we must look for the true origin of all arts and sciences, and that the moment evil ceases, the society must be spoiled, if not totally dissolved.[30]

As I have stated in more detail elsewhere,[31] this is a sociological application of Leibniz's theodicy. Leibniz, indeed, held at the metaphysical level that the existence of some evil is a *necessary condition for* the maximization of the good, whereas his contemporary, Malebranche, held the more timid view that evil is an *inevitable by-product* of the good. At the sociological level Leibniz, however, did not take the consequence of his metaphysics. He held, for example, that luxury must be accepted as a regrettable by-product of a prosperous life, whereas Mandeville went the whole way and actually said that luxury and prodigality are the causes of prosperity.

Substitute 'self-interest' for 'evil' in the passages just quoted, and you have Adam Smith. He shared with Mandeville the conviction that the invisible hand is not only sufficient, but also necessary for the promotion of the common good:

> By preferring the support of domestic to that of foreign industry, [every individual] intends only his own security; and by directing that industry in

such a manner as its produce may be of the greatest value, he intends only his own gain, and he is in this, as in many other cases, led by an invisible hand to promote an end which was no part of his intention. Nor is it always the worse for society that it was no part of it. By pursuing his own interest he frequently promotes that of the society more effectually than when he really intends to promote it. I have never known much good done by those who affected to trade for the public good.[32]

Marx is sometimes said to have stood Hegel upon his head; more importantly, at least for our purpose, they both stood Adam Smith on his head. For Hegel and Marx history works itself out through the negative rather than the positive unintended consequences of human actions; through counterfinality rather than the invisible hand.[33] For Adam Smith a paradigmatic case would look like this: each actor has an amount y_1 of y and does x in order to get y_2; when they all do this, they all get y_3, where $y_3 > y_2 > y_1$. Hegel and Marx would rather set $y_2 > y_3 > y_1$, or even $y_2 > y_1 > y_3$. I submit that whenever we see the invisible hand its mysteries perform, we are dealing with a situation where (i) all the actors have a dominant strategy, and (ii) the outcome that results when all actors use their dominant strategies dominates all other outcomes. The first feature implies that the actors do not really have to take account of the behaviour of others; they may, perhaps, entertain incompatible beliefs about each other, but these beliefs are inessential to their choices. The second feature implies that the outcome really is in everyone's best interest. Counterfinality, by contrast, may obtain when one of these features are lacking, as we shall see below. I would also suggest here that Nozick is inconsistent when he refers to theories of the trade cycle or of the non-provision of public goods as cases of 'invisible-hand explanations'. They are both cases of counterfinality (or perhaps suboptimality, to be discussed in the next section) and no one could possibly think that they seem 'to be the product of someone's intentional design'. Nozick is quite right when drawing attention to the fact that beneficial effects of actions often are not (and indeed sometimes cannot be) the motivating effects of these actions. I return to this idea below. Where he goes wrong, is in the examples he singles out to illustrate his point.

The notion of counterfinality should be made more precise still before we go on to examples. Four remarks seem to be in order. In the first place, the notion of 'acting upon an assumption' may, but should not necessarily be interpreted in a psychological manner. What I am trying to capture is the notion of what is needed for the action to make sense, and this is not always the same thing as the explicit belief system of the actors. For example, in the cobweb model (to be discussed below) each farmer acts upon an assumption about next year's prices without necessarily relating this to any assumptions about the other farmers' behaviour. Nevertheless I impute to each farmer the assumption that the other farmers will act in a certain way, because a *rational* price expectation must be grounded in some expectations about what the others will do. If we assume, as in the simplest cobweb model, that each farmer acts upon the assumption that prices next year will be the same as current prices, this assumption may be generated by an assumption that all the other farmers will produce exactly the same amounts as in the current year, but it may equally well be just an assumption *faute de mieux*, a convenient focal point for a choice that has to be made. Another possibility is that each farmer acts upon some vague assumption that things in general will stay roughly the same, without having any clear idea of what things in particular would make a difference if they did *not* stay the same.

The remaining three remarks are intended to make precise my deliberate restriction of the notion of unintended consequences. For, in the second place, I limit the term 'unintended consequences' to consequences that arise *instead of* the intended and thus exclude those that arise *in addition to* the intended result. I am not concerned with cars generating pollution, but rather with anti-pollution machinery generating pollution. In the third place I deal with unintended consequences that have an impact upon the actors themselves, and not with the unintended consequences that are felt by other people only. I am not concerned with factories polluting the air for consumers, but with factories polluting the air for themselves, by causing rust, etc. I believe that the degree of overlap or inclusion between actors and victims is an important variable in many contexts, but it is not only for simplicity that I limit myself to the case where the group of actors is wholly included in (and in some cases identical with) the group of victims. The basic task of the social scientist must surely be to *explain how people react to situations of their own making.* If this is accepted, *a priori* limitations are imposed upon the choice of object by the scientist. As observed in the last paragraph of Chapter 4, he should not content himself with passing the buck, but rather search for an object undergoing an endogenous process of change. He will certainly be unable to circumscribe a wholly autonomous object that could be studied independently of *all* exogenous factors, influences, or parameters, but he should strive for a *local maximum* of autonomy, in the sense that both a small increase and a small reduction of scope would make the object less amenable to an immanently causal study.

Finally I would like to stress the crucial difference between counterfinality and those negative unintended consequences that arise from a single action. When, for example, Adam Smith chided the mercantilists for acting 'contrary to the very end which they propose',[34] he did not have in mind the counterfinality that arises from the statistical summation of many individual (and rational) actions, but only the fact that an uninformed economic policy may bring about the contrary result to that intended. By 'uninformed' I here refer to lack of insight into technical ends–means relationships, whereas counterfinality goes with correct technical rationality, but incorrect assumptions about initial conditions. To illustrate the distinction we may look to two recent studies of urban economics. Jay Forrester's work on 'counterintuitive effects' of urban policy deals with the unintended consequences that stem from a single planning decision (such as the decision to create new jobs for the unemployed) when indirect and long-term effects on the urban system are neglected.[35] In a quite different vein, Thomas Schelling has shown how racial segregation may arise in a city not because of misguided (i.e. technically uninformed) action by the city authorities, but as the unintended by-product of innumerable individual decisions, a typical case being that 'everyone lives in a neighbourhood in which his own color predominates by an average ratio somewhat greater than five to one', as a result of 'individuals *seeking* a ratio not less than five to four'.[36] Needless to say, the two types of unintended consequences may be produced simultaneously, to reinforce or possibly to annul each other. I shall not, however, explore this issue.

Most of the examples in the following catalogue of cases are given rather brief treatment only, leaving only two for more prolonged discussion: the cobweb model and the Marxist theory of the falling rate of profit. I close the section with some comments upon what I propose to call 'the structuralist fallacy in the social sciences' and upon a closely related fallacy that is found in functionalist sociology.

(a) In a lecture hall where everyone gets to his feet in order to get a better view of the speaker, no one is able to do so. Paul Sweezy[37] uses this example as a paradigm for the logic of capitalism, but it should be clear—and will be shown by the examples below—that counterfinality is a more general mechanism and not confined to a single mode of production.

(b) When everyone simultaneously want to deposit their money or to withdraw the deposits, no one will achieve what they wanted (interest and their money, respectively).

(c) Jean-Paul Sartre takes erosion as his paradigmatic case of counterfinality.[38] Each individual Chinese peasant (in his example) seeks to obtain more land by cutting down trees, but a general deforestation induces erosion with *less* land available to each peasant than at the outset. Other cases where counterfinality passes through the 'practical–inter field' (Sartre's term for material structures) include overexploitation of resources, the tragedy of the commons, pollution, and species extinction.

(d) Population growth and poverty are linked through the mechanism of counterfinality. In many peasant societies, past and present, a large number of children has been an advantage to the individual as a means of insurance against old age, but in the aggregate the widespread adoption of large families has the effect of reducing *per-capita* incomes.[39]

(e) Many social systems have been based upon export of manpower or of capital; this is true of the ancient Greek states, of the older slave states of the American South, and of 19th-century England. This, clearly, is not a solution that can be generalized to all systems. Moses Finley[40] calls it a 'stop-gap'; Eugene Genovese sees the impossibility of all slave-holders to be slave-sellers simultaneously as the 'most important contradiction' in the last stage of the slavery system;[41] Hegel, in some remarkable paragraphs of the *Philosophy of Right*[42], noted that a system of states each of which depends upon others as markets for excess production must give rise to imperialist wars and ultimately break down. Emigration of manpower, export of surplus goods, and exploitation of colonies are all zero-sum games: thus if the take-off into industrial growth depends on some or all of these, then either some nations will never make it or—as suggested by Veblen and Gerschenkron—latecomers to the industrialization process may enjoy advantages of backwardness that offer a way out of the trap.

(f) Counterfinality may also arise in the political system. We might assume, for example, that some voters that normally vote for a given party feel so confident that their party will win that they permit themselves the—otherwise unheard-of—luxury of voting for another party in order to give their own party a swing to the left or to the right. If there is a sufficiently large number of people acting in this way, each sophisticated voter counting upon the sincerity of all the others, counterfinality may be the result. The impact of opinion polls upon voting is important in this context. Polls have a well-documented impact upon voting, and we may assume that the impact is mediated by the assumption, for each voter, that he is the only one to read the predictions—or at any rate the only one to change his voting as a result of having read the predictions. Herbert Simon has shown that given certain conditions it is possible for the predictors to take the effect of the prediction into account so that the polls are confirmed by the actual voting, but these conditions are not, perhaps, very plausible ones.[43]

(g) A more complex example is the well-known cobweb cycle from economic theory. We may start by distinguishing between two forms that counterfinality may assume in agriculture. In pre-capitalist economic systems the supply curve of agricultural produce is usually assumed to be backward-sloped, at least in part: peasants may prefer leisure over extra consumption, and in any case the family members cannot work more than 24 hours out of 24. This may generate counterfinality in the following manner: an initial year with below-equilibrium prices makes all peasants increase their production for next year, on the assumption that prices will remain at the same low level. By doing this, however, they bring the prices even further down, so that they will have to produce even more for the following year, and so on in a cumulative movement of lower prices and larger volumes. Conversely, initial above-equilibrium prices will generate a cumulative movement of higher prices and smaller volumes produced.[44]

With the forward-sloping supply curve typical of capitalist agriculture, counterfinality takes the form of a cobweb cycle. Let us assume that supply and demand are linear functions of price: $S = -a + bp, D = c - dp$, all constants positive. Then it is easy to show, and intuitively obvious, that if the initial price differs from the equilibrium price (obtained by setting $S = D$), prices and volume will change in a cyclical pattern. Initial above-equilibrium prices will generate above-equilibrium volumes for next year, always assuming that the farmers assume constant prices from one year to the next; this makes for low prices, with below-equilibrium volumes and above-equilibrium prices for the year after that, and so on in a process that, mathematically at least, may go on for ever. The cyclical movement may be damped, constantly repeated, or explosive, as b is smaller than, equal to or greater than d. In the first case the equilibrium is stable; in the third unstable; in the second case it is neutral, but structurally unstable.[45] If the movement is damped, the counterfinality will disappear after some time, if not completely, then at least sufficiently for the unintended consequences to be confused with the noise that pervades any social system. With an explosive movement we may assume that after some time the farmers will come to understand that the cyclical fluctuations are due neither to the vagaries of the weather nor to government intervention, but to their own actions. They will come, that is, to *learn* and to modify their behaviour accordingly.

The logic of this learning process is important for our analysis. The usual textbook analysis[46] assumes that at a first level of learning each farmer believes that next year's prices will be some weighted average of this year's prices and last year's prices, so that if prices have risen from $t - 1$ to t they will be expected to fall from t to $t + 1$, and vice versa. These price expectations, however, will generate actions that invalidate the expectations, so that a new cycle is produced. The chances are better for this cycle to be damped than in the original case; even with $b > d$ the oscillations may die out of themselves.[47] If they do not, or if they take too long a time doing so, a second-level learning may take place, so that the farmers also take account of the price level of the year before the last. This second-level learning, in its turn, may or may not be successful; in the latter case the farmers may go on to a third level, and so on in a process that, mathematically at least, may go on for ever. In actual cases, of course, one of two things will happen: either the process will come to a stop at some level, or the farmers will realize that this mode of learning is inherently contradictory. They may come to learn, that is, that this is not the way to learn. In that case they have taken the decisive step to a *strategic* situation, where no one believes that prices change in some mysterious and autonomous fashion.

I am not quite satisfied with this textbook version of the learning process, because it is not rooted in an analysis of the change of expectations about the behaviour of others. To assume that the prices will move in the opposite direction to what they have done recently, without linking this assumption to some idea about *why* they should do so, is a piece of fetichism that is certainly frequent, but not very rational. A case of 'rational' (even if contradictory) learning would be the following. If the simple cobweb cycle is explosive, or not sufficiently damped, each farmer may come to understand that they are all acting upon the assumption that prices will remain the same from one year to the next. He will then assume that the others will continue acting upon this assumption, so that he—as the only one—can adjust optimally to the prices that will then prevail. When everyone does this, however, we immediately have a new contradiction, for *each farmer cannot be the only one to have learned*. In fact, the resulting process will model itself upon the original cobweb cycle, but skipping every second year, so that we get a cumulative upwards or downwards movement (as in the pre-capitalist case) rather than a cycle. In year t each farmer acts upon the assumption that prices in year $t + 1$ will be what they would have been had everyone but him acted upon the assumption that they will remain the same as in year t, and this will immediately bring it about that prices in year $t + 1$ at this first level of learning coincide with prices in year $t + 2$ of the original cycle. At the second level of learning each farmer will assume that he—as the only one—has understood what goes on at the first level, and so on in a movement that soon becomes rather complex. Either the process comes to a halt at some level, or the farmers make the transition to the strategic mode; they come to learn, that is, that this is not the way to learn.

Brief mention may be made here of another case in which a hierarchy of inconsistent beliefs also occurs, viz. in the analysis of duopoly. In the so-called 'Cournot solution' to the duopoly problem each duopolist strives to maximize profits on the assumption that the other will keep output constant at its present level. Following Alan Coddington[48] the rule 'keep output at present level' may be called rule A, and the rule 'maximize profits on the assumption that the other duopolist will adopt rule A' may be called rule B. It is then only a short step to define rule C as 'maximize profits on the assumption that the other duopolist will adopt rule B'; when both adopt rule C the so-called 'Stackelberg disequilibrium' is the result. In both cases counterfinality will, of course, be a prominent feature. In principle we might go on to define rules D, E, F, etc.; in principle we might also ask what will happen when the duopolists finally understand that the use of such rules leads to a bilateral assumption of unilateral advantage and therefore is contradictory. The problem, however, is that the corresponding game does not have a solution in the non-cooperative mode. Again the reader is referred to the next sections for further comments.

(h) Marx also explained the (purported) fall in the rate of profit as the result of measures (labour-saving inventions) taken to counteract the falling rate of profit. He argued that when the economy grew at a higher rate than the rate of growth of the labour force, there would come a point where the whole reserve army of the unemployed was absorbed by production and where a scarcity of labour, with rising wages, would set in. He further argued that for *each* capitalist labour-saving inventions are the rational response to a fall in profit due to higher wages,[49] but that when *all* capitalists cut down on labour there ensues a reduction of aggregate surplus-value and a fall in the rate of profit. To each capitalist the worker is a costly factor of production subject to the usual economizing, especially when scarce, but to the totality of all capitalists the workers are the only and ultimate source of surplus-value and thus of profits. Thus the argument has two parts: a motivational analysis of the actions of the individual entrepreneur, and an aggregate analysis of the net effect produced when all entrepreneurs act simultaneously on the same motive. Both parts of the argument are fallacious. Nevertheless the fallacies are *interesting* fallacies, and will help us bring out some logical points worth making.

The motivational analysis is inadequate because the individual capitalist, when confronted with higher wages, will certainly have an incentive to innovate in order to cut costs, but no special incentive to search for innovations with a labour-saving bias, because in perfect competition (which is what Marx wrote about) the individual entrepreneur's demand for labour cannot influence the wage level.[50] *If* all capitalists did in fact bias their innovative search to the labour-saving side, this would profit them all by the impact on the aggregate demand for labour and thus on the wage level, but it is axiomatic that in a world of purposive–parametric price-takers (see Appendix 2 below) an action will not be undertaken if its efficacy depends on all other actors' doing the same thing. It is no doubt true, as stressed by both Marx and Neil Smelser,[51] that capitalists were motivated to introduce machinery that could replace particularly recalcitrant or combative groups of workers, but this does not give a general mechanism. Perhaps the attempt by William Fellner to rehabilitate the link between rising wages and labour-saving innovations can be seen as a generalization of the Marx–Smelser argument. Fellner has proposed a rationale that could motivate the individual capitalist to bias his search, viz. the expectation that wages will go on rising in the future, in which case it is rational to pre-empt the future increase by using less labour. 'In some cases a preference may develop for inventions which are particularly factor-saving in the resource that is getting scarcer, because a *learning process* may induce atomistic firms to behave as if they were big enough to notice that *macroeconomically* the factors of production are *not* in infinitely elastic supply.'[52]

We must ask, however, why the individual capitalist should have any expectations that wages will go on rising. Such expectations may certainly just be an extrapolation from past evidence,[53] but if they are to have a rational basis this must be the assumption that other capitalists are *not* going to bias their search. This means that each capitalist gives a labour-saving bias to his search on the assumption that the other capitalists are not going to do so: a clear-cut case of contradictory belief systems, resulting in the unintended consequence that wages go down instead of going up. This looks like a marriage of contradictions and the invisible hand, but actually the case is more complex, as also recognized by Paul David.[54] In the next period the capitalists will unlearn their belief that wages will continue rising and they will therefore not bias their innovations, as a result of which wages *will* rise, and so on in a cycle somewhat similar to the cobweb. It is, however, different from the cobweb, and more related to the duopoly problem, in that the game which ensues does not have a solution. Setting 'xy' for the situation 'I adopt strategy x and all others adopt y', where the variables range over the set (C, D) or (Cooperate, Defect), the above situation is described by the following preference structure (common to all capitalists): $(D,C)P(C,C)P(C,D)P(D,D)$, where defection is interpreted as no bias and cooperation as a labour-saving bias in the search for innovations. This is the structure of the no-solution game of Chicken (see Appendix 1 below). Thus, if capitalists are price-takers, they will not bias their innovations; if they learn, their learning will be in the contradictory mode; if they understand that their learning is in the contradictory mode, they will not converge towards a (non-cooperative) equilibrium.

In order to see the error or errors in the second part of Marx's argument, it is necessary to deal in some detail with the link between labour-saving inventions, the wage level, the organic composition of capital, and the rate of profit. We now accept, for the sake of argument, that a capitalist will adopt labour-saving techniques in the face of higher wages. From this assumption Marx's conclusion to the fall in the rate of profit is the following two-step argument. Firstly, he assumes that the average (economy-wide) rate of profit must be given by the formula

$$r = \frac{\sum_i S_i}{\sum_i C_i + \sum_i V_i} = \frac{S}{V} = \frac{S/V}{(C/V) + 1},$$

where S is the surplus-value, C the constant capital, and V the variable capital, subscript i indicating sector i of the economy and symbols without subscripts being aggregate quantities. (For simplicity annual replacement of all constant capital is assumed.) From the last expression for the rate of profit, it is obvious that if the organic composition C/V rises while the rate of exploitation is constant, then the rate of profit must fall. The second step in Marx's argument, then, is to assume that labour-saving inventions must be synonymous with rising organic composition of capital. From this it at once follows that with a constant rate of exploitation, a bias towards labour-saving innovations must imply a fall in the rate of profit.

Now both steps in this argument are fallacious. We shall see below that the rate of profit must be determined simultaneously with the relative prices, so that the formula given by Marx does not produce the correct result. (This is related to a better-known error in the transformation of values to prices,[55] viz. Marx's attempt to derive prices by taking the sum of constant and variable capital (measured in labour time) multiplied with $(1 + r)$. This is incorrect because prices must equal *costs* (in money terms) times $(1 + r)$, as capitalists calculate profits on their monetary outlays rather than on the values of the factors of production, these values being unknown to them.) I shall, however, concentrate upon the second step and the fallacy underlying the reasoning here. We may observe at the outset that the assumption of a constant rate of exploitation is a rather strange one, because—given technical progress—it also implies rising real wages, the very thing the labour-saving bias was supposed to prevent. I shall therefore first argue that given constant real wages (and an increasing rate of exploitation) the second step in the argument is not valid. Inventions that are labour-saving *ex ante*, may turn out to lower the organic composition *ex post*. (What this means, will soon be made clear.) I then go on to show that the same possibility obtains with a constant rate of exploitation.

We assume that each of the n sectors of the economy produces a homogeneous good with fixed coefficients of production, so that in order to produce one unit of good j we need a_{ij} units of good i and a_{0j} units of labour. We further set b_i for the amount of good i that enters into the consumption basket that represents the wages of labour per unit of labour time. This implies fixed coefficients of consumption. The value x_j (measured in labour time) is then determined by the following set of equations:

$$x_j = \sum_i a_{ij} x_i + a_{0j}, \qquad j = 1,2\ldots n.$$

The prices p_j and the profit rate r are determined simultaneously by another set of equations:

$$\left(\sum_i a_{ij} p_i + \sum_i b_i a_{0j} p_i \right)(1 + r) = p_j, \qquad j = 1,2\ldots n.$$

In the last set of equations we set $p_1 = 1$, taking the first good as a numéraire. Each equation in the first set says that value in must equal value out, each equation in the second set that costs + profits must equal prices. The conditions for these equations to have economically meaningful solutions are well known (some variant of the Hawkins–Simon conditions).[56] Actually I do not believe that we really need the values x_j for our purpose, because we are dealing with the options that confront the individual entrepreneur, for whom only prices have subjective reality. My definition of the organic composition of capital will then be made in price terms rather than in the usual value terms:

$$O_j = \frac{\sum_i a_{ij} p_i}{\sum_i b_i a_{0j} p_i},$$

which is the ratio of the cost of machinery to the wage outlays. We further assume that firms only adopt labour-saving innovations and that in each sector there is one firm that makes the innovational breakthrough, while the others follow suit after some time. For the innovational firm in sector j there is present, therefore, a production possibility $(a'_{1j}, a'_{2j} \ldots a'_{nj}, a'_{0j})$, with the properties

$$a'_{ij} \leqslant a_{ij} \quad \text{for all } i,$$

$$O'_j = \frac{\sum_i a'_{ij} p_i}{\sum_i b_i a'_{0j} p_i} > O_j.$$

The first property is implied by the assumption of fixed coefficients of production. If one of the inequalities $\leqslant$ were replaced by $>$, the choice between the old technology and the new could not be made unambiguously on technical grounds alone. Instead one would have to take prices into account, which means that one would have to abandon the central assertion of Marxian economics that values can be determined independently of prices.[57] The second property states that the organic composition of capital in the new technology is higher than that of the old technology *when both are calculated in the old prices*. The relevance of this condition should be clear. If we are to define labour-saving innovations in terms that are related to individual entrepreneurs and their motives, it must be done in terms of the prices that confront them at the moment of choice. Thus O'_j is the *ex-ante* organic composition of capital in the new technology and $O'_j > O_j$ is the condition of a labour-saving bias. On the other hand, when all firms in all sectors have adopted the new methods, there will be a new set of prices p'_j, given by

$$\left(\sum_i a'_{ij} p'_i + \sum_i b_i a'_{0j} p'_i \right)(1 + r') = p'_j, \qquad j = 1, 2 \ldots n,$$

and a new organic composition,

$$O''_j = \frac{\sum_i a'_{ij} p'_i}{\sum_i b_i a'_{0j} p'_i},$$

for each sector. My point is now simply that we may very well have $O'_j > O_j > O''_j$ for all j, as may be shown by a simple two-sector example. Indeed, setting $b_1 = 0$, $b_2 = \frac{1}{6}$, $a_{11} = \frac{1}{2}$, $a_{21} = 0$, $a_{01} = 1$, $a_{12} = \frac{1}{2}$, $a_{22} = 0$, $a_{02} = 2$, $a'_{11} = \frac{1}{8}$, $a'_{21} = 0$, $a'_{01} = \frac{1}{5}$, $a'_{12} = \frac{1}{2}$, $a'_{22} = 0$, $a'_{02} = \frac{7}{4}$, we get approximately $O_1 = 2 \cdot 3$, $O_2 = 1 \cdot 15$, $O'_1 = 2 \cdot 9$, $O'_2 = 1 \cdot 3$, $O''_1 = 0 \cdot 5$, $O''_2 = 0 \cdot 2$. Thus the conclusion from a labour-saving bias *ex-ante* to a rise in the organic composition *ex post* is not valid. Purists might want to object that Marx, in his references to the change in the organic composition of capital, always talks in terms of values. Setting $\bar{O}$ for the organic composition in value terms, a counterexample would then have to exhibit the following structure: $O'_j > O_j$ and $\bar{O}_j > \bar{O}''_j$. The same coefficients as above give $\bar{O}_1 = 6$, $\bar{O}_2 = 3$, $\bar{O}''_1 = \frac{40}{87}$, $\bar{O}''_2 = \frac{128}{609}$. If now we turn to the case of a constant rate of exploitation, this implies that among the adjustments that must be made to the new technology is a change in the b_i. Firstly, that is, we have to find a set of b'_i such that $\Sigma_i b_i x_i = \Sigma_i b'_i x'_i$, where x'_i is the value of one unit of good i in the new technology, and secondly we must calculate the new set of prices p''_i from the equations

$$\left(\sum_i a'_{ij} p''_i + \sum_i b'_i a'_{0j} p''_i \right)(1 + r'') = p''_i, \qquad j = 1, 2 \ldots n,$$

from which the organic compositions can be calculated. Once again the same example can be used to show that labour-saving innovations across the board may go together with a fall in the organic compositions *ex post*, even with constant rate of exploitation.

Now the reason why this is an *interesting* fallacy, is that Marx neglects the very interaction effects to which he attributes the counterfinality of capitalism. According to Marx the crises of capitalism are due to each individual's making his decision on a partial-equilibrium basis, wrongly assuming that all other actors can be treated as parameters for his decision problem. In his own reasoning, however, Marx himself commits the error of concluding from partial to general equilibrium, i.e. he commits the fallacy of composition, when he neglects the distinction between the organic composition of the new technology when calculated in the old prices and when calculated in the new prices. From the fact that a given innovation is labour-saving when all other things are kept constant, Marx illegitimately concludes that this remains true when all innovations are considered simultaneously. In addition to the fallacy of composition we may speak here of the pathetic fallacy: the contradiction that Marx discerned in the capitalist economy is nothing but the outward projection of an error in his own reasoning.

The fallacy is all the more surprising because Marx knew very well the importance of simultaneous calibration in economics. Indeed I believe that his recognition of this notion is the first in the history of economic thought and a decisive step forwards from the 'historical' view of value.[58] Nevertheless, Marx was also too much of a Hegelian to liberate himself completely from the historical mode of thought. To be precise, I suggest that the Hegelian theory of the Objective Spirit—the dead hand of the past, as incarnated in present institutions—may be at the root of the fallacious theory of the falling rate of profit. Subjectively, for the worker, the capital goods come to dominate him more and more, until he is transformed into a mere appendix to the machine.[59] In the development of Marx's thought the psychological step from this qualitative domination of labour by capital to a quantitative domination (i.e. a rise in the organic composition of capital) may have been shorter than the corresponding logical step. The increase in the *physical volume* (and in the subjectively felt importance) of 'machines per worker' may have hindered the recognition of a possible decrease in the *value* of constant capital per unit of variable capital.

I conclude this section with a few remarks about what I propose to call *the structuralist fallacy in the social sciences*, a fallacy that in an unjustified manner equates the relation between motives, actions, and consequences in sociological analysis with the corresponding relation in individual rationality. Let us look at the following modes of inference, where it is supposed that the actions x are feasible and that all actors are rational:

(1) When actor a does x, this has the known and desired effect y.
Therefore, a will do x.
(2) Actor a did x.
When actor a does x, this has the known and desired effect y.
Therefore, actor a did x in order to obtain y.
(3) When all members of group A do x, this has the known and desired effect y.
Therefore, all members of A will do x.
(4) All members of A did x.
When all members of A do x, this has the known and desired effect y.
Therefore, the members of A did x in order to obtain y.

Of these inferences the first two may be assumed to be valid by the definition of a rational actor. Someone might want to question the second inference on the grounds that we may do x in order to obtain z, even if we foresee that this also will have the beneficial effect y. This is rather like a cause of causal overdetermination, as in the simultaneous presence of two causal factors y and z each of which is sufficient to cause x. I submit that if someone were to say 'I do x in order to obtain z, but I foresee that I shall also get y, and if I thought that x would not bring me z, then I would nevertheless do x in order to get y', then he really does x also in order to obtain y, so that the second inference is justified. The third inference, which has been labelled the anarchistic fallacy and the liberal fallacy,[60] is obviously wrong, as is brought out at once by invoking the Prisoner's Dilemma. We know that people often do not act in a collectively optimal manner, but it is tempting to conclude that when they *do* act optimally, they do so in order to bring about the optimal result. This conclusion is the structuralist fallacy, i.e. the fourth inference above. Some examples will justify, or so I hope, the addition of yet another fallacy to an already long list of invalid modes of inference.

The first example is the Marx–Fellner problem just referred to, which arises if we let 'x' stand for 'the search for labour-saving innovations' and 'y' for 'reduction of the wage level'. A second example is given by Eric Hobsbawm, when he warns against the fallacious explanation of the origins of capitalism that turns external economies into motivations for individual entrepreneurs.

> The very process which reorganized the social division of labour, increased the proportion of non-agricultural workers, differentiated the peasantry and created classes of wage-earners, also created men who depended for their needs on cash purchases—customers for goods. *But this is the analyst's way of looking at the matter, not the entrepreneur's, who decided whether or not to revolutionize his production.*[61]

A third example is slightly more complex. Here the fallacy is committed by E. P. Thompson in an otherwise important article on peasant revolts in pre-industrial England. He states that there were recurring revolts, and observes that while unsuccessful in their immediate objectives, they had a long-term success in making the propertied classes behave more moderately than they would have done otherwise. From these two propositions he seems to conclude that the long-term success provides a *motivational* explanation of the revolts. This, at any rate, is how I interpret his rhetorical question whether the revolts 'would have continued over so many scores, indeed hundreds of years, if they had consistently failed to achieve their objectives'.[62] This explanation, while not impossible, assumes a rather improbable degree of intergenerational solidarity. A more parsimonious approach would be to explain the persistence of the revolts by the persistence of their causes. In any case the motivational statement cannot be deduced from non-motivational premises. From the fact that each generation did revolt and the fact that it is to the benefit of all that all revolt, we cannot conclude that they revolted in order to realize this benefit.

A last example is very different, but exhibits the same general structure. It is taken from the methodological controversies raging in the foundations of evolutionary theory. In the most important single work from the early phase of that discussion George Williams denounced the 'misconception....that when one demonstrates that a certain biological process produces a certain benefit, one has demonstrated *the* function, or at least *a* function of the process'.[63] From the examples he gives it is clear that what Williams has in mind is beneficial effects that arise from interaction between individuals. An example may be taken from a textbook by Stanley Salthe:

> Another example involving a supraindividual structure can be seen in the spacing of individuals during colonial nesting in a heron rookery. Each pair has a small territory in which their nest is located. Any individual other than the mate who passes into this territory is attacked and driven out. Young fledglings are also not welcome in any pair's territory, including that of their parents. They occupy narrow spaces in between the territories. This places most of them in relatively safe areas in respect to attack by most sorts of predators. Their parents are no longer concerned with pro- tecting them, but will attempt to drive off predators venturing close to their nests. If successful, they will also 'unintentionally' have protected any fledgling occupying the spaces around their territory.[64]

In the formalism of inference (4) above, we have x = parents defending their territories and y = the protection of fledglings: the external economies or spill-over effects of the individually adaptive action x could not in themselves set up a selectional pressure for this behaviour. Another example involving this biological fallacy might be the 'unintentional' effects arising from pleiotropy, i.e. from the fact that a single gene may influence several phenotypic features. We may assume, for example, that gene a is expressed in features A and B. A is a feature that confers reproductive advantage on the organism in some straightforward manner, without any interaction effects. B is an altruistic feature whose benefit to the individual is similar in structure to the Prisoner's Dilemma: for each organism the best (in terms of reproductive capacity) would be to be the only one without the feature, the next best that all organisms should have it, the third best that no one should have it, and the worst fate would be to be the only organism having the feature. (Williams[65] cites schooling in fishes as a possible example of 'egoistic' properties of organ- isms; other examples include aggression and discriminatory warnings.) Such a gene a could never have been selected on the account of B alone, at least not if we abstract from the possibility of group selection. On the contrary any organism exhibiting B would—*ceteris paribus*—be a loser in the struggle for reproductive advantage, so that the feature would soon disappear from the population. If, however, the advantages conferred by A were sufficiently large, the loss implied by B might be tolerable. In this case an apparently 'beneficial' feature, such as altruistic behaviour in the Prisoner's Dilemma, does not really 'have a function' (i.e. has not been selected for), but is only an 'uninten- tional' side-effect of a gene whose main product has been selected for. I take it that this is one of the points Robert Nozick was also hinting at in his discussion of invisible-hand explanations: what looks like intentional (or functional) adaptations may just be an accidental by-product of actions (or selections) undertaken for other ends (or 'ends').

The paradigm of functionalist explanation in sociology involves a line of reasoning that to my mind is quite close to the structuralist fallacy, while being nevertheless distinct from it. The common feature of both modes of reasoning is that favourable objective consequences of some set of actions are seen as *explaining* the actions. In the structuralist fallacy these consequences are transformed into individual *motives* for actions, whereas the functionalist explanations postulate some causal *feedback* from effect to cause. Drawing upon the standard expositions of functionalist sociology by Robert Merton and Arthur Stinchcombe,[66] I believe that a paradigm of functionalist explanation would be the following. We say that *phenomenon X is explained by its function Y for group Z* if and only if:

(1) *Y* is an effect of *X*;
(2) *Y* is beneficial to *Z*;
(3) *Y* is unintended by the actors producing *X*;
(4) *Y* is unrecognized by the actors in *Z*;
(5) *Y* maintains *X* by causal feedback passing through *Z*.

It is rarely recognized how seldom theories are proposed that satisfy all these criteria. Quite often criteria (1), (2), (3), and (5) are satisfied while criterion (4) is not. Here we might talk of *filter-processes*, or perhaps of *artificial selection*. The phenomenon in question is maintained precisely because some group perceives it as beneficial, even if the actors producing it may be quite unaware of—and perhaps opposed to—that effect. When the US Department of Defence allocates funds to scientists, each of which applies for a project that to him seems the most interesting on purely scientific grounds, the end result will be a bias in the composition of research even if each individual scientist feels that he is following his personal bent only.[67] In other cases criteria (1), (2), (3), and (4) are satisfied, while criterion (5) is not. For example, Marx and Mandeville argued[68] that criminality had a beneficial impact on the capitalist economy, even if this was neither intended by criminals nor recognized by legislators or businessmen. The only convincing case I have come across where criteria (1)–(5) are satisfied simultaneously is the explanation of profit-maximizing behaviour in firms that postulates that the firms not using profit-maximizing rules of thumb will go out of existence, so that only profit-maximizers are left.[69] This, indeed, is a case of *natural selection* operating at the social level, but I submit that such cases are extremely rare.

Now the fallacy involved in functionalist reasoning is the inference of a causal feedback from properties (1)–(4). If, for example, one can demonstrate that the apparent neutrality of the state in modern capitalist societies actually is better suited to capitalist purposes than an overtly biased government would have been, then a well-known Marxist–functionalist argument tends to conclude that this beneficial effect *explains* the neutrality of the state.[70] Unless one imputes the feedback to the filtering offices of some hidden executive committee of the bourgeoisie, it is hard to see how it can operate. The feedback must be *demonstrated* rather than merely *postulated*, in contradistinction to the biological case where the existence of a beneficial effect does give a prima-facie reason for thinking that it is the product of natural selection. I argued above that it is a fallacy to think that it *must* be the product of natural selection, but at any rate there does exist in evolution a general mechanism for causal feedback. No such mechanism exists in societies, for which reason the step from (1)–(4) to (5) cannot even be justified as a regulative idea.[71] The structuralist fallacy proper would have explained the neutrality of the state by imputing certain Machiavellian intentions to its officials. In the face of the increasing empirical plausibility of this line of argument, Marxists have tended to retreat to the impregnable fortress of functionalism by postulating or implicitly assuming some causal feedback. That is, from a falsified position they have retreated to an unfalsifiable one. Indeed, Karl Popper has shown that all positive existential statements such as 'There exists a finite sequence of Latin elegiac couplets such that, if it is pronounced in an appropriate manner at a certain time and place, this is immediately followed by the appearance of the Devil'[72] are non-falsifiable (although verifiable) and thus outside the range of science. Similarly, a statement that there exists some causal feedback is non-scientific if supported neither by general reasoning that could lend it some prima-facie plausibility nor by the demonstration of some specific mechanism.

Suboptimality

The second variety of social contradictions I propose to call 'suboptimality': it is *the deliberate realization of a non-cooperative solution that is Pareto-inferior to some other payoff set obtainable by individual choices of strategy*, i.e. when all the players adopt the solution strategies, fully aware that the others will do so as well and that they could all have obtained at least as much, and one of them more, than in the solution if some or all of them had diverged from the solution strategies. (Games without a non-cooperative solution are discussed in the next section.) The paradigm example of suboptimality is, of course, the Prisoner's Dilemma. Before proceeding to examples, two general problems must be examined: What is the relation between counterfinality and suboptimality, and what justifies the term 'contradiction' in the case of suboptimality? It turns out that the answer to the second question depends heavily upon the answer to the first: suboptimality is subsumed under the heading of contradictions because in many cases it is indistinguishable from counterfinality.

Suboptimality as defined is a game–theoretic notion. It presupposes perfect information and correct anticipations. It should be stressed, however, that the transition from a pre-strategic to a strategic situation often does not modify the behaviour of the actors. In a Prisoner's Dilemma, for example, counterfinality is generated when everyone does x in the hope of being the only one to do x, and suboptimality when everyone does x out of fear of being the only not to do x. The hope of being a free rider does, when generalized, generate counterfinality; the fear of being a sucker does not. There is no difference in the observed behaviour of the actors, only in the expectations of the actors. In cases of sub-optimality the consequences are foreseen rather than unexpected, intended rather than unintended.[73] In other cases, however, the transition from parametric to strategic rationality (see Appendix 2) *does* make a difference to the behaviour of the actors. The cobweb model illustrates this case. Here the competitive price is the solution of the game, being the only equilibrium point. This, however, does not mean that all contradictions have disappeared. As observed by Luce and Raiffa,[74] the competitive strategy can also be seen as the non-cooperative behaviour in a Prisoner's Dilemma, as opposed to the cooperative behaviour of monopolistic restriction or joint profit maximization. With imperfect information, the farmers are constantly frustrated because their expectations and plans come to nought; with perfect information they are frustrated because they understand that they could all have improved their lot by acting differently from that which rationality requires them to do.

The crucial difference between a Prisoner's Dilemma and the cobweb game is that only in the former do all actors have a *dominant strategy*. In games with a dominant strategy it may be difficult to decide whether a given behaviour is a case of counterfinality or of suboptimality, unless one has direct evidence about the expectations of the actors. If, however, a suboptimal solution is realized in a game without dominant strategies, we can immediately conclude that this is a case of suboptimality and not of counterfinality, for the solution strategies will be chosen only on the (correct) assumption that the others are choosing them as well. It is not easy to say how often the solution is realized in real-life games without dominant strategies. The severe information require-ments for the solution to be realized makes it *a priori* rather improbable that the actors will take the chance of acting upon the assumption that the others are taking the same chance. With the smallest element of uncertainty, the normal course will be to fall back upon a maximin-strategy. Some exceptions to this general conclusion may be mentioned. Firstly, the group may be so small and so stable (see also the last section below and Appendix 1) that people really come to know and trust each other. Secondly, the relevant information may be supplied by some outside agency, such as the government. If, for example, a given situation really is an Assurance Game, whereas each actor wrongly believes that for all other actors it is a Prisoner's Dilemma, then the govern-ment may supply information about the real preference structure that will make the actors converge upon the solution. This could conceivably be impor-tant in cases such as tax-evasion or work effort. (For further discussion of the Assurance Game see Appendix 1 below.) Thirdly, repetition of the situation in essentially the same form may give rise to a *learning process*, as in the cobweb case.

A special case of games without dominant strategies is when the solution requires the actors to use *mixed strategies*. This notion is crucial in some of Raymond Boudon's recent work, to be discussed below. As far as I know, there is no empirical evidence that people deliberately choose mixed strategies in real-life situations involving such large numbers of people as in the cases discussed by Boudon. It would be very interesting indeed if such evidence could be found, for — as further discussed in Appendix 2 below — this could bridge the gap that exists at present between the intentional and the causal images of man in the social sciences. It is certain, however, that we are still very ignorant in these matters.

It is now possible to explain why I propose to subsume suboptimality under the general heading of social contradictions. The main argument is that in many cases counterfinality and suboptimality are identical as regards overt behaviour. An additional argument is the following. As I try to show in the next section, both counterfinality and suboptimality tend to generate collective action, in the first case because of the tension between *the intention and the result*, in the second because of the tension between *the actual and the possible*. These tensions are in themselves not contradictions in the rigorous sense of the term used here, but they nevertheless point to the need for a unified terminology. There is both a formal overlap and a substantial affinity between counterfinality and suboptimality. I should add, perhaps, that I do *not* want to defend my thesis that contradictions generate collective action by renaming 'contradictions' all causes of such action, but rather to persuade the reader that the very small extension implied in the step from counterfinality to suboptimality has the advantage of simplifying and unifying the discussion. If the reader remains unconvinced, this does not matter very much for the substance of the argument that is set forth in the remainder of the chapter. I now proceed, as before, to use a number of different examples to make some conceptual points that seem important.

(a) The standard examples of suboptimality arising in situations having the general form of the Prisoner's Dilemma, are externalities, public goods, and organizations. As these are exhaustively treated in Mancur Olson's modern classic on the subject as well as in many other works,[75] I shall be rather brief in my coverage at this point. Externalities—such as pollution—may arise both as counterfinality and as suboptimality, whereas I submit that the non-provision of public goods most often arises in the mode of suboptimality. Typically, I think, people will either be unaware of the very existence and possibility of the public good in question (the absence of pollution control was not felt in ancient Greece) or they will understand that the free-rider problem will prevent the realization of the good. The intermediate case, where each actor hopes to be the only one to have the benefits of the good without contributing to the costs, does not seem very plausible. The fear of being a sucker is more likely to animate the actors than the hope of being a free rider.[76] This is a difficult point, and not very important. The main idea I want to get across is that we should not talk about suboptimality when the strategies that would give the Pareto-superior outcome do not belong to the subjective possibilities of the actors.

Suboptimality may also stem from the absence of organizations, as may be seen in the cobweb example. It is better for all the farmers if they form a cartel to maximize collective profits than if they all maximize individually, but for the individual farmer it would be even better to break the cartel agreement and increase production in order to exploit the high prices that are made possible by the cartel restriction of production. Since all farmers understand this, no cartel will be formed. A similar argument goes for labour union formation as analysed by Mancur Olson. Even if the workers understand that they will all be better off if they are all organized than if each is left to negotiate for himself (an insight that took quite some time to emerge in 19th-century Europe, where there was a widespread belief that the only effect of unions was to redistribute income within the working class), the individual worker may be tempted to try to have his cake and eat it, as a free rider. During a strike, for example, the strike-breaker will not only get the usual (i.e. pre-strike) wages, but may even be able to claim higher wages because of his temporary monopoly of labour power. After the strike, of course, he will benefit by the higher wages obtained by the strikers. If, however, everyone reasons in this manner, no one will get any benefits at all. In the next section I discuss this problem in more detail.

(b) An interesting use of the logic of counterfinality and suboptimality is found in the recent work of Raymond Boudon on the sociology of education. In contrast to the classical approach to education as a public good that makes for a free-rider problem in that everyone wants to have the benefits (through increased productivity) of the others' education—a Prisoner's Dilemma with too little education as the solution—Boudon argues that in modern industrial societies there is a tendency towards too much education, in that everyone wants to have more education than the others in order to enjoy an income differential:

> The famous cobweb theorem suggests that people can behave rationally (i.e. can make decisions apparently well adapted to their objectives) and yet by doing so obtain a result contradictory to these objectives. This is exactly what we found: every individual has a definite advantage in trying to obtain as much education as possible—the higher the educational level, the more favorable the status expectations. But as soon as all individuals want more education, the expectations associated with most educational levels tend to degenerate, and this has the effect of inciting people to demand still more education in the next period.[77]

The problem, as stated here, is one of counterfinality and not of suboptimality, but this is not essential. (The reference to the cobweb model is misleading, because in that model the difference between a pre-strategic and a strategic context is essential, as we saw above. Also the cobweb model describes a cyclical movement, whereas the model of the demand for education generates a cumulative upward movement of demand.) In another paper Boudon and his co-workers have explored in more explicit detail the logic of suboptimality in education.[78] Trying to explain why French students do not seek (in the large numbers foreseen by the educational authorities) the shorter road in higher education made available by the Instituts Universitaires de Technologie, but rather prefer the long road of the classical higher educational institutions, they propose a model incorporating the following assumptions. In a cohort of 20 students a choice has to be made between the long road and the short road. They know that at the end of the short road they are certain to get a job at 1 franc, whereas the remuneration at the end of the long road depends upon the number of students who have chosen it. Specifically, it is assumed that for students with the long-road education there are available six jobs of 2 francs and eight jobs of 1 franc. These jobs are automatically filled if there are qualified candidates for them; if there are too many candidates, the surplus will get no job at all.

Given these assumptions it is easy to see that the total remuneration of the students (and the expected remuneration of each student) is maximized if not less than 6 and not more than 14 students take the long road, so that 6 would seem to be the minimal capacity for the short road. This reasoning, however, overlooks that things may look very different from the point of view of the individual student. If x students were to take the long road ($6 \leqslant x \leqslant 14$), each student would have to use a mixed strategy and choose the long road with probability $x/20$ and the short road with probability $1 - x/20$. This set of mixed strategies, unfortunately, is not an equilibrium point. In fact it is easy to see that the long road is a *dominant strategy*, so that the short road will not be chosen by anyone, leaving a surplus capacity of six. Total remuneration will fall from 26 to 20 francs and expected remuneration from 1·3 to 1, a clear case of suboptimality. This line of argument is ingenious and interesting, but the results depend too much upon the specific numerical assumptions made. Boudon and co-workers affirm[79] that the conclusion is not materially changed if we assume that at the end of the short road the student is certain to get 1·5 francs, but this statement is not correct. In this case there is no dominant strategy, and the solution of the game requires that each student choose the long road with probability 0·6 and the short road with probability 0·4, whereas the collectively optimal mix would be (0·3, 0·7), giving expected payoffs of 1·5 and 1·65, respectively. Thus *if* the students choose the mixed strategies of the solution, we are dealing with a case of suboptimality as defined here; but I have argued that is a big *if* indeed. More probably each student will choose his educational strategy on the maximin principle, or on the basis of some assumption concerning the behaviour of the others, e.g. the assumption that the other students of the cohort will choose in the same proportion as the preceding cohort. The latter possibility could generate a true cobweb cycle, with alternately too few and too many students choosing the short road.

In the paper just discussed, there is no explicit mention of the notion of a mixed strategy. One of the cases discussed by Boudon turns out to require mixed strategies, and this to my mind constitutes an objection to his argument.[80] In a later work[81] Boudon has turned the tables on his critics, and exploited the notion of mixed strategies to a very interesting purpose, viz. the reinterpretation of the classical findings of *The American Soldier* concerning the unexpected correlation between possibilities of promotion and level of frustration.[82] Imagine a cohort of 20 MPs and another cohort of 20 air force members. The first belongs to a group characterized by small possibilities for promotion and low level of frustration, whereas in the second both promotion potential and frustration are high. Let us further assume that in order to participate in the 'promotion game' you have to stake 1 franc's equivalent of effort. The promoted receive the equivalent of 5 francs in remuneration. Here, 5 out of 20 air force members will be promoted, whereas only 2 out of 20 MPs achieve this. It is then easy to see that all the 20 air force members will stake 1 franc, which results in 15 out of 20 being disappointed, whereas only 10 MPs will enter the game, of which 8 are necessarily disappointed. The mechanism that brings it about that 10 MPs enter the game is, of course, that each of the 20 uses the mixed strategy of entering the game with probability 0·5. Greater potential for promotion leads not only to more participants in the promotion game, but to a difference in participation that exceeds the difference in potential for promotion, which again means more frustration. Again I can only affirm that the validity of this elegant analysis depends crucially upon the empirical plausibility of mixed strategies in real-life situations.

(c) The remaining examples will turn in various ways upon dynamic considerations, i.e. suboptimality over time. The first of these examples is the problem of inconsistent time preferences discussed in chapter 4, where I promised that a further analysis would be forthcoming here. I shall restate the problem as one of a game between successive generations. Let us first assume that each generation is interested in its own consumption only; then for all generations it is better if all undertake some investment than if no one does so, but for each generation it is even better to consume all of current output while benefiting from previous generations' investment. For the case of two generations A and B (A preceding B) the payoff matrix would have the following ordinal structure:

		B	
		Invest	Consume
A	Invest	10, 10	10, 15
	Consume	15, 5	15, 8

We see that the no-investment strategy dominates the investment strategy for each generation. The 'game' is not a Prisoner's Dilemma, for A cannot be hurt by B's retaliation. In other cases, however, it is possible to give a sense to such retaliation, namely if the utility of any given generation is a function not only of its own consumption but also of the consumption enjoyed by subsequent generations. This, of course, does not imply that future behaviour can have an impact upon present utility, only that present expectations about future behaviour can have such an impact. Assuming an infinite sequence of generations, the problem of an intergenerational game–theoretic equilibrium[83] may then be put in the following manner: does there exist a sequence s_i of saving ratios such that for all i it is true that if generation i expects its successors to choose ratios $s_{i+1}, s_{i+2} \ldots$, it will itself choose s_i for utility maximization?

To see how this problem arises we recall that a 'naive' generation would try to maximize utility by fixing both its own savings ratio and the ratio of all future generations. The snag, as we saw in chapter 4, is that the next generation may very well find it desirable to change the savings ratio planned for it, so that *ex post facto* the first generation would not have its expectations fulfilled. In this—slightly strained—sense we may say that later generations can retaliate against its precedessors, or that a generation may be 'deceived' by its successors and experience counterfinality. We have also seen that such continual revision of the plans will in fact take place if time preferences are non-exponential in form, i.e. if the present values of one utility unit in future years do not form an exponentially decreasing series. One way in which this may arise is the following. Let us assume that there are two kinds of discounting of the future. Firstly, there is a time-independent discounting of all future utilities, irrespective of the time at which they are experienced, so that generation t accords to one unit of utility experienced by generation $t + T$ the present value $(1 + r_1)^{-1}$. Secondly, there is an exponential and time-dependent discounting that gives to one unit of utility experienced at $t + T$ the present value $(1 + r_2)^{-T}$. Compounding the two gives a non-exponential discounting of the future, with the need for a continual revision of naive plans.

There is, of course, no logical impossibility in the assumption that some generation might be able to impose its wish upon the future, even if it is hard to see how this could be realized institutionally. There is, however, a logical impossibility in the assumption that all generations might be able to do so if they all have non-exponential time preferences. If all try to maximize 'naively', they will all be deceived in the *ex post facto* sense. Here, as in the cases examined in the previous section, non-universalizable assumptions about the behaviour of others lead to unintended consequences. Before I go on to consider the transition from counterfinality to suboptimality that is observed when the naive generations achieve a more sophisticated outlook, I would like to observe that we are dealing here with a basic problem in the theory of democratic planning. Francis Sejersted talks about an 'inner conflict'[84]—a contradiction, in our terms—in the notion of democracy. By extending the scope of the current exercise of power to the limit, democracy also undermines the efficacy of power. In the limit complete democracy means that each generation is free from the obligations handed over by its predecessors, but this also implies that it is itself unable to bind its successors. In other terms: stability and efficiency require permanent rules that transcend the span of a single generation; democracy and participation require for each generation a full say in all matters concerning its members; but is not instant power also an objectless power?

A 'sophisticated' generation, that assumed all subsequent generations to be equally sophisticated, would adopt a game–theoretic approach to the problem and seek for a sequence s_i as defined above. Phelps and Pollak have shown[85] that in some cases this equilibrium sequence exists and (in a certain sense) implies undersaving and Pareto-suboptimality. That is, each generation will adopt the same saving ratio s_1 while there exists a ratio s_2 $(s_2 > s_1)$ such that all generations would derive larger utility if all adopted s_2 than when all adopt s_1. We should observe here that the ratio s_1 is not a dominant strategy, in contrast to the game that results when each generation's utility is a function exclusively of its own consumption, for then a savings ratio of zero dominates all other ratios. In this case the realization of the solution in a game without dominant strategies is more plausible than in most other situations, for once one generation has adopted the strategic point of view it can reasonably expect its successors to do so as well; Phelps and Pollak speak of eating from the fruit of knowledge. Sophistication is contagious in time, if not in space.

(d) In some cases static and dynamic suboptimality may be considered together, as reinforcing each other, as annulling each other, or as alternatives to each other. I first mention briefly an example where the two work in the same direction, viz. investment in fundamental research. For the individual country, especially if it is small,[86] it is preferable to be a free rider and exploit the scientific advances made elsewhere, at least to the extent that it is able to do so without doing more than a modicum of research itself. At the same time the investments made by any single generation will depend very heavily upon the time preferences of the government. Because of the lack of correlation in space and time between the investment in basic research and the return to that investment, both chauvinism and myopia will make for underinvestment and suboptimality.

(e) In other cases the two mechanisms may work in opposite directions, as in the 'imperialism of free trade'.[87] Let us assume that there exist two groups of countries, group A and group B, and that group B for some reason is unable to form a cartel. The problem, then, is whether the members of group A should trade with group B countries on a non-cooperative (competitive) basis or on a cooperative basis (cartel prices). At any given moment the aggregate profits of group A will be maximized by adoption of the cartel strategies, even if for the individual A country it is even better to be a free rider and break the cartel. Assuming that a stable cartel is somehow maintained, this may be seen as a suboptimal strategy over time, because the countries in group B that face monopoly and monopsony prices will be motivated to develop their own industries and refineries if this can be done at prices below the world prices, even if initially they lack the resources or the technological sophistication to do so at competitive prices. This is a variant of the infant industry argument, the difference being that we assume here that the governments and the industries of B are so myopic that they will not undertake production unless it is *immediately* feasible to produce at prices below world market prices.

The preceding assumptions imply that for maximization of long-term aggregate profits the countries of group A should adopt the competitive strategy; at any given moment there will be a temptation to break out of the intertemporal cartel for low prices and form instead an instantaneous cartel for high prices in order to maximize short-term aggregate profits; this, however, may be annulled by the temptation for any given country to break the instantaneous cartel and use competitive prices in order to maximize short-term individual profits. The cooperative behaviour in the long-term game coincides with the non-cooperative behaviour in the short-term game, so that nationalism and myopia somehow annul each other. This 'imperialism of free trade' also demonstrates that, in sociological parlance, 'universalism is the particularism of the rich'. I would like to add that even if the use of competitive prices *may* be the outcome of a Machiavellian 'anti-cartel cartel', it may also (and will normally) be the less sophisticated outcome of an atomistic market situation. The reader should recall at this point the structuralist fallacy criticized above: from the fact that nations behave in a way that maximizes their long-term aggregate profits, we cannot conclude that this is what motivates them to action.

(f) The preceding examples may be referred to as 'hierarchical Prisoner's Dilemmas', in the sense that we are dealing with an inter-temporal game between actors that do themselves involve internal subgames. Static and dynamic suboptimality may also, however, interact in a different manner, as *alternatives* to each other in the kind of dilemma that is basic to the institutional arrangements of capitalism. Drawing upon the insights of Joseph Schumpeter and Kenneth Arrow,[88] two cases will be mentioned. Firstly, the patent system, by internalizing the economic benefits of an invention, is dynamically optimal in the sense of maximizing the creation of new technological possibilities, but at the same time it is statistically suboptimal in the sense of preventing the best exploitation of the existing possibilities.[89] Secondly, a similar dilemma between the exploitation and the creation of possibilities arises from the risk aversion of the entrepreneur. By maximizing utility rather than profits he prevents the realization of the static Pareto-optimum, but at the same time it is his identification with the firm (and the subsequent maximization of utility rather than profits) that makes the entrepreneur into the heroic figure of capitalism from the dynamic point of view.[90]

(g) In direct prolongation of this discussion, we may try to unravel the meaning of the third and last among the main occurrences of the term 'contradiction' in the corpus of Marx: the 'contradiction between the forces of production and the relations of production'.[91] Let us start out by observing that Marx never uses that favourite phrase of vulgar Marxism, 'the contradiction between the social means of production and the private relations of production', which by itself is no more of a contradiction than a marriage between a tall woman and a short man. The contradiction, if contradiction it be, should not rely upon this kind of verbal sleight-of-hand. Secondly, in the phrase to be interpreted all the terms—and not just the term 'contradiction'—are very difficult to understand. I shall simplify the problem by stipulating that productive forces are merely technology and relations of production the institutional property arrangements, thus disregarding the tendency of Marx to speak as if everything (relations of production included) is in some sense a 'force of production' if it has an impact upon productive efficiency.[92]

In what is probably the best-known (or next-to-best-known) paragraph that Marx ever wrote, he states—given the above interpretation of some key terms—that in each mode of production the property relations are initially 'forms of development' for technology, while later on they become 'fetters' for this same development. The latter expression strongly suggests some kind of suboptimality, either of static exploitation or of dynamic development of technology. Unfortunately it is very hard to understand what Marx had in mind, even if we limit ourselves to the capitalist mode of production. As far as I know there is only one text that points concretely to a possible mechanism. Here Marx states that 'In a communist society there would be very different scope for the employment of machinery than there can be in a bourgeois society',[93] because in the former machinery would be used in all cases where the labour value of the machine is smaller than the value created by the workers who are replaced by the machine, whereas in the latter, machinery is employed only in the cases where the labour value of the machines is smaller than the value of the labour power of the workers replaced by the machine. This static suboptimality would seem, however, to be a permanent feature of capitalism and not—as required by the argument—a feature that appears only (or increasingly) in the later phases of capitalism.

The most natural interpretation, from the modern economist's point of view, is perhaps the following argument: competitive capitalism offers high incentives to invent; new technology typically requires large-scale production and extensive use of machinery; the resulting economies of scale create a tendency towards oligopoly; oligopoly in turns reduces the incentive to invent. Of these four propositions the first and the last are partially endorsed by Arrow.[94] The third proposition is hard to refute, as one cannot simultaneously have increasing returns to scale, profit maximization, and perfect competition. The second proposition is more dubious, in that it abstracts from the possibility of capital-saving innovations. Over and above this problem, however, there is the exegetical difficulty that Marx explicitly states[95] that under capitalism technical progress will take place at an ever-increasing rather than at a decreasing rate.

A last interpretation could argue that the dynamic suboptimality should not be understood—as in the last paragraph—as a decline in the absolute rate of change of technology, but rather as a decline relative to the rate of change that would have been possible—at the same stage in the development of the productive forces—in a communist organization of society. This, I think, comes closest to what Marx had in mind. The details of the argument are not worked out, but roughly something like the following may have been intended. In conditions of material well-being, innovation is a natural activity for man and springs from the very source of his being, but in conditions of scarcity and poverty, incentives are required if innovations are to come forth. In the early stages of capitalism there was indeed a great deal of scarcity and poverty, and unavoidably so, as the material conditions for the universal satisfaction of wants were lacking. Under these conditions the patent system was the best and most progressive arrangement, even if it subordinated progress to profits. This system, however, inevitably created the conditions for its own demise. In later phases of capitalism there is still a great deal of poverty, but avoidably so. Given the technology developed by capitalism itself, it is materially feasible to install a regime where the level of material well-being is so high that innovation as a spontaneous activity comes into its own—at a rate far in excess of anything that has existed before. In this interpretation, therefore, it is possible to characterize the rate of technical change under capitalism as increasing *and* as suboptimal.[96]

I will not dwell upon the intrinsic merits of this argument, except to state that personally I tend to accept it. I do not, on the other hand, accept the corollary that was certainly implied by Marx, that this 'contradiction between the forces and the relations of production' can also serve as a lever for social change. I submit that if the gap between the potential and the actual is to act as a social force in a given society, it must coincide with a gap between what is actual in that society and what is actual in another and not yet realized in the first. Of course I do not deny the power of Utopian thought in social movements, but I think it would be a misrepresentation of that thought to see it as a theory of suboptimalities. When men strive to realize Utopia, they do not work to realize the optimum relative to given preferences, but more often to change men and their preferences. This strand of thinking is also very important in Marxism, but for the purposes of the present argument I am focusing—as I think Marx did himself in the theory now under discussion—upon the inefficiency of capitalism rather than upon its perversion of wants.

To restate the above argument negatively, I do not believe that a suboptimality defined relatively to a mere possibility that is nowhere realized can be an important agent in social change. The point is well brought out in Alexander Gerschenkron's comparative analysis of European industrialization, where he singles out 'the tension between the actual state of economic activities in the country and the existing obstacles to industrial development on the one hand, and the great promise inherent in such a development, on the other'[97] as a key variable. This tension or suboptimality does not, however, enter into the analysis of the *English* industrialization, only in the explanation of the forms assumed by the industrialization of Germany, Italy, Russia, etc. Once the Industrial Revolution had taken place in England, the results obtained there could stand out as 'promises' for other countries and define for these countries the gap between the actual and the potential, but for the first country one cannot usefully talk about such a gap. And once communism has been successfully introduced in one country, the gap between the achievements of that country and the drab realities of other countries might serve as a lever for social revolution in the latter, but the crucial *first* communist revolution cannot come about in this way. (Cf. also the fallacy of composition inherent in diffusionist thought.)

(h) My last example of suboptimality is Kelvin Lancaster's model of capitalism as a differential game exhibiting suboptimality.[98] In a two-person differential game each actor controls, within certain constraints, the value of a variable $x_i(t)$, $i = 1, 2$. A strategy is a time profile $x_i(t)$ of a variable, defined for a period (t_0, t_1). The payoff may be defined in various ways, but here we deal with the case where the payoff is a cumulative function of the strategies used up to the point in time when the payoff takes place. We assume that both actors want to maximize the payoff for the whole period (t_0, t_1). The notions of an equilibrium point and a solution are defined analogously to the static case, for which see Appendix 1 below. We must take care, however, to interpret correctly the notion of one strategy being better than another: against a given $x_2(t)$ a strategy $x_1(t)$ is better than $x_1'(t)$ if it gives a larger payoff at the end of the period, which does not imply a larger accumulated payoff at each moment during the period.

In Lancaster's model it is assumed that the workers control the ratio of current worker consumption to output, either directly by controlling the wage rate or indirectly by controlling taxes on profits. The control is constrained by upper and lower limits, which may be arbitrarily close to 100% and 0 respectively. The capitalists control what proportion of the output not consumed by the workers shall be invested and what proportion used for capitalist consumption, with similar constraints. For modern capitalist economies this model seems to me superior to the traditional Marxist one, because it brings together several facets of exploitation. In the capitalism of Marx's time the upper limit to the workers' control variable was at a very low level, and this in itself would seem to be a form of exploitation. (I assume that this upper limit is set by the relative bargaining powers of the two classes.) The exploitation is especially severe if the capitalists choose a low value for the rate of reinvestment out of profits, but I would argue that we should talk about exploitation even if a large part of the sacrifice imposed upon the workers is reinvested to the benefit of future workers. In modern capitalism the upper limit to the workers' control variable is at a very high level, but as the workers do not control the investment process they have to choose a value for the control value well below this upper limit; a sacrifice that it chosen rather than imposed, or imposed by the structure of the game rather than by the capitalist class. The crucial point is that the workers have to keep their control variable well below the upper limit if there is to be any investment and any increase in future consumption, even if they cannot be certain that the capitalists will actually reinvest the surplus rather than spend it upon immediate consumption. A similar dilemma holds for the capitalists, for if they do invest out of profits they have no guarantee that they will obtain their share of the increased output later on.[99]

Now the mathematical analysis of this game (or rather of an important special case) demonstrates that it has a solution with several interesting features. Firstly, the time profiles of the control variables are discontinuous; there exists a time t $(t_0 < t < t_1)$ such that up to t both classes consume minimally whereas from t onwards both consume maximally. Secondly, the solution is Pareto-suboptimal: there exist $x_1(t)$ and $x_2(t)$ that give a larger total consumption for both classes than the consumption defined by the solution strategies, the snag being of course that $x_1(t)$ and $x_2(t)$ are not optimal against each other. Lancaster has shown that the feature of suboptimality is preserved even if we introduce various modifications to make the model more realistic. I am not quite sure that these modifications suffice to make the model more than a stylized approach to some aspects of modern capitalism; in particular I can see nothing in actual economies corresponding to the 'bang-bang' feature of discountinuity exhibited by the solution to the game. Nevertheless the model suggests the very important idea that in modern economies of the mixed type the workers have the political power and the capitalists the economic power; the workers the power over the saving decisions and the capitalists the power over the investment decisions; *the workers the power over the present and the capitalists the power over the future.* It also suggests that in some cases, the importance of which is uncertain, this separation of powers makes for Pareto-suboptimality. In my view, however, the indictment of capitalism stems from the unequal access to investment decisions itself and not from the inefficiency that may or may not be a consequence of this inequality.

A dual theory of social change

In the last section of this chapter I shall bring together some of the strands from the preceding pages in a theory—or, more modestly, an explanatory scheme—of social change. The argument turns upon the relation between change, contradictions, structural conditions, and political action. The main thesis is that given certain structural conditions, such as spatial proximity between group members or low turnover rates within the group, contradictions tend to generate collective action for the purpose of overcoming the contradictions. This collective action may have the effect of reversing or halting the process of change, viz. if the contradiction to be overcome is itself a vehicle of change. If, on the other hand, the contradictions are stable configurations of society, the political process will bring about a change if successful. As collective action, therefore, may both prevent and generate change, the conditions for such action may function both as conditions for stability and as conditions for change. In this sense I am proposing a *dual* theory of social change.

It is not hard to see how some of the contradictions referred to above do in themselves constitute a form of change. This is the case for all the examples of counterfinality, and indeed I believe that this link holds in virtually all cases.[100] If erosion, a falling rate of profit or a self-reinforcing demand crisis are not examples of social change, then nothing is. We can speak here of an *economic variety of change*, resulting from the statistical interaction of innumerable individual choices. Most cases of suboptimality, on the other hand, are not in themselves cases of change. This certainly holds good for the non-provision of public goods or for the absence of organizations. It is not true for the external diseconomies such as pollution or 'the tragedy of the commons', and it is neither obviously true nor obviously false for the other examples of suboptimality discussed above. For simplicity I shall speak as if suboptimalities never constitute change and as if counterfinality always does, which implies, among other things, that an externality will be classed as an example of counterfinality (which, of course, it often is). Given a suboptimality, then, a collective action for the purpose of attaining the Pareto-optimum will represent the *political variety of change*, a departure from the *status quo*. But given a counterfinality, the purpose of a political action will be to restore the *status quo* and thus to counteract change.

These are the bare bones of the argument, which must now be fleshed out. Let me start by observing that, as in Hegel's *Phenomenology of Mind*, the responses to contradictions can be ordered hierarchically, involving several *levels* and *modes* of learning. Hegel speaks of the itinerary of the spirit as a series of 'Momente' (consciousness, self-consciousness, reason, mind, religion) within each of which several *Gestalten* may be distinguished. Within each 'Moment' or mode of consciousness, each *Gestalt* or level represents a particular form of the contradiction specific to that moment. The contradictory desires of the master, for example, are but a particular form of the general contradiction that defines the mode of self-consciousness, and that might roughly be characterized as the desire to have your cake and eat it. In each attempt to transcend the contradiction at a given level a new contradiction is created, until finally it is seen that the mode as a whole is contradictory, an insight that leads to a new mode arising. (The notion of hierarchical and inherently contradictory learning is also found in Gregory Bateson's work on 'deutero-learning', where it is suggested that 'the creature is driven to [learning at] level III by "contraries" generated [by learning] at level II'.[101]

We have already seen this logic at work in the analysis of the cobweb cycle. At the zero'th level of learning we simply have behaviour according to the supply and demand schedules; this 'learning' may be said to be successful if the oscillations die away sufficiently fast. At the first level of learning we then get the behaviour generated by the assumption that all other producers are acting according to their supply and demand schedules; at the nth level the behaviour generated by the assumption that all other producers are at the $n - 1$th level. At any level in the hierarchy the oscillations may become sufficiently damped for the process to come to an end, but there is also the possibility that the actors realize that the hierarchy itself is inherently contradictory and that they are all at the same level. In that case we have a transition to a new *mode*, viz. the strategic or game–theoretic one. If, however, this mode also exhibits some variety of contradictions, only the step to the (third and last) mode of collective action can overcome the contradiction. In Hegel's philosophy all contradictions are finally reconciled in the mode of Absolute Knowledge; I suggest that the Marxist equivalent would be organized collective action. The three modes, then, are defined respectively by a shared assumption of unilateral advantage, a shared assumption of strategic rationality, and the solidarity of organized action. As pointed out in Appendix 2 below, strategic rationality is in one sense a vehicle of collective freedom, but from a formal point of view only. From a substantial point of view the Prisoner's Dilemma tells us that even in the transparent rationality of game theory the actors may be compelled to act in a collectively disastrous manner. There is the frustration of being in the grip of causal forces that one does not understand, but it may be equally intolerable to understand that one is deliberately contributing to a Pareto-inferior state. To sum up, then, the first mode of social existence necessarily generates contradictions, which may or may not be eliminated by the transition to the second mode; if they are not, only the step to the third mode can resolve the dilemma. Needless to say, this sequence is a logical one only; in any actual case of change one or more of the steps may be skipped.

At this point some words are required to explain the role of *games without a non-cooperative solution* to which reference was made in the preceding section. These games are of two main types: games without equilibrium points and games with several equilibrium points none of which can be singled out as the solution. (For these notions, see Appendix 1 below.) As an example of a game without an equilibrium point we may perhaps take hyperinflation, where the largest payoff goes to the player foreseeing and acting upon a larger price increase than the increase foreseen by others. A formal model of this game is the following: 'Each player writes down a number. The player who has written the largest number receives from each of the other players a sum of money equal to the difference between the largest number and the number written down by that player.' It is intuitively clear, and can be proved rigorously,[102] that in this *fuite en avant* there can be no equilibrium point and *a fortiori* no solution. More important are probably the games with several equilibrium points but with no solution. The provision of public goods may serve as an example here. If there are many actors involved, all of approximately the same size, the provision of public goods in a *n*-person Prisoner's Dilemma. If among the actors there is one much larger than the others, he may find it in his interest to provide the good in question even if he cannot prevent the others from being free riders; this was referred to above as the exploitation of the great by the small. If, finally, there are two large actors, each of whom would act as sole provider of the good were he certain that no one else would provide it, we have a game of Chicken, i.e. a game without a solution. We have already observed that the duopoly problem and the Marx–Fellner analysis of the bias of technical change lead to similar no-solution games: better-known examples are bargaining by threat, the arms race, etc.

Games without a solution are *sui generis*, sharing some features with counterfinality and with suboptimality, while coinciding with neither. As there is no rational thing to do, the actors *must* form some psychological hypotheses about what the others are likely to do, even if they are all aware of the fact that they are all trying to outguess each other. These hypotheses may, of course, be contradictory and generate counterfinality. I submit that this is a particularly intolerable form of counterfinality, because each actor knows that the others are rational and still has to treat them as if they were not. In the pre-strategic mode each participant acts upon the sincere (even if naive) belief that he is really one step ahead of all the others, but the post-strategic counterfinality found in games without a solution is more perverse in that everyone is fully aware of the possibility that he may be outguessed. Even random behaviour, of course, is of no avail, because the absence of a solution covers the case of mixed strategies. Thus, in games without a solution the pressure towards a cooperative behaviour should be especially strong. 'In cases where the equi-

librium concept does not lead to a unique mode of behaviour, the players probably do well to contemplate the cooperative game.'[103] Whenever I talk about
contradictions below, I also include the games without a non-cooperative solution, which may indeed be said to constitute a third variety of contradictions.
I do not think they compare in importance with the two other varieties. It was
thought for a long time that the class of games without a solution was much
larger than it actually is,[104] but the introduction by von Neumann of the
notion of mixed strategies vastly increased the number of cases in which 'the
equilibrium concept does lead to a unique mode of behaviour'.

I now state and discuss the four propositions that form the substance of
my approach:

(1) *If the actors perceive that they are behaving in a contradictory manner,*
they will try to organize themselves for the purpose of overcoming the contra-
diction.

I shall expand upon this idea, which may seem banal (or empty) at first glance.
A similar notion has been proposed by Arrow, who suggests that 'when the
market fails to achieve an optimal state, society will, to some extent at least,
recognize the gap, and nonmarket social institutions will arise attempting to
bridge it'.[105] In *Exit, Voice and Loyalty* Albert Hirschman quotes approvingly
from the same passage, immediately after the following quotation from his own
earlier work on *The Strategy of Economic Development*:

> Tradition seems to require that economists argue forever about the
> question whether, in any disequilibrium situation, *market forces acting*
> *alone* are likely to restore equilibrium. But as social scientists we surely must
> address ourselves also to the broader question: is the disequilibrium situa-
> tion likely to be corrected at all, by market or nonmarket forces, or by both
> acting jointly? *It is our contention that nonmarket forces are not necessarily*
> *less automatic than market forces.*[106]

Another approach heavily influenced by Arrow's observation is the 'theory
of institutional change' devised by Douglass North and Lance Davis, who
'postulate that economic institutions are innovated or property rights are
revised because it appears profitable for individuals or groups to undertake
the costs of such charges; they hope to capture some profit which is unattainable
under the old arrangement'.[107] These references seem to prove that at any rate
discussion of the first proposition above is not a mere waste of time.

We may observe, firstly, that all of these authors are mainly concerned with
suboptimalities, especially the non-provision of public goods and the lack
of organization. Only Hirschman refers in passing to political intervention
in the business cycle. Secondly—and in spite of the misleading word 'automatic'
in the passage quoted from Hirschman—these authors are all very careful
to point out that market failures do not *always* generate successful political
action for the purpose of attaining the optimum or the equilibrium. North and

Davis, in fact, do more than just issue a general warning against this misconception, as they try to specify the conditions that tend to further or prevent such action. I return to some of their ideas below. Here I would only like to stress as much as possible that the first proposition above does *not* imply a cybernetic view of society as an ultrastable system.[108] The passage from Hirschman, if read in isolation from the immediately following caveat, seems to imply that the political process is a second-order regulatory mechanism that is switched on when the first-order mechanism of the market fails to achieve optimum or equilibrium. This view was in fact held by the now extinct school of systems theorists in political science,[109] but is not today, or so I think, taken very seriously. There are indeed some built-in automatisms in societies, such as the quasi-automatically forthcoming measures when inflation or unemployment rates exceed certain levels, but the process that established these mechanisms was in itself far from automatic. One misses the essence of history if one thinks that the creation of new institutions shares the 'automatic' character of the everyday functioning of these institutions once established. (Cf. also the distinction between routine politics and creative politics discussed in Chapter 3 above.) Far from being automatic, the attempt to reach Pareto-optimality or to restore equilibrium may fail utterly, for reasons to be discussed below.

It is, of course, crucial in this context that the contradictions be *perceived*. If the farmers (in the cobweb cycle) blame the weather for the cyclical price fluctuations, they are not going to do very much except talk about it. I also stressed above that the absence of a public good has a motivating and mobilizing power only if it is a *felt* absence, and that this typically means the absence of something that is present elsewhere. I have likewise mentioned in passing that for the free-rider problem in union formation to be a *problem*, the workers must perceive that joint adoption of the cooperative strategy is Pareto-superior to the lack of organization and that the wage game is not zero-sum. I shall not discuss separately the conditions for the contradictions to be perceived, as I believe these coincide largely with the conditions for organization that are discussed at some length below.[110]

The problem of dynamic suboptimality must be treated separately, as the notion of successive generations coming together for an organized attack on, say, the suboptimal investment level is implausible to say the least. Here the transition to the cooperative behaviour must be made by a single actor (i.e. a single generation) in the hope that the successors will follow suit. The individuals belonging to the crucial generation will have nothing to gain from the switch to cooperation, whereas in the static case all will experience a gain from cooperation. I am not very sure about this problem but I would suggest that two sets of conditions enhance the probability of the switch. In the first place the crucial generation must satisfy the conditions spelled out in propositions 2 and 3 below. In the second place it must be in a position to somehow oblige its successors to follow suit, e.g. by establishing a constitution that cannot easily (or legitimately) be undone by later generations for their benefit. If the welfare of future generations enters into the utility function of the present generation, then a sacrifice for the sake of *all* later generations will presumably be more attractive than a sacrifice for the next generation only. Be this as it may, I believe that the first proposition concerning the *tendency* to cooperate is valid also in the intergenerational case, even if the conditions for this tendency to be realized are more stringent.

We may also observe here that it is not always easy to decide whether we are dealing with a case of counterfinality (or static suboptimality) or a case of dynamic suboptimality. Take erosion: if the effects of deforestation are not felt in the current generation, we are dealing with an intertemporal Prisoner's Dilemma, where the collective short-term interest and the individual short-term interest both require a non-cooperative behaviour, as opposed to the cooperative behaviour required by the collective long-term interest. If, however, the time span of the causal mechanism is shorter than the time horizon of the individuals, the collective and the individual interests will diverge even in the short term. The same point is brought out by Marx's analysis of the English Factory Acts, which he explained as being partly the result of the political activity of the workers and partly as the defence of the capitalist class against its own members,[111] the idea being that overexploitation of the workers might threaten their physical reproduction and thus capitalism itself. The latter explanation either requires the collective interests of the capitalists to overcome their individual interests or their long-term interest to overcome their short-term interest. Both ideas, however, are hard to square with what Marx says elsewhere about the possibility of solidarity between capitalists.[112]

As a last remark on the bearing of the first proposition upon dynamic suboptimality we may note that in cases such as free-trade imperialism the proposition asserts that there is a tendency both for a cartel and for an anti-cartel cartel to be formed. These assertions may be true simultaneously, even if, of course, the tendencies cannot be realized simultaneously (as, however, they should be according to the cybernetic theory). Here the conditions for intergenerational solidarity are not so stringent, as it may ally itself with the short-term individual interests.

(2) *The probability of success in the attempt at organization varies inversely with the communicational distance between the members.*

I think of 'communicational distance' as some function of spatial distance and of transport technology, so that the members of a densely populated society with poorly developed communications may be more isolated from each other than the members of a sparsely populated country with good transport. The rationale behind proposition (2) (and proposition (3)) is the simple observation that trust is necessary to overcome the contradictions, and for people to come to trust each other they must be together for some time. The importance of spatial proximity for group solidarity has often been noted, of course. According to the Federalist Papers, 'The natural limit of a democracy is that distance from the central point which will just permit the most remote citizens to assemble as often as their public functions demand.' In the 18 *Brumaire* Marx explained the lack of class consciousness among the French peasants by their isolated mode of existence. The emergence of class consciousness—the transition from the class in itself to the class for itself—is indeed a special case of the main problem discussed in this section, the transition from individual maximization to group maximization or from non-cooperative to cooperative behaviour. In contrast to the isolation of the peasantry, the physical proximity of the workers to each other in the factory enhances their solidarity; they are 'disciplined, united, organized by the very mechanism of the process of capitalist production itself'.[113] Marx also states that 'The dispersion of the rural labourers over larger areas breaks down their power of resistance while concentration increases that of the town operatives'[114], and in terms very similar to those of proposition (2) he also postulates that 'the power of resistance of the labourers decreases with their dissemination'.[115]

It will be said—and I agree—that these are obvious notions indeed. It is possible, however, to go a step further by observing that class organization, in addition to the goal of overcoming the contradictions of the class itself, also has the purpose of perpetuating the contradictions of the opposed class. This may be done, of course, by simply outlawing working-class associations, as attempted by the English ruling classes through the Combination Acts. It is generally agreed that these acts were of doubtful efficiency, and they may even have helped to bring forth the very associations they tried to forbid.[116] In other situations outlawing unions or killing off working-class leaders may be more efficient, but a simpler and often more intelligent expedient is to repress the exploited class by controlling the structural conditions that are relevant for the success of organization. Resistance to railroads among the ruling classes of the ante-bellum South[117] or of pre-1860 Russia[118] can be explained along these lines, contrary to what is implied in a recent survey article where transportation systems are 'considered facilitating agents for integrating or maintaining society'.[119] If we look at the class structure rather than just at 'society', a transportation system that has an integrating effect upon *all* classes may have a negative net effect upon the ruling classes (the marginal utility of transportation being larger for the classes that before had less access to it) and therefore a destabilizing effect upon society as a whole. At the micro level the spatial layout of factories is sometimes designed so as to minimize the possibilities of prolonged interaction between workers. This is usually justified in the name of productive efficiency, but certainly also has the effect, which may be intended or not, of hampering the development of the workers' class consciousness and combativity.

Two apparent exceptions to proposition (2) permit a further conceptual development. In his important work on *The Yenan Way in Revolutionary China* Marx Selden attempts to refute the hypothesis linking revolution to urbanization (and thus to a highly developed transportation system) by observing that the Chinese Revolution failed utterly in the most developed areas and was ultimately successful in the remote Shensi province with poor internal communications.[120] Selden admits, however, that the revolutionary movement first *emerged* in the more developed areas, and this concession may be sufficient for our purpose. A telling counterexample to proposition (2) would be the demonstration that countries with uniformly poor communications are more favourable to revolutions than countries with at least some developed regions, but this does not seem to be the case. The use of *mean* communicational distance may be too crude for a valid generalization to emerge, just as we shall see that the *mean* duration of group membership is not always the relevant variable in proposition (3). A second problem is provided by Georg Simmel's analysis of the spatial distribution of the Jewish people during the Diaspora.[121] By dispersing throughout the world the Jews ensured the survival of the group because no single persecution could hit them all; at the same time the Jews in any given city assembled in ghettos in order better to defend themselves. The last fact is well in line with my argument, but the first looks like a counterexample. For persecuted minority groups dispersal may be a condition for survival and hence for organization. The exception, however, may only be apparent. For, in the first place, we might apply the same reasoning as in the discussion of the first counterexample and argue that the *decision to disperse* could not itself have emerged in a dispersed community. In the second place it may be that it is precisely the truth of proposition (2) that renders persecution more probable in the case of concentration; by appearing to be weak you may be able to preserve what little strength you have. (This line of counter-argument to the counterexample would fail, however, if concentration of the victims renders the persecution more efficient and not just more probable.)

Proposition (2) implies that a small group is—*ceteris paribus*—more likely to achieve optimum than a larger group. Other things, however, are not likely to be equal, because the gap between the non-cooperative and the cooperative equilibria is smaller for small groups.[122] To the extent that the probability of success is related to strength of motivation and the latter to the potential gain from organization, smaller groups are *less* likely to be successful. It is not easy to say *a priori* what will be the net effect of these opposing tendencies.

(3) *The probability of success in the attempt at organization varies inversely with the rate of turnover in group membership.*

The proposition again relies on the very simple idea that if members of the contradiction-generating group never stay members long enough to come to know and trust each other, it is hardly to be expected that they will be able to overcome the contradiction. I believe that for modern societies this is the main obstacle to successful organization, while spatial isolation was more important in the past. Unsuccessful student rebellions are today's analogy of the unsuccessful peasant rebellions of yesterday. I also believe that the very same causes that have reduced the importance of spatial isolation have also increased the turnover rates, so that the net capacity for collective action may or may not have been enhanced. One can agree, certainly, with Mark Granovetter when he makes a case for the 'strength of weak ties'[123] and argues that collective action will be more easily generated in communities where most people have many friends that do not know each other (and between whom they serve as bridges) than in communities that can be broken down in isolated clusters of people who all know each other quite well. This correlation, however, is presumably subject to a *ceteris paribus* clause that may not always obtain, viz. that the number of *strong* ties should be the same in both cases. Mobility is among the forces that generate weak ties, but also among the dissolvents of strong ties, so that the net effect of mobility may go both ways even in the most favourable of cases, viz. geographical mobility within a fairly small area.

The idea behind proposition (3) is often given casual mention in the literature, but a systematic discussion is hard to come by.[124] A survey of the field points to the need for at least three distinctions. In the first place one should distinguish clearly between the conditions for (say) union *membership* and the conditions for union *formation*. Mancur Olson observes that, 'Compulsory membership cannot... explain the creation of the first, small, local unions, as it can account for the viability of the later, larger, national unions'.[125] Seymour Lipset and Joan Gordon found that there was a positive correlation between mobility and union membership,[126] but this does not mean, of course, that the unions could have been organized in the first place by highly mobile workers. The relation between union membership studies and union formation studies is similar to the relation between partial and equilibrium analyses in economics. The analysis of membership must take the unions as given and explain how individual workers relate to them, just as partial equilibrium analysis takes prices as given and examines how firms and consumers adapt to them. In economics it has long been recognized that there is a need for a more general analysis that also explains price formation, and similarly I would argue that more attention should be given to the general problem of union formation.

In the second place the impact of mobility upon collective action may be studied at many different levels. Correlations may be found at the levels of the *individual*, of the *role*, or of the *group*. The last is our primary concern here, but a few words about the other levels may be in order. The well-known finding that downwardly mobile individuals are typically more conservative than the other members of the group of arrival[127] is formulated at the level of the individual. The corresponding hypothesis on the group level would be that groups having a larger-than-average proportion of downwardly mobile members also would be more-than-average conservative, which would neither imply nor follow from the finding at the individual level. An example of correlations at the role level is Georg Simmel's analysis of elected officials in the US. According to Simmel this institution presents the prima-facie paradox that it was designed to serve the people while actually serving the office holders. When judges, etc. are elected, they tend to consider the office as a piece of private property which they may legitimately exploit for their own purposes. Simmel argues that the paradox disappears when we look at the alternative to elected officials, viz. permanent officials. From the point of view of the people it is better to have an unstable ruling class that can never consolidate its hegemony than a bureaucracy that acquires a professional and stable role structure, even if the spoils system inherent in the former has no analogue in the latter. 'The all-and-out democrat will not be governed, even if this means that he cannot be served either.'[128]

In the third place we should distinguish between 'the sheer experience of mobility'[129] and the direction of that mobility; between the scalar and the vector aspects, so to speak. The very fact of being on the move, socially, geographically, or occupationally, may have an impact that is independent of the question whether mobility is horizontal or vertical, or, if vertical, upwards or downwards. In proposition (3) I am mainly concerned with the scalar aspect of mobility. We shall see that in at least one important case the amount of mobility and the direction of mobility tend to reinforce each other, but this need not always be the case.

The turnover rate as a variable in social analysis is important for time spans of very different orders. If it is correct, as suggested for example by Arrow, that norms for social behaviour such as taboos or customs are 'reactions of society to compensate for market failures',[130] one would expect several generations to be required for these norms to be firmly established. The argument may be generalized to cover class-specific customs such as solidarity, and here the time span becomes a crucial variable. If, for example, a given class is a 'transition class' whose members typically have parents and children in classes different from their own, then it will not acquire cumulative traditions and norms. A pure case of such a transition class is the group of freedmen under Roman law, 'an evanescent status restricted by law to a single generation'.[131] (This example also points to the fact that a transition class may quite well be a permanent feature of the social structure, if there is a constant inflow to the class in question.) A more important case is the middle class of modern capitalism. A famous controversy between Rosa Luxemburg and Eduard Bernstein may be interpreted in the terms of proposition (3). Bernstein showed[132] that the absolute and even the relative numbers of small capitalist firms had no tendency to decline, contrary to what he took to be the opinion of Marx. Luxemburg countered[133] that one could indeed observe the polarization predicted by Marx, but in a sense different from the one imputed to him by Bernstein. Even though the number of small firms was constant, the life span of the individual small firm was becoming steadily shorter, which also implied a more rapid metabolism for the whole class of small producers. New possibilities for small firms were being created by technical progress at an ever faster rate, but the emerging small firms were also absorbed by large-scale capitalist enterprise at an equally fast rate, the net result being a numerically constant, but 'evanescent' class of small producers.

Thus, Marx was right in predicting the diminishing political importance of the middle class: not because of an absolute or relative decline in numerical strength, but because of the steadily more pronounced character of being a transition class with small potential for autonomous organization. This is a temporal analogy to the spatial obstacles to class consciousness among the

French peasantry, and it is not surprising that later Marxists[134] have used the 18 *Brumaire* as a paradigm for the explanation of the rise of fascism, with the middle class in the place of the peasants and high turnover rates in the place of geographical distance. In these interpretations Bonapartism and fascism serve the *interests* of capital, while relying on the popular support of the peasantry and the middle class, respectively. Also both regimes are seen as expressions of the functional necessity for capitalism to have an apparently anti-capitalist government. As mentioned above, the difficulty with this explanation is that it is hard to see how this 'functional need' is transformed into action and actors.

Many examples can also be adduced to show the impact of turnover rates upon collective action within shorter time spans. In the previously cited article on pre-industrial revolts E. P. Thompson argues that the *market* had a privileged place in the genesis of rebellions. 'The market was the place where the people, because they were numerous, felt for a moment they were strong.'[135] *For a moment*: the market is not a place where prolonged interaction can generate the cumulative class consciousness that is required for successful action, and indeed Thompson shows that the bread riots rarely achieved their immediate objectives. We have already questioned his implicit assertion that the riots were perpetuated by their long-term benefits, but this does not mean that such benefits may not have existed. As observed by Thompson the regularity of the bread riots may have acted as a deterrent and kept exploitation at a lower level than would have been the case in the absence of the revolts. We here have an interesting exception to proposition (3). In some cases the nuisance value of a failure may be so great as to confer the same benefits as those achieved by a fully realized organization. The point obviously turns upon an ambiguity in the notion of 'successful' attempts at organization. If by success we mean that the objectives of the movement are achieved, bread riots are an exception to proposition (3), but if we also require that the objectives shall be achieved *in the intended way* the counterexample disappears. In the analysis of power and political possibility in Chapter 3 above, *intentional and intelligent production of desired results* was seen as the key notion, and if this approach is also adopted here the bread riots and similar phenomena (such as the 'successes' of the student movements) do not constitute exceptions to proposition (3).

Another apparent counterexample turns upon an ambiguity in another notion, viz. the idea of 'radicalism' or class consciousness. It has been argued that at least in some cases the most radical segments of the working class are the itinerant workers of the construction industry,[136] which would seem to be incompatible with proposition (3). Here, however, I would like to bring together some Leninist notions and argue that the 'infant malady' of the labour movement is its inability to take 'one step backwards, two step forwards'. Radicalism is defined by the impatient desire to exploit maximally the possibilities of the present moment, at the expense of the optimal creation of new possibilities. A fully class-conscious labour movement should be able to mark time and even to make tactical retreats, whereas the radical segments will always urge for immediate action.[137] No doubt the mode of existence of the itinerant labourers was such that it favoured group solidarity and a capacity for short-term action, such as strikes, but this is not the same thing as a capacity for *organization*. To put the matter in slightly different terms: solidarity between all workers at any given moment does not suffice for the acquisition of durable gains; in addition there must also develop a feeling of solidarity between workers of successive moments. The reader will recall the importance of intertemporal solidarity in the analysis of exploitation above: the radical working-class leaders will in fact be unable to perceive the historical roots of exploitation and will be unable to understand why 'capital' and 'labour' should not be on a par as regards the right to a reward.

It is not true, of course, that an itinerant mode of existence always generates a radical attitude; only the special conditions of the construction workers favour this development. In the typical case, being on the move (geographically) hinders the development of any sort of class consciousness, be it for short-term or long-term gains. In developing countries where factory workers typically are peasants that stay some time in the city before returning to the countryside, union formation is much delayed. A similar 'life-cycle hypothesis' has been advanced for 19th-century Norway, and been linked up with the problem of class consciousness.[138] Stephan Thernstrom has discussed at some length the 'permanent transients' of American society, 'unable to sink roots and to form organizations'.[139] It seems, however, that Thernstrom's discussion takes place at the level of the individual rather than of the group. He is not concerned, as I am here, with identification of the groups having a particularly high proportion of members with short membership duration, but rather with the individuals that rarely stay more than a few months in a given job. For this reason it is hard to understand why the capacity to 'form organizations' should be relevant, unless he means that the proportion of these transients in the whole working-class community was so large that *any* kind of unionization was retarded.

The relative infrequency or lack of success of organization among certain groups of modern societies finds at least a partial explanation in the high turnover rates that characterize them. Recruits, students, the temporarily unemployed,[140] house seekers, consumers, users of public transportation, immigrant workers, tourists, pensioners—all come in this category of groups with numerical constancy (or growth) and evanescent membership. In the words of Thernstrom they are 'disorganized, pulverized, alienated, invisible and impotent'.[141] They look solid enough as groups in the statistics formed on the 'pile-of-snapshots' model of social change, but they evaporate before the eye on the longitudinal 'bunch-of-life histories' model. Take student revolts as a typical example. These are certainly frequent, but rarely gather the momentum that is required for durable results; they do not learn from past mistakes nor accept the necessity in some cases of temporarily marking time. This is not, I think, a question of each student having a time horizon that ends at the date of his final examination. The dynamic suboptimality resulting from political myopia is a cause for organization rather than an obstacle to it. The problem is rather one of the students having insufficient time to acquire experience and develop bonds of solidarity. Three different time spans are involved in such cases: the duration of the individual's group membership, the minimum time required for emergence of solidarity, and the time required for the detrimental effects of non-cooperative behaviour to make themselves felt. If the third exceeds the first, we have a dynamic analogue of the Prisoner's Dilemma, but if the second exceeds the first the difficulty is rather one of how to overcome the static dilemma.

Two additional remarks will be made here concerning the problem of *time*. Firstly, if the individuals in the group have strong preferences for the present, their effective time horizon may be even shorter than the duration of group membership, so that the latter is not really an operative constraint at all. In this case the scope for dynamic suboptimality is, of course, even greater. Secondly a testable version of proposition (3) would have to specify, among other things, how the duration of membership is to be measured. Should we take the mean, the median, or some measure such as the proportion of group members with very short or with very long membership? The choice, say, between mean duration and the proportion of group members with long membership involves important substantial issues. The existence of a hard-core minority of permanent members may do more for solidarity than a larger mean duration with a small dispersion around the mean. The reader will recall a similar point made in the discussion of proposition (2) above, that the existence of some regions with highly developed communications may have greater importance for revolutionary potential than a communicational system that on the average is better—even if more uniformly—developed.

In the preceding pages I have tried to relate collective action to the 'sheer experience of mobility' regardless of direction. As already mentioned, the direction may have an additional impact of its own, that may or may not coincide with the impact of the amount of mobility. The traditional interpretation, that may be the correct one in many cases, has been to assume that working-class upwards mobility (to restrict ourselves to this important special case) has had negative effects upon working-class solidarity, thereby reinforcing the effect of mobility as such. Two distinct mechanisms have been invoked to justify this assumption. In the first place it has been conjectured that the potential organizers of a class are the first to leave it. 'The more a ruling class is able to assimilate the foremost minds of a ruled class, the more stable and dangerous becomes its rule.'[142] In the second place—and this is the more frequently mentioned hypothesis—the possibility of upwards mobility may act as a safety-valve, whose efficiency may be relatively independent of the actual mobility rates, as observed in Chapter 2 above. Here, however, the findings from the *American Soldier*, as explained for example by Boudon, are of relevance, for if mobility aspirations grow more rapidly than actual mobility possibilities, upwards mobility may act so as to increase rather than reduce discontent. I cannot enter here into a discussion of this problem, but only observe that if mobility rates are *very* high it may be presumed that both the net effect and the effect of each separate mechanism will be to reduce the capacity for collective action.

In this connection the possibility of *countermobility*, to use Roger Girod's term,[143] is especially important. If, for example, the upper-class children whose parents had middle-class parents more frequently become middle-class than the upper-class children whose parents come from upper-class homes, and similarly for other transitions, each move away from one's own class would tend to be opposed by a counter-move in the following generation. If this goes on at a large scale, there may be a great deal of apparent mobility—enough to act as a safety-valve—but little durable mobility. In one of the rare studies of social mobility over three generations Ramkrishna Mukherjee concluded that this was indeed the case. His 'analysis suggests that the society contains both a solid core of "stable elements" and, at the same time, a group of "unstable" elements. The latter may perhaps comprise only a small proportion of the total members of society, but they are so unstable as to be involved in reverse shifts in status in successive generations'.[144] This statement would seem to imply that some family lines should be inherently unstable. An alternative explanation of the data might be through the mechanism described by Marx in the text quoted above. If moving to or staying in a class different from 'one's own' (a notion that would have to be made precise) depends upon deviations from average ability and if ability is less than perfectly heritable so that there is a regression towards the mean, countermobility would be the expected result.

Moving now towards some concluding comments upon proposition (3), we should observe that the general processes of increasing factor mobility and technological change have brought more people closer together for shorter periods of time, reducing the relevance of proposition (2) and enhancing that of proposition (3). In traditional societies each person had permanent communicational access to a very small subset of the persons whose behaviour—jointly with his—generated the contradictions in which he was trapped. In modern societies each person has access to all the persons concerned, but the time during which this access is at all relevant is restricted by the short—and increasingly shorter—duration of group membership.

This conceptual framework permits, I think, a theory of the 'objectively capitalist nature of the modern state'. Let us first observe that in most capitalist countries—and certainly in the most advanced ones—there can be no question of a subjective alliance between the state and the interests of capital. Too many state activities are directly opposed to the capitalist interests and directly geared to working-class interests for this conspiratorial explanation to hold water. Neither should one lend credence to the degenerate explanations that make such activities fit into the conspiratorial framework by postulating a long term—very long, if need be—in which the anti-capitalist activities of the state are seen as a functional prerequisite of capitalism. 'Notoriously any argument can be turned to any effect by juggling with the time scale.'[145] Finally, we recall that a functionalist explanation that does not *specify* the causal feedback from the economic effects of state activities to the maintenance of these activities is vacuous and worthless.

The modern state and its officials certainly have a sincere wish to act as neutral brokers between the conflicting groups rather than to further the interests of any particular group. The catch, however, lies in the power to decide which are the groups to be admitted to the negotiations. For the modern government official it is second nature that only organized groups can be admitted, and that their organization is, so to speak, a condition of their being taken seriously at all. Granted, therefore, that the state is approximately neutral when mediating between the organized groups, a bias in the capacity for organization will be reflected in the outcome of the mediation. This is a case of non-decision-making as defined by Peter Bachrach and Morton Baratz: 'When the dominant values, the accepted rules of the game, the existing power relations among groups, and the instruments of force, singly or in combination, effectively prevent certain grievances from developing into full-fledged issues which call for decisions, it can be said that a non-decision-making state exists.'[146]

To the four causes of non-decision-making cited in this passage—values, rules, power, and force—we may add the structural group attributes that form the subject of propositions (2) and (3). These attributes are certainly not uniformly distributed over all contradiction-sharing groups in society, but have a distinct bias that results in owner and manager interests being better organized than worker interests, with a correspondingly greater impact on final decisions. I do not deny that workers in industrialized countries are heavily organized, but usually the horizon of the union stops at the factory gate. Unions are little concerned with workers as perpetrators and victims of congestion and pollution, nor with the conditions of their wives and children. There is, for example, no organization that could push forward the obvious claim that the time of the journey to work should be included in the number of working hours that is subject to collective bargaining. Car producers are better organized than automobile workers, workers better than car owners, owners better than car victims, victims better than the potential victims. From the fact that capitalist class interests are over-represented in most mediations, it follows that the neutrality of the state between the various claims set forward, or even a slight bias in the favour of the workers (as in countries with social-democrat governments), will produce a set of final outcomes that is also skewed in the direction of capitalist interests.

The preceding paragraph made a case for 'the objectively capitalist nature of the modern state'. I think it is possible to go a step further, and argue that the skewed representation is maintained by its own effects. Not only is the set of final outcomes biased to the capitalist side, but this bias also tends to regenerate its own causes. This feedback loop follows from the fact that a high degree of factor mobility is a very important part of the interests of the capitalist class, so that the final decisions will tend to perpetuate and accelerate the high turnover rates that were responsible for the decision bias in the first place. The seeming innocence of the state turns out to be, on this analysis, part of a vicious circle where skewed representation and impartial brokership generate an even more skewed representation.

(4) *The probability of success in the attempt at organization varies inversely with the irreversibility of the contradictions.*

This simply means that when the actors finally agree upon a cooperative strategy, it may already be too late. In addition to the various time spans discussed above, we here introduce the time that can be allowed to pass before the situation has irreversibly deteriorated. There comes a time when the population size of a threatened species falls below the minimum required for sustained reproduction, and if this occurs before group solidarity has developed, no amount of later cooperation can re-create the extinct species. In other cases the irreversibility is slightly less radical. Deserts can be made to flower, even if at enormous cost; the life of destroyed lakes may be restored. For thousands of years such irreversible counterfinality has been perhaps the main factor in social change. The history of China or of the Mediterranean countries shows that erosion and deforestation are second to none as agents of change. These are cases of irreversible degradation, but irreversible accumulation is equally important. *Knowledge*, once obtained, cannot be erased—with some unimportant exceptions. This also goes for technological knowledge, which explains why Marx—in contrast to Keynes—did not think capitalism would be able to overcome the contradictions of the system. The main contradiction that Marx saw in the capitalist mode of production—the fall in the rate of profit— was linked to technical progress in such a manner as to make it virtually irreversible. The Keynesian theory of demand crises has no implication of irreversibility, and indeed the crises can be reversed by suitable government intervention; the multiplier works both ways. I add without argument that in my opinion the word 'materialist' in the phrase 'the materialist conception of history' can be given a precise meaning only through this notion of irreversibility, with the twin aspects of irreversible degradation and irreversible accumulation.

I do not claim, of course, that propositions 2–4 exhaust the set of variables that may explain the success or failure of attempts at organization. Among the factors discussed by other authors the following may be given brief mention. Granovetter stresses the sociometric structure of the group in question, with special emphasis upon the weak ties that serve to bring two members together through a third member ('bridges').[147] North and Davis mention, among other things, the potential gain from organization and the degree of uncertainty associated with the outcome. They also discuss a problem that was briefly touched upon in Chapter 3 above, viz. that the probability of successful collective action is greater 'the more equal is the distribution of potential profits among [the] group'.[148] They could have added that this problem is especially acute if the cooperative game in question is solved along the lines known as the 'Nash solution',[149] where the greatest benefits from organization accrue to those members who were best off in the first place. In the discussion above I have deliberately abstracted from this problem, and assumed that all members of the contradiction-generating group stand to gain the same amount if the contradictions are overcome. Kenneth Arrow has emphasized the information structure of the group as an important variable in organization, observing that 'The concept of class interest and identification may be related to ease of communication among individuals with similar life experiences'.[150]

When I have singled out spatial distance, turnover rates, and irreversibility as crucial variables, I have done so because these all involve *time* in a manner that I believe to be essential. (That spatial distance has implications for time is obvious from the fact that the time required for a given group to develop trust and solidarity will depend very much upon the communicational distance between its members.) For contradictions to be overcome, a number of distinct processes must be synchronized. The time required for emergence of class or group solidarity must not exceed the duration of group membership nor the length of time beyond which the contradictions are irreversible. Making temporal considerations central to the analysis also permits a new and immediately *causal* interpretation of that often-quoted saying, 'Plus ça change, plus c'est la même chose.' The more rapid the change *within* the structure, the less probable is a change *of* the structure. It is a commonplace to observe that the idea of a structure maintaining itself through a flux of matter is basic to much of modern scientific thinking. The notion of the *steady state*—so different in its implications from the notion of equilibrium—pervades chemistry, biology, and indeed much of the social sciences. We tend to think, however, that the structure maintains itself *in spite of* the constantly changing elements that make it up. In the perspective I suggest it is rather the other way around, that a rapid metabolism is a condition for the maintenance of the system.

The last remarks of the preceding paragraphs were intended to apply to *suboptimal* systems only. At this point the reader should recall that we are dealing here with a *dual* theory of social change. To the extent that the phenomena discussed in propositions 2–4 prevent the overcoming of *counterfinality*, we should rather reverse the argument and say that too much change *within* the structure prevents the actors from preventing a change *of* the structure. Depending upon the kind of contradiction involved, the structural conditions for political organization may function both as obstacles to change and as agents of change.

APPENDIX 1 TO CHAPTER 5

Some notions and problems in game theory

This appendix has two purposes, one elementary and the other more advanced. In the first place it offers to the reader unacquainted with game theory the basic notions required for understanding of the above sections on suboptimality and counterfinality. In the second place it points to a gap in the reasoning of the last section, and sketches some ways in which it may be closed. The gap, roughly, has to do with the precise mechanism of the transition from non-cooperative to cooperative behaviour. The theory embedded in propositions (2)–(4) of the last section is in a sense a 'black-box theory', because it only states that given certain conditions the initial state of non-cooperation tends to be transformed into a final state of cooperation, leaving unspecified the psychological details of that transformation. I do not pretend to be able to resolve this problem, but the reader may want to know about some of the solutions and discussions found in the literature.

A *game*[151] includes a number of *actors*, each having the choice between a certain number of *strategies*. For each combination of strategies—one strategy for each actor—the rules of the game define a *payoff* to each actor. Thus, in the general case the payoff to *each* is determined by the choice of *all*. The actors can choose their strategies *cooperatively* or *non-cooperatively*. Which strategies they actually choose will also depend upon their *information*—information about their own payoffs, about the other players' payoffs and about the other players' information. Under certain conditions the game will have a *solution*, by which we mean either a unique and predictable set of strategies that will be chosen by the players, or a unique and predictable set of outcomes (i.e. payoffs to the players). These are the bare bones of game theory; I now proceed to some filling-in.

For simplicity we shall assume that there are two actors only. This may seem a rather drastic assumption in a discussion of the usefulness of game theory for the *social* sciences, but actually it is less serious than it appears. For, in the first place, many of the two-person games discussed in greater detail below generalize easily to the *n*-person case.[152] Also, in the second place, many two-person games can be usefully interpreted as a game between myself and 'all others'. Nevertheless the reader should know that the limitation to two-person games excludes what is potentially, perhaps, the part of game theory with the greatest relevance for the social sciences, viz. the *theory of coalitions* in *n*-person coopera-tive games. In economics this theory already plays an enormously fruitful role, and later on I believe that it will almost certainly find profound applications in sociology. At present, however, the state of the art seems to justify this exclu-sion. We also assume, less drastically, that each actor has the choice between a finite number (most often two) strategies only. Finally, I shall mainly be con-cerned with variable-sum games, to the exclusion of zero-sum games. The latter are defined by the feature that the sum of the payoffs to all players is constant (and by redefinition of the game this constant may always be taken to be zero), whereas in the former the sum of the payoffs depends upon the strategies actually chosen. Zero-sum games are games of pure conflict, whereas the games that are of relevance here are games featuring both conflict and cooperation.

The notion of a *choice of strategy* can be made quite complex. The simplest case is when each player individually chooses a uniquely predictable strategy among his 'pure strategies', i.e. in the given set (here assumed to be finite) of strategies. A more difficult notion is when each actor chooses individually, but at random, according to a certain probability distribution over the set of

152

pure strategies. This distribution is then called a *mixed strategy*. If a game has a solution in mixed strategies, this means that the probability distributions that govern the choice of pure strategies are uniquely predictable, even if the pure strategies themselves are not. Before I spell out an example of a game that has no solution in pure strategies, but does have a solution when mixed strategies are admitted, some notation must be introduced. I shall suppose that we are dealing with players Row and Column, who have the choice between strategies r_i and c_i, respectively. In matrix form each cell represents a combination of strategies, the first number in a given cell representing the payoff to Row and the second the payoff to Column. With these conventions it is easily seen that the following (zero-sum) game requires mixed strategies for its solution:

$$\begin{array}{ccc} & c_1 & c_2 \\ r_1 & 3,-3 & 1,-1 \\ r_2 & 2,-2 & 4,-4 \end{array}$$

In addition to the extension from pure to mixed strategies we now introduce the extension from individual to joint choice of strategies. Especially important is the notion of *jointly mixed strategies*. If, for example, Row and Column have the choice between (r_1, r_2) and (c_1, c_2) respectively, they may agree upon the jointly mixed strategy of choosing (r_1, c_1) with probability $\frac{1}{2}$ and (r_2, c_2) with probability $\frac{1}{2}$. This, for example, might be a useful procedure if both (r_1, c_2) and (r_2, c_1) have disastrous consequences, as illustrated in an example below. If both actors chose according to individual mixed strategies, it would not be possible to steer clear of these two outcomes while retaining the first two. The use of jointly mixed strategies is a crucial feature of cooperative games.

Another important and complex notion of game theory is that of the *solution* to a game. Restricting ourselves to the non-cooperative case, this notion is defined as follows. First we define the notion of an *equilibrium point*: it is a pair of (pure or mixed) strategies (r_i, c_j) such that r_i is Row's best answer to c_j, and c_j is Columns best answer to r_i. If a game has exactly one equilibrium point, this is the solution of the game. If there is no equilibrium point, the game does not have a solution. (Cf. the discussion in the last section above of hyperinflation as a possible example of a game without an equilibrium point.) If there are several equilibrium points, the game has a solution if and only if all equilibrium points that are not dominated by another equilibrium point are interchangeable and equivalent. This statement presupposes the following notions. That two equilibrium points are *equivalent* means that they give the same payoffs to all actors. That equilibria (r_i, c_j) and (r_m, c_n) are *interchangeable* means that (r_i, c_n) and (r_m, c_j) are also equilibrium points. That (r_i, c_j) *dominates* (r_m, c_n) means that the first is Pareto-superior to the second, so that both actors get at least as much in the first case and one of them strictly more. In some numerical examples below I explore the implications of this definition of the solution-concept.

Suffice it to say here that it tries to capture the notion of what rational actors with perfect information would do in a non-cooperative game.[153]

The five games below will serve to bring out some of the problems that can arise in variable-sum games:

Prisoner's Dilemma

	c_1	c_2
r_1	5,5	$-10, 10$
r_2	$10, -10$	0, 0

Assurance Game

	c_1	c_2
r_1	10, 10	$-10,5$
r_2	$5, -10$	0, 0

Battle of the Sexes

	c_1	c_2
r_1	2, 1	$-1, -1$
r_2	$-1, -1$	1, 2

Chicken (I)

	c_1	c_2
r_1	1, 1	$-2, 2$
r_2	$2, -2$	$-5, -5$

Chicken (II)

	c_1	c_2
r_1	1, 1	$-2, 6$
r_2	$6, -2$	$-5, -5$

These games have all been extensively studied in the literature.[154] The best known is certainly the Prisoner's Dilemma, which is at the root of a variety of important social situations, as observed above. The solution is (r_2, c_2) — it is the only equilibrium point — which is clearly suboptimal. We should observe here that both Row and Column have their second strategies as *dominant strategies*. For Row r_2 is the best regardless of what Column does, and similarly c_2 is best both against r_1 and r_2. The other games all have several equilibrium points, and do not have dominant strategies for any players. The Assurance

Game has the equlibria (r_1, c_1) and (r_2, c_2), of which the first must be the solution since it dominates the second. (Please note the difference between a dominant strategy and a set of strategies that dominates another set.) The Assurance Game may also generate suboptimality, viz. if the actors lack the information that is required for them to converge upon the solution. If, in the Assurance Game, each player knows his own payoffs only, but suspects that the payoff structure of the other player is that of the Prisoner's Dilemma, or that the other player suspects *his* structure to be that of the Prisoner's Dilemma, each will expect the other to choose his second strategy and will therefore have to choose his second strategy himself. Thus, suboptimality may result from lack of information (as in the Assurance Game) or be deeply rooted in the non-cooperative mode of choice itself (as in the Prisoner's Dilemma).

The Battle of the Sexes and Chicken are games without a solution, even when mixed strategies are admitted. They have several equilibria: (r_1, c_1) and (r_2, c_2) in the Battle of the Sexes; (r_1, c_2) and (r_2, c_1) in the game of Chicken. These equilibria are all undominated, non-equivalent, and non-interchangeable.[155] What *will* happen in the Battle of the Sexes or in the game of Chicken is a matter of psychology rather than of rational choice, unless we are prepared to make yet another extension of our framework. The introduction of the notion of mixed strategies was motivated by the existence of games without a solution in pure strategies, and similarly the existence of non-cooperative games without a solution in mixed strategies can motivate the introduction of cooperative solutions to the game. There are a number of solution concepts for two-person cooperative games, but space does not permit details. Instead I shall concentrate upon the Battle of the Sexes and the two versions of Chicken in order to get across what I believe to be the essential ideas. In Chicken (I) it is intuitively clear that two cooperating players will agree upon the strategy pair (r_1, c_1). In Chicken (II), however, the gain obtained by unilateral use of the second strategy is so great that a different cooperative solution will be sought, viz. the jointly mixed strategy where the players toss a coin between (r_1, c_2) and (r_2, c_1), giving an expected payoff of 2 to each player. (The difference between Chicken (I) and Chicken (II) also shows, incidentally, that if we measure payoffs in ordinal units only, as it is sometimes proposed that we do, the 'natural' cooperative solution may be undetermined.[156]) In the Battle of the Sexes the cooperative solution is also a jointly mixed strategy, with the chances equally divided between the two equilibria.

The preceding remarks conclude the elementary part of this appendix and permits a transition to more complex (or at any rate less standard) material. The problem, as already mentioned, is how to analyse the passage from non-cooperative to cooperative behaviour. Let us start out by observing that this question may be interpreted in two distinct ways. Firstly, we may ask under what conditions we shall observe a shift from the non-cooperative to the cooperative *strategy* in, say, the Prisoner's Dilemma. Secondly we may ask under which conditions we shall see a shift from the non-cooperative to the cooperative *mode of decision* in, say, the Battle of the Sexes. As we shall see below, the first of these questions harbours further ambiguities, but still I shall argue that the subquestions that emerge permit fairly definite answers. The second question, however, seems more intractable, and I shall not have much to say about it.

In the Prisoner's Dilemma it is standard practice to refer to the strategies r_1 and c_1 as *cooperative* or *altruistic*, and the strategies r_2 and c_2 as *non-cooperative* or *egoistic*. The switch from altruism to egoism has been analysed along three distinct lines. In the first place we may adopt the causal rather than the intentional image of man (cf. Appendix 2 below) and discuss the conditions under which we may expect to find deviations from rational behaviour. Much of the work done by social psychologists on the Prisoner's Dilemma fall under this heading. One should especially mention here the empirical and theoretical work associated with the name of Anatol Rapoport.[157] For a typical specimen of this approach, we may cite the application of the Asch–Cohen model to sequences of Prisoner's Dilemmas.[158] Here it is assumed that each of the two players who are involved in the successive games will always be in one of the following states:

s_1: if the player is in this state, he will subsequently use the cooperative strategy in all games;

s_2: if the player is in this state, he will use the cooperative strategy in the next game, but may use the non-cooperative strategy in subsequent games;

s_3: if the player is in this state, he will use the non-cooperative strategy in the next game, but may use the cooperative strategy in subsequent games;

s_4: if the player is in this state, he will subsequently use the non-cooperative strategy in all games.

In addition, we assume that the process of transition is a Markov chain. From these assumptions we may deduce various conclusions concerning the expected behaviour of the players, and these may be checked against empirical evidence. The characteristic feature of this approach clearly is that the players are not seen as rational actors, but as the vehicles of causal processes; as the bearers of 'states' rather than of 'intentions'. It is difficult to say whether the many interesting results obtained by this and similar approaches carry over to real-life, many-person cases, and at any rate I shall not have more to say about them here.

In the second place we may postulate that repeated playing of the game leads to a change in the preference structure, so as to make the altruist behaviour the rational one. This simply means that after repeated playing the game no longer *is* a Prisoner's Dilemma, but has been transformed into another game, such as the Assurance Game. If we content ourselves with observing the behaviour of the actors, it may look as if they choose the cooperative strategy in a Prisoner's Dilemma, but there may be things going on inside their skulls that make a difference to the situation. More specifically, we may assume that as the actors come to know each other and gain affection for each other, they

(i) draw some positive utility from the welfare of others, (ii) draw some negative utility from their own use of the egoist strategy ('bad conscience'), and (iii) come to draw some positive utility from income equality as such. If the material payoff structure (as measured, say, in money) is a Prisoner's Dilemma, the real preference structure may be quite different if it reflects one or several of these mechanisms. The real preference structure may be such as to make cooperation into a dominant strategy or, more realistically perhaps, as to make cooperation a solution without being a dominant strategy (as it is in the Assurance Game). Presumably it is the very same conditions—explored in propositions (2) and (3) in the last section above—that transform the game from a Prisoner's Dilemma *and* that make the actors capable of realizing a solution that does not consist of dominant strategies. Affection for others and information about them grow *pari passu*, or approximately so.

The approach spelled out in the last paragraph has at any rate the virtue of simplicity, even if it will be said that it solves the dilemma in a rather trivial way. A more ambitious approach would be to argue that it may be rational to use the cooperative strategy even if the game is a Prisoner's Dilemma in the strict sense. The first line of argument sketched above resolved the dilemma by renouncing rationality, the second by changing the game; we now come to the third approach that refuses to take any of these easy ways out. This approach exists in two main variants, the 'metagame' theory proposed by Nigel Howard[159] and the 'supergame theory' set forward by Martin Shubik and Michael Taylor.[160] As I do not think many students of the field would now accept that the metagame theory really has any resolving power, I shall only offer some brief comments upon the much more promising supergame approach. Once again sequential Prisoner's Dilemma is at the heart of the matter. It is well known that in a sequence of such games the non-cooperative behaviour will be chosen in each game if (i) all games count equally (no time discounting of the future), and (ii) the number of games is fixed in advance and known by the players.[161] Conversely the cooperative behaviour may be the rational choice if either (i) there is a preference for the present, (ii) the number of games is fixed in advance but unknown to the players, or (iii) the number of games is determined by a stochastic process.[162] Of these possibilities the first is at the heart of the Shubik–Taylor approach. Michael Taylor, in particular, has shown how certain conditions will make *conditionally cooperative strategies* emerge as the solution to a sequential Prisoner's Dilemma.

I must refer the reader to the original for details of Taylor's approach. Here I shall only stress the crucial fact that these conditionally cooperative strategies are not dominant strategies, which means that the probability of their being realized in real-life games is rather doubtful. Taylor himself is very much aware of this point: the

> requirement of a high degree of awareness on the part of the conditional cooperators is itself 'more likely' to be met in a small group of players than in a large group—and even more likely in the sort of small community

in which people have contact with and can observe the behaviour of many of their fellows and which is fairly static, in the sense that there is little mobility in and out.[163]

This, while very much in agreement with the reasoning behind propositions (2) and (3) in the last section above, is perhaps subject to the objection that the kind of group favouring the solution—a small community with little mobility—is also the kind of group favouring abolition of the game to which it is the solution. By interacting closely people may change their preferences so as to make irrelevant the fact that interaction also permits a solution to the dilemma created by the old preferences.

I believe that the choice between the three approaches to the 'transition problem' discussed in the preceding paragraphs is a research problem that is amenable to analysis in a fairly straightforward way. Hard work will certainly be required to determine which approach is best suited to which cases, but there does not seem to be any inherent conceptual obstacles to the analysis. Such obstacles, on the other hand, present themselves as soon as we formulate the problem of a transition from the non-cooperative to the cooperative decision. J. F. Nash[164] has suggested that the decision to cooperate should itself be seen as a move in a larger non-cooperative game, because the latter is somehow more fundamental. I believe that this view is indeed sound, and follows from the principle of methodological individualism, but I also agree with the critics who point out that it lacks persuasive power so long as it has not been spelled out in detail.[165] A typical problem is the confusion over the two aspects of Nash's own solution to the bargaining problem. The most well-known part of this solution tells us how to find the cooperative solution *given the no-trade or* status quo *payoffs*. If we know, that is, the payoffs that would accrue to the players if they did not engage in any bargaining at all, then we can argue that the cooperation solution is uniquely determined. The solution, however, also has another aspect, viz. the determination of the no-trade point itself. By the use of threats, each player will strive to obtain a no-trade point that makes the cooperative solution come out as favourable to himself as possible. Conceptually it seems very hard to understand whether the non-cooperative game (using the threats as strategies) or the cooperative game (using jointly mixed strategies) is the more basic one. Until further clarification of these and related issues, one should probably be rather cautious in the use of cooperative game theory for empirical purposes.

APPENDIX 2 TO CHAPTER 5

Causality and intentionality: three models of man

In this appendix I try to bring together some standards from Chapters 4 and 5, exploring the relation between contradictions, intentionality, causality, strategic thinking, and freedom. The basic postulate from which I start is that *the goal of the social sciences is the liberation of man*. They should permit him to free himself from the causal forces that both form and pervert his intentions; enable him to realize unobstructedly his freely chosen goals. Now this is a tall order indeed, and one of the conclusions of the analysis will be that it cannot be filled. Nevertheless I believe that such is the regulative idea that should always guide the social scientist.

As I see it, there are four main obstacles to the realization of this idea. In the first place man sometimes sets himself inconsistent or contradictory goals, as discussed in Chapter 4. In the second place the individual is traversed by causal processes that escape him and which he does not understand. The endogenous change of preferences discussed in Chapters 2 and 4 belongs to this problem. In the third place a group of persons each of whom has consistent preferences and freely chosen goals, may nevertheless be unable to get their way because of the problem of counterfinality. In the fourth place we have seen that the transition to the strategic mode of thought does not ensure the ability to realize one's goal, because the ensuing game may be a game without a solution. It is tempting to add suboptimal solutions as a fifth obstacle, but this would bring in a *substantive* problem that goes beyond the strictly *formal* problems inherent in the first four obstacles. Both at the collective and at the individual level freedom may be used to bad as well as to good purposes; just as suicide can presumably be an act that fulfils all the formal requirements of a free action, so can the choice of the non-cooperative strategy in the Prisoner's Dilemma.

Thus I submit that the obstacles to freedom can be summed up as mental contradictions, subintentional causality, social contradictions (= supraintentional causality) and games without solutions. For the present purposes, however, this can be simplified so that only two classes of obstacles remain. The contradictions of the mind can be subsumed under the heading of subintentional causality, because in such cases there must be some causal mechanism that determines which of the contradictory desires will get the upper hand in a given situation. Also I think that games without a solution are covered by the notion of supraintentional causality, because in such games the outcome will be determined by the (unpredictable) causal interaction between the actions generated by a-rational assumptions about the behaviour of others.

Thus we are left with the classical problem of causality versus intentionality in the analysis of human actions, or of explanation versus understanding. I shall not deal with the thorny philosophical questions of this discussion, except to make the following observations. In the first place I am arguing for a trichotomy rather than for a dichotomy: instead of the simple distinction between intentionality and causality, I propose to split the latter into subintentional and supraintentional causality. (A similar distinction is useful in biology, where exceptions to the statement 'Everything has a function' may be found both at the subfunctional and at the suprafunctional level.[166]) In the second place I believe that intentional accounts of human actions cannot be reduced to causal accounts, neither in the sense of a reduction to the neurophysiological language of proximate causes[167] nor in the sense of a reduction to the evolutionary language of ultimate causes.[168] In the third place I believe that the preceding statement is fully compatible with two statements that prima facie seem to contradict it: that some forms of human behaviour are amenable only to causal analysis and not to intentional understanding, and that all forms of human behaviour can in principle be explained along purely causal lines. As mentioned in Chapter 1 above, the conclusion from materialism and determinism to reductionism is a fallacy similar to the conclusion from 'Everything has a cause' to 'There is something which is the cause of everything'.

Implicit in what has been said above is that in various contexts one of three distinct models of man will be appropriate. I shall call them the causal, the purposive–parametric, and the purposive–strategic images of man. The purposive–strategic man is the actor of game theory who knows that his environment is composed of other strategic actors and that he is part of their environment. He will be able, therefore, to realize his goals without any danger of counterfinality. *Strategic action is the incarnation of collective freedom*, the fully transparent rationality that incorporates into itself the expectations of other rational actors in order to converge upon some predictable course of action. Purposive–parametric behaviour, by contrast, stems from a more opaque state of mind. The purposive–parametric actor assumes that he is free to adjust optimally in a constant or parametric environment. This assumption is in itself quite consistent, as we have seen, but if entertained simultaneously by all actors it generates counterfinality and is to that extent an obstacle to freedom. It seems to me quite clear that the social sciences can go a long way towards bringing about a transition from a society of purposive–parametric actors to one composed of purposive–strategic actors. I repeat that this collective freedom does not guarantee collective rationality, in the sense of realizing Pareto-optimal situations; the Prisoner's Dilemma exhibits the possibility of freely chosen self-destruction. Nevertheless, I do not think that the transition to strategic thinking can ever make the situation worse than it was before, and in many cases—such as in the Assurance Game—the transition may be sufficient for the collectively rational behaviour to emerge.

The problem of subintentional causality is a darker one. For the present purposes it may be split into several subproblems, that all have negative implications for the problem of freedom. These are the problems of contradictory goals, the problem of non-goal-directed behaviour, and the problem of goal-formation. Enough has already been said about the first to permit brevity here. In this case, the difficulty is that we have *too many intentions*. Even if the social sciences, psychology, and various forms of therapy in particular, can presumably be of help in resolving the mental knots examined in Chapter 4, the existence of several inconsistent intentions makes it hard to say exactly *who* is being helped. Should the paternalistic slave-owner be liberated from the sadistic one, or vice versa? And can such a person liberate 'himself'? There seems to be a conceptual difficulty here that eludes me for the moment.

In the second problem, the difficulty is rather that we have no intentions at all. I believe that some examples are needed at this point in order to get across how action can be non-goal-directed. Actually there are two distinct ways in which the reality of intentional choice between alternatives can be denied. To explain the distinction we must first observe that any realized action can be seen as the result of two successive filtering processes. In the first place there are the objective constraints that narrow down the set of abstractly possible courses of action to a small subset, *the feasible set*. In the second place we must postulate some mechanism to explain why one action rather than another is realized from the feasible set. In rational-choice theory this mechanism is, of course, the maximization of some objective function. From this two-step model it at once follows that the reality of rational choice can be denied *either* by postulating that the set of constraints effectively define a feasible set with only one member, or more realistically a set that is so small that it is hardly possible to distinguish its members from each other; *or* by arguing that the realization of one action rather than another in the feasible set is not made through a rational choice. I believe that some of the writings of the French structuralist school can be interpreted along the lines of the first possibility, as can also some of Marx's arguments concerning fixed coefficients of production and of consumption.[169] I shall not dwell upon this, however, as my main interest for the present purpose is in the second possibility. Gary Becker[170] has distinguished between two sub-cases here: irrational behaviour may either mean that the realization of one member from the feasible set is governed by *tradition* or that it happens more or less at *random*. Let us look at these two cases in turn.

Even if, as implied by the above remarks, there are several alternatives to the rational-choice model, the alternative most frequently cited is probably the norm-oriented model. According to the rational-choice approach the realized action will typically change if there is a change in the constraints that define the feasible set, whereas the norm-oriented model denies that this is the case. As observed by Becker, there is a serious inconsistency here, for if the constraints change so as to make the old course of action lie outside the new feasible set, there *must* be some change in observed behaviour. Occupation cannot be inherited from father to son if technical progress makes the father's occupation obsolete; consumption habits must change if the old consumption point lies above the new budget line. In addition to this conceptual problem, there are many pertinent empirical objections that can be made to the pure norm-oriented model. A good example here is the discussion of the 'economics of crime'. William Cobb and Gordon Tullock,[171] among others, have distinguished between two hypotheses that purport to explain why some people become criminals: the 'economic' hypothesis that assumes maximization of expected utility and the 'sociological' hypothesis (also called the 'sickness' hypothesis) that link criminal activities to subculture-specific norms that more or less inexorably force some individuals into crime. The first explanation is intentional, relating an action to its expected consequences in the future; the second is causal, linking the action to conditions in the past.

An empirical consequence of the sociological hypothesis is that the choice of a criminal career should not be significantly affected by changes in the probability of conviction or the severity of punishment. Several studies have found this to be false; according to Tullock[172] many of the sociologists that started out to prove the hypothesis that punishment does not deter crime ended up by finding that it does have a deterrent effect. In addition to this empirical objection against the sociological hypothesis and the conceptual argument cited in the last paragraph, there is also the following theoretical point that tells against it. One should certainly accept the contention that norms are subculture-specific, but this does not mean that they *directly* determine courses of actions. Rather the link is an indirect one: norms determine preferences, preferences + the feasible set determine actions. Here we touch upon the problem of preference formation, to which I return below. I would like to point out, however, that between the pure rational-choice model and the pure norm-oriented model there may be some intermediate schemes. To the extent that adjustment to changes in the reward system is not instantaneous, the lag may be due to some psychic inertia that is a purely causal phenomenon. I know that in some settings inertia may be a rational strategy, and that in other settings it may (perhaps) be explained by invoking the 'psychic costs' of adjustment. I would deny, however, that *all* cases of apparently irrational behaviour can be explained as governed by some higher-order rationality.[173]

Turning now to Becker's second subcase, it would seem at a first glance that all probabilistic models of individual actions must rely on the causal rather than the intentional image of man. The models of social mobility, for example, seem to assume that man is but a vehicle for transition probabilities; rather than being *attracted* by some occupation he is *pushed* towards it with a probability that depends upon his occupational background. Recently, however, there have been several attempt to get intentionality and rationality into mobility models.[174] Of these the most promising one seems to be that of Raymond Boudon. The reader will recall from the discussion earlier on of Boudon's work that his way of reconciling intentionality and probability was through the notion of a mixed strategy. From the two-step approach to action sketched above it follows that there could also be another way of reconciling the two, viz. by placing the probabilistic element at the level of the feasible set rather than at the level of the choice itself. That is, if we are going to predict the choice of a rational actor who will have to choose within a feasible set subject to variation according to some probability distribution, then the prediction must also be a probabilistic one. (In principle, of course, probability might enter at both levels simultaneously.) Nevertheless, I would not want to argue that *all* probabilistic explanations of action can be transformed into intentional explanations through one of these mechanisms. There certainly are causal processes at work in the mind that take on a stochastic character at the level of observed behaviour; the Asch–Cohen–Rapoport model for the Prisoner's Dilemma cited in Appendix 1 above is but one of of the many examples of such processes in experimental psychology. Still I want to repeat that the social scientist should study such processes for the purpose of liberation rather than manipulation.

I conclude this appendix with some remarks upon the third of the subproblems inherent in subintentional causality, the question of preference formation and endogenous preference change. At this point the notion of *freedom* requires a less cursory discussion than has been forthcoming above. I believe that the idea behind the Kantian idea of freedom is that man should somehow be able to *choose himself*; to be free not only in the weak sense of acting according to consistent preferences, of whichever level, but also in the stronger sense of having chosen these preferences. This is analogous to the problem raised by Sidney Winter in his profound discussions of profit maximization. His contribution can be seen as the fourth and decisive step in a series of attempts to understand what business rationality really means. The first attempt was the standard model of profit maximization, assuming costless information and no transaction costs. The second was Herbert Simon's model of 'satisfaction' that argued that in actual practice businessmen search for a satisfactory level of profits rather than for the maximal one.[175] The third step was a retort by the 'maximization school' that satisfaction emerges as a variety of maximization once the costs of acquiring and evaluating information are taken into account.[176] Winter then, in a surprisingly ignored paper, argued that this retort creates an infinite regress, for how do you solve the problem of finding the optimal amount of information? The 'choice of a profit maximizing information structure itself requires information, and it is not apparent how the aspiring profit maximizer acquires this information, or what guarantees that he does not pay an excessive price for it'.[177] In a later paper Winter returns to the problem in these terms: a true maximization would be an 'optimization whose scope covers all considerations including its own costs'.[178]

The problem of freedom is analogous to the problem of profit maximization. In the first place the same information paradox arises. Aristotle said that you can be held responsible for your ignorance,[179] but how can you know how much you should know? In the second place, and this is the deeper problem, the fact that you choose according to your preferences does not mean that you choose your preferences. If there could exist some *fixed-point preferences* that could, so to speak, justify themselves, this might solve the problem. But, firstly, until the possibility of such preferences has been exhibited in detail I do not know whether the notion is at all meaningful; and, secondly, there might be several fixed points the choice between which would be hard to explain rationally. (This problem partly corresponds to some well-known difficulties in the Cartesian notion of God's choice of one world among the many possible worlds.[180]) Pending a solution to these problems, I think, therefore, that the problem of preference formation and the endogenous preference change is the greatest obstacle to complete freedom. Still there can be a never-ending process of liberation, for at any given level of, say, endogenous preference change, it is always possible to move one level up and exploit the psychic causality for your own strategic purposes at this higher level. Every such process must ultimately come to a halt at some level, and in this sense freedom is impossible;

but there is no level at which every process must come to a halt, and in this sense freedom as a regulative idea is a meaningful notion indeed.

Notes

1. Robinson (1956, p. 78); see also Keynes (1971, p. 143–145). Because part of my intention is to link up the analysis of contradictions with the work of Hegel and Marx, I shall give a long quote from Marx to show that he was very much aware of this problem, even if he did not see it as the essential paradox of capitalism: 'no economist will deny that if workers *generally*, that is as *workers* (what the individual worker does or can do, as distinct from his genus, can only exist as *exception*, not as *rule*, because it is not inherent in the character of the relation itself), that is, if they acted according to [the demand to save] as a *rule* (apart from the damage they would to general consumption—the loss would be enormous—and hence also to production, thus also to the volume of the exchange which they could do with capital, hence to themselves as workers), then the workers would be employing means which absolutely contradict their purpose. . . . Each capitalist does demand that his own workers should save, but only *his own*, because they stand towards him as workers; but by no means the remaining *world of workers*, for these stand towards him as consumers' (Marx, 1857–58, pp. 285, 287). The reason why Marx imputes to the individual capitalist a wish that his workers should save is that this would permit him to lower wages during a recession.
2. Lazarsfeld and Menzel (1969, p. 507).
3. Lazarsfeld and Menzel (1969, p. 507).
4. Exceptions are Vendler (1967) and Geach (1972, pp. 1–12). The fallacy is not touched upon in the surveys by Hamblin (1970) and Mackie (1967).
5. Ullman-Margalit (1976); cf. also Sobel (1967) for some of the same points, even if less clearly stated.
6. For this argument see Singer (1963), Lyons (1965), and Sobel (1967).
7. P. and T. Ehrenfest (1959, p. 4).
8. Geach (1972, p. 1).
9. See Guilbaud (1952) for a brilliant analysis of the Quetelet–Cournot controversy over this notion. Briefly the idea is that it may be physically impossible for any single individual to have the average value on *all* variables simultaneously. If, for example, there are increasing returns to scale, then in a population of efficient firms there will be no firm that has both average size and average income.
10. Winch (1958, p. 16).
11. Hume (1748, Section IV, Part II).
12. Wittgenstein (1953, 345). Referring back to the discussion of the various kinds of universalizability, we see that Wittgenstein here is telescoping two of these into the single inference $(\exists x)\ (M(Fx)) \supset M(\forall x)(Fx)$.
13. The contradiction, however, does enter in a different manner. As mentioned above, Kant does not tell us to avoid a maxim if we cannot *imagine* it to be made into a general law, but rather to avoid it if we cannot *will* that it be generalized. In the terms of Chapter 4, we are appealing to the notion of inconsistent desires rather than to that of inconsistent beliefs. Now Kant's argument may be interpreted as saying that given a Prisoner's Dilemma (or, for that matter, an Assurance Game) we cannot consistently prefer the lower right-hand corner to the upper left-hand corner in the payoff matrix, as this would mean preferring x to y and y to x.
14. This is a reversal of the procedure in Hughes and Cresswell (1972, pp. 77–78), who offer an interpretation in which a world with telephones would not be conceivable from and therefore not accessible from a telephone-less world.

15. Marx (1867, p. 163).
16. Cf. Schumpeter (1954, p. 739).
17. Coleman (1973a, p. 67), italics added.
18. Vernon (1971, p. 138).
19. Clark (1899) is usually cited as the *locus classicus* for the notion that each factor ought to be rewarded according to its marginal product. With important reservations, the theory of justice elaborated by Nozick (1974) can be seen as a sophisticated outgrowth of this tradition; cf. also note 21 below.
20. Brief mention should be made here of the so-called 'capital controversy', the most important result of which is that the use of homogeneous capital as a factor of production is hard to justify analytically; cf. especially Harcourt (1973) and Bliss (1975). Some authors, such as Nuti (1970), argue that the inadequacy of the function $P = f(K, L)$ as a representation of the process of production implies the need for a functional $P(t) = F(L(t))$, where capital has been replaced by the stream of labour inputs that have produced it. This, however, cannot be rigorously true; present processes must be governed by present causes only. At the ontological level we know that some representation such as $P = f(K_1, K_2 \ldots K_n, L)$, where K_i is capital at some lower level of aggregation, *must* be possible. (Cf. also Elster, 1976 a) One cannot argue from the *need* for the functional $F(L(t))$ to political conclusions about income distribution, but the denial of a right to reward for capital presupposes the *possibility* of this functional.
21. The notion of end-result principles is taken from Nozick (1974, pp. 153 ff.). Different as they are in all other respects, the Marxist theory of exploitation and Nozick's theory of justice share the feature of being *historical* theories, as opposed to end-result theories. As the marginal productivity theory of income is itself an end-result theory, the need for the 'important reservations' in note 19 above should be clear.
22. Marx had an acute eye for this: '*the individual capitalist . . .* has the choice of making use of his capital by lending it out as interest-bearing capital, or of expanding its value on his own by using it as productive capital, regardless of whether it exists as money-capital from the very first, or whether it still has to be converted into money-capital. But to apply it to *the total capital* of society, as some vulgar economists do, and to go so far as to define it as the cause of profits, is, of course, preposterous. The idea of converting all the capital into money-capital, without there being people who buy and put to use means of production, which make up the total capital outside of a relatively small portion of it existing in money, is, of course, sheer nonsense' (Marx, 1894, pp. 377–378, italics added).
23. If the reader will refer back to the example of the Laputans and the Ruritanians of Chapter 4 above, he will appreciate the relevance of the following observation: 'The Laputans may believe that they will be attacked by the Ruritanians without therefore believing that they believe it, for each of them may be unaware that the others believe it. Our theory, however, is designed to be applicable to what an individual human being believes (and knows), and not to what a number of individuals are said to believe (and know)' (Hintikka, 1961, p. 29).
24. For other historical accounts of this idea see Merton (1936) and Hayek (1967).
25. Unfortunately Haavelmo's work on this topic has mainly been published in Norwegian, an exception being the brief statement in Haavelmo (1970). It seems that much of the current theory of public goods and the Prisoner's Dilemma was first worked out by Haavelmo, so that future histories of economic thought should take account of this pioneering effort.
26. Bossuet's *Discours sur l'Histoire Universelle* dates from 1681, the first edition of Vico's *Scienza Nuova* from 1725.
27. Nozick (1974, p. 19).
28. Keynes (1936, pp. 359 ff.) contrasts the following passages: 'As this prudent economy, which some people call *Saving*, is in private families the most certain method to

increase an estate, so some imagine that, whether a country be barren or fruitful, the same method if generally pursued (which they think practicable) will have the same effect upon a whole nation, and that, for example, the English might be much richer than they are, if they would be as frugal as some of their neighbours. This, I think, is an error' (Mandeville). 'What is prudence in the conduct of every private family can scarce be folly in that of a great Kingdom' (Adam Smith). The first passage should, I think, be read as a refutation of the fallacy of composition in the precise sense given here to this fallacy; it is not, however, absolutely certain that the second passage asserts that fallacy *in that sense*.

29. Mandeville (1729, vol. I, p. 89).
30. Mandeville (1729, vol. I, p. 428).
31. Elster (1975a, pp. 193 ff.).
32. *Wealth of Nations*, IV: II.
33. A profound and very difficult analysis of counterfinality is found in Hegel's *Phenomenology of Mind*, Chapter V. C. a; for (somewhat divergent) interpretations, see Hyppolite (1946, pp. 286 ff.) and Chamley (1963, pp. 23 ff.). The concept of the ruse of reason is by comparison an exoteric one, and more related to the Vico–Bossuet interpretation of history; cf. here d'Hondt (1970, pp. 22 ff.) and Avineri (1971). Among the many texts, especially in the *German Ideology* and the *Grundrisse*, where Marx discusses counterfinality, the following seems to be of particular salience: 'This reciprocal dependence is expressed in the constant necessity for exchange, and in exchange value as the all-sided mediation. The economists express this as follows: Each pursues his private interest and only his private interest; and thereby serves the private interests of all, the general interest, without willing or knowing it. The real point is not that each individual's pursuit of his private interest promotes the totality of private interests, the general interest. One could just as well deduce from this abstract phrase that each individual reciprocally blocks the assertion of the others' interest, so that, instead of a general affirmation, this war of all against all produces a general negation. The point is rather that private interest is itself already a socially determined interest, which can be achieved only within the conditions laid down by society and with the means provided by society; hence it is bound to the reproduction of these conditions and means. It is the interest of private persons; but its content, as well as the form and means of its realization, is given by social conditions independent of all' (Marx, 1857–58, p. 156). Observe that Marx in this passage makes two important conceptual points. Firstly there is the distinction between counterfinality and the invisible hand; secondly the idea that 'private interests' are not formed at random, contrary to what is implied by Parsons (1949, p. 493) who talks about 'the implicit assumption of the randomness of ultimate ends' in the thought of Marx.
34. *Wealth of Nations*, IV: IX.
35. Forrester (1969).
36. Schelling (1971, p. 150).
37. Sweezy (1962).
38. Sartre (1960, pp. 232 ff.).
39. Cf. for example Benedict (1972, pp. 81 ff.) and Neher (1971) for empirical evidence and theoretical analysis, respectively.
40. Finley (1973a, p. 175).
41. Genovese (1965, p. 165). It is shown in Chapter 6 that as an empirical assertion this cannot be substantiated. It would seem that Genovese has had better intuitions about the mental contradictions generated by slavery than about the social contradictions.
42. Paragraphs 243–246. I rely here on the interpretation offered by Weil (1966, p. 99).
43. Cf. Simon (1954a) and Brams (1976, Chapter 3) for discussions of self-fulfilling prophecies. In these discussions it is assumed that actual voting **y** is a function $f(\mathbf{x})$ of predicted voting **x**, where **x** and **y** are vectors indicating the percentages of the

vote going to the various parties. The set of such vectors is compact and convex, and if the function f is continuous we can then invoke the Brouwer fixed point theorem to assert the existence of a prediction $\bar{x}$ such that $\bar{x} = f(\bar{x})$, i.e. a prediction taking itself into account. Now there are two problems inherent in this elegant and justly famous demonstration. In the first place, as already observed in Chapter 3 above, the function $f(x)$ must not be made available to the public, for if the voters were told how they would react to the prediction, their reaction and (in the typical case) the fixed point would change, so that the same problem would arise at one remove. For the approach to work, *something must be kept secret*, be it the first-order prediction of the voting, the second-order prediction of how the first-order prediction will influence the actual voting, the third-order prediction of how the second-order prediction will influence the reaction to the first-order prediction, etc. In the second place the continuity assumption is certainly debatable. For an example that brings this out, we may take the case where the opinion survey gives a continuous distribution over some issue rather than a discrete repartition of voters over parties. Recent work in catastrophe theory (Isnard and Zeeman, 1974) has shown how discontinuities may arise in this case. Let us suppose that the opinion distribution initially is bimodal, and that the individuals react to the published distribution by moving closer to the mode that is nearest to their own opinion. If the distribution is continuously changed into a unimodal one, there will be a discontinuity (a catastrophe) in the reaction function at the point where one of the modes disappears. Exactly the same kind of discontinuity may arise in the vector-space case.

44. For the backward-sloped supply curve, see Chayanov (1966, pp. 80 ff.).
45. A dynamic system is structurally stable if the global behaviour of the system remains the same for any sufficiently small perturbation of the system parameters; in the case of $b = d$ above, it is clear that the smallest change in either b or d will change the global properties of the trajectories.
46. Allen (1966, pp. 13–14).
47. Allen (1966, pp. 197).
48. Coddington (1968, pp. 58 ff.); cf. also p. 64 for a very explicit comment upon the distinction I have tried to express by contrasting the first and the third theses on contradictions in the preceding chapter. Cf. also Leijonhufvud (1976, p. 103) for a similar observation.
49. Marx believed that production in industry took place with fixed coefficients, so that factor substitution was not a relevant possibility. The imputation to Marx of a theory of fixed coefficients is sometimes questioned (see for example Samuelson, 1957), but the documentation adduced in Maarek (1975, pp. 42–43), to which a number of other passages could be added, suffices to eliminate all doubt.
50. This was first recognized, it seems, by Salter (1960, pp. 43–44). A partial recognition of the same fact is found in Sweezy (1962, p. 88), who sees that the wage-reducing effects of mechanization is an extra bonus or a side-effect of actions undertaken for other motives, but does not explain what these other motives could be—why the innovations should have a labour-saving bias.
51. Marx (1867, p. 435); Smelser (1959, p. 235).
52. Fellner (1961, p. 307).
53. Cf. the discussion of 'irrational' versus 'rational' learning in the remarks on the cobweb model above.
54. David (1975, pp. 36 n. 2, and 54). David is aware of the free-rider problem that arises as soon as each capitalist understands that the other capitalists are acting in a way that will benefit him regardless of what he does himself, but his discussion does not bring out that the ensuing game is without a solution.
55. Cf. Morishima (1973) for this problem.
56. See for example Takayama (1974, Chapter 4) or von Weiszäcker (1971b).

57. I believe that we may distinguish between four distinct meanings of that elusive notion 'the labour theory of value':

(a) Prices are proportionate to values.
(b) The sum of all prices equals the sum of all values.
(c) Values may be determined independently of prices, but not vice versa.
(d) Prices are independent of the composition of final demand.

The local identity of prices and values implicit in interpretation (a) is asserted in *Capital I*, only to be abandoned in *Capital III*. As is well known by now, this is not the 'great contradiction' that Böhm-Bawerk (1898) thought it was, but only a case of analysis by successive approximations. The global identity of prices and values is asserted in *Capital III*, but as values are absolute and prices relative this is either meaningless or just a definition of a numéraire. Interpretation (c) stems from the Hegelian distinction between the essence (values) and the appearance (prices), whereas interpretation (d) goes back to the Ricardian ancestry of Marxism. For a precise analysis of the conditions under which statements (c) and (d) are valid, see Hoel (1974).

58. 'What determines value is not the amount of labour time incorporated in products, but rather the amount of labour time necessary at any given moment' Marx, 1857–58, p. 135). For comments upon the general problem of simultaneous versus. historical theories of value, see Dorfman *et al.*, (1958, p. 234); for Marx's use of 'circular reasoning' defended against his critics, see Bródy (1974, p. 84).

59. For this 'real subsumption of labour under capital', see especially Marx (1933).

60. The first label is used by Olson (1963, p. 131), the second by Barry (1973, p. 118).

61. Hobsbawm (1954, p. 56). The same point is also abundantly made in North and Thomas (1973, *passim*).

62. Thompson (1971, p. 120).

63. Williams (1966, p. 209).

64. Salthe (1972, p. 339).

65. Williams (1966, pp. 212 ff.). For any school of given density, the best for the individual fish is to be in the middle of the school where it is best protected against predators, but the more fish that seek towards the middle the greater the density of the school and the greater the vulnerability to predators.

66. Merton (1957), Stinchcombe (1968).

67. See Glantz and Albers (1974) for a case study.

68. Mandeville (1729, *passim*); Marx (1862–63, vol. 3, pp. 363–364).

69. Cf. Winter (1964) and Winter (1975) for detailed explorations of this model.

70. I believe that most readers will have come across a more than sufficient number of examples of this reasoning, so that documentation is superfluous. We may observe that Marx himself (see for example Marx, 1871, pp. 338, 541, 592, 594) used this line of argument in his analysis of the Second Empire in France; not, in my opinion, one of his glories. As a matter of fact Marx's empirical analysis of the capitalist state tend to oscillate between the conspiratorial mood (as in the diatribes upon Palmerston in Marx (1857, pp. 278 ff.) and the vacuously functional one.

71. Cf. Elster (1977a) for further discussion.

72. Popper (1963, p. 249).

73. Kenny (1970) makes a case for a distinction between foresight and intention, but I believe that in the present case the two notions coincide. The reasons why we may feel that the players in a Prisoner's Dilemma do not really intend (i.e. want) the suboptimal outcome is that we tend to compare the diagonal entries in the payoff matrix, but from the point of view of the actors only horizontal and vertical comparisons are relevant.

74. Luce and Raiffa (1957, p. 97).
75. See Olson (1963); Riker and Ordeshook (1973, Chapter 9); Staaf and Tannian (1972); Arrow and Scitovsky (1969).
76. Thus I am rather sceptical towards the following statement: 'Since no [feudal] lord could capture even a small portion of the social product of improved agricultural processes and technology, each had little incentive to try. The rational response would be to wait for some other landowner to bear the research and development costs and then to simply imitate his procedures should they prove successful. Each lord, of course, chose to wait and little progress was made' (North and Thomas, 1973, p. 62).
77. Boudon (1974, p. 198).
78. Boudon (1977, Ch. IV).
79. Boudon (1977, p. 265).
80. Cf. Elster (1976b).
81. Boudon (1977, Ch. V).
82. See Stouffer *et al.* (1949), and the explanations offered by Merton (1957, pp. 225 ff). and Hirschman (1973, p. 552, n. 9).
83. Phelps and Pollak (1968), on which I rely heavily in what follows. See also Elster (1976d).
84. Sejersted (1975); see also Elster (1976d).
85. Phelps and Pollak (1968). Their result really is somewhat ambiguous, and the interested reader must consult the original for details.
86. This is a case of the 'exploitation of the great by the small' as discussed by Olson (1963, p. 29).
87. Gallagher and Robinson (1953). In this article and in the subsequent discussion the term has been used to denote the informal empire that *accompanied* free trade, whereas I use it here for the informal control obtained *by means of* free trade. The term is also used in this latter sense by Kindleberger (1975, p. 33 sq.), referring to and quoting from 'the political economists who sought free trade as a means for slowing down the development of manufacturing on the Continent'. I hardly need to stress the analogy to the reverse free-trade imperialism exerted today by the oil-producing countries, where the oil-importing industrialized countries have found it in their interest to impose a *minimum* buying price of oil in order to make possible the development of alternative sources of energy. To an opponent who may try to ruin you by selling cheap it is rational to retort by buying dear.
88. Schumpeter (1953, p. 83) states the problem in its full generality: 'A system—any system, economic or other—that at *every* given point of time fully utilizes its possibilities to the best advantage may yet in the long run be inferior to a system that does so at *no* given point of time, because the latter's failure to do so may be a condition for the level or speed of long-run performance. 'An elaboration of the idea is given by Arrow (1971a). The argument has also been extended to the case of political behaviour, where there is a whole school of thought that sees apathy (i.e. short-term political suboptimality) as a condition for democracy (i.e. long-term political optimality). A flavour of this position and of the criticism levelled at it may be given by the following two quotes: 'The discovery that citizens do not normally use more than a fraction of their political resources came originally as a surprise and a disappointment to political scientists who had been brought up to believe that democracy requires for its functioning the fullest possible participation of all citizens. But soon enough a degree of apathy was found to have some compensating advantages inasmuch as it contributes to the stability and flexibility of a political system '(Hirschman, 1970, p. 14.). 'My argument is that, far from being a healthy necessary condition of democracy, apathy is a withdrawal response to the imbalance in the access of different interest-groups to those who make the decisions' (Finley, 1973b, p. 67). My sympathy here is on Finley's side, though I think there is a confusion

in the passage quoted between the causes of apathy and the effects of apathy —but then the same confusion is at the root of the functional analysis that sees the stabilizing effects of apathy as the cause of its persistence. (I do not know whether Hirschman would accept this analysis.) Lest it should be thought that my own criticism of radicalism and political impatience in the last section of the chapter also makes a virtue out of apathy, I would like to point out the difference between self-imposed restraint and externally induced apathy.

89. The importance of the patent system has recently been stressed by North and Thomas (1973) as perhaps *the* main condition for the rise of capitalism and the Industrial Revolution. In my work on Leibniz (Elster, 1975a, Chapter III) I discuss in some detail how the dilemma between the static and the dynamic suboptimalities was articulated in late 17th-century Germany. The knowledge industry at that time and place was suboptimal from both points of view: the craftsmen guarded their secrets so jealously that the static utilization was even worse than it would have been with a patent system, and at the same time the absence of a patent system gave small returns to knowledge and a weak incentive to innovate. Leibniz proposed a system whereby the artisans could be forced to reveal their secrets against compensation by the state. A crucial point would concern the principles governing the amount of compensation. An ideal system would link the reward to the productivity increases that the invention would bring about, but Leibniz seems rather to have had in mind a scheme whereby the craftsman would receive an amount equivalent to what he could otherwise have obtained by keeping his skills to himself. The latter system, while eliminating static suboptimality, would not have made any difference from the dynamic point of view.

90. See Arrow (1971a, p. 147 and *passim*). The deviation of utility-maximization from profit-maximization may come about even in the absence of risk, viz. if the entrepreneur's leisure-income trade-off changes with level of income; cf. Quirk and Saposnik (1968, p. 35). As observed by Scitovsky (1971, p. 153) this source of deviation of utility from profit is less important in the case of the classical 'puritarian' entrepreneur than for the modern managerial type, whereas the opposite presumably is true for the source mentioned in the text.

91. Young (1976) offers an extensive analysis of this phrase which, if valuable at the exegetical level, is not to my mind very convincing at the conceptual level. He denies that the Marxist notion of a contradiction has anything to do with logical contradiction, and argues that it should rather be understood as 'the relation between the two elements in a polar structure or two phases in a polar process'. Unfortunately, this notion is not very much clarified by the examples adduced, and I do not think it really achieves the status of an intersubjective and fairly operational concept.

92. These exegetical and terminological matters are further discussed in Elster (1972).

93. Marx (1867, p. 393).

94. Arrow (1971a, pp. 156 ff.).

95. 'The rapidity of the change in the organic composition of capital, and in its technical form, increases' (Marx, 1867, p. 631).

96. For substantiation of this interpretation I would especially point to the following passage: 'Although limited by its very nature, [capital] strives towards the universal development of the forces of production, and thus becomes the presupposition of a new mode of production, which is founded not on the development of the forces of production, for the purpose of reproducing or at most expanding a given condition, but where the free, *unobstructed*, progressive and universal development of the forces of production is itself the presupposition of society and hence of its reproduction' (Marx, 1857–58, p. 540). The word that I have italicized shows that Marx did not foresee any problem of a lack of incentive to innovate in communist society. What calls for an explanation would be the low rate of innovative activity

in pre-communist societies rather than the high rate that will prevail under communism.

97. Gerschenkron (1966, p. 8).
98. Lancaster (1973).
99. Setting x_1 for the rate of workers' consumption out of output, x_2 for the rate of reinvestment out of profits and u_1 for the upper limit of x_1, we may distinguish between the following modes of exploitation:

   (1) Low u_1, low x_2.
   (2) Low u_1, high x_2.
   (3) High u_1, low x_1, low x_2.
   (4) High u_1, low x_1, high x_2.

   The first form is typical of pre-capitalist societies (if we generalize the approach so as to include exploitation in slave societies and feudalism), the second is typical of early capitalism, the last of modern capitalism. The third is not very plausible, because the workers can retaliate with a high x_1 against a low x_2.
100. If the non-provision of public goods could be a form of counterfinality rather than of suboptimality, we would have a counterexample to this proposition, but I have given my reasons for doubting this possibility. Again I stress that nothing substantial is at stake here.
101. Bateson (1972, p. 305).
102. Owen (1968, p. 72).
103. Luce and Raiffa (1957, p. 107).
104. Rémond de Montmort wrote in his classical treatise *Essai d' Analyse sur les Jeux de Hasard* (2nd edn, 1713): 'These questions are very simple, but I believe them to be insoluble. If this proves to be the case, it will be a great pity, for this difficulty occurs quite often in civil life. For example when each of two persons in some transaction (*ayant affaire ensemble*) wants to align himself on the behaviour of the other.' More recently Latsis (1976, p. 31) writes that, 'In oligopoly each decision-maker is involved in guessing the other's expected behaviour; and if perfect knowledge on both sides is assumed, we should be led to an infinite regress.' (In fairness to the author it should be mentioned that the oligopoly game is in fact a game without a solution, but neither the quoted sentence nor the context shows any awareness of the distinction between games with and without non-cooperative solutions.) Such statements neglect both the possibility of arriving at a solution even when no dominant strategy is forthcoming and the notion of mixed strategies.
105. Arrow (1971a, p. 184).
106. Hirschman (1970, p. 18), quoting from Hirschman (1958, p. 63).
107. North and Davis (1971, p. 10).
108. For the notion of ultrastability see Ashby (1960).
109. Well-known adherents of this view are Easton (1965) and Deutsch (1963). For an explicit use of the notion of ultrastability, see Kaplan (1967, p. 161): 'The political system has the metatask capacity to act as the ultrastable regulator of the larger system in which it functions.' The basic fallacy of the approach is simply the belief that societies are systems. We may usefully talk about systems that have been teleologically fashioned by man or teleonomically fashioned by natural selection, but societies are not the result of design or of evolution in any sense resembling natural evolution. The criteria of identity of societies are ill-defined, as are also the criteria of 'health', 'sickness', 'birth', or 'death' of societies. We may talk, if we like, about societies as adapting to problems, but this adaptation differs from organic adaptation (i) in that it is not automatic, and (ii) that it is not restricted to a set of responses that have been programmed by evolution.

110. Perception and organization are, for example, discussed under the same heading by North and Davis (1971, p. 57).
111. Marx (1867, p. 239). The only author (to my knowledge) that has drawn attention to the curiously un-Marxist implications of this passage is Smelser (1959, p. 393).
112. 'So long as things go well, competition effects an operating fraternity of the capitalist class, as we have seen in the case of the equilization of the general rate of profit, so that each shares in the common loot in proportion to the size of his respective investments. But as soon as it no longer is a question of sharing profits, but of sharing losses, everyone tries to reduce his own share to a minimum and to shove it off upon another. The class, as such, must inevitably lose. How much the individual capitalist must bear of the loss, i.e. to what extent he must share in it at all, is decided by strength and cunning, and the competition then becomes a fight among hostile brothers. The antagonism between each individual capitalist's interest and those of the capitalist class as a whole then comes to the surface' (Marx, 1894, p. 253). This passage is fairly confused, as the last sentence suggests a variable-sum game between capitalists, and the preceding statements a zero-sum game. On the basis of other passages I believe that the last sentence should be stressed.
113. Marx (1867, p. 763).
114. Marx (1867, p. 506).
115. Marx (1867, p. 462).
116. Thompson (1968, pp. 566–567); Perkins (1969, p. 188).
117. Genovese (1965, p. 176).
118. Gerschenkron (1965, p. 710); Portal (1965, p. 804).
119. Smith (1968).
120. Selden (1971, pp. 35 ff., 54 ff.).
121. Simmel (1908, p. 460 ff.).
122. Olson (1963, p. 28).
123. Granovetter (1973, pp. 1373 ff.).
124. A brief survey of the papers brought to light by a search of the literature may be useful for some readers. For the first edition of *Class, Status and Power* Seymour Lipset and Joan Gordon (1953) wrote a paper that touches upon several aspects of the relation between turnover rates and collective action. The article was not retained in the second edition, perhaps because some of the remarks about the relation between mobility and lack of class consciousness were not confirmed in the later work of Lipset and Bendix (1959). Another important early work is Kerr and Siegel (1964), who find horizontal mobility a key factor in the analysis of the propensity to strike. More recently Thernstrom (1970) argues along similar lines. Fellin and Litwak (1963) studied the impact of mobility on neighbourhood cohesion, but the capacity for collective action enters only marginally in the latter notion. A well-known paper by Germani (1966) on various consequences of mobility has surprisingly little to say about our problem; this also holds for the work of North and Davis (1971) on the conditions for institutional change. The work of Granovetter (1973) is very stimulating, but uses an approach that is somewhat oblique to the present one.
125. Olson (1963, p. 69).
126. Lipset and Gordon (1953).
127. Wilensky and Edwards (1959) discuss 'the skidder' and his ideological adjustments in some detail.
128. Simmel (1908, p. 431). The quoted passage is a somewhat free translation of the following: 'Der prinzipielle Demokrat aber will nicht beherrscht werden, selbst um den Preis, dass ihm damit gedient wird.' Cf. also Peyrefitte (1976, p. 42).
129. Lipset and Gordon (1953).
130. Arrow (1971b, p. 22).

131. Finley (1973a, p. 77).
132. Bernstein (1899, pp. 73 ff.).
133. Luxemburg (1899, pp. 386–387).
134. Thalheimer (1930).
135. Thompson (1971, p. 135).
136. Bjørgum (1976) gives evidence for Norway. Kerr and Siegel (1964, n. 10) cite the 'itinerant but occupationally specialized sheepshearers in the western United States' as another example of a group where horizontal mobility does not prevent the development of class consciousness.
137. See Meisner (1967, p. 169) and Elster (1977) for further remarks on this point.
138. I am referring to the work of Sivert Langholm and his students, especially Jan Myhre.
139. Thernstrom (1970, p. 227).
140. If we adopt the so-called Cornell mobility model (for which see Boudon, 1973, pp. 85–95) unemployment tends to create the conditions for its own perpetuation ('cumulative inertia') in the sense that the longer a person has been out of work, the smaller become the chances that he will get a job in the next period. (We assume that this is a real after-effect and not just an effect of sampling.) To the extent that this is due to changes in the person himself (and not to attitude changes in potential employers), it will presumably take the form of increased despondency and lack of motivation, which again means that in the group of the unemployed the persons with longest membership will not necessarily be more motivated to collective action.
141. Thernstrom (1970, pp. 234–235) (running quotation).
142. Marx (1894, p. 601).
143. Girod (1971, pp. 51 ff. and *passim*). See also Thernstrom (1973, pp. 77, 94 ff.) and Blau and Duncan (1967, pp. 54 ff.).
144. Mukherjee (1954, p. 286). For other remarks upon mobility over more than two generations, see Schumpeter (1951, p. 169) and Lipset and Bendix (1959, pp. 74–75).
145. Brooke (1972, p. 93).
146. Bachrach and Baratz (1963).
147. Granovetter (1973).
148. North and Thomas (1971, p. 60).
149. See Luce and Raiffa (1957, pp. 124 ff).
150. Arrow (1974, p. 42).
151. For further reading the standard works of Luce and Raiffa (1957 and—in a more mathematical vein—Owen (1968) are recommended.
152. See especially Sen (1967) for n-person extensions of the Prisoner's Dilemma and the Assurance Game.
153. The above remarks rely heavily upon Luce and Raiffa (1957, pp. 106 ff.). Nevertheless I believe that the solution concept offered here is more natural than both the 'solution in the strict sense' and the 'solution in the sense of Nash' which are their main alternatives. The Assurance Game is not solvable in the sense of Nash, whereas the Prisoner's Dilemma is not solvable in the strict sense; nevertheless I believe that on intuitive grounds both these games should be solvable, in the sense that rational and fully informed actors will converge upon a unique mode of behaviour.
154. For the Prisoner's Dilemma, see Rapoport and Chammah (1965) and Taylor (1976). For the Assurance Game see Sen (1967) and Sen (1973). For the Battle of the Sexes, see Luce and Raiffa (1957, pp. 90 ff., p. 115 ff.). For Chicken, see Rapoport (1966, pp. 137 ff.).
155. For a discussion of a strange 'quasi-solution' in the Battle of the Sexes and Chicken, see Luce and Raiffa (1957, pp. 93–94) and Rapoport (1966, pp. 140 ff.).
156. See Luce and Raiffa (1957, Chapter 2) for a discussion of utility theory as used in the theory of games.
157. See Rapoport and Chammah (1965) *et al.* and Rapoport (1976) for some of his work in experimental game theory.

158. Rapoport and Chammah (1965, pp. 123 ff..

159. Howard (1971), criticized (correctly in my opinion) in Taylor (1976, pp. 64 ff.).

160. Shubik (1970), Taylor (1976); see also Taylor (1977) for extensions to biology.

161. The argument for this conclusion is very simple. Each player knows that in the last game both will choose the non-cooperative strategy, for after that game there is no future in which cooperation can be rewarded. This, however, means that the next-to-last game effectively becomes the last, and the same consideration then applies here, and so on backwards in time to the first game. I believe this notion can be generalized: would we not all give up some years of our life in order to remain ignorant of the number of years we have to live?

162. Luce and Raiffa (1957, p. 102).

163. Taylor (1976, p. 93).

164. As quoted in Luce and Raiffa (1957, p. 165).

165. Luce and Raiffa (1957, p. 165).

166. Mutations, senescence and cancer are subfunctional phenomena (Williams (1966, pp. 138 ff., 225 ff.)); suprafunctional phenomena were discussed in the biological examples of the structuralist fallacy.

167. Davidson (1973).

168. Elster (1977). Two features are mentioned here as separating intentional from functional adaptation: the human capacity for attaining global maxima even if this should require waiting or even temporary retreat from a local maximum, and the human capacity for realizing the solution in a game where there are no dominant strategies.

169. Thus, I largely agree with the following observation: 'The besetting weakness of the Marxian system, omissions apart, is to this writer what many another critic considers a pillar of strength. This is its structuralism, which is to say, its tendency to take important relations as technically determined behind the back of the price systems, leaving that latter with few functions beyond equating profits' (Bronfenbrenner, 1965, p. 223). It is only fair, however, to add that the Marxist theory of the falling rate of profit is—mathematical errors part—a model of actor-oriented analysis.

170. Becker (1962).

171. Cobb (1973). Tullock (1974).

172. Tullock (1974).

173. Innumerable recent discussions, often very subtle and fascinating and sometimes conceivably valid, could be cited that purport to prove the underlying rationale of apparently irrational behaviour. I do indeed believe that as a regulative idea in the social sciences one should always start out by looking for some *meaning* or *purpose* behind every piece of behaviour, but one should always endeavour to *test* rational-choice explanations against other explanations instead of just postulating unobservable entities (such as 'psychic costs') that make all behaviour come out as rational per definition. In particular, if one is talking about a *choice*, this is in itself an act that takes place in time and space and not something that can be imputed to its observed results on the assumption of rationality. For an example of an analysis that to my mind is definitely wrong (or vacuous) the following may be cited: 'People act in terms of general ideological positions rather than incur the costs of acquiring information on a particular issue even when it would pay them to do so. Thus, they react as liberals, conservatives, radicals, or reactionaries. Ideologies are a way of economizing on the cost of information and therefore are in general a rational response to the costs of information about the broad range of issues that face them' (North, 1971, p. 122). In the first place, does 'response' in this context mean a datable event or is it just an analytical invention? In the second place, do people *never* act stupidly out of stupidity and rigidly out of rigidity? In the third place, how do they get the information that enables them to economize optimally on the costs of information?

174. An interesting approach that is rather oblique to the present problem is that of McFarland (1976). An approach more directly geared to our problem is that of Coleman (1973b), who errs, however, in confusing the substantive intentionality of human actions with the 'as-if intentionality' of physical processes, such as the apparent intentionality exhibited by the least-time principle in physics.
175. Simon (1954b).
176. See for example Riker and Ordeshook (1973, Chapter 2).
177. Winter (1964, p. 262).
178. Winter (1975, p. 83).
179. *The Nicomachean Ethics*, 1113–1114.
180. Elster (1975a, p. 72, n. 85). The problem is the following. On the one hand Descartes says that God is not bound—in his choice of world—by any pre-existing criteria of perfection, but on the other hand Descartes also tries to justify the evil in the world by the traditional kind of arguments. The contradiction can be resolved by supposing that the present world is the best of all possible worlds *according to its own (created) criteria of perfection.*

6

COUNTERFACTUALS AND THE NEW
ECONOMIC HISTORY

The notion of counterfactual (or contrary-to-fact) propositions has recently become important in two unrelated disciplines: philosophical logic and economic history. In both cases interest in counterfactuals stems from a concern with causation: with the *notion* of causality in the case of the philosopher, with the *evaluation* of the relative importance of causes in the case of the historian. I shall first briefly explain how these concerns have led to the notion of a counterfactual. Then I shall go on to discuss some selected aspects of the notion, offering first a sketchy and patchy history of the concept, a tentative analysis of historical counterfactuals and finally a number of examples drawn from recent controversies in economic history.

The starting point for all analyses of causation is Hume's view that causation means constant conjunction between events. This 'regularity theory of causation' has since been refined in various ways, so that 'in present-day regularity analyses, a cause is defined (roughly) as any member of any minimal set of actual conditions that are jointly sufficient, given the laws, for the existence of the effect'.[1] Now on Hume's theory there is an obvious difficulty in distinguishing causation from mere correlation, and similar problems arise also in the case of the more elaborate versions.[2] To distinguish causation from correlation we may point out that the former warrants the statement that if the cause had not occurred, then the effect would not have occurred, whereas no such counterfactual is implied by the latter. To *define* causation through the notion of counterfactuals has seemed, however, to most philosophers a case of *obscurium per obscurius*, because the logical status of counterfactuals has not been very well understood. In particular, several of the problems that create difficulties for the regularity theory of causation also seem to constitute insuperable obstacles to most of the traditional accounts of counterfactuals. It is only with the recent emergence of a theory of counterfactuals in terms of possible worlds that this approach to causation has begun to appear a plausible one. The details of this approach will be spelled out below.

The reason why the historian is concerned with counterfactuals is a quite different one. Let us observe for a beginning that the historian has traditionally entertained two incompatible beliefs. On one hand he has assumed as a matter of course that some causes are more important than others, but on the other hand he has been wont to talk about 'the seamless web of history' and to criticize the rare historian that has indulged in speculations about the 'might-have-beens' of history. Now these two beliefs are hard to reconcile, for in a non-experimental and non-comparative discipline one can hardly discuss the relative importance of causes without engaging in some kind of thought experiment where one removes successively and separately each of the causes in question and evaluates what difference the absence of this cause would have made to the phenomenon in question.[3] Some historians have come to recognize, therefore, that they have been talking counterfactually all the time without recognizing it, but I do not know whether they are by now a majority in the profession. The controversy over counterfactuals in history does not depend upon the choice we make between the theories of causation discussed in the preceding paragraph. If we hold a counterfactual theory of causation—be it one of the traditional varieties or the possible world variety—we are of course committed to saying that causation involves counterfactuals, but this commitment also holds for the proponents of the regularity theory. On the latter theory any statement about causation *implies* a counterfactual statement, even if the theory does not accept that causation should be *defined* in terms of counterfactuals. What has troubled the historians, viz. the idea that statements about causation implies statements about counterfactuals, has been taken for granted by the logicians; and the problem of the latter, whether causation should be defined in terms of counterfactuals or whether the link is a non-definitional one only, has been too esoteric for the former.

Three chapters from the history of the notion

The logical problem of counterfactuals and possible worlds has a complex historical background. Even if I had the space, I would lack the competence to offer the reader an adequate account. I shall restrict myself, therefore, to a brief exposition of some thinkers whose contributions—and mistakes—remain relevant for our purposes. After a highly selective account of the Leibnizian doctrine of modality, I shall have something to say about the views of John Stuart Mill and Max Weber on counterfactual reasoning in the social and the historical sciences.

Between Aristotle and the recent developments sketched in Chapter 1 above, Leibniz certainly is the most important figure in the history of modal logic. The definition of necessity as *truth in all possible worlds* stems from his work, as do also the analogy between deontic and alethic modal logic (the analogy, that is, between obligation and necessity) and the distinction between possibility and compossibility. This latter distinction, however, is worked out in a way that makes it very hard for Leibniz to admit counterfactual statements as meaningful. To see this, we must sketch—again in thumbnail format—some of Leibniz's metaphysical doctrines. As is well known—and distinctly less well understood—Leibniz held the universe to be composed of *monads* or individual substances.

An individual substance is completely described by the corresponding individual concept that includes everything that will ever happen to that individual and all properties that can truthfully be ascribed to it. Thus, all true statements are analytic, i.e. the predicate only repeats what is already included in the subject. From this thesis it at once follows that counterfactual statements asserting, either in the antecedent or in the consequent, that an individual of the actual world would have acted differently or been different in another world, are meaningless, for then he would not have been *that* individual.

Actually the restriction on counterfactuals imposed by Leibniz's theory are stronger still, as I shall now explain. Given a possible substance—i.e. a complete notion of an individual—we know that it can be actualized, but we do not yet know under which conditions. Not all possible substances can be realized simultaneously, i.e. in the same world; they constrain each other mutually in various ways. A possible world is a maximal set of compossibles, i.e. a consistent set of possible substances such that the addition of one further substance would make the set incoherent. Now in some texts Leibniz speaks as if one substance could be a member of several possible worlds,[4] but Nicholas Rescher has argued persuasively that this idea is not really compatible with the Leibnizian metaphysics.[5] Because Leibniz argues that the notion of an individual substance contains a reference to all other substances in the world in which it is realized, transplantation of a substance from one world to another is impossible. Formally, the relation of compossibility is an equivalence relation (reflexive, symmetrical, and transitive) that partitions the set of abstractly possible substances into equivalence classes or possible worlds. Thus, not only is it illegitimate to attribute to an individual actions or properties that are not found correlated with him in the actual world, but one cannot even assume him to be living in a possible world differing from the actual one in some insignificant details apparently unrelated to that individual, such as the location of a grain of dust at the far side of the moon. Or, more properly, the point is that no details are insignificant; there is no way of modifying a set of individual substances without modifying each of the substances.

This theory may look far-fetched, and I suppose that it is. Still it may serve to bring out the inherent difficulties of what we may call, barbarically, 'ontological counterfactualization'. In the next section much of the discussion will turn upon a distinction between this way of interpreting counterfactuals and the 'epistemological counterfactualization'. The first, which might also be called a 'parallel worlds theory', assumes that any small counterfactual change at some point of time implies the counterfactualization of the whole universe prior to (and perhaps subsequent to) that time. Possible worlds, on this account (and excluding worlds with non-deterministic laws of nature), have no common points where they converge or diverge, but always run parallel to each other. The second interpretation might be dubbed a 'branching worlds theory', as it permits two worlds to be identical up to a point and to diverge from that point onwards (and eventually to reconverge later on). On the second theory, there is no problem of 'trans-world identity', that is of determining which individuals are common to several worlds. Accepting the notion of Kripke and Dummett that the essential properties of an individual are the properties that are somehow linked to his origins, a sufficient condition for two individuals in two worlds to be the same individual is that they were the same individual before the branching point. On the first theory, however, it is hard to see how such unambiguous criteria of trans-world identity could be forthcoming. One might, certainly, lay down some criteria such as DNA-sequence, but by assuming suitable changes in the environment two individuals with the same sequence can be made nearly as different phenotypically as you want. Leibniz, then, is just cutting the Gordian knot: from the fact that on a parallel worlds theory all criteria of identity must be arbitrary, he draws the conclusion that individuals are completely bound to one world and that transplantation is impossible.

One way out would be to argue that identity can be a matter of degree, as is the case in David Lewis's theory of counterparts that has also been read into Leibniz.[6] According to this theory, an individual living in one world cannot also crop up in another, but we may find one or even several *counterparts*, i.e. persons resembling him more or less closely in some aspect or aspects. Counterfactual propositions, then, are to be read as being about the counterpart (s) of the person in some possible world. More specifically, the proposition, 'If Sextus had not raped Lucretia, he would have lived a happy life', is to be read as saying that the individual that (i) did not rape Lucretia and (ii) otherwise differs minimally from the actual Sextus also (iii) led a happy life. This obviously turns crucially upon the phrase 'differs minimally', about which more in the next section.

In the social sciences I do not know of any treatment of counterfactuals before John Stuart Mill. In the first methodological discussion of what was then known as the 'moral sciences', Mill rejects the Method of Difference in the social sciences, on the ground that we cannot imagine a society changing in some particular aspect while all other aspects remain the same. The entire passage is worth quoting:

If two nations can be found which are alike in all natural advantages and disadvantages; whose people resemble each other in every quality, physical and moral, spontaneous and acquired; whose habits, usages, opinions, laws and institutions are the same in all respects, except that one of them has a more protective tariff, or in other respects interferes more with the freedom of industry; if one of these nations is found to be rich and the other poor, or one richer than the other, this will be an *experimentum crucis* – a real proof by experience which of the two systems is most favourable to national riches. But the supposition that two such instances can be met with is manifestly absurd. *Nor is such a concurrence even abstractedly possible. Two nations which agreed in everything except their commercial policy would agree also in that.*[7]

This is a rather strange argument, as it would seem to be equally valid for other examples of the Method of Difference. In his general discussion of the method Mill glosses over this difficulty, by conceding that 'this similarity of circumstances needs not extend so such as are already known to be immaterial to the result',[8] a clause that is rather dubious in itself—for how can we know in advance what is material and what is not?—as well as being inconsistent with the discussion of the social sciences, where *total* similarity is required. Mill does, however, try to justify this inconsistency, by arguing that the inapplicability of the Method of Difference in the social sciences is due to the distinguishing feature (such as interference in industry and trade) being here 'an effect of pre-existing causes' rather than a 'property of Kinds'.[9] If, then, we turn to the discussion of properties of Kinds,[10] these are properties that can be taken as an *index* of other properties with which they are constantly conjoined, without being the *cause* of these properties. Thus mankind is a Kind, because the properties that are specific to man are independent of each other, even if always found together. By contrast the class of Christians is not a Kind, because all properties specific to members of this class stem from their property of being Christian. This implies that the Method of Difference—i.e. the comparative method—is inapplicable to Kinds, because Kinds always differ in more than one feature. On the other hand the counterfactual method *is* applicable to Kinds, because the features are assumed to be independent of each other and can therefore be freely varied in the imagination.

In the social sciences, however, neither the comparative method nor the counterfactual thought experiments have any place. The reason why Mill deems counterfactuals illegitimate in the study of societies is that here all parts are assumed to be interdependent to such a degree that no single part or subset of parts can be varied in the imagination, the other being held constant. This, I submit, is an instance of a pre-theoretic attitude, because it neglects to relate the interdependence to a specific theory. At the ontological level we may no doubt hold that all things somehow hang together in a vast causal network, but science is a search for *specific* interdependence. When discussing the impact of free trade upon national prosperity, one has to use a theoretical framework with a finite number of specified variables, and it is not at all absurd to assume that two societies might have the same values for all but one of these variables, for this does not imply that they are also similar in all other aspects not included in the theory.

There is a complementary pre-theoretic attitude that instead of assuming that no counterfactuals are legitimate in the study of society, tends to hold that all counterfactuals are equally and completely legitimate. This attitude is, I believe, found in a famous article by Max Weber on objective possibility and causal adequacy in the historical sciences. The notion of objective possibility clearly is a species of the notion of a counterfactual, but Weber does not sufficiently stress the aspects in which it differs from merely subjective possibility. Before I come to my critical comments, it must be said that there is much that may still be read with profit in Weber's analysis of counterfactuals. An important idea, to which I return below, is his observation that the choice of counterfactuals *ex post* is often guided by the range of subjective options open to the actors *ex ante*. Whether a given act shall be characterized as an objective possibility often depends on whether it belonged to the subjective repertory of the agents. The apparent contradiction in the previous sentence, where subjective factors are included among the objective elements, disappears on closer reflection. The contrast 'objectively present in the historical situation' versus 'subjectively created by the historian' does not coincide with the opposition 'material and structural aspects of the situation' versus 'psychological and cultural elements of the situation'. Also observe that on a branching worlds theory the subjective range of possibilities is a natural joint in which to insert the wedge of counterfactualization, though I would not argue that there are no other branching points than those located at moments of choice.

Another important insight provided by Weber's essay is his observation that juridical reasoning and practice is a paradigm for the analysis of the causal importance of several factors in a complex historical situation. It is not quite clear, however, that he is also right when he sees a difference between the two fields in that the juridical problem of subjective intention is of less importance to history, whose concern is with the deed rather than with the doer. Indeed the contrast may be reversed. In the study of social contradictions in Chapter 5 we saw that decisive importance must be attached to the intentions of the actors, for only through them can we understand which of the observed set of events constitute *un*intended consequences. Conversely, the attribution of subjective guilt does not always proceed by examination of the actual thoughts of the culprit; at least sometimes it relies on a reconstruction of the counterfactual thoughts that a 'reasonable man' would have had in the same situation.

Finally, Weber is quite right in emphasizing that in the assessment of the consequences of a counterfactual assumption we must rely upon nomological knowledge rather than upon our subjective empathy. The defect in Weber's analysis lies in the virtually total absence of what I shall call the problem of legitimacy: are all counterfactual assumptions equally justified? From a careful reading of Weber's text I have found only one passage[11] that shows *some* awareness of the problem, and the main message seems indeed to be that any 'factor' or 'element' can be freely varied at will. The simple point that Weber overlooked was this: the nomological laws that we use in concluding from the antecedent to the consequent of a counterfactual statement must also be used in order to ensure that the antecedent itself is compatible with the elements that are *not* assumed to vary. The theory that forms the framework of the analysis may leave us *some* liberty (*pace* Mill) to vary the situation, but (*pace* Weber) they do not give us complete freedom. Both Mill and Weber neglect the importance of having a *specific theory* that can circumscribe the set of legitimate counterfactual assumptions: Mill by appealing to a universal theory (metaphysical determinism) and Weber by not appealing to any theory at all. These errors look opposed, but in the pre-scientific mode they are two sides of the same coin. When all is possible, nothing is possible.[12]

The problem of historical counterfactuals

By the preceding remarks I have implicitly committed myself to a particular analysis of counterfactual statements. In the present section this analysis will be spelled out in more detail, and contrasted with the alternative analysis offered by Robert Stalnaker and David Lewis. It should be stated at the outset that I do not pretend to give a general analysis of counterfactuals and their logic. The Stalnaker–Lewis theory is one such analysis, which I believe to be wrong, for reasons given below. Some of these reasons are quite general, whereas others are related to the lack of relevance of their analysis for the specific problem of historical counterfactuals. I try to argue that for the historian the account offered here is more satisfactory, but I do not pretend that this account solves the general problem of counterfactuals. To put the matter somewhat differently, I believe that a valid general theory of counterfactual statements must be compatible with the present analysis of historical counterfactuals, but I have no inkling as to how the extension should be made.

Two distinctions may be useful in order to impose a structure upon the various analyses of counterfactual statements offered. In the first place we may distinguish between the *ontological* and the *meta-linguistic* theories of counter-factuals. An ontological theory says that counterfactuals are *about* possible worlds, and are rendered true or false by virtue of the features of these worlds, much in the same manner as the statement 'snow is white' is rendered true or false by the presence or the absence of white snow in the actual world. A meta-linguistic theory, on the other hand, makes *statements* about the world rather than (non-linguistic) features of the world the crucial explanatory element. Roughly the meta-linguistic analysis of the counterfactual 'If p had been the case, then q would have been the case' turns upon the existence of some set S of empirical and law-like statements such that the conjunction of S and p logically implies q. Following David Lewis we can make a further distinction within the meta-linguistic approaches, according as the counterfactuals are analysed in terms of *truth conditions* or in terms of *conditions of assertability*. A paraphrased quotation from Lewis will explain the distinction better than I could hope to do:

> Most previous theories of counterfactuals are *meta-linguistic*: a counter-factual is true, or assertable, if and only if its antecedent, together with suitable further premises, implies its consequent. Either the counterfactual is a sentence meaning that some such argument exists, or it is itself an elliptical presentation of such an argument. On the former version, the counterfactual can be evaluated as true or false according as there do or do not exist suitable premises S which, together with p, imply q. On the

latter version, it cannot be evaluated as true or false, but only—after the omitted premises S have been restored—as valid or invalid.[13]

I submit that for the working historian conditions of assertability are all that matters; the theory set forth below, therefore, is a meta-linguistic theory of the conditions of assertability of counterfactual statements. The crucial point is that the counterfactual statements must be explained in terms of some *actual* theory T that the speaker, if challenged, could produce to back his assertion. This, I think, makes good sense when dealing with historical counterfactuals. The mere existence of some—possibly unknown and perhaps unknowable—theory that would make the inference valid is totally irrelevant in actual historical research. A quite different problem is whether my analysis in terms of conditions of assertability should be supplemented, for the purpose of logical analysis, by an account of truth conditions. That is, can an analysis in terms of conditions of assertability be a *complete* account of the logic of counterfactuals or does it only work as an account of how some such counterfactuals are actually used in scientific work? Lewis argues that some theory of truth-conditions must be forthcoming, because otherwise we should not be able to make sense of non-asserted counterfactuals, serving for example as the antecedent of an ordinary counterfactual. ('If it is the case that the Second World War would never had occurred if Hitler had not been born, then all diagnosed psychopaths should be shot in order to prevent future wars.') I am not sure that we have very firm intuitions about such cases, and I would not exclude *a priori* that on closer analysis they would turn out to be meaningless. No such analysis, however, is proposed here. If I could give a reasoned argument for the view that counterfactuals can be wholly analysed in terms of assertability, I would have given an alternative to the Lewis–Stalnaker theory. This, to repeat, is not my ambition. I try (i) to demolish the Lewis–Stalnaker theory of truth conditions in terms of possible worlds, (ii) to offer an analysis of conditions of assertability, but not (iii) to prove that the very notion of truth conditions for counterfactuals is suspect.

For the analysis of historical counterfactuals I believe that a more specific version of the meta-linguistic account is required. By introducing a dynamic aspect in the theory that is part of the set S of statements permitting the inference from p to q, some points can be made that would not easily emerge in a more general account. I shall say, then, that a theory T explains a process P when:

(1) The process P is at each moment of discrete time described exhaustively through the variables $x_1 \ldots x_n$ ($\mathbf{x}$ in vector notation).
(2) The theory T states that
    (i) for each variable x_i there exists a set X_i of singly admissible values;
    (ii) there exists a set X of jointly admissible values of the variables, X being a subset of the Cartesian product $X_1 X_2 \ldots X_n$;
    (iii) for each admissible vector $\mathbf{x}(t)$ there exists at least one admissible vector

such that T excludes that the process can be represented by that vector at $t + 1$.

(3) The sequence of vectors $x(t)$ describing P is compatible with requirements (2) (i)–(2) (iii).

Condition (2) (ii) is a requirement of *static compatibility*. It says that among the many abstractly possible vectors that can be formed by combining elements in the X_i, only a subset of vectors can represent the process. It is natural to require that this be a proper subset, so that at least one possible combination of values can never occur as a state of the process. Condition (2) (iii) is a requirement of *dynamic compatibility*. It states that there are some minimal restrictions on the states that can succeed each other. I believe that these are the absolutely minimal requirements of any scientific theory. They are based upon the idea that *knowledge proceeds by exclusion*, the narrowing of the set of abstractly possible configurations to a set that is smaller by at least one member.[14] Most people have in mind substantially stronger requirements when they refer to scientific theories, usually according to some idea that *the goal of knowledge is determination*. They would like, probably, to replace (2) (iii) by

(2) (iii)′: For each admissible $\mathbf{x}(t)$, T excludes all but one vector in X as possible values of $\mathbf{x}(t + 1)$

This is the usual approach in systems dynamics, where one traces deterministically the trajectory of the system over time. I believe, however, that for many purposes this is too stringent. A general argument for using (2) (iii) rather than (2) (iii)′ is the following. As stated in Chapter 3 above, any description of reality must be under-specified, and under-specification of the present implies a possible under-determination of the future. Instead of using deterministic and almost invariably inexact models, we might prefer to use a non-deterministic and exact one. With the recent development of the mathematical tools for analysing correspondences or set-valued functions[15] the last option should be more attractive than it has traditionally seemed, though I would not suggest that it should be employed in all or even in a substantial minority of cases. More specific arguments can be adduced for the use of set-valued functions in the social sciences.[16] On the practical level there is simply the dearth of theories that are both deterministic and reasonably exact. I do not argue that social facts are inherently less subject to causal determinism than natural facts, only that we must at present treat them as if they were, constructing our theories so as to admit more degrees of freedom than is usual in the natural sciences. On a more speculative level I think that in some cases the process *must* be treated as if it were inherently non-deterministic, even if we know that in 'reality itself' it must be completely determined.[17]

The link to counterfactuals may now be forged in the following manner. We assume that at time t the actual historical configuration of the values of the variables $x_1 \ldots x_n$ was $A_1 \ldots A_n$. Then the general form of a *static counterfactual* is the following (we assume without lack of generality that only the last k variables vary independently):

If at time t the variables $x_{n-k+1}, x_{n-k+2} \ldots x_n$ had taken on the values $B_1 \ldots B_k$, then at time t the variables $x_{i_1}, x_{i_2} \ldots x_{i_p}$ would have taken on the values $C_1 \ldots C_p$, with $i_r < n - k + 1$ for all r.

We may ask two distinct questions concerning this counterfactual: about meaningfulness and about assertability. Instead of meaningfulness, I shall also speak of the *legitimacy* of the antecedent. As a minimum requirement there must be some $\mathbf{x}$ in X such that $x_r = B_r$ for $r = n - k + 1, n - k + 2 \ldots n$. This is the condition of static legitimacy. In addition we might want to impose some condition of dynamic legitimacy, for example that there should be some k such that from the actual state of the process at $t - k$ there is a *permitted trajectory of states* (i.e. a sequence of states satisfying condition 2 (iii) above) leading up to a state $\mathbf{x}$ such that $x_r = B_r$ for $r = n - k + 1, n - k + 2 \ldots n$. The problem is whether we shall require that a counterfactual antecedent must be capable of insertion into the real past. I shall argue that this is indeed a natural requirement, but the reader must wait to the end of this section and to the examples of later sections for the details of the argument. As for the problem of assertability, I shall defer discussion till I have set forth the essentials of the ontological theory of counterfactuals.

The general form of a dynamic counterfactual is the following:

If at time t the configuration had been $A_1 \ldots A_{n-k} B_1 \ldots B_k$, then at time $t + t'$ the subset $x_{i_1}, x_{i_2} \ldots x_{i_p}$ of the variables would have assumed the values $C_1 \ldots C_p$,

Again the same questions may be asked, with roughly the same answers. For the antecedent to be legitimate, we must impose the static requirement that the configuration at t be a member of X, and (or so I shall argue) the dynamic requirement that the configuration be capable of insertion into the real past. For the problem of assertability, I once again refer the reader to the discussions further on.

Before turning now to a detailed presentation of the ontological view of counterfactuals, we should note some features of the account just given. One crucial aspect is that the theory T emerges as something more than just an instrument that permits us to conclude from the hypothetical antecedent to the hypothetical consequent: it also serves as a filter for the acceptance or the rejection of the antecedent itself. This double role of the theory T in the assessment of a counterfactual creates what I think is *the basic paradox of counterfactuals*: the stronger (i.e. the more deterministic) the theory T, the better grounded is the conclusion from antecedent to consequent, but the more vulnerable is also the legitimacy of the antecedent. With a weak theory many antecedents are permitted by the filter, but it may be impossible to prove the assertability of the conditional. Thus for a successful counterfactual analysis a delicate balance must be struck: the theory must be weak enough to admit the counterfactual assumption, and also strong enough to permit a clear-cut conclusion. To use an example to be discussed later on: when evaluating the consequences of a non-railroad economy in 19th-century America, we can hardly ask whether the internal combustion engine would have been invented before it actually was, for this would require a theory of technical change that might prevent the non-railroad assumption itself from being meaningful. The problem is not that it is difficult to know whether the internal combustion engine would have been invented,[18] but rather that if it were possible to answer this question, it should not have been put in the first place.

The basic paradox of counterfactuals may also be referred to as the paradox of *the unimportance of the inevitable*. In order to assess the causal importance of some historical event or social fact, the mental removal of that element must be statically and dynamically legitimate; conversely, any element that cannot be subjected to this thought experiment is inherently unfit to causal assessment. A very different example that brings out this difficulty can be taken from the conceptual analysis of power. Alvin Goldman[19] has argued that, 'To say that S is powerful is not to say that he usually gets what he in fact wants, but that whatever he wanted he could get, no matter what he might happen to want.' The reason why we want to impose this condition is that otherwise we should have to ascribe extreme power to the *chameleon*, i.e. to the person who always changes his (sincere) preferences so as to always be on the winning side. On the other hand I believe that this counterfactualization of power leads us into the basic paradox just discussed. Take the two contrasting examples of

— Nixon had the power to end the Vietnam War: therefore the Vietnam War would have gone on had Nixon so wanted.
— De Gaulle had the power to safeguard France's independence: therefore France would have lost her independence had de Gaulle so wanted.

The counterfactual assumption implied in the statement about Nixon seems perfectly legitimate; there is nothing inherently improbable, as far as we know, in the idea of Nixon's wanting the Vietnam War to go on. (This is not to say, of course, that the counterfactual as a whole is assertable.) On the other hand it seems to me clearly absurd to assume that de Gaulle *could* have wished for France to lose her independence, at any rate if we want to ascribe to de Gaulle the power that we feel that he had. We may certainly assume a counterfactual world where de Gaulle was a different kind of person altogether, the kind of person who might have wished for France to lose her independence, but *that* de Gaulle would probably not have had any power at all, because the power of (the real) de Gaulle mainly stemmed from the fact that he visibly was not the kind of person that *could* form such a wish. Thus we are in a dilemma: we accept that de Gaulle was a powerful person indeed; we accept the need for a counterfactual analysis of power statements; but the counterfactual statement about de Gaulle's power is either absurd (having an illegitimate antecedent) or false (if we assume a de Gaulle that could have wished differently). De Gaulle, it seems, was powerless because he could not have wished to act differently from what he did. I do not at present see any way out of this dilemma.

The double role of the theory as a filter and as a deductive machinery points to an important difference between counterfactual statements and factual statements. When new theories emerge in addition to the old (I abstract from the new theories that *replace* old theories) the impact on the set of true (factual) causal statements will be unambiguously in the direction of an increase, but the impact on the set of assertable counterfactual statements is harder to assess. Some counterfactuals previously accepted will now appear as illegitimate, and some formerly seen as legitimate but unassertable will now be assertable. This, however, holds in the short run only. If we impose some dynamic condition of legitimacy, we know that the emergence of more and better theories will *ultimately* reduce the set of assertable counterfactuals, for in the limit—an all-embracing and deterministic theory of the universe—no branching points will exist where the wedge of counterfactualization can be inserted.

I now turn to the Stalnaker–Lewis theory of counterfactuals, referred to above as 'the ontological theory of counterfactuals'.[20] As in modal logic generally, this theory assumes that relatively to any given world, including the actual one, there exists a set of possible worlds. In addition, and this is the crucial point, we assume that we have defined some measure for the *distance* between the given world and the worlds that are possible relative to it. With a slight simplification of Lewis's argument we then say that 'If p had been the case, then q would have been the case' is true in world x if (1) p is not the case in any world that is possible relatively to x, or (2) q is the case in the closest world to ours where p is the case.[21] This does not exclude that there may be worlds where p is the case and q is not the case; the analysis only implies that such worlds are always further away from our world than at least one world where p and q are both the case.

I want to praise the general idea behind this account, and to criticize the particular ('ontological') interpretation of the possible-world notion used by Lewis. As for the praise, it is indeed important to point out that for 'If p had been the case, then q would have been the case' to be true (or assertable, as the case may be), we should not require that q would have been the case in *all* circumstances where p had been the case. To argue that if Hitler had died just after birth, the Second World War would not have occurred, does not commit us to the proposition, 'If Hitler had died just after birth and if he had also had an identical twin that survived and grew up, the Second World War would not have occurred.' What we want to say is that the Second World War would not have occurred if we assume the early death of Hitler and *a minimum of other changes*, the assumption of a twin brother being probably beyond this minimum. As to exactly what *is* the minimum, I would argue that on the meta-linguistic theory of conditions of assertability there is no need to assume any change at all in addition to the mental removal of Hitler, at least for the purpose of exploring the consequences for the Second World War. This is so because relative to a socio-economic theory at the macro-level the existence of a particular individual is an accidental or exogenous fact. The impact of an individual of a given type upon a social process is subject to sociological explanation, but not the emergence of that individual, unless it can be shown that as a type he was characteristic of his times and not just an idiosyncratic deviation.

On the ontological theory of truth conditions for counterfactuals matters are not that simple. Assuming the death of Hitler at birth requires—*but not in a uniquely defined manner*—a number of other and concomitant changes. The death of Hitler can be assumed to have taken place in a number of distinct ways, each of which would require some rewriting of the past, and it may be very difficult to tell which of these ways implies the minimum of change. My contention, briefly stated, is that the relation 'implying more change than' is a partial ordering only, whereas Lewis must hold that it be complete. That is, if for two 'possible worlds' x' and x'' it is the case that x'' differs from the actual world x in all aspects where x' differs from x, but not vice versa, then we can say unambiguously that x'' implies a greater change than x'. If, on the other hand, there are some aspects shared by x and x' but not by x'' and some (different) aspects shared by x and x'' but not by x', then no unambiguous ordering can be possible. Lewis's answer to this obvious objection is to invoke some rough but not (he thinks) wholly arbitrary notion of *importance* which may be used to weigh the different aspects. It is a bit difficult to refute this answer, as I am not sure that I have understood it. Nevertheless I think the following consideration carries some weight: if the aim of the historical counterfactual is to arrive at an evaluation of the relative importance of causes, then we cannot use our intuitive feelings about importance as a basis for weighing variables in a comparison between possible worlds. We cannot explain causation through counterfactuals and then analyse counterfactuals through a notion of importance that inevitably includes causal importance.

In addition to this problem of circularity I would like to draw attention to a difficulty in Lewis's theory that is related to the full-bodied (even if shadowy) nature of his possible worlds. On the interpretation sketched here (and in Chapter 3 above) a possible world is a mere skeleton of a state, as described by a finite number of variables. To use a concept explored in Chapter 4, *it is possible for all that I believe* (*theoretically*); a configuration of variables compatible with a given theory T that I believe to be true. Lewis's possible worlds, however, are full-bodied entities with no blanks to be filled in. If they have a three-dimensional spaces (some have not), then every point in space is either empty or filled with some specific matter. Now this solid existence (or subsistence, or whatever) of the possible worlds makes it hard to see how one could construct a distance measure by attaching different weights to different features. This procedure is meaningful for a skeleton world with a *finite* number of features, but not for the filled-in worlds of Lewis's theory—at least if we accept Ernest Nagel's assertion that 'no finitely long statement can possibly formulate the totality of traits embodied in any concretely existing thing'.[22] There are just too many aspects for us to be able to count them, let alone attaching weights to them.

A similar problem crops up in Fabricio Mondadori's analysis (directly inspired by Lewis) of the role of counterfactuals in the philosophy of Leibniz. As mentioned above, he suggests that a counterfactual proposition about Sextus involves the notion of an individual satisfying a certain condition and otherwise 'differing minimally' from the real Sextus, where this notion is explained roughly as 'has more properties in common with the real Sextus than any of his counterparts'.[23] Now it is well known that according to Leibniz a complete individual concept is resolvable only 'at infinity', in an infinite number of simple properties. If several of Sextus's 'counterparts' satisfying the condition in question share an infinite number of his properties and also differ from him in an infinite number of properties, while there is no counterpart satisfying the condition and differing from Sextus in a finite number of properties only, then the explanation may not be well defined.

It is instructive to look at some of the problems that Lewis claims to have solved, and to see how these solutions are applied to historical problems. Among the difficulties that have baffled both the regularity theory of causation and many traditional theories of counterfactuals, the problem of epiphenomena and the problem of pre-empted potential causes[24] seem particularly important. The first refers to the following situation: an event c is a sufficient cause (given some of the actual circumstances) for event e and a necessary cause (given others of the actual circumstances) for event f. (We also assume that e precedes f in time.) Then we can infer that if e had not occurred, f would not have occurred and—or so it would seem—that e is the cause of f. This confusion between correlation and causation can be dispelled, according to Lewis, by assuming that, 'It is less of a departure from actuality to get rid of e by holding c fixed and giving up some of the other laws and circumstances in virtue of which c could not have failed to cause e, rather than to hold these laws and circumstances fixed and get rid of e by going back and abolishing its cause c'.[25] Yes: this must be so if Lewis's theory is correct, but one cannot argue for this or for any other theory by pointing out the problems it would permit us to solve if it were correct.[26] If Lewis could provide us with *independent* criteria of what constitutes a 'large' departure from actuality, then we could check whether the quoted assertion holds in any particular case, but no such criteria have been forthcoming.

T. A. Climo and P. G. A. Howells[27] have applied Lewis's theory to historical causation. The epiphenomenon problem is illustrated by a case where c is a fall in overseas demand for British goods, e a fall in the prices for these goods, and f a rise in unemployment. The problem, as before, is how we can avoid accepting the statement 'If e had not occurred, then c would not have occurred' which, given the truth of 'If c had not occurred, then f would not have occurred' implies that 'If e had not occurred, then f would not have occurred' and therefore 'e caused f'. The authors seek to resolve this problem in the following passage, which I quote in full because I find it rather hard to understand:

The fall in export demand, c, is only one of some alternative events which could be said to have caused e, the fall in prices (c is a sufficient condition for e). However...given that home demand continued rising, the only other possible cause of f, the rise in unemployment, is absent. Therefore the rise in unemployment could have been caused only by the fall in export demand. Hence if asked whether *if not e then not c* or *if not e then c* departs least from actuality, we would feel entitled to claim that the latter does. The criterion used here is the strength of the tie between the fall in demand and the fall in prices compared with the strength of the tie between falling export and unemployment. In effect we should be saying that it is less of a departure from actuality to abandon falling export demand as the cause of falling prices and to dredge up some alternative cause—the government's deflationary policy perhaps—than it is to countenance falling prices as the cause of rising unemployment in this case.[28]

Whereas Lewis's solution had at least the virtue of Gordian simplicity, this account seems to make the knot even tighter than it was before. Even though the intention of the authors is to apply Lewis's theory to historical problems, their analysis differs from his in at least three respects.

(1) On Lewis's theory it is not a question whether *if not e then not c* or *if not e then c* differs least from actuality, but whether *c but not some other laws and circumstances* or *not c* departs least from the actual world.

(2) On Lewis's account the problem of epiphenomena is resolved without making any appeal whatsoever to the effect f, whereas Climo and Howells make the strength of the tie between c and f relative to the strength of the tie between c and e a crucial factor in their explanation. Specifically, they seem to argue that the tie between c and e is weaker than the tie between c and f, because the latter represents a causal condition that is both sufficient and (given the assumption of rising home demand) necessary, whereas the former is a sufficient cause only.

(3) On Lewis's account the alternative involving the smallest departure from reality does not imply the substitute of a new cause c' for c, nor does any such substitute enter into his analysis on any other way. In the actual world c caused e; in the closest possible not-e world nothing caused e at all; it is hard to see why we should invoke a world where c' caused e and c caused f. Pending further clarification (I may have misunderstood the argument) we must conclude that something went wrong in the Climo–Howells analysis at this point.

The problem of pre-empted potential causes is this: 'Suppose that c_1 occurs and causes e; and that c_2 also occurs and does not cause e, but would have caused e if c_1 had been absent.... In virtue of what difference does c_1 but not c_2 cause e?'[29] The problem is that here a true statement about causation (c_1 caused e) seems to imply a false counterfactual (if c_1 had not occurred, then e would not have occurred). Lewis's solution roughly is this. Assume that c_1 caused e through the intermediate cause d. It is then possible to hold that c_1

might have failed to cause d, but still prevented c_2 from causing e, so that e would not have occurred. In this analysis there is an ambiguity. When Lewis writes that 'thanks to c_1 there is no causal chain from c_2 to e', this may either mean that c_1 prevents c_2 from being the cause of e by some actual inference in the causal efficacy of c_2 or that c_1 prevents c_2 by the very fact that e cannot be caused twice over. If c_1 is a bullet reaching a man's heart at time t_1 and c_2 another bullet reaching the same man's heart at a later time t_2, we have the latter case. If, to take a fanciful example, the bullet c_1, before reaching the man's heart, also passes through the heart of another man who, on falling down, blocks the way between the bullet c_2 and the first man, we have the former case. Lewis's account is adequate at most for this fanciful example. In addition to its inadequacy for examples of the other type, the theory is beset with the general difficulties discussed above.

The Climo–Howells example is the following. c_1 is the Second World War, c_2 the increase in employment from pre-war levels, e the price rise during the war, d the reduction in imported supplies and p_a the package of government controls aimed at limiting demand and rationing supply. If c_1 had not occurred, c_2—through the intermediary of an increase in purchasing power—would have caused e, but c_1 also caused p_a which in the actual world prevented the intermediary from coming about. (Thus we have a case analogous to the fanciful example of the previous paragraph.) The authors proceed by rejecting the counterfactual *if not d then not c_1 and not p_a* on the grounds that 'it is easier to conceive of a world close to our own in which there was a war but in which for one reason or another imports were not reduced, than of one in which the imports were maintained but there was no war'.[30] This assertion seems to hinge upon the massive importance (according to which criteria?) of a war as compared to a mere reduction in imports, but this is surely an accidental feature of this example. It would be easy to construct a formally similar example where d was the war and c_1 some 'intrinsically negligible' (whatever that should mean) feature, such as the length of Cleopatra's nose. Again I must conclude that the possible-world explanation has no resolving power when applied to concrete cases.

I am now in a better position to complete my own account of historical counterfactuals. This account depends crucially upon the notion of dynamic legitimacy. I shall follow Lewis in the formal structure of the theory, appealing to possible worlds and the distance between worlds, but I shall try to do so in a manner not open to the objections specified above. Now with a theory T an apparently plausible notion of relatively possible worlds could be the following: a state s_t' is possible relatively to s_t if in the past history of s_t there is a state s_{t_1} such that there is a permitted trajectory from s_{t_1} to s_t'; that is, if there is some branching point from which the process may diverge to either s_t or s_t'. This definition works quite well if s_t is a state of the actual world history, for we know the past of such states. It does not work, however, if s_t itself is an unactualized world, for states are not, in general, given with the pasts that have led up to them. This difficulty could be resolved,[31] but instead I shall urge that it be ignored. The historian, surely, is interested in the assertability of counter-factuals uttered in the actual world; the assertability of counterfactuals uttered in some possible world presumably leaves him cold. In order to determine the relative importance of causes in the actual world he must postulate a world where one or more of them are absent, but he is under no obligation to find out how important are the various causes in *that* world too.

Now the dynamic criterion of legitimacy permits a natural measure of the distance between the actual world and some possible state: if in the past history of the real system there is some state s_{t_1} from which permitted trajectories lead both to the actual state s_t and to the hypothetical state $\acute{s}_t$, but no permitted trajectory from $s_{t_1 + 1}$ to the state $\acute{s}_t$, then $(t - t_1)$ is the distance between the actual world and the alternative world in question. That is, the further back we have to go in order to insert the possible state in the real history, the greater is the distance to that state. A state of the economy with twice the gross national product of the actual economy is possible, but only distantly so, because we would have to adjust the savings and investment decisions for a very long period in the past if this state is to be at the end of some permitted trajectory. Using this distance measure we can also define in a natural manner the conditions of assertability for historical counterfactuals: the counterfactual as a whole is assertable if the consequent holds in the closest world(s) where the antecedent obtains. If, for example, the antecedent may be inserted into the real world at t_2, whereas we must go back to an earlier time t_1 in order to find a branching point from which a permitted trajectory leads to a state where both the antecedent and the consequent obtain, then the counterfactual is not assertable. Take the statement: 'If it had not been for slavery, the GNP of the US South in 1860 would have been twice as high as it actually was.' This statement would not be assertable if a non-slave South could stem from a branching point no later than, say, 1750, whereas a GNP of the required size would require counterfactual changes going back to 1700.

We should add a brief definition of the conditions of assertability of *might-counterfactuals*. The statement 'If p had been the case, then q might have been the case' is assertable if there is *at least one world* x such that (i) p obtains in x, (ii) q obtains in x, and (iii) there is no world closer than x where p obtains. The corresponding requirement for would-counterfactuals is that condition (ii) obtains for *all* worlds x satisfying (i) and (iii). That is, the distinction between might-counterfactuals and would-counterfactuals requires the possibility of several equally and minimally distant worlds.

The crucial problem in this account is the need for a dynamic criterion of legitimacy, the requirement that the alternative state be capable of insertion into the real past. My main arguments will derive from the concrete examples discussed in subsequent sections, and here I can only state that the historian's concern with the real past makes it difficult for him to accept alternatives that could not (as far as he knows) have come about as the end product of some process starting at some point in the real past. In order to imagine an American economy without slavery in 1860, it is not sufficient to convert all slave-owners into some capitalist or semi-feudal equivalent and all slaves into wage workers or sharecroppers or whatever is thought to be the closer form, and to leave everything else unchanged. Even if this alternative were statically legitimate, we know that it could not have come into being except on premises that differ enormously from the real pre-1860 period, but then we would no longer be dealing with American Negro slavery.

The main idea behind this argument may perhaps be better brought out by taking the simpler example of an individual with his properties, actual and counterfactual. Some of these properties will be closely linked to his genetic constitution, even if intrinsically unimportant: fingerprint patterns might be a good example.Other properties will be independent of the DNA-sequence, but massively important for the personality of the individual: we may think of various character traits that are only slightly constrained by genetic factors. On Lewis's account I suppose that a person without my fingerprints but similar in all other respects is 'closer' to me than is a person with my fingerprints but without my arrogance or jealousy or whatever. On the Kripke–Dummett account discussed in previous chapters this would not be the case, for someone without my fingerprints could not have been born of my parents, given their genetic make-up. The problem is that Lewis does not search for *me* in other worlds, only for some person looking more or less like myself. On the Kripke– Dummett analysis, statements about what I would have done in various hypothetical cases are statements about *me*, which require full and not only partial identification. I submit that this is also how the historian tends to see counterfactual statements: they are statements about the American economy, the one we know, the one and only; not statements about some economy differing minimally from the actual one.

Imperialism and colonialism

In the remainder of this chapter I shall go from theory to applications, and discuss in some detail five examples of counterfactual reasoning in history. The first two represent a search for the *best past* or the *optimal counterfactual*: could the development of Africa and the industrialization of Great Britain have taken place with smaller costs? The last three deal with counterfactuals as a tool in positive rather than in normative analysis: what was the causal importance of the Navigation Acts for the American Revolution, of the railroads for American economic growth, of slavery for the development of the Old South? I hope that the case studies will be of interest in their own right, in addition to permitting further clarification and substantiation of the theses advanced in the preceding section.

My first case concerns the consequences of—and the alternatives to— European colonization in Africa. This is not a field with which I am familiar, so I rely heavily upon some stimulating work by Jarle Simensen.[32] The basic problem discussed in the literature cited by Simensen is the following: Could recent African history have taken another course than the actual one, and what would the consequences have been for the modernization and the economic development of the continent? Building upon Patrick Manning's typology of the main hypothetical alternatives put forward in the debate,[33] Simensen lists the following possibilities:

(1) *Autonomous development* = modernization + economic autonomy + political independence (example: Japan).
(2) *Peripheral, independent development* = modernization + peripheral (i.e. world-market-dependent) economic development + political independence (example: Ethiopia).
(3) *Benign colonialism* = modernization + economic autonomy + foreign rule.
(4) *Peripheral stagnation* = stagnation + peripheral development + political independence (example: some African societies, ravaged by the slave trade about 1850).
(5) *Autonomous stagnation* = stagnation + economic autonomy + political independence (example: some African societies before any contact with the West).

The actual course of events, by contrast, is said to have been characterized by modernization, economic dependence, and foreign rule. For the discussion of these alternatives, the distinction between economic imperialism and political colonialism is crucial, and especially the fact that the former antedated the latter by decades or even more. Thus, given the integration of many African societies in the world market, especially through the slave trade, political domination may have been a necessary feature for the modernization of Africa; what Europeans had destroyed, only Europeans could rebuild. If, on the other hand, we go further back in time, the possibility of autonomous modernization becomes more realistic. According to Simensen, 'Critics of colonial rule... tend to employ a longer time perspective than apologists, going far back to find points where wholly different hypothetical courses of development may branch off.'

Let us now look at the following counterfactuals:

(A) If country X had not been under colonial rule in 1920, it would not have been modernized.
(B) If country X had not been integrated in the world market in 1920, the country would not have been modernized.

On the analysis proposed in the preceding section, these counterfactuals should be explained along these lines:

(A′) If time t_A is the latest date at which there is a branching point from which a permitted trajectory leads to a non-colonized X in 1920, then all non-colonized states of X at the end of a trajectory branching off at t_A or later are non-modernized.
(B′) If time t_B is the latest date at which there is a branching point from which a permitted trajectory leads to a non-integrated X in 1920, then all non-

integrated states of X at the end of a trajectory branching off at t_B or later are non-modernized.

On the account proposed by Lewis the analysis, presumably, rather goes like this:

(A'') Among the non-colonized states of country X the state (states) having the greatest overall similarity to the actual 1920 X is (are) non-modernized.

(B'') Among the non-integrated states of country X the state (states) having the greatest overall similarity to the actual 1920 X is (are) non-modernized.

If we accept the historical account sketched above, (A) is assertable and (B) is not just because (A') is true and (B') is not. On the other hand there does not seem to be any reason why (A'') should be true and (B'') false. Perhaps one could argue that a no-colonization world could be made consistent with known laws (supposing we want to retain *them*), either by renouncing on modernization and keeping everything else intact or by retaining modernization and making suitable changes in the educational and administrative subsystems, but I fail to see why the former adjustment should be smaller than the latter, as it would have to be for (A'') to explain (A). Also it seems to me that (B'') is true rather than false; presumably the simplest way of doing away with integration in the world market is to remove all export–import activites and to relocate the workers in local trade or manufacture, which would surely do away with modernization as well. In an autonomously modernized country (starting at t_B) the modern sectors of the economy would not necessarily be linked to foreign trade, but in the actual world modernization and integration in the world market were so intertwined that to abandon the latter and retain the former would take us very far away from the actual state. Obviously I do not feel very confident in making these assertions, as they presuppose a notion of overall similarity whose usefulness and even meaningfulness I reject; nevertheless it seems to me that they are the kind of assertions that a defender of Lewis's theory would have to accept.

Other conceptual problems also arise in this context. It is natural, for example, to ask which of the alternative states listed above are at all plausible. The *benign colonialism* that would presumably have led to a maximum of modernization with a minimum of costs is for example rejected by Manning as a 'contradiction in terms', which may indeed be an apt expression if the phrase is understood in an absolute sense (cf. the analysis of the master–slave contradiction in Chapter 4 above). But some colonial policies surely were more benign than others, or at least stemmed from the long-term interests of the colonizers rather than from their myopic short-term calculations. It may be worth while, therefore, to discuss whether some alternative policy could have been followed and, if so, what the consequences would have been. One possible criterion (suggested by Simensen) could appeal to the policies which were considered realistic by well-informed contemporaries and actually proposed by some interest groups. The discussion of political possibility in Chapter 3 above has shown, however, that this criterion is both too wide and too narrow. It is too wide because it does not permit the possibility that even well-informed observers might have been wrong, and too narrow because it glosses over the ambiguous or border-line cases where no *ex ante* evaluation of political possibility can be made. Nevertheless, as observed in the discussion of Max Weber above, these subjective possibilities form one natural wedge for counterfactualization.

If—or to the extent that—'benign colonialism' is a contradiction in terms, this has nothing to do with our knowledge about the colonized nation; the impossibility stems from our assumptions about the colonizer. This distinction becomes crucial when we assess the plausibility of autonomous modernization (or of continued autonomous stagnation). From the point of view of the Europe-an nations, continued expansion and ultimately contact with African countries was inevitable, which means that the assumption that the latter could be kept outside the world market is an illegitimate one. From the point of view of the African countries, however, there was no inherent necessity that led to integra-tion in the world market. In this sense the counterfactual 'If Africa had not met the West, it would have undergone an autonomous modernization' is legitimate, whereas the counterfactual 'If the West had not met Africa, European industrialization would have been retarded' is not. This seeming paradox is resolved when we recall how much depends upon our choice of object to be studied. If the 'system' is defined as the African continent and the rest of the world is simply regarded as a constant environment, then the expan-sion of that system into the environment does not follow from the theoretical assumptions we make concerning the system. If, on the other hand, Europe is the system of variables considered, then the expansion into the environment follows at once from an analysis of capitalism in terms of reinvestment of profits. From the point of view of the African economy, European expansion was an exogenous element in much the same sense as the 1923 earthquake was an exogenous shock to the Japanese economy; they can both be safely assumed away for the purpose of causal analysis, even if there exists a theory telling us that they were inevitable.

To this something must be added. When assessing the causal importance of an exogenous factor for the development of a system, the factor may be assumed not to have been present, even if on other grounds we know it to have been inevitable. Certainly we must ensure that the theory we use when going from the antecedent to the consequent does not itself exclude the antecedent as being illegitimate, but theories concerning an *exogenous* antecedent need have no impact upon a world where the antecedent is assumed to be absent. On the other hand we cannot assume the absence of exogenous factors if, as in the present case, we are also concerned with a search for 'the best past'. We may discuss causality as if the impossible were possible, but not morality. More precisely, the distinction between theories concerning the system and theories concerning the environment has no relevance for the welfare issues involved. If we argued that it would have been better for the Africans if the Europeans (*per impossibile*) had colonized them in a completely benign manner or had left them completely alone, then we could also say that it would have been better if the Africans had refused to involve themselves in the slave trade or had set up study groups to assimilate Western technology. The relevant standard against which to compare the actual development is the feasible options *on both sides* that would have led to the best development for Africa.

Optimism and pessimism[34]

For some 20 years or more, British historians have been engaged in the search for *their* best past, in what is called the controversy of optimism versus pessimism in the interpretation of the consequences of the Industrial Revolution in Britain. Actually I do not think this terminology very useful. A number of distinct issues are involved, and I shall argue that in order to sort them out it is better (as well as more correct from the etymological point of view[35]) to talk of optimism versus non-optimism and of pessimism versus non-pessimism. Briefly, I shall speak of pessimism versus non-pessimism as a controversy over the actual development: Did the standard of living of the British workers rise or fall during, say, the period 1820–40? The debate over optimism versus non-optimism, on the other hand, concerns the counterfactual issue whether the trend in real wages could have been higher than it actually was, and if so under which institutional arrangements. I shall deal in turn with the three questions raised by Richard Hartwell and Stanley Engerman in a recent contribution[36] to the debate:

1. Did the working classes improve their standard of living during the Industrial Revolution?
2. Given some set of exogenous changes, were the working classes better off than they would have been in the absence of industrialization?
3. Given the Industrial Revolution, could there have been some other institutional arrangement which would have made the working classes better off than they actually were?

The first of these questions concerns the issue of pessimism as defined above. For simplicity I shall interpret the problem of standards of living as a problem concerning the trend in real wages, even though numerous other aspects—both quantitative and qualitative—are relevant. A comparison of two states of the economy can then be carried out in several distinct ways, three of which shall be briefly covered here. In the first place we may use the 'puristic' method of Samuelson and Sen, discussed in Chapter 2 above. The peculiar feature of this approach, it will be recalled, is that it requires that some counterfactualization be carried out even for the intra-world comparison of two actual states. The point is that a reduction in actual want satisfaction may be accompanied by an increase in the potential for want satisfaction, if, for example, some of this potential is diverted to military uses. This, however, leads us into the second of the three questions raised by Hartwell and Engerman; we return to this problem below. In the second place we might adopt the maximin criterion proposed by

John Rawls in a rather different context: according to this criterion the 1840 workers were better off than the 1820 workers if the least well-off subset of the first group was better off than the least well-off subset of the second, where 'least well-off' may be defined as 'all persons with less than half of the median income and wealth'.[37] This may seem ill-defined, as there may be significant differences within this subset, but Rawls tells us to take the average of the subset as representative for the subset as a whole. To compare average incomes of the least well-off *groups* in this sense is not the same as to compare the incomes of the worst-off *persons*, even though Rawls is often paraphrased in the latter terms. A high value for the first quantity may quite well go together with a very low value for the latter; indeed some critics of Rawls have argued that this is a typical case in modern societies.[38] Disregarding this problem, however, I do not think historians would be very happy with the maximin-criterion. To abstract *completely* from the fate of *all* groups above the worst-off is too heroic a simplification for the social historian who is concerned with the whole complex picture.

In the third place, therefore, we must look for some way of weighing the changes in income for different income groups. Instead of saying (as Rawls would have us do) that a reduction in the income in the least well-off group cannot be compensated by *any* increase, be it of astronomical dimensions, in the income of other groups, we must somehow define a trade-off between income groups. It goes without saying that these trade-offs cannot be determined in a scientific manner, no more than we can evaluate scientifically the relative importance of equity and efficiency[39] in modern societies. In both cases there will be agreement as to the need for some trade-off, but irreducible political disagreement as to the quantitative weights to be used. This, no doubt, explains the heated ideological nature of the standards of living controversy.

For simplicity we may assume that we are interested only in average income and the dispersion around the mean. If the income of the relatively less well-off counts for more in the social welfare function than the income of the better off, then we have a trade-off between average and dispersion: a rising trend in average incomes may be offset by a trend towards a more unequal income distribution, not only between workers and non-workers, but also, as observed by Eric Hobsbawm,[40] between different strata within the working class. The distinction between average and dispersion is important in at least two other respects. In addition to the problem of distribution between individuals there is, firstly, the issue of regional distribution and, secondly, the issue of temporal distribution. As to the first, constant and even falling average values may mask an improvement in welfare caused by better transportation, permitting the rapid transfer of goods from regions with a temporary surplus to regions with a temporary deficit. It is quite possible for investment in railways to lower average consumption (*qua investment* in railways) and to raise average welfare (*qua* investment in *railways*). As to the second, we may note that the trade-off between temporal average and dispersion is more amenable analytically than the inter-personal trade-off, at least to the extent that we are dealing with the same individuals in both states. This is so because we can make use here of the time preferences of the individuals themselves: if an individual alive in both 1820 and 1840 prefers the small fluctuations around the low average in former period to the larger fluctuations round the higher average in the latter (assuming that this was indeed the pattern), then we should feel justified in saying that he experienced a deterioration in his standards of living. (Assuming, of course, that his preferences are constant, which may be rather unrealistic when the individual is aging and his environment changing.)

Actually two distinct problems are involved in the temporal dispersion: diminishing marginal utility of consumption and risk aversion. Consumption of $A + a$ in year 1 and of $A - a$ in year 2 is for most people a less preferred alternative to an equal consumption of $A - e$ in both years, for some positive e.[41] Thus R. M. Hartwell seems justified in accusing E. Hobsbawm of 'double talk' when the latter tries to reduce the 'optimist' (or 'non-pessimist') implications of reduced mortality by pointing out that this may be due to greater regularity of supply rather than to an increase in average consumption.[42] If we are interested in the welfare of individuals rather than in aggregate consumption (and the quoted observation by Hobsbawm about a rising average being offset by a greater dispersion shows that this is indeed his concern), then increased regularity of supply may partially or wholly compensate for reduced average supply. As for risk aversion, it has been argued[43] that the very insecurity created by the irregular supply may have reduced the all-over welfare level. An analogy to this in the inter-personal case is envy, as will now be shown.

It is usually (but not universally[44]) assumed that individual-welfare-at-a-point-in-time is a function exclusively of individual-consumption-at-a-point-in-time. In the preceding paragraph I have indicated that the pattern of consumption in the past may enter into present utility,[45] and in an analogous manner other people's consumption may have an impact upon my own welfare. If, for example, all individuals try to increase (by working extra hours and thus forgoing leisure) the difference between their own consumption and average consumption, no one will actually achieve this, but everyone will have to work harder in order to stay at the same level. It would seem certain that this externality was less important during the period in question than it is today, but it would be rash to conclude that only the absolute levels of income mattered.

I observed above that the political positions of the protagonists in the controversy are reflected in their evaluation of the standard of living. Typically non-pessimists are conservative or libertarian thinkers who tend to attach greater weight to the average than to the dispersion around the mean, while pessimists are egalitarian to a greater extent. In addition to this nuance, there is also the choice of average versus aggregate welfare as the proper maximand, disregarding all problems of distribution. Non-pessimists, I think, have stressed total rather than average welfare, which does indeed favour a non-pessimist view in an age of rapidly increasing population. In one of the more blatantly ideological contributions to the debate, F. A. Hayek writes that, 'The proletariat which capitalism can be said to have "created" was thus not a proportion of the population which would have existed without it and which it had degraded to a lower level; it was an additional population which was enabled to grow up by the new opportunities for employment which capitalism provided.'[46] This, I think, should be read as a defence of capitalism in terms of aggregate welfare maximization. It is impossible to refute this by referring to the usual meaning of the term 'standard of living' which surely is independent of population size, for the real underlying question is whether industrialization was on the whole a good or a bad thing for the working class. I do not pretend to be able to resolve the hard question whether many poor workers are better (*ceteris paribus*) than few poor workers, except to offer the obvious comment that to wish existing workers out of existence now differs crucially from wishing that they had never been born, and even more from wishing before they were born (and before anyone knew that they would be they) that they would not get born. Taking the *ex-ante* view, I believe that an argument can be made for the average welfare measure, but I am not very confident about this.

Rather than exploring further dimensions of the controversy over pessimism, I now turn to the two counterfactuals set up for discussion by Hartwell and Engerman. As to the fate of the workers in the absence of industrialization, Hartwell and Engerman very pertinently observe that the notion of exogenous factors must be resolved before we can give an answer. One of their examples concerns the Napoleonic Wars, which clearly had a negative effect on living conditions, by diverting some of the potential for want satisfaction. Should these wars be treated as exogenous, so that they should be part of the world where no industrialization took place? Or should we rather argue that industrialization and the Napoleonic Wars were both caused by capitalism (and that there was no pre-empted potential cause waiting in the wings that would have caused the wars even in the absence of capitalism), so that we cannot assume away the one without removing the other? This example is purely hypothetical, as no historian (to my knowledge) has held the latter view. A better example of historical controversy over exogenous factors is provided by the fall in the death rate. R. M. Hartwell argued that the lower mortality should be imputed to industrialization itself, whereas H. J. Habakkuk on more recent evidence concludes that it was due to inoculation against smallpox and would have taken place even in the absence of industrialization.[47] This, by the way, is also relevant to the question discussed in the preceding paragraph. To the extent that population grew because people (i.e. the same people that would have been around in any case) lived longer than formerly, this is unambiguously an increase in welfare even if standards of living (as measured by instantaneous criteria such as real wages) were constant, but to the extent that the increase stemmed from increasing fertility, the ambiguity remains.

As to the issue of optimism versus non-optimism raised by this counterfactual, we have only two alternatives to compare: the actual development and the development without industrialization and its concomitants, whatever they are. Presumably the optimists will tend to classify as exogenous the elements with an adverse impact upon the standard of living, such as the wars, and as endogenous the positive elements such as the fall in mortality rates. When we turn to the counterfactual question whether industrialization could have taken a smoother course if suitable changes are assumed in the institutional setting, more alternatives emerge and the search for the best past becomes more complex. The actual Industrial Revolution in Britain took place in the context of imperfect capitalism: a mode of production based upon private property of the means of production, wage labour, and profit-maximizing entrepreneurs, but with imperfect factor mobility, some monopolistic elements, and a large enclave of domestic industry and handicraft. As far as I can see no one has argued that this actual setting was the best possible setting, so that the participants in the debate are all various kinds of non-optimists. One variety holds that the social consequences of industrialization were unnecessarily harsh because of the capitalist context in which it took place, whereas another contends that the misery was due to the process taking place in the context of *imperfect* capitalism. The latter position, roughly, tends to see the actual process as better than what would have taken place in the absence of capitalism and as worse than what would have taken place in a context of perfect capitalism.

Thus W. O. Henderson and W. H. Chaloner stress explicitly,[48] as do many optimists implicitly, that the worst conditions were found in the sectors of domestic industry rather than in the factories, the conclusion presumably being that what was good during the period in question was due to industrial capitalism and what was bad to surviving sectors from the ancient system. As correctly pointed out by Hobsbawm,[49] this comparison between two systems coexisting at a given point of time cannot serve as a basis for a comparison between the two hypothetical 'pure' or unadulterated systems, as one system may have an impact upon the other and even create parts of the other. If wages were low in the domestic sector, this may have been due to the impact from the factory sector. More importantly, the case of the handloom weavers can be cited to show that a vast class of domestic workers may owe its very existence—its initial prosperity and subsequent misery—to the factory system. As observed already by Marx and Rosa Luxemburg, 'pure capitalism' is a fiction. The capitalist mode of production has always generated—and later on reabsorbed— small handicrafts and service sectors working on a quasi-artisan basis in the interstices between the capitalist firms.[50] Thus, the very assumption made is an illegitimate one, making the assertability or non-assertability of the counterfactual quite irrelevant. The same argument can be made to bear upon the contention of Hayek[51] that imperfect factor mobility and monopolistic elements were the 'true sources' of the social disaster. Even if capitalism *per impossibile* had come full-blown into life in perfect form, it would soon have developed the monopolistic elements that according to Hayek were a legacy of the past. Hayek's separation of capitalism from its imperfections is doubly doubtful: using dynamic criteria of legitimacy it is meaningless, and using static criteria it is not assertable.

The Navigation Acts

The problem of quantifying the burden of the Navigation Acts arose in the context of determining the causes of the American Revolution, where it was thought that the importance of the economic grievances among the causes of the revolution could be assessed by measuring the economic loss suffered by the colonies as a result of having to ship all their exports and imports via England. As a preliminary point we may observe that this approach presupposes that one is also able to specify the link between objective economic losses and subjectively felt grievances. This link cannot be the same in all historical situations; there can be no general law stating that when exploitation losses exceed $x\%$ of GNP, revolution will occur. In the first place the even or uneven distribution of the loss over the population is crucial for the revolutionary potential of the loss;[52] in the second place the magnitude of the loss must be correctly estimated by the groups involved; in the third place the loss must be correctly ascribed to exploitation; in the fourth place the conditions for collective action, as discussed in Chapter 5, must be present. Thus in the absence of direct evidence on individual motivations, the chain of reasoning must go approximately as follows:

(1) For group X the exploitation loss was large.
(2) For group X the structural conditions for correct perception and interpretation of the loss were present.
(3) For group X the structural conditions for collective action were present.
(4) Collective action took place.
(5) Therefore there is some probability that group X, motivated by the exploitation loss, participated in the collective action.

Here we do not commit the structuralist fallacy discussed in Chapter 5, as it is explicitly assumed that the capacity for overcoming the free-rider problem is at hand. Now the counterfactual analysis of the Navigation Acts has not gone further than the first link in the chain, or perhaps not even this far, as no effort has been made to determine the distribution of the total loss over the various economic groups in the colonies. If it should turn out that some of the structural conditions were absent, the attempt to calculate the objective loss will probably have been a total waste of time, an attempt to obtain precision in the second decimal while ignoring the first.

In the first studies of the impact of the Navigation Acts, a rather simplistic approach was followed. Let us assume that the actual price per unit sold was p_1, the loss per unit of routing via England was c, and the volume of sales was v. Then the total loss to the colonies due to English exploitation was calculated as cv, the assumption being that in a counterfactual world without the Acts the price would have been $p_1 - c$ and the volume of sales v. Now both parts of this assumption are invalid, the second most obviously so. To assume constant sales with a different price may either be solemnly characterized as an implicit assumption of a completely inelastic supply curve,[53] or just recognized as an instance of the pre-theoretic *ceteris-paribus* fallacy discussed in the first section above. The first part of the assumption is invalid for more subtle reasons. In the present example, as in much of cost–benefit analysis generally, the losses or benefits of the counterfactual situation may be split in two: the impact *upon* the activities undertaken in the actual situation and the impact *of* the additional activities undertaken in the counterfactual situation. Nor only is it incorrect to discuss losses or benefits on the basis only of the former; it may even be impossible to determine the former without taking account of the latter. In the present case the fall in unitary price induced by the elimination of the extra transport costs will be smaller than these costs, because the additional buyers will push the price up. Figure 1 will make the point clear:

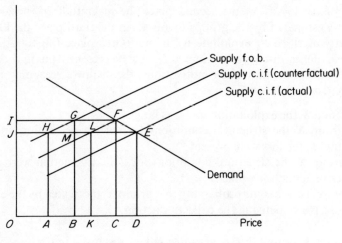

Figure 1.

Here the distance *KD* represents the cost of routing via England. In the actual world supply and demand equate (in Amsterdam) at price *OD* and volume *DE*, giving a f.o.b. price in Philadelphia of *OA* and total producer income of *OA·DE*. In the counterfactual situation supply and demand equate at price c.i.f. *OC* with volume *CF*, giving a price f.o.b. of *OB* and total producer income *OB·CF*. It is easy to see that the difference in income (i.e. the difference between the rectangles *OAHJ* and *OBGI*) has nothing to do with actual sales multiplied by transportation costs (rectangle *KDEL*), nor with the preceding magnitude plus extra sales multiplied by actual price plus transportation costs, nor with any other conceivable magnitude. If the estimated difference in income in this case coincides with the simplistic measure *KDEL*,[54] this can be no more than an accident. It is quite possible to draw the curves so that the simplistic measure cannot even serve as a minimum estimate of the loss. In many contexts the impact of the counterfactual assumption upon the existing activities may indeed serve as a minimum estimate, but not if interaction effects are present. Take the example of a new motorway, which by reducing the distance will both save money (i.e. gasoline) for existing motorists and create benefits for additional motorists. If we consider monetary costs only, the savings created for the existing motorists can serve as a minimum estimate for the total savings. If, however, the additional motorists attracted by the motorway generate extra costs in *time* for the existing motorists by increasing congestion on the road, interaction effects are present and it might conceivably be the case that the nuisance effect of the new motorists for the old more than offset the gain for the new, so that the simplistic measure will not serve as a minimum estimate.

The point may also be put in terms of partial equilibrium analysis versus general equilibrium analysis. What one does in the simplistic approach is to assume that a single unit was routed directly from the American colonies to its destination in Europe, *all other units being routed via England.* In this partial analysis we take the price as given and then calculate the benefit that would accrue to the single producer that could act in this way. By generalizing the result of the partial equilibrium analysis one then arrives at an obviously incorrect conclusion about the general equilibrium that would arise if everyone were able to ship directly to destination. The marginal producer cannot influence prices; each producer can be seen as the marginal producer; therefore the conclusions valid for the marginal producer are valid for all producers taken simultaneously. This, of course, is merely the fallacy of composition once again. I submit that in many counterfactual analyses this fallacy is at work, when aggregate counterfactualizations are estimated by multiplying the impact of a counterfactual change on a single unit by the number of units.

Another error of a related kind is found in the attempt by R. P. Thomas to determine the sales and prices in the counterfactual 1770. He writes[55] that, 'The price that would have existed in the colonies in the absence of the Navigation Acts can be estimated ... by dividing the observed Amsterdam price of Virginia tobacco before the revolution by the ratio of Amsterdam to Philadelphia tobacco prices after the Revolution.' In other words, the counterfactual price f.o.b. 1770 is the actual price c.i.f. 1770 multiplied by

$$\frac{\text{actual price f.o.b. 1790}}{\text{actual price c.i.f. 1790}}.$$

This is an attempt to pull counterfactual rabbits out of actual hats; even if we accept the dubious notion that the ratio of f.o.b. to c.i.f. prices would have been the same in the counterfactual 1770 as in the actual 1790, the counterfactual price f.o.b. can only be obtained if we know the *counterfactual* c.i.f. price of 1770. The procedure proposed by Thomas amounts to an assumption that the counterfactual c.i.f. price of 1770 would have been the same as the actual c.i.f. price of 1770, which is equivalent to assuming a completely elastic demand curve, an assumption that is no less arbitrary than the assumption of a completely inelastic supply curve.

Railroads and American economic growth

This is the title of a book by Robert Fogel that involves what is certainly the most ambitious attempt at wholesale counterfactualization ever undertaken by a serious historian.[56] Assuming that the railroad did not exist, Fogel asks whether this would have made any substantial difference to the American GNP of 1890. In his attempt to answer this question, Fogel explicitly chooses the method of inserting a no-railroad economy into the real past, by going back to the point in time (about 1830) where one could legitimately assume a branching point without railroads. At the level of intentions, at least, he follows the procedure proposed above. We shall see, however, that it is doubtful whether he actually draws all the implications that follow from this choice. In some respects his procedure is closer to what would presumably be recommended by Lewis: take the actual 1890 economy, remove the railways, and assume a minimum of other changes, and recalculate the GNP. In other respects he takes the method very seriously by discussing in astonishing detail the alternative developments to the railroad that would have come about during the period leading up to 1890.

As always we begin with the question of legitimacy, for if this cannot be answered in the affirmative, the issue of assertability does not arise. Is it, then, legitimate to suppose that the railroad was never invented? The answer to this question depends upon which of the currently contending theories of technological change we prefer: a supply-oriented one or a demand-oriented one; a theory stressing the inevitability of inventions or a theory of inventions as being as essentially random as biological mutations. On non-deterministic theories all (or, on moderately non-deterministic theories, many) counterfactuals concerning the non-invention are legitimate. Rather surprisingly we shall see that both varieties of the deterministic approach also allow some leeway for the mental removal of actually made inventions.

On the deterministic demand theory of Jakob Schmookler[57] a growth industry induces an inevitable and predictable increase in the inventive effort directed towards that industry and in the number of inventions actually made for that industry. This determinism, however, concerns mainly the receiving end and not the producing end of the invention. We can predict that when the railroad industry grows, there will be an increasing number of patents for improved railroad technology, but we cannot say very much concerning the techniques used in these inventions; whether their principles will be mechanical, electrical, or thermodynamical. This ignorance concerning the material and technical details of the invention is not simply a matter of the logical impossibility to predict in detail a future invention (if we could predict it we would have made it). Schookler's point is rather that the details are objectively random, in the sense that we are not permitted to assert any counterfactual statement that if the inventor had not made this invention, then someone else would have. All we can say is that some functionally equivalent invention would probably have been made. If we are mainly interested in the functional aspects of the invention, this is not a serious restriction. For some purposes, however, we are equally concerned with the material substrate of the invention. When Fogel attempts to determine the importance for the American economy of the demand for pig-iron induced by the railroad, we are dealing with a material and not with a functional aspect of the railroad. If we assume that in the absence of the railroad the internal combustion engine and the whole automobile industry would have developed some 50 years before they actually did, this is an alternative that is in some respects functionally equivalent (it does many of the same things), but materially very different (it implies a smaller demand for iron and a larger demand for rubber). Of course Schmookler's theory does not permit us to assume that the internal combustion engine would have appeared on the technological scene, only that *some* functional equivalent with probably different material requirements would have done so.[58]

On a deterministic supply theory such as the one proposed by Robert Merton and other students of simultaneous inventions,[59] not only the functional but also the material aspects of an invention are inevitable, in the sense of permitting counterfactual statements to the effect that someone else would have made it had its inventor not done so. At most a time lag is admitted, the role of the genius being to make discoveries appear somewhat sooner than they would have done otherwise. Now this kind of theory may seem to exclude all assumptions of the no-railroad kind, but on closer reflection matters are not so simple. Namely, if progress of science and technology is seen as a largely autonomous process, little or not at all influenced by the social and economic environment (which is certainly influenced by it), then we can permit assumptions of the no-railroad kind much as we can accept assumptions of the no-earthquake kind mentioned above. It is only if science, technology, economy, and society form one system of interrelated variables, no subsystem of which can be separated out and solved independently of the rest, that we must impose severe restrictions upon counterfactuals about technological change and its impact on economic development. Of course the notion of an internally determined process is a rather implausible one for technological development, and only slightly less so for the progress of science. The technological concept of a chain reaction (or of a combinatorial accumulation of ideas) should not be used to characterize the process of technological change itself.

There is also a third kind of deterministic theory that will probably appeal more to most people than either of the preceding ones; a mixed supply–demand theory stating that the joint effect of the demand conditions and of the state of the arts was to render inevitable the emergence of the inventions that actually did emerge.[60] This theory has the advantage of permitting an assessment of the alternative transport technologies that would have developed in the no-railroad economy, but only at the cost of making the very assumption of a world without railroads an illegitimate one. As stated above, if the question about substitutes can be answered, then it should never have been put in the first place. Actually it is much better for Fogel to concede that no substitutes would have developed and attempt to prove that even then the no-railroad economy would have had a 1890 GNP not much smaller than the actual one (which is the thesis for which he is arguing), than to set out to prove the same thesis by arguing that the substitutes that would have developed would have been roughly equivalent to the railroad itself. The former line of argument (which is the one followed in the book) is perfectly consistent. It does not imply that Fogel has a positive belief that no alternatives would have developed (such a belief would require a *theory*, that might enter into conflict with the no-railroad assumption), only that he is willing to accept an assumption that in any case is biased against the conclusion he wants to prove. If he attempted to strengthen his conclusion by the second line of argument, he could be sawing off the branch he is sitting on. In this kind of exercise it is often the case that more is less and that ignorance is strength.

Assuming now that the question of legitimacy has been answered in the affirmative, we must go on to examine whether the unimportance-of-the-railways conclusion follows; whether the GNP of the no-railroad economy would have been approximately of the same magnitude as the actual one. The argument roughly goes like this. Fogel first subdivides the total contribution of the railroads to American economic growth in their contribution *qua* suppliers of transport services (related to the functional aspect) and their contribution *qua* users of various inputs, notably pig-iron (the material aspect). Because Fogel claims to have shown (and I have no quarrel with this) that the last contribution was negligible, the total contribution can be equated with the impact on the supply side. Fogel exclusively deals with the transport of *goods*, leaving passenger conveyance unexplored. With the importance attached in recent economic theory to transaction costs, this neglidgence is hard to justify. With the railroads face-to-face discussions were facilitated, contracts could be more rapidly concluded, inventories more rapidly adjusted, etc. I shall return to some aspects of this problem, but let us first look at Fogel's treatment of the transportation of goods. Within the general category of goods he actually only considers agricultural goods, and within this subcategory he further restricts himself to corn, wheat, pork, and beef. I shall accept his contention that if his mode of reasoning is valid for these commodities, it is valid for all commodities.

A crucial distinction in the argument is between interregional transport (from the producers in the Middle West to the consumers in the East and the South) and intraregional transport (from the producers to the distribution centres and from the distribution centres to the consumers). For interregional transport he finds that the social savings generated by the railroads were about 0·6% of the GNP in 1890 (this figure, as all others, is intended as an upper bound). For intraregional transport he finds that the savings were about 1·2%, so that the total for the four agricultural commodities would be about 1·8%. The generalization to all commodities then gives an all-over total of well below 5% of GNP. The main counterfactual adjustments made by Fogel in order to get from the antecedent to the consequent are the following. Firstly, he assumes that a large number of additional storehouses would be built in order to ensure the supply of meat in the secondary markets (East and South) during the five months of the year when the canals could not be used because of freezing. Secondly, he assumes that the spatial pattern of agricultural production would have been modified, so as to exclude locations that would have been too far from transport facilities in the no-railroad world. Thirdly, he assumes that a number of new canals would have been built in the absence of the railroads and that the roads would have been much improved; in both cases the actual technologies are assumed to have prevailed.

The main defect of Fogel's analysis has been well brought out by Paul David:[61] it is the confusion of *introduction gains* with *withdrawal losses*. To lose something is very different from never having had it; the loss may be better (as in the present case) or worse (as in the loss of a child). On Lewis's account of counterfactuals, the notions of similarity and of distance invoke the idea of withdrawal loss, so that the closest possible world is the one where this loss is minimized, subject to the condition of the antecedent. On my account, however, the idea of the lost introduction gains is the more relevant one. When discussing the importance of the railways for the 1890 GNP we do not want to know what would have happened if, say, it suddenly turned out that structural fatigue in the rails made this mode of transport too dangerous for continued use, all other things remaining the same. We want to know which of the features of the 1890 economy would still have been around had there never been any railroads in the first place.

It should be repeated that Fogel's *intention* is to answer precisely this question, but—as convincingly argued by David—some of his arguments really deal with the instantaneous loss from the withdrawal of the railroad rather than with the cumulative losses from the non-introduction of the railroad. One example— not mentioned by David—concerns refrigeration techniques. In 1890 it would have been perfectly feasible to have large amounts of meat in cheap cold storage for long periods, but prior to 1875 the necessary technique for the mechanical production of ice was not available. Arguing along the lines of Schmookler one might contend that in a no-railroad world the demand for storage facilities would have led to the ammonia machine being invented earlier, or at least to some functionally equivalent device, but if we prefer (as I think we should) a mixed supply–demand theory of inventions, this line of argument may be closed to us. We should then have to accept that for a long period the consumption of meat in the secondary markets would have been restricted to the summer half of the year, when live cattle could be shipped by water. It should not be necessary to dwell upon the implications of this for the development of American agriculture—implications that would still make themselves felt in the hypothetical 1890.

David's main example concerns the existence of irreversible economies of scale in production, due to learning by doing. If the smaller transportation costs of the railroad led to lower prices of—and greater demand for—transported goods, mass-production techniques may have developed that—in the case of an instantaneous withdrawal of the railroads in 1890—would still have larger efficiency at the *smaller* volume of production than the initially given techniques. If you step in and measure the importance of the ladder at the point where it has become possible to kick it away, you should not be surprised if it turns out to be negligible. A plausible case may be made for the proposition that no great harm (and possibly some benefits) would result if today we were to abandon the assembly-line system and return to methods that give larger scope to individual decisions, but from this one should not conclude that the economy would have been pretty much the same today had the assembly line never been introduced.

A last remark will be made upon what I take to be Fogel's implicit assumption that the course of the hypothetical economy would have been a sequence of equilibrium states. An actual economy is never in equilibrium, but for long stretches of time it may operate near equilibrium if the mechanisms that make for stability are sufficiently sensitive and rapid. It seems evident to me that the adjustment to disturbances would have been much slower in a canal economy than in a railroad economy. The enormous amounts of food that would have to be stored for winter could make for extremely large inventory cycles, with a corresponding loss of efficiency. Bottlenecks in interindustry relations would have constituted a much more serious problem than they actually did; the increased transaction costs implied by the absence of rapid passenger transportation have already been mentioned. The point is that the importance of the railroad was much broader than just the reduction of transport costs: by permitting quasi-instantaneous adjustment and communication, flexibility, and previsibility, the reilroad was part and parcel of the general conditions for economic development. If there had been perfect foresight and total certainty associated with all economic decisions, this would not have mattered much, but in a world where unintended consequences are perpetually generated it is of the utmost importance that these fluctuations become quickly damped and are not permitted to propagate themselves for the long reaction time of a canal economy. The dual theory of social change proposed in Chapter 5 included good communication facilities among the conditions that facilitate collective action for the purpose of restoring the equilibrium, and it is obvious enough that they are also crucial for the efficacy of the mechanisms that restore equilibrium through the individual actions in the market.

American slaves and their history

I conclude the present chapter, and the book, by an exposition of some counter-factual statements that have been proposed in the discussion of American Negro slavery. This discussion has recently been brought to a new pitch by the publication of Robert Fogel and Stanley Engerman's *Time on the Cross*,[62] which presented itself as a drastic revision of virtually all tenets of the conventional wisdom on American Negro slavery. Was slavery profitable? Were slave-owners rational? Were slaves efficient? The conventional wisdom says No, Fogel and Engerman Yes. Was the economic growth of the South retarded by slavery? Were slaves treated cruelly? The conventional wisdom says Yes,

Fogel and Engerman No. Such is at any rate the self-image of the authors, even if it has since been shown[63] that no one has ever held simultaneously all the views imputed to the conventional wisdom and that many of these views were abandoned long ago by most scholars in the field. This historiographic discussion, however, is but one and probably the least important of the four main dimensions to the debate that has been raging around *Time on the Cross*. A second dimension concerns the question whether Fogel and Engerman got their basic facts right, whether their samples are representative, their understanding of the sources correct. A third dimension concerns the logic of their inference from facts or purported facts, such as their use of aggregate data as foundation for inferences about motivation. The fourth dimension is the ethical one, where critics have argued that the 'shrill' anti-racism of the authors is just a more subtle variety of the very stance they are attacking and that the effect, if not the intended effect, of their work is to obliterate the fundamental distinction between freedom and subjection.

In what follows I deal with a small subset of problems within the third dimension, and not exclusively with the work of Fogel and Engerman. This subset concerns the use of counterfactual analysis for answering two distinct questions. In the first place we may ask how the Southern economy would have been about 1860 in the absence of slavery; in the second place we may assume that slavery was never abolished and ask what follows. Underlying both questions is a preoccupation with the relation between slavery and economic growth: did slavery actually impede economic growth in the South, or would it eventually have done so had it been allowed to go on? An affirmative answer to the first question implies that slavery was *stagnating*, whereas the same answer to the second implies that it was *moribund*. It is perfectly possible to state than an economy has been vigorously growing up to time t *and* that it would not have continued to do so; this is indeed the argument of the school of thought that sees the use of non-renewable resources as the essential condition for the economic growth of the ante-bellum South.

Fogel and Engerman answer both questions negatively. In addition they also raise a third problem, concerning the expectations of the slave-holders on the eve of the Civil War. They argue that slave-holders were optimistic and that they were justified in their optimism, in the sense that if the war had not taken place their expectations would have been confirmed. From a methodological point of view this procedure seems sound, and indeed indispensable if we are to assess fully the thesis of a moribund Southern economy. I submit that we should have to accept this thesis if it could be proved either that the slave-owners held a dark view of the future or that their future would have been dark; conversely the thesis can be disproved only by refuting both of these propositions. If, for example, the future would have been rosy, but for reasons that could not have been foreseen by the slave-owners in 1860, such as an exogenous change in the demand for cotton, the system was moribund in an *ex-ante* sense, and slave-owners would have acted as if it were moribund. The comparison between the expected outcome and the counterfactual outcome is probably the summit of abstraction in historical reasoning. We often compare anticipated outcomes with the actual ones, and sometimes at least the actual outcome with the counterfactual one, but I do not know of any other case where there has been occasion and indeed a need for comparing the outcome anticipated on the basis of certain assumptions with the outcome that would have been realized if these assumptions had turned out to be correct. We are not concerned with 'the capacity of the slave-holding class to read crystal balls',[64] for we know already that the Civil War proved them wrong. Rather we want to know whether they would have been right if the war had not taken place.

Before entering into the details of this comparison, however, I shall take up the first counterfactual mentioned above, concerning the hypothetical state of the Southern economy in, say, 1860 in the absence of slavery. It is extremely hard to determine which of the no-slavery worlds is the closest to the actual one, but here are some of the more plausible candidates:

(1) Take the actual 1860 economy; replace slave owners with large agricultural proprietors and slaves with sharecroppers and day labourers; eliminate all features of society that stem *directly* from the *present* institution of slavery.
(2) Take the actual 1860 economy; make the same substitutions as in the preceding case; eliminate all features that directly *or indirectly* stem from the present institution of slavery.
(3) Take the actual 1860 economy; make the same substitutions as in the preceding cases; eliminate all features that directly or indirectly stem from the present or *past* institution of slavery.
(4) Go back in time to the latest branching point at which slavery could have been abolished and develop an alternative economy from that point up to 1860.
(5) Go back in time to the latest branching point from which a development could have begun where slavery was never introduced, and develop an alternative economy from that point up to 1860.

Of these possibilities the first two invoke the static criterion of legitimacy only, and are more or less along the lines of David Lewis's theory. The last two, on the other hand, correspond to the approach advocated by the present author. The third is somewhat ambiguous, but is fundamentally a variant of the first two. The difference between (1), (2), and (4) on the one hand, and (3) and (5) on the other, is that the former permit the counterfactual economy to retain all the features (racism, etc.) that follow from a past history of slavery, whereas the latter define a no-slavery economy in a more rigorous manner as one without any 'hysteresis traces'[65] from a slavery past. The difference between (1) and (2) is the difference between a non-equilibrium and an equilibrium state. When we remove slavery, we must also remove the aspects of society that are immediately and conceptually linked to that institution, such as police for tracking down fugitive slaves, stud farms for slaves, separate legal status for slaves, etc. Whether or not also to remove the aspects that (in equilibrium) are *causally* linked to slavery, is another matter. A society without slavery, but with the political and ideological features of a slave society, is quite possible, but it would not be in equilibrium. Also the transition from slavery to non-slavery would presumably require some changes in the nature and location of economic activities, due to the suddenly created factor mobility and to changes in motivation. The distinction between (1) and (2) corresponds, *mutatis mutandis*, to a distinction between the actual South of 1865 and the actual South of 1880 or some other date when it can be assumed that an approximate no-slavery equilibrium had been reached.

As far as I can understand or guess, the world of alternative (1) must be the closest no-slavery world if we accept Lewis's account, but this world is extremely uninteresting if we are asking about the importance of slavery for Southern economic growth. If someone asked for a proof of the purported inefficiency of socialism, he would not be very impressed if we pointed out to him the problems that beset an economy immediately after a violent socialist revolution. In order to evaluate the performance of an institutional arrangement, we must step in at a point in time—whether actual or counterfactual—where the system has operated for a sufficiently long period for the implications of that arrangement to have worked themselves out. I do not imply that Lewis's notion of the *closest* no-slavery world coincides with the state that immediately *succeeded* slavery (or would have succeeded it had it been abolished). In Lewis's theory there is no requirement that there be a feasible path from the actual world to the closest possible world. Nevertheless, I can see no objection to the interpretation that the closest possible world to an equilibrium state may be a non-equilibrium state, just as the state immediately succeeding an interrupted equilibrium is also out of equilibrium.

We may now proceed to link up this somewhat arid analysis with some actual counterfactual statements about the Old South. An example of a not uncommon mode of reasoning can be taken from an article by Robert Russel where he tries to refute the thesis that slavery was harmful to the non-slave-holding Whites:

> In slavery days the cities and towns of the South, being neither numerous nor large, derived their support principally from plantation districts, where there were many slaves, rather than from small-farming regions, where there were few. It was chiefly the planters who bought, sold, borrowed, travelled, and sent their children to academies and colleges. It seems quite certain therefore, that if it had not been for plantations and slavery, the cities and towns of the South would have been even fewer and smaller, resulting in even fewer opportunities for nonslaveholding whites.[66]

Russel's 'therefore', linking the factual part of the passage to the counterfactual part, is breathtaking. In the first place, how could you in a no-slavery economy distinguish the slave-holding from the non-slave-holding Whites? How do you identify the counterfactual persons that in the actual world were respectively the one and the other? One possibility is to look at the functionally equivalent persons, i.e. owner-non-workers and owner-workers respectively, and see whether the fate of the latter would have been better or worse than the fate of the actual non-slave-holding Whites. On alternative (1) above this is plausible, for in that case you know that you are dealing with the same individuals in different roles. On alternatives (2)–(5), however, you have no assurance that this is the case, and then any statement about the counterfactual distribution of income does not imply anything about the fate that would have befallen the non-slave-holders. As I have argued that alternative (1) is itself implausible, this question is left without a satisfactory answer. (Another possibility, presupposing alternatives (4) or (5), would be to identify the counterfactual persons with actual persons by looking at their common ancestry before the branching point, but in that case there is the difficulty that many of the actual non-slave-holders might never have been born at all in the counterfactual world.) In the second place, we distinctly receive the impression that according to Russel the slave-holders would just have disappeared without any substitute in the counterfactual world, as he seems to rule out the idea that the counterfactual homologues for the planters, such as large capitalist farmers, might have been functionally equivalent in providing support for the cities and towns.

Identically the same *contresens* is found in a well-known article by Robert Fogel, 'The specification problem in economic history'. In the course of a discussion of Eugene Genovese's contention that the industrial development of the Old South was retarded by slavery, Fogel writes that

the statement that the size of the Southern market for goods was limited by the existence of slavery implies the counterfactual proposition that in the absence of slavery the Southern market for manufactured goods would have been larger than it actually was. Given the consuming groups into which Genovese divides the population, the basic condition for his proposition to be valid is

$$(D_0' - \bar{D}_0') + (D_0'' - \bar{D}_0'') + (D_s - \bar{D}_s) + (D_f - \bar{D}_f) > 0,$$

where
D_0' = the slave-owners' demand function for manufactured goods to be used in the maintenance of slaves;
D_0'' = the slave-owners' demand function for manufactured goods for all other uses;
D_s = the slaves' demand function for manufactured goods;
D_f = the demand function for manufactured goods of non-slave-holding free persons.

Symbols with bars refer to the slave period; those without bars refer to the abolition period.

Obviously the basic condition could have been satisfied in a multitude of ways. If only ordinal comparisons of the paired functions are allowed, there are 240 ways of satisfying the inequality. Genovese did not clearly specify which of these alternatives he had in mind. The most that can reasonably be inferred from his discussion is that $D_s - \bar{D}_s > 0$ and that $D_f - \bar{D}_f > 0$. The restrictions reduce the theoretical alternatives, but the number remaining, sixty, is still large.[67]

With enemies like this, Genovese does not need friends. Fogel is so eager to make fun of Genovese's lack of sophistication that he is led to invoke theoretical constructs devoid of meaning. The notion D_0', for example, is not at all meaningful. (Or perhaps one could argue that it should be identically equal to zero, which would then cut down even more the number of alternatives.) More importantly, the distinction between D_0'' and D_f is impossible to draw, for the reasons given above. Fogel curiously refers to the counterfactual situation as 'the abolition period', but of course the actual post-1865 period cannot serve as a proxy for the counterfactual 1860; nor is it obvious that this counterfactual 1860 must be a world where slavery had been *abolished* rather than a world where it had quietly disappeared or just never been introduced.

The points made here can be generalized in the following manner: under all plausible conditions it is impossible to evaluate the impact of an economic system on groups that are defined in terms of notions specific to that system, for these groups cannot be identified in words where the system is assumed to be absent. We may enquire about the fate of small agricultural producers or of owner-workers in a capitalist South, but not about what would have happened to the non-slave-holding free. The attempt to prove that the latter were victims of slavery is just as meaningless as Russel's attempt to prove the contrary. Similarly we cannot determine the impact of capitalism on workers, whereas it *is* possible to analyse the impact of capitalist agriculture upon the precapitalist forms that coexist with it or the impact of early capitalism on the artisan sectors, because in the latter cases it is possible to assume away the environment without removing also the conditions for identifying the groups in question. The problem may be linked to Sen's analysis of national income, as briefly discussed in Chapter 2 above. The one case where we can say unambiguously that the non-slave-holding free would have been (say) better off without slavery, is when it can be shown that the counterfactual South would have been better than the actual one on *all* imputations of the consumption baskets of the former to members of the latter. I think, however, that in all interesting cases the highest income of one state will be higher than the lowest income of the other, so that unambiguous comparisons can in practice never be made on these grounds. On the other hand I have just argued that it is not possible to find a privileged imputation that preserves personal identity; in particular rank-preserving imputations will not in the general case preserve personal identity of some independently defined subgroup.

Even if we avoid making comparisons for functionally defined subgroups, we might try to tackle the problem of aggregate entities such as GNP *per capita* or growth rates. In that case, however, we at once hurt ourselves on the stumbling-block of racism. The causal relationship between slavery and racism, the persisting character of racism once created (even in the absence of the original cause) and the negative effects of racism upon economic performance, require a branching point so far back in time that counterfactual reconstruction crosses the borderline between science and science fiction. The upshot of my discussion of the first counterfactual problem, viz. the impact of slavery upon Southern economic growth, is thus wholly negative. The large problem—the impact of slavery upon GNP or the growth rate of the economy—cannot be resolved for practical reasons; the smaller problems—the consequences of slavery for subgroups defined in terms of the system—cannot be resolved for conceptual reasons. To invoke comparative evidence in order to prove that the Old South could hardly have had a higher rate of growth without slavery, as do Fogel and Engerman,[68] is not very relevant. In particular there is a trade-off between low levels of GNP *per capita* and relatively high rates of growth, at least in certain stages of economic development, that could equally well be invoked to prove that without slavery the 1860 South would have had a larger *per-capita* income.

I turn now to the second counterfactual problem, concerning what would have happened to the Southern economy in the absence of the Civil War. This question is inextricably linked up with the analysis of the rationality, the profitability, and the viability of slavery. This discussion has in recent years become increasingly complex, and I can offer only a simplified sketch of the arguments. I shall approach the problem by means of a distinction between the various rates of profits (or of interest) that are conceptually important to the analysis. These are

$r_1 =$ the prevailing rate of interest that investors in 1860 obtained outside slavery, e.g. in railroads and manufacture;

$r_2 =$ the rate of interest that would have prevailed if slavery had gone out of existence;

$r_3 =$ the internal rate of return upon slave-rearing, defined as the rate that equalizes the value at birth of expected future gross earnings from a slave and value at birth of expected maintenance costs for the slave during his life (risk neutrality being assumed for simplicity);

$r_4 =$ the revealed rate of profits in slave production, defined as the rate that equalizes current slave prices and present value of expected future net earnings, both prices and earnings being defined relative to a slave of a given age (risk neutrality still assumed).

In order to determine the last two rates, we need some ideas about the slave-holders' expectations about future earnings. It will not do simply to extrapolate current earnings into the future, for then we obtain only the special case that slave-holders anticipated no change in earnings. (Current earnings are relevant only for the question whether *past* prices, based on past expectations, were justified or not.) Rather we must follow Fogel and Engerman, who use the available data to measure the 'sanguinity of slave-holders' by looking at the relative movements of slave hire rates and slave prices. An increase in hire rates relative to prices would indicate that planters had a pessimistic outlook on future earnings.[69]

If slave-holders were 'rational' in the sense understood by Fogel and Engerman, i.e. moved solely by the desire to maximize the return on their investment, then we must have $r_4 = r_1$ in equilibrium. Alfred Conrad and John Meyer, in their path-breaking contribution to the problem,[70] required that $r_4 = r_2$, but most later authors have argued that for motivational analysis of the individual planter this general equilibrium approach of wholesale counterfactualization is irrelevant. Even if it were the case that all planters would have been better off if they had all left slavery, the discussion of Chapter 5 showed that this could have had a motivational impact only if (i) all planters recognized the fact, recognized that it was recognized by all, etc., and (ii) no individual advantage could be obtained by being the only one not to leave slavery. With these assumptions (plus the assumption that it was not to the advantage of the individual planter to be the only one to leave slavery, which is sustained by the fact of slavery itself) the situation would look roughly like an Assurance Game. The difficulty, of course, lies in assumption (i); it is indeed unlikely that the structural conditions for the required information were present.

If $r_4 < r_1$, this could be a sign of the irrationality of slave-holders, in the sense of their being swayed by other than purely business considerations. On Fogel and Engerman's interpretation these non-business motives are taken to be conspicuous consumption, i.e. the pride and prestige attached to slave-holding. In their analysis of this notion, they seem to commit two conceptual errors, which I shall now discuss briefly. Firstly, they argue that

> To show that the ownership of slaves and prestige were positively correlated does not settle the issue of causality. Was the price of slaves high because the ownership of slaves brought prestige, or did the ownership of slaves bring prestige because their price was high? To distinguish between these alternatives one needs to find whether the expected return to slaves was below or above alternative rates.[71]

As the authors find that the return on slaves was comparable to return on other investments, they opt for the second alternative: prestige was the effect rather than the cause of high slave prices. This argument seems to rest upon a confusion between general equilibrium reasoning and partial equilibrium reasoning. The prestige attached to highly productive assets is surely a general equilibrium phenomenon, in the sense that a slave-holder would derive prestige from his slaves not because *his* slaves were especially productive, but because slaves *in general* were highly productive. From the point of view of the individual planter (partial equilibrium) it would therefore have been desirable to increase his holding of slaves beyond the profit-maximizing point, because the fall in productive efficiency of *his* slaves would entail but an infinitesimal loss of prestige. As all planters would presumably act likewise, there would be a general loss of efficiency up to the point where all prestige had disappeared.

At this point the individual planter would prefer to reduce his holdings of slaves; when everyone does this the prestige of slave-holding would rise again, which could induce the cycle to begin all over again. We are, in fact, dealing with a game without a (non-cooperative) solution.

Secondly, and this is a more fundamental difficulty of their approach, Fogel and Engerman take it for granted that the only alternative to profit-maximizing is the 'conspicuous-consumption' model; at any rate they seem to take it as a matter of course that all other alternatives would imply deviations from profit-maximizing. I believe that there exists another alternative to profit-maximizing, which might behaviourally give the same observed results as profit-maximizing. (Thus here, as in other cases, the deduction of profit-maximizing motivations from profit-maximizing behaviour is unjustified.[72]) This is the Hegelian master–slave dialectic discussed in Chapter 4 above. In this model, the master's power over the slave is inseparable from his conspicuous consumption of the objects produced by the slaves (which is not the same thing as conspicuous consumption *of* slaves). For the master to derive social prestige from his slaves, mere possession is not enough; he must also have a correspondingly high level of consumption. For simplicity we may assume that slaves and ordinary consumption goods must be held in fixed proportions, so that at any given number of slaves an increase in consumption goods beyond the proportional magnitude gives no extra satisfaction and vice versa. The proportions may be constant, so that the corners of the indifference curves lie on a straight line, but in general we need only assume that more slaves require more consumption goods. But if the planters' consumption is an increasing function of the number of slaves used on the plantations, this means that *planters' consumption can be analytically classified as costs of production*. Eugene Genovese has been much criticized for his statement that the planters' outlays on vacations, education for their children, etc. should be seen as costs of production (to be deduced before profits),[73] but I submit that his procedure can be justified along the Hegelian lines just sketched. Hegel can be read as saying that in a slave economy the scale of consumption is directly linked to the scale of production, so that the two are determined simultaneously rather than successively, whereas in the standard analysis of the capitalist entrepreneur it is assumed that consumption depends upon net income, commodity prices, and preferences, the gross volume of production being irrelevant.[74] On the Hegelian model $r_4 = r_1$ is not a sufficient condition for planters' rationality, for it is quite possible that the function linking consumption to number of slaves would make them want to hold exactly the profit-maximizing number of slaves.

By these remarks I do not claim to have refuted what Fogel and Engerman say about the rationality of slave-holders. Their conclusions may be correct, even if there are some holes in their argument. I only claim to have shown (i) that rationality is incompatible with prestige as an effect of high slave prices, and not only with prestige as the cause of high slave prices; and (ii) that from the observed fact that $r_4 = r_1$ we cannot automatically conclude that slave-holders were rational, even though this conclusion would be valid if the conspicuous-consumption model were the only alternative to profit-maximizing. Given the fact of $r_4 = r_1$, we can conclude only that slavery was profitable. If Fogel and Engerman commit the error of concluding from profitability to rationality, they must be credited, however, with the avoidance of the conclusion from profitability to viability. I now turn to this problem.

The profitability of slavery means only that no over- or undercapitalization of net returns from slaves was observed, but on this definition any moribund enterprise is bound to seem profitable.[75] Given the expected stream of net returns, however small (but positive), and the prevailing rate of interest r_1, the market will automatically fix the present value of the productive assets so as to show the same profitability as other assets. (Here I assume profitability *and* rationality, in order to show that they do not jointly imply viability.) The problem of the viability of slavery must therefore be defined in terms of the cost of production of slaves rather than in terms of the prices of slaves. For a 20-year-old slave, the present value of future net earnings (discounted at r_1) may be positive even if the value at birth of his future net earnings (discounted at r_1) is negative. This is so because up the age of ten the outlays on a slave exceed the income produced by the slave, so that the stream of net returns will have some negative elements that may outweigh the positive elements, especially as the former, corresponding to earlier years and reduced by a smaller mortality coefficient, count more heavily than the latter in the discounted present value. To say that the value at birth of a slave is negative when discounted at the prevailing rate of interest $(r_3 < r_1)$, means that slavery is not viable. Fogel and Engerman found this to have been the case in Jamaica, where slavery can be said to have been non-viable in the sense of requiring a continuous stream of adult slaves from Africa, whereas for the United States they found $r_3 > r_1$.

To the extent that slavery was viable in this *ex-ante* sense, we can also justify the assumption that the Civil War did not take place and ask whether it would have been viable in the *ex-post* sense. The point here is the following. Some traditional interpretations of slavery have argued that the Civil War was caused by the internal contradictions of slavery; that slave-holders had the subjective choice between an expansionist war and a steady decline in prospects. If slavery had turned out to be non-viable in the *ex-ante* (subjective) sense, this interpretation could not be ruled out of court. And if we accept that the main cause of the war was economic contradictions in the South rather than abolitionist sentiment in the North, then the war cannot be treated as an exogenous event to the slavery states and the assumption of its absence (for the purpose of predicting the future course of Southern economic development) would not have been justified. With sanguine slave-holders, on the other hand, this assumption seems legitimate, and then we can go-on to ask whether their sanguinity would in fact have been justified.

As stated above, I hope that the use of these lengthy examples is justified by their being of interest in their own right, in addition to their importance for the conceptual analysis of historical counterfactuals. It may perhaps be useful if at this point I briefly summarize some of the main ideas. I have been arguing for a specific interpretation of historical counterfactuals, and against the general interpretation of all counterfactuals proposed by David Lewis. I have not tried to offer an alternative general theory. My objections to Lewis's theory have been of two kinds. In the first place I have argued, quite generally and without reference to historical counterfactuals, that to explain causality by counterfactuals and counterfactuals by similarity is a circular procedure, as causal importance is an element in our intuitive notions about similarity. In the second place I have argued that even if we waive this objection and try to make some intuitive sense of the notion of similarity, Lewis's account is quite misleading when applied to the specific problem of historical counterfactuals, and as it is intended as a general theory for all kinds of counterfactuals this would seem to be a criticism of some import. The main problem is that on Lewis's theory the closest possible world satisfying a certain condition may very well turn out to be a world that could never have branched off from the actual past; indeed, restricting ourselves to the worlds where the laws of nature, even if different from ours, are deterministic in form, there can be no branching-off at all. When the historian, however, makes a counterfactual assertion, I submit that it is intended as, and must be analysed as, a statement about what could have happened (for all that we believe) to the *real* past. This implies the need for a genetic theory of counterfactuals, and for a theory of assertability rather than of truth. The theory is strengthened, I think, by its congruence with the genetic account of essential properties advanced by Saul Kripke and Michael Dummett. Instead of looking for counterparts to the actual worlds or to individuals in it, we must interpret counterfactuals about collective or individual actors as statements about *them*.

Notes

1. Lewis (1973 a).
2. For one such version, see Mackie (1965); for objections see Sosa (1975).
3. A few words about the comparative method may be in order at this point. In some privileged cases the relative importance of causes can be determined directly on comparative grounds. When arguing that cause A was more important than cause B for the emergence of effect C in country I, we do not always have to compare a counterfactual country I without A, a counterfactual country I without B and the actual country I; with a large amount of luck we may be able to settle the question by comparing the actual country I with actual country II exactly similar (in the respects defined by the underlying theory) to country I except for the absence of A and with actual country III similar to country I except for the absence of B. In the general case, however, comparisons play a more indirect (even if absolutely crucial) role, as the empirical basis for the generalizations which are needed for the evaluation of the counterfactuals. Comparative evidence may be used, for example, to establish the generalization that in traditional societies the supply-curve of labour is negatively sloped; in the analysis of a given traditional society, for which we have no direct evidence on this point, this generalization may then be used in order to determine what the effect on production would have been if a certain wage increase had occurred; and the answer to this problem may in turn tell us something about the relative importance of the wage

level as compared to other causes that influence the level of gross national product. It may be useful to stress, for later reference, that counterfactual propositions are law-users and not law-confirmers. If, on the basis of a certain generalization, a counterfactual proposition is asserted, this does not constitute further proof of the generalization. To think that it does, would be to lay oneself open to the devastating criticism of Adler proffered by Popper (1963, p. 35): 'Once, in 1919, I reported to him a case which to me did not seem particularly Adlerian, but which he found no difficulty in analysing in terms of his theory of inferiority feelings, although he had never seen the child. Slightly shocked, I asked him how he could be so sure. "Because of my thousandfold experience", he replied, whereupon I could not help saying: "And with this new case, I suppose, your experience has become thousand-and-one fold."'

4. Leibniz (1948, pp. 285–286).
5. Rescher (1967, p. 17); see also Mates (1968).
6. Lewis (1968), Mondadori (1973).
7. Mill (1967, p. 575).
8. Mill (1967, p. 256).
9. Mill (1967, p. 575).
10. Mill (1967, pp. 80–81).
11. Weber (1968, p. 276).
12. For similar assertions, cf. Hegel (1970, vol. 16, p. 290) and Merleau-Ponty (1963, p. 45).
13. Lewis (1973b, pp. 66 ff.).
14. Here I follow Ashby (1971, p. 130).
15. See Berge (1963) for an exposition.
16. An ambitious attempt (the only one to my knowledge) to formulate a theory of historical change in these terms is Rader (1971).
17. Cf. here Davidson (1973), as paraphrased in Appendix 2 to Chapter 5; also Elster (1976a).
18. This, I take it, is the point made by McClelland (1975, pp. 161 ff.) when he emphasizes the elusive but important role of substitutes that might have emerged instead of the factor mentally removed in the counterfactual assumption.
19. Goldman (1972, p. 223).
20. Stalnaker (1968), Lewis (1973b).
21. Actually this simplification of Lewis's theory gives us the original formulation by Stalnaker. Lewis wants to hold open the possibility that there may be no A-world that is *the* closest, either because there are A-worlds arbitrarily close to ours or because there may be several A-worlds equally and minimally distant from ours. The latter idea is the most important one; without it the distinction between would-counterfactuals and might-counterfactuals collapses.
22. Nagel (1963, p. 214).
23. Mondadori (1973); the quote is not exact.
24. In addition Lewis (1973 a) lists *the problem of effects*: assuming that c is a sufficient cause of e (given the laws and some of the actual circumstances), we must conclude that if e had not occurred, then c would not have occurred, so that e turns into a cause of c. This problem is solved by the same method as the problem of epiphenomena.
25. Lewis (1973a, p. 566).
26. Cf. the remarks at the end of note 3 above.
27. Climo and Howells (1976).
28. Climo and Howells (1976, pp. 11–12).
29. Lewis (1973a, p. 567).
30. Climo and Howells (1976, p. 14).
31. The obvious way of defining the accessibility relation between two unactualized worlds is to say that s'_t is possible relatively to s''_t if there is some states s_{t_1} in the actual past from which both s'_t and s''_t might have emerged, at the end of permitted trajectories.

220

It is not obvious, however, which measure of the distance between s'_t and s''_t would then be the appropriate one. Given that s'_t and s''_t are at distances d' and d'' respectively from the actual state s_t, then $(d' + d''), |d' - d''|$ and max (d', d'') are all possible candidates for the measure of the distance between s'_t and s''_t.

32. Simensen (1977).
33. Manning (1974).
34. The following account draws heavily upon Elster (1975b).
35. The term 'optimism' was coined in 1737 to denote the Leibnizian doctrine that the actual world is the best of all possible worlds; it is thus fitting to apply this term to the counterfactual aspect of the controversy. The term 'pessimism' was used by Schopenhauer in 1819 to denote his own doctrine that the actual world is the worst of all possible worlds, but a far more common acceptation is the idea that the evil in the world outweighs the good, which is an intra-world comparison similar to the one denoted here by the same term.
36. Hartwell and Engerman (1975).
37. Rawls (1971, p. 98).
38. Barry (1973, p. 50).
39. Cp. Okun (1975).
40. Hobsbawn (1963, p. 112).
41. Thus the following statement is open to doubt: 'the labourer suffered more sharply under the pressure of industrial distress, though he gained *equally* substantially when business activity moved upwards' (Taylor, 1960, p. 29, italics supplied).
42. Hobsbawm (1957, p. 46), criticized by Hartwell (1961, p. 413 n. 2).
43. 'It is necessary to take account not only of prosperous and depressed years but also perhaps of the new insecurity which the changing character of the business cycle brought with it' (Taylor, 1960, p. 29). Against this we may note the risk preference of the very poor.
44. For recent statements to the contrary see Pollak (1976b) and Haavelmo (1970); also Leibenstein (1976, Chapter 4).
45. Please observe that this is not the same thing as the dependence of my present preferences upon past consumption, as explained in the section on endogenous change of tastes in Chapter 2 above.
46. Hayek (1954, p. 16).
47. Hartwell (1961, p. 412); Habakkuk (1971, p. 34).
48. Henderson and Chaloner (1958, p. xiv).
49. Hobsbawm (1963, pp. 127–128).
50. Marx (1933, p. 120); for Rosa Luxemburg, see the discussion in Chapter 5 and the reference in note 133 to that chapter.
51. Hayek (1954, p. 28).
52. Loschky (1973).
53. Walton (1971).
54. This is the contention of Thomas (1965, p. 637, n. 53).
55. Thomas (1965), criticized by Walton (1971, p. 537).
56. Fogel (1964).
57. Schmookler (1966).
58. We may observe here that the distinction between functional and material aspects of an invention permits a simple proof of the thesis that it is impossible to predict technological development. At time t_1 it is logically impossible to predict the material details of the inventions that will be made at t_2, for a successful prediction would be equivalent to making the invention. We may assume, at least for the sake or argument, that it is possible at t_1 to predict the functional aspects of the inventions that will be made at t_2, but we cannot at t_1 predict the material or the functional aspects of the inventions that will be made at t_3, for some of these will arise directly out of the (unpredictable)

material aspects of the t_2 inventions and are therefore as unknowable at t_1 as are the latter.

59. Merton (1973, Part 4); Kroeber (1952).
60. Rosenberg (1974).
61. David (1969).
62. Fogel and Engerman (1974).
63. Stampp (1976).
64. Fogel and Engerman (1974, vol. II, p. 76).
65. The term is taken from Georgescu-Roegen (1971, p. 126), who asks 'Can socialist man be created so as not to show any hysteresis trace of his bourgeois or peasant past?' cf. also Elster (1976a).
66. Russel (1966).
67. Fogel (1967, p. 287).
68. Fogel and Engerman (1974, vol. I, pp. 247 ff.). The authors argue that the South had both a high income *per capita* and high rates of growth compared to most other countries, but the most relevant comparison would seem to be with the North, where income *per capita* was 40% higher than in the South, even if the growth rate was only 82% of that of the South.
69. For these problems, with full references to the literature, see Fogel and Engerman (1971) and Fogel and Engerman (1974, vol. II, pp. 54 ff.).
70. Conrad and Meyer (1958).
71. Fogel and Engerman (1971, vol. I, p. 71).
72. Cf. David and Temin (1976, p. 40) for a similar observation.
73. Genovese (1965, p. 278), criticized by A. H. Conrad (1967, p. 520) and Fogel and Engerman (1971, p. 321).
74. An exception being Marx (1867, p. 594): 'When a certain stage of development of capitalism has been reached, a conventional degree of prodigality, which is also an exhibition of wealth, and consequently a source of credit, becomes a necessity to the "unfortunate" capitalist. Luxury enters into capital's expenses of representation.' For details of the Hegel–Genovese model, see Elster (1976c).
75. Here and below I follow Yasuba (1961), as well as the further development of his work by Fogel and Engerman in the work cited in note 69 above.

References

Acton, H. B. (1967). Dialectical materialism, *The Encyclopedia of Philosophy*, New York: Macmillan.

Ainslie, G. (1975). Specious reward, *Psychological Bulletin*, **82**, 463–496.

Allen, R. G. D. (1966). *Mathematical Economics* 2nd edn. London: Macmillan.

Althusser, L. (1965). *Pour Marx*, Paris: Maspero.

Arrow, K. (1971a). *Essays in the Theory of Risk-Bearing*, Amsterdam: North-Holland.

Arrow, K. (1971b). Political and economic evaluation of social effects and externalities, in M. D. Intriligator (ed.), *Frontiers of Quantitative Economics*, Amsterdam: North-Holland.

Arrow, K. (1974). *The Limits of Organization*, New York: Norton.

Arrow, K. and Scitovsky, T. (eds.) (1969). *Readings in Welfare Economics*, London: Allen and Unwin.

Ashby, W. R. (1960). *Design for a Brain*, London: Chapman and Hall.

Ashby, W. R. (1971). *Introduction to Cybernetics*, London: Chapman and Hall.

Avineri, S. (1969). *The Social and Political Thought of Karl Marx*, Cambridge: Cambridge University Press.

Avineri, S. (1971). Consciousness and history: *List der Vernuft* in Hegel and Marx, in

W. E. Steinhaus (ed.), *New Studies in Hegel's Philosophy*, New York: Holt, Rinehart, and Winston.

Balacz, E. (1968). *La Bureaucratie Celeste*, Paris: Gallimard.

Bachrach, P. and Baratz, M. (1963), Decisions and nondecisions, *American Political Science Review*, **57**, 632–642.

Balibar, E. (1966). Les concepts fondamentaux du matéralisme historique, in L. Althusser *et al.*, *Lire le Capital*, vol. II, Paris: Maspero.

Bar-Hillel, Y., Perles, M., and Shamir, F. (1964). On formal properties of simple phrase structure grammers, in Y. Bar-Hillel, *Language and Information*, Reading, Mass.: Addison-Wesley.

Barnes, J. (1971). *Three Styles in the Study of Kinship*, London: Tavistock.

Barry, B. (1973). *The Liberal Theory of Justice*, Oxford: Oxford University Press.

Bateson, G. (1956). Towards a theory of schizophrenia, *Behavioral Science*, **1**, 251–264.

Bateson, G. (1972). *Steps to an Ecology of Mind*, New York: Ballantine Books.

Becker, G. (1962). Irrational behavior in economic theory, *Journal of Political Economy*, **70**, 1–13.

Benedict, B. (1972). Social regulation of fertility, in G. A. Harrison and A. J. Boyce (eds.), *The Structure of Human Populations*, Oxford: Oxford University Press.

Berge, C. (1963). *Topological Spaces*, Edinburgh: Oliver and Boyd.

Bernstein, E. (1899). *Die Voraussetzungen des Sozialismus*, quoted here after the 1967 edn. Hamburg: Rowohlt.

Bjørgum, J. (1976). Fagopposisjonen av 1911, *Tidsskrift for Arbeiderbevegelsens Historie* (Oslo), No. 1, 63–131.

Blau, P. and Duncan, O.D. (1967). *The American Occupational Structure*, New York: Wiley.

Bliss, C. J. (1975). *Capital Theory and the Distribution of Income*, Amsterdam: North-Holland.

Bloch, E. (1954). *Das Prinzip Hoffnung*, Berlin: Aufbau.

Böhm-Bawerk, E. von (1898), Karl Marx and the Close of his System, London: Unwin.

Boudon, R. (1973). *Mathematical Structures of Social Mobility*, Amsterdam: Elsevier.

Boudon, R. (1974). *Education, Opportunity and Social Inequality*, New York: Wiley.

Boudon, R. (1977). *Effects Pervers et Ordre Social*, Paris: Presses Universitaires de France.

Bourdieu, P., Chamboredon, J.-C. and Passeron, J.-C. (1968). *Le Métier de Sociologue*, Paris: Mouton.

Brams, S. (1976). *Paradoxes in Politics*, New York: Free Press.

Bródy, A. (1974). *Proportions, Prices and Planning*, Amsterdam: North-Holland.

Bronfenbrenner, M. (1965). *Das Kapital* for the modern man, *Science and Society*, **29**, 419–438.

Brooke, M. (1972). Problems in the decision-making process, in M. Brooke and H. Remmers (eds.), *The Multinational Company in Europe*, London: Longman.

Canarella, G. and Tomaske, J. (1975). The optimal utilization of slaves, *Journal of Economic History*.

Čapek, M. (1972). The fiction of instants, in J. T. Fraser *et al.* (eds.), *The Study of Time*, Berlin: Springer.

Chamley, P. (1963). *Economie Politique et Philosophie chez Steuart et Hegel*, Paris: Dalloz.

Chayanov, A. V. (1966). *The Theory of Peasant Economy*, Homewood, Ill.: Irwin.

Chomsky, N. (1957). *Syntactic Structures*, The Hague: Mouton.

Chomsky, N. (1959). On certain formal properties of grammars, *Information and Control*, **2**, 137–167.

Chomsky, N. (1964). Current issues in linguistic theory, in J.A. Fodor and J.J. Katz (eds.), *The Structure of Language*, Englewood Cliffs, NJ: Prentice-Hall.

Chomsky. N. and Miller, G. A. (1963). Finitary models of language users, in R. D. Luce, R. R. Bush, and E. Galanter (eds.), *Handbook of Mathematical Psychology*, vol. II, New York: Wiley.

Church, A. (1956). *Introduction to Mathematical Logic*, Princeton: Princeton University Press.

Clark, J. M. (1899). *The Distribution of Wealth*, New York: Macmillan.

Climo, T. A. and Howells, P. G. A. (1976). Possible worlds in historical explanation, *History and Theory*.

Cobb, W. E. (1973). Theft and the two hypotheses, in S. Rottenberg (ed.), *The Economics of Crime and Punishment*, Washington: American Enterprise Institute for Public Policy Research.

Coddington, A. (1968). *Theories of the Bargaining Process*, London: Allen and Unwin.

Cole, J. and Cole, S. (1973). *Social Stratification in Science*, Chicago: Chicago University Press.

Coleman, J. (1973a). *The Mathematics of Collective Action*, London: Heinemann.

Coleman, J. (1973b). Theoretical bases for parameters of stochastic processes, in P. Halmos (ed.), *Stochastic Processes in Sociology*, Monographs of the Sociological Review, No. 19.

Conrad, A. J. (1967). Contribution to 'Symposium on slavery as an obstacle to economic growth', *Journal of Economic History*, **27**, 518–560.

Conrad, A. J. and Meyer, J. (1958). The economics of slavery in the ante-bellum south, *Journal of Political Economy*, **66**, 95–122.

Cripps, T.F. and Tarling R. J. (1974). An analysis of the duration of male unemployment in Great Britain 1932–63, *Economic Journal*, **84**, 289–316.

David, P. (1969). Transport innovation and economic growth, *Economic History Review*, **22**, 506–525.

David, P. (1975). *Technical Choice, Innovation and Economic Growth*, Cambridge: Cambridge University Press.

David. P. and Temin, P. (1976). Capitalist masters, bourgeois slaves, in P. David *et al.*, *Reckoning with Slavery*, New York: Oxford University Press.

Davidson, D. (1963). Actions, reasons and causes, *Journal of Philosophy*, **60**, 685–700.

Davidson, D. (1969). How is weakness of the will possible?, in J. Feinberg (ed.), *Moral Concepts*, Oxford: Oxford University Press.

Davidson, D. (1970). Mental events, in L. Foster and J. W. Swanson (eds.), *Experience and Theory*, Cambridge, Mass.: University of Massachusetts Press.

Davidson, D. (1973). The material mind, in P. Suppes *et al.* (eds.), *Logic, Methodology and Philosophy of Science IV*, Amsterdam: North-Holland.

Deutsch, K. (1963). *The Nerves of Government*, Glencoe, Ill.: Free Press.

Dorfman, R., Samuelson, P., and Solow, R. (1958). *Linear Programming and Economic Analysis*, New York: McGraw-Hill.

Dubarle, D. (1970). Logique formalisante et logique Hégélienne, in J.d'Hondt (ed.), *Hegel et la Pensée Moderne*, Paris: Presses Universitaires de France.

Dummett, M. (1973). *Frege: Philosophy of Language*, London: Duckworth.

Duncan, O. D. (1966). Methodological issues in the analysis of social mobility, in N. J. Smelser and S. M. Lipset (eds.), *Social Structure and Mobility in Economic Development*, Chicago: Aldine.

Easton, D. (1965). *A Systems Analysis of Political Life*, New York: Wiley.

Eckstein, A. (1968). Economic fluctuations in Communist China, in Ping-ti Ho and Tang Tsou (eds.), *China in Crisis*, vol. I, Chicago: Chicago University Press.

Ehrenfest, P. and T. (1959). *Conceptual Foundations of Statistical Mechanics*, Ithaca, NY: Cornell University Press.

El-Safty, A. E. (1976). Adaptive behavior, demand and preferences, *Journal of Economic Theory*, **13**, 298–318.

Elster, J. (1972). Production et reproduction. Essai sur Marx, unpublished Thèse d'Etat, Université de Paris V.

Elster, J. (1975a). *Leibniz et la Formation de l'Esprit Capitaliste*, Paris: Aubier-Montaigne.

Elster, J. (1975b), Optimism and pessimism in the discussion of the standard of living during the Industrial Revolution in Britain, report to the XIV International Congress of the Historical Sciences, San Francisco.

Elster, J. (1976a). A note on hysteresis in the social sciences, *Synthese*, **33**, 371–391.

Elster, J. (1976b). Boudon, education and the theory of games, *Social Science Information*, **15**, 733–740.

Elster, J. (1976c). Some conceptual problems in political theory, in B. Barry (ed.), *Power and Political Theory*, London: Wiley.

Elster, J. (1976d). Ulysses and meta-rationality, paper presented to the ECPR Workshop on Political Theory, Louvain.

Elster, J. (1977). Beyond gradient-climbing, paper presented to the Fourth International Congress of the International Organization for the Study of Human Development.

Fararo, T. S. (1973). *Mathematical Sociology*, New York: Wiley.

Farquhar, J. E. (1964). *Ergodic Theory in Statistical Mechanics*, London: Wiley.

Feller, W. (1968). *An Introduction to Probability Theory and its Applications*, 3rd edn, vol. 1, New York: Wiley.

Fellin, P. and Litwak, E. (1963). Neighborhood cohesion under conditions of mobility, *American Sociological Review*, **28**, 364–376.

Fellner, W. (1961). Two propositions in the theory of induced innovations, *Economic Journal*, **71**, 305–308.

Festinger, L. (1957). *A Theory of Cognitive Dissonance*, Stanford: Stanford University Press.

Festinger, L. (1964). *Conflict, Decision and Dissonance*, London: Tavistock.

Finley, M. I. (1973a). *The Ancient Society*, London: Chatto and Windus.

Finley, M. I. (1973b). *Democracy: Ancient and Modern*, London: Chatto and Windus.

Fogel, R. W. (1964). *Railroads and American Economic Growth*, Baltimore: Johns Hopkins Press.

Fogel, R. W. (1967). The specification problem in economic history, *Journal of Economic History*, **27**, 283–308.

Fogel, R. W. and Engerman, S. (1971). The economics of slavery, in R. Fogel and S. Engerman (eds.), *The Reinterpretation of American Economic History*, New York: Harper and Row.

Fogel, R. W. and Engerman, S. (1974), *Time on the Cross*, Boston: Little, Brown.

Forrester, J. (1969). *Urban Dynamics*, Cambridge, Mass: MIT Press.

Freedman, J. L. and Sears, D. O. (1965). Selective exposure, in L. Berkowitz (ed.), *Advances in Experimental Psychology*, vol 2, New York: Academic Press.

Freud, S. (1968). Die Verneinung, in S. Freud, *Gesammelte Werke*, vol. XIV, Frankfurt a. M.: Fischer.

Gallagher, J. and Robinson, R. (1953). The imperialism of free trade, *Economic History Review*, **6**, 1–15.

Geach, P. (1972), *Logic Matters*, Berkeley and Los Angeles: University of California Press.

Genovese, E. (1965), *The Political Economy of Slavery*, New York: Pantheon Books.

Genovese, E. (1974), *Roll, Jordan, Roll*, New York: Pantheon Books.

Georgescu-Roegen, N. (1950), The theory of choice and the constancy of economic laws, *Quarterly Journal of Economics*, **64**, 125–138.

Georgescu-Roegen, N. (1968), Utility, in *The International Encyclopedia of the Social Sciences*, New York: Macmillan.

Georgescu-Roegen, N. (1971), *The Entropy Law and the Economic Process*, Cambridge, Mass.: Harvard University Press.

Germani. G. (1966), Social and political consequences of mobility, in N. J. Smelser and S. M. Lipset (eds.), *Social Structure and Mobility in Economic Development*, Chicago: Aldine.

Gerschenkron, A. (1965), Agrarian policies and industrialization: Russia 1861–1917, in H. J. Habakkuk and M. Postan (eds.), *Cambridge Economic History of Europe*, vol. VI, Cambridge: Cambridge University Press.

Gerschenkron, A. (1966), *Economic Backwardness in Historical Perspective*, Cambridge, Mass.: Harvard University Press.

Girod, R. (1971). *Mobilité Sociale*, Genève: Droz.

Glantz, S. A. and Albers, N. V. (1974). Department of Defense R & D in the university, *Science*, **186**, 706–711.

Godelier, M. (1966). Système, structure et contradiction dans *Le Capital*, *Les Temps Modernes*, **22**, 828–864.

Goldman, A. (1972). Toward a theory of social power, *Philosophical Studies*, **23**, 221–268.

Gorman, W. M. (1967). Tastes, habits and choices, *International Economic Review*, **8**, 218–222.

Graaff, J. de V. (1971). *Theoretical Welfare Economics*, Cambridge: Cambridge University Press.

Granovetter, M. (1973). The strength of weak ties, *American Journal of Sociology*, **78**, 1360–1380.

Guilbaud, G. Th. (1952). Les théories de l'intéret général et le problème logique de l'agrégation, *Economie Appliquée*, **5**, 501–584.

Günther, G. (1959). *Idee und Grundriss zu einer nicht-Aristotelischen Logik*, Hamburg: Felix Meiner.

Haavelmo, T. (1944). The probability approach in econometrics, *Econometrica* (Supplement), **12**, 1–118.

Haavelmo, T. (1970). Some observations on welfare and economic growth, in W. A. Eltis, M. Scott and N. Wolfe (eds.), *Induction, Growth and Trade: Essays in Honour of Sir Roy Harrod*, Oxford: Oxford University Press.

Haavelmo, T. (1971). Forventninger og deres Rolle i Økonomisk Teori, memorandum fra Sosialøkonomisk Institutt ved Universitetet i Oslo.

Habakkuk, H. J. (1971). *Population Growth and Economic Development since 1750*, Leicester: Leicester University Press.

Hamblin, C. L. (1970). *Fallacies*, London: Methuen.

Hammond, P. J. and Mirrlees, J. A. (1973). Agreeable plans, in J. A. Mirrlees and N. H. Stern (eds.), *Models of Economic Growth*, London: Macmillan.

Harcourt, G. C. (1973). *Some Cambridge Controversies in the Theory of Capital*, Cambridge: Cambridge University Press.

Hartwell, R. M. (1961). The rising standard of living in England 1800–1850, *Economic History Review*, **13**, 397–416.

Hartwell, R. M. and Engerman, S. (1975). Models of immiseration: The theoretical basis of pessimism, in A. J. Taylor (ed.), *The Standard of Living in Britain in the Industrial Revolution*, London: Methuen.

Hayek, F. A. (1954). Introduction to F. A. Hayek *et al.*, *Capitalism and the Historians*, Chicago: Chicago University Press.

Hayek, F. A. (1967). The results of human action but not of human design, in F. A. Hayek, *Studies in Philosophy, Politics and Economics*, London: Routledge.

Heal, G. M. (1973). *The Theory of Economic Planning*, Amsterdam: North-Holland.

Hegel, G. W. F. (1961). *The Science of Logic*, London: Allen and Unwin.

Hegel, G. W. F. (1970). *Werke in 20 Bänden*, Frankfurt a. M.: Suhrkamp.

Henderson, W. O. and Chaloner, W. H. (1958). Introduction to F. Engels, *The Conditions of the Working Class in England*, Oxford: Oxford University Press.

Hintikka, J. (1961). *Knowledge and Belief*, Ithaca, NY: Cornell University Press.

Hintikka, J. (1967). *Cogito, ergo sum*: Inference or performance?, in W. Doney (ed.), *Descartes*, London: Macmillan.

Hintikka, J. (1972). Leibniz on plenitude, relations and the 'Reign of law', in H. G. Frankfurt (ed.), *Leibniz*, New York: Anchor Books.

Hintikka, J. (1973). *Logic, Language-Games and Information*, Oxford: Oxford University Press.

Hirschman, A. O. (1958). *The Strategy of Economic Development*, New Haven: Yale University Press.

Hirschman, A. O. (1970). *Exit, Voice and Loyalty*, Cambridge, Mass.: Harvard University Press.

226

Hirschman, A. O. (1973). Changing tolerance for inequality, *Quarterly Journal of Economics*, **87**, 544–566.

Hobsbawm, E. (1954). The general crisis of the 17th-century, *Past and Present*, No. 5, Part I, 33–53; No. 6, Part II, 44–65.

Hobsbawm, E. (1957). The British standard of living 1790–1850, *Economic History Review*, **10**, 46–61.

Hobsbawm, E. (1963). The standard of living during the Industrial Revolution, *Economic History Review*, **16**, 120–134.

Hockett, C. F. (1955). *A Manual of Phonology*, Baltimore: Memoir 11 of *International Journal of American Linguistics*.

Hoel, M. (1974). Kryssløp, Arbeidsverdier og Priser, *Statsøkonomisk Tidsskrift*, **88**, 57–88.

d'Hondt, J. (1970). Téléologie et praxis dans la logique de Hegel, in J. D.'Hondt (ed.), *Hegel et la Pensée Moderne*, Paris: Presses Universitaires de France.

Howard, N. (1971), *Paradoxes of Rationality*, Cambridge, Mass.: MIT Press.

Hughes, G. E. and Cresswell, M. J. (1972), *An Introduction to Modal Logic*, London: Methuen.

Hull, D. (1965). The effect of essentialism on taxonomy, *British Journal for the Philosophy of Science*, **15**, 314–326.

Hume, D. (1748), *An Enquiry into Human Understanding*.

Husserl, E. (1913). *Logische Untersuchungen*, vol. I: *Prolegomena*, 2nd edn, Tübingen: Max Niemeyer.

Husserl, E. (1966). *Husserliana*, vol. X, Haag: Martinus Nijhoff.

Husserl, E. (1967). *Husserliana*, vol. XI, Haag: Martinus Nijhoff.

Hyppolite, J. (1946). *Genèse et Structure de la Phénoménologie de l'Esprit de Hegel*, Paris: Aubier-Montaigne.

Hyppolite, J. (1966). Commentaire parlé sur la 'Verneinung' de Freud, in J. Lacan, *Ecrits*, Paris: Editions du Seuil.

Ishiguro, H. (1972a), Leibniz's theory of the ideality of relations, in H. G. Frankfurt (ed.), *Leibniz*, New York: Anchor Books.

Ishiguro, H. (1972b). *Leibniz's Philosophy of Logic and Language*, London: Duckworth.

Isnard, C. A. and Zeeman, E. C. (1974). Some models from catastrophe theory in the social sciences, in L. Collins (ed.), *Use of Models in the Social Sciences*, London: Tavistock.

Jakobson, R. and Halle, M. (1963). Phonologie et phonétique, in R. Jakobson, *Essais de Linguistique Génerale*, Paris: Editions de Minuit.

Johansson, I. (1936). Der Minimalkalkül, *Compositio Mathematica*, **4**, 119–136.

Kalecki, M. (1943), Political aspects of full employment, *Political Quarterly*, **14**, 322–331.

Kanger, S. and Kanger, H. (1966). Rights and parliamentarism, *Theoria*, **32**, 85–115.

Kaplan, M. (1967). Systems theory, in J. C. Charlesworth (ed.), *Contemporary Political Analysis*, New York: Free Press.

Kemeny, J. G., Snell, J. L., and Thompson, G. L. (1966). *Introduction to Finite Mathematics*, 2nd edn. Englewood Cliffs, N J: Prentice-Hall.

Kenny, A. (1963). *Action, Emotion and Will*, London: Routledge.

Kenny, A. (1965–66). Happiness, *Proceedings of the Aristotelian Society*, **66** (N. S.), 93–102.

Kenny, A. (1970). Intention and purpose in law, in R. S. Summers (ed.), *Essays in Legal Philosophy*, Oxford: Blackwell.

Kerr, C. and Siegel, A. (1964). The inter-industry propensity to strike. in C. Kerr, *Labor and Management in Industrial Society*, New York: Anchor Books.

Keynes, J. M. (1936). *The General Theory of Employment, Interest and Money*, London: Macmillan.

Keynes, J. M. (1971). *A Treatise on Money*, vol. V of *The Collected Works of John Maynard Keynes*, London: Macmillan.

Kindleberger, C. (1975). The rise of free trade in Western Europe 1820–75, *Journal of Economic History*, **35**, 20–55.

Körner, S. (1976). *Experience and Conduct*, Cambridge: Cambridge University Press.

Koyre, A. (1971), *Etudes de l'Histoire de la Pensée Philosophique*, Paris: Gallimard.

Kripke, S. (1972). Naming and necessity, in D. Davidson and G. Harman (eds.). *Semantics of Natural Language*, Dordrecht: Reidel.

Kroeber, A. (1952). The superorganic, in A Kroeber, *The Nature of Culture*, Chicago: Chicago University Press.

Lacan, J. (1966). *Ecrits*, Paris: Editions du Seuil.

Lancaster, K. (1973). The dynamic inefficiency of capitalism, *Journal of Political Economy*, **81**, 1092-1109.

Laplanche, J. (1970). *Vie et Mort en Psychanalyse*, Paris: Flammarion.

Latsis, S. (1976). A research programme in economics, in S. Latsis (ed.), *Methods and Appraisal in Economics*, Cambridge: Cambridge University Press.

Lave, C. A. and March, J. G. (1975). *An Introduction to Models in the Social Sciences*, New York: Harper and Row.

Lazarsfeld, P. A. and Menzel, H. (1969). On the relation between individual and collective properties, in A. Etzioni (ed.), *A Sociological Reader on Complex Organizations*, New York: Holt, Rinehart; and Winston.

Lee, H. P. D. (1936). *Zeno of Elea*, Cambridge: Cambridge University Press.

Leibenstein, H. (1976). *Beyond Economic Man*, Cambridge, Mass.: Harvard University Press.

Leibniz, G. W. (1875-90). *Die Philosophische Schriften*, ed. Gerhardt, Berlin: Weidmannsche Buchhandlung.

Leibniz, G. W. (1903). *Opuscules et Fragments Inédits*, ed. Couturat, Paris: Presses Universitaires de France.

Leibniz, G. W. (1948). *Textes Inédits*, ed. Grua, Paris: Presses Universitaires de France.

Leijonhufvud, A. (1976), Schools, 'revolutions' and research programmes in economic theory, in S. Latsis (ed.), *Methods and Appraisal in Economics*, Cambridge: Cambridge University Press.

Lévi-Strauss, C. (1958). *Anthropologie Structurale*, Paris: Plon.

Lévi-Strauss, C. (1967). *Les Structures Elémentaires de la Parenté*, Paris–The Hague: Mouton.

Lévi-Strauss, C. (1967-71). *Mythologiques*, I–IV, Paris: Plon.

Lévi-Strauss, C. (1973). *Anthropologie Structurale Deux*, Paris: Plon.

Lewis, C. I. and Langford, C. H. (1932). *Symbolic Logic*, New York: Dover.

Lewis, D. (1968). Counterpart theory and quantified modal logic, *Journal of Philosophy*, **65**, 113-126.

Lewis, D. (1973a). Causation, *Journal of Philosophy*, **70**, 556-567.

Lewis, D. (1973b). *Counterfactuals*, Oxford: Blackwell.

Lindbeck, A. (1976). Stabilization policy in open economies with endogenous politicians, *American Economic Review: Papers and Proceedings*, **66**, 1-19.

Lipset, S. M. and Bendix, R. (1959). *Social Mobility in Industrial Society*, Berkeley and Los Angeles: University of California Press.

Lipset, S. M. and Gordon, J. (1953), Mobility and trade union membership, in S. M. Lipset and R. Bendix (eds.), *Class, Status and Power*, Glencoe, Ill.: Free Press.

Loschky, D. J. (1973). Studies of the Navigation Acts: New economic non-history, *Economic History Review*, **26**, 689-691.

Luce, R. D. and Raiffa, H. (1957). *Games and Decisions*, New York: Wiley.

Luxemburg, R. (1899). *Sozialreform order Revolution?*, in *Gesammelte Werke*, vol. 1/1, Berlin: Dietz, 1970.

Luxemburg, R. (1906). *Massenstreik, Partei und Gewerkschaften*, in *Gesammelte Werke*, vol. 2, Berlin: Dietz, 1972.

Lyons, D. (1965). *Forms and Limits of Utilitarianism*, Oxford: Oxford University Press.

Maarek, E. (1975). *Introduction au Capital de Karl Marx*, Paris: Calmann-Lévy.

McClelland, P. D. (1975). *Causal Explanation and Model-Building in History, Economics and the New Economic History*, Ithaca, NY: Cornell University Press.

228

McFarland, D. (1970). Intergenerational social mobility as a Markov process, *American Sociological Review*, **35**, 463–476.

McFarland, D. (1976). Putting goal-oriented actors into Harrison White's vacancy chains, paper presented to the Annual Meeting of the American Sociological Association, New York.

McGuire, W. J. (1966). The status of cognitive consistency theories, in S. Feldman (ed.), *Cognitive Consistency*, New York: Academic Press.

MacIntyre, A. (1962). A mistake about causality in the social sciences, in P. Laslett and W. C. Runciman (eds.), *Politics, Philosophy and Society*, 2nd Series, Oxford: Blackwell.

Mackie, J. L. (1965). Causes and conditions, *American Philosophical Quarterly*, **2**, 245–264.

Mackie, J. L. (1967). Fallacies, *The Encyclopedia of Philosophy*, New York: Macmillan.

Mandeville, B. (1729). *The Fable of the Bees*, 6th edn, London.

Manning, P. (1974). Analysing the costs and benefits of colonialism, *African Economic History Review*, **1**, 15–22.

Marx, K. (1845–46). *Die Deutsche Ideologie*, in *Marx-Engels Werke*, vol 3, Berlin: Dietz.

Marx, K. (1847). Die moralisierende Kritik und die kritisierende Moral, in *Marx-Engels Werke*, vol. 4, Berlin: Dietz.

Marx, K. (1850). *The Class Struggles in France*, quoted after the edition New York: International Publishers, 1935.

Marx, K. (1857). The secret diplomatic history of the 18th century, quoted from the reprint in R. Payne (ed.), *The Unknown Karl Marx*, New York: New York University Press.

Marx, K. (1857–58). *Grundrisse der Kritik der politischen Ökonomie*, quoted from the Pelican translation, London 1973.

Marx, K. (1862–63). *Theorien über den Mehrwert*, in *Marx-Engels Werke*, vol. 26, Berlin: Dietz.

Marx, K. (1867). *Capital I*, New York: International Publishers.

Marx, K. (1871). *The Civil War in France*, quoted after the edition Moscow: Foreign Languages Publishing House, 1952.

Marx, K. (1879–80). Randglossen zu Adolph Wagners 'Lehrbuch der politischen Ökonomie', in *Marx-Engels Werke*, vol. 19, Berlin: Dietz.

Marx, K. (1894). *Capital III*, New York: International Publishers.

Marx, K. (1933). Resultate des unmittelbaren Produktionsprozesses, *Arkhiv Marksa i Engelsa*, II (VII).

Mates, B. (1968), "Leibniz on possible worlds", in B. van Rootselaar and J. F. Staal (eds.), *Logic, Methodology and Philosophy of Science III*, Amsterdam: North-Holland.

Meisner, M. (1967). *Li Ta-chao and the Origins of Chinese Communism*, Cambridge, Mass.: Harvard University Press.

Merleau-Ponty, M. (1945). *Phénoménologie de la Perception*, Paris: Gallimard.

Merleau-Ponty, M. (1963). *La Structure du Comportement*, Paris: Presses Universitaires de France.

Merton, R. (1936). The unanticipated consequences of purposive social action, *American Sociological Review*, **1**, 894–904.

Merton, R. (1957). *Social Theory and Social Structure*, Glencoe, Ill.: Free Press.

Merton, R. (1973). *The Sociology of Science*, Chicago: Chicago University Press.

Milgram, S. (1974), *Obedience to Authority*, London: Tavistock.

Mill, J. S. (1967), *A System of Logic*, London: Longman.

Mondadori, F. (1973), Reference, essentialism and modality in Leibniz's metaphysics, *Studia Leibnitiana*, **5**, 74–101.

Moore, G. E. (1922), External and internal relations, in G. E. Moore, *Philosophical Studies*, London: Routledge.

Morishima, M. (1973). *Marx's Economics*, Oxford: Oxford University Press.

Mortimore, G. W. (ed.) (1971). *Weakness of Will*, London: Macmillan.

Mukherjee, R. (1954). A study of mobility between three generations, in D. Glass (ed.), *Social Mobility in Britain*, London: Routledge.

Nagel, E. (1963). Assumptions in economic theory, *American Economic Review*, **53**, 211–236.

Nathan, A. (1976). Policy oscillations in the People's Republic of China: A critique, *China Quarterly*, **68**, 720–733.

Needham, R. (1962). *Structure and Sentiment*, Chicago: Chicago University Press.

Neher, P. (1971). Peasants, procreation and pensions, *American Economic Review*, **61**, 380–389.

Nordhaus, W. (1975). The political business cycle, *Review of Economic Studies*, **42**, 169–190.

North, D. (1971). Institutional change and economic growth, *Journal of Economic History*.

North, D. and Davis, L. (1971). *Institutional Change and American Economic Growth*, Cambridge: Cambridge University Press.

North, D. and Thomas, R. P. (1973). *The Rise of the Western World*, Cambridge: Cambridge University Press.

Nozick, R. (1969). Newcomb's problem and two principles of choice, in N. Rescher (ed.), *Essays in Honor of Carl G. Hempel*, Dordrecht: Reidel.

Nozick, R. (1974). *Anarchy, State and Utopia*, Oxford: Blackwell.

Nuti, D. M. (1970). Capitalism, socialism and steady growth, *Economic Journal*, **80**, 32–57.

Nutini, H. G. (1970), Some considerations on the nature of social structure and model building, in E. N. Hayes and T. Hayes (eds.), *Claude Levi-Strauss: The Anthropologist as Hero*, Cambridge, Mass. : The M. I. T. Press.

Okun, A. (1975). *Equality and Efficiency: The Big Trade-Off*, Washington: The Brookings Institution.

Olson, M. (1963). *The Logic of Collective Action*, Cambridge, Mass.: Harvard University Press.

Ollman, B. (1976). *Alienation: Marx's Concept of Man in Capitalist Society*, 2nd edn, Cambridge: Cambridge University Press.

Owen, G. (1968), *Game Theory*, Philadelphia: Saunders.

Parsons, T. (1949). *The Structure of Social Action*, Glencoe, Ill. : Free Press.

Pen, A. (1959). *The Wage Rate under Collective Bargaining*, Cambridge, Mass.: Harvard University Press.

Perkins, H. (1969). *The Origins of Modern English Society: 1780–1880*, London: Routledge.

Peyrefitte, A. (1976). *Le Mal Francais*, Paris: Plon.

Phelps, E. S. and Pollak, R. A. (1968). On second-best national saving and game-equilibrium growth, *Review of Economic Studies*, **35**, 185–199.

Pollak, R. A. (1968). Consistent planning, *Review of Economic Studies*, **35**, 201–208.

Pollak, R. A. (1976a). Habit-formation and long-run utility functions, *Journal of Economic Theory*, **13**, 272–297.

Pollak, R. A. (1976b). Interdependent preferences, *American Economic Review*, **66**, 309–320

Popper, K. (1940). What is dialectic?, *Mind*, **49**, 403–426.

Popper, K. (1963). *Conjectures and Refutations*, London: Routledge.

Pörn, I. (1970). *The Logic of Power*, Oxford: Blackwell.

Portal, R. (1965). The industrialization of Russia, in H. J. Habakkuk and M. Postan (eds.), *Cambridge Economic History of Europe*, Cambridge: Cambridge University Press.

Postal, P. M. (1964). Limitations of phrase structure grammars, in J. A. Fodor and J. J. Katz (eds.), *The Structure of Language*, Englewood Cliffs, N. J.: Prentice-Hall.

Prior, A. N. (1967), *Past, Present and Future*, Oxford: Oxford University Press.

Quine, W. V. O. (1953). *From a Logical Point of View*, Cambridge, Mass.: Harvard University Press.

Quine, W. V. O. (1959). *Methods of Logic*, New York: Holt-Dryden.

Quine, W. V. O. (1960). *Word and Object*, New York: Wiley.

Quirk, J. and Saposnik, R. (1968). *Introduction to General Equilibrium Theory and Welfare Economics*, New York: McGraw-Hill.

Rabin, M. and Scott, D. (1959). Finite automata and their decision problems, *IBM Journal of Research and Development*, **3**, 114–125.

Rader, T. (1971). *The Economics of Feudalism*, New York: Gordon and Breach.

Raiffa, H. (1968). *Decision Analysis*, Reading, Mass.: Addison-Wesley.

Rapoport, A. (1966), *Two-Person Game Theory*, Ann Arbor: University of Michigan Press.

Rapoport, A. (1975), Comment on Bram's discussion of Newcomb's problem, *Journal of Conflict Resolution*, **19**, 613–619.

Rapoport, A. and Chammah, A. (1965), *Prisoner's Dilemma*, Ann Arbor: University of Michigan Press.

Rapoport, A. Guyer, M. and Gordon, D. (1976). *The 2 × 2 Game*, Ann Arbor: University of Michigan Press.

Rawls, J. (1971). *A Theory of Justice*, Cambridge, Mass.: Harvard University Press.

Rescher, N. (1967). *The Philosophy of Leibniz*, Englewood Cliffs, NJ: Prentice-Hall.

Rescher, N. and Urquhard, A. (1971). *Temporal Logic*, Vienna New York: Springer.

Riker, W. and Ordeshook, P. C. (1973). *An Introduction to Positive Political Theory*, Englewood Cliffs, NJ: Prentice-Hall.

Robinson, J. (1956). *The Accumulation of Capital*, London: Macmillan.

Rorty, R. (1967). External and internal relations, *The Encyclopedia of Philosophy*, New York: Macmillan.

Rosenberg, N. (1974). Science, invention and economic growth, *Economic Journal*, **84**, 90–108.

Russel, R. (1941). The effects of slavery upon nonslaveholders in the ante-bellum South, in H. D. Woodman (ed.), *Slavery and the Southern Economy*, New York: Pantheon.

Russell, B. (1905). On denoting, *Mind*, **14**, 479–493.

Russell, B. (1910). Some explanation in reply to Mr. Bradley, *Mind*, **19**, 373–378.

Russell, B. (1938). *Power*, London and New York: Norton.

Salter, W. (1960). *Productivity and Technical Change*, Cambridge: Cambridge University Press.

Salthe, S. N. (1972). *Evolutionary Biology*, New York: Holt, Rinehart, and Winston.

Samuelson, P. (1950). The evaluation of real national income, *Oxford Economic Papers*, **2**, 1–29.

Samuelson, P. (1957). Wages and interest, *American Economic Review*, **48**, 884–912.

Sartre, J. P. (1943). *L'Etre et le Néant*, Paris: Gallimard.

Sartre, J. P. (1960). *Critique de la Raison Dialectique*, Paris: Gallimard.

Schelling, T. S. (1971), Dynamic models of segregation, *Journal of Mathematical Sociology*, **1**, 143–186.

Schmookler, J. (1966). *Inventions and Economic Growth*, Cambridge, Mass.: Harvard University Press.

Schumpeter, J. A. (1951). *Imperialism and Social Classes*, New York: Kelley.

Schumpeter, J. A. (1953). *Capitalism, Socialism and Democracy*, London: Allen and Unwin.

Schumpeter, J. A. (1954). *A History of Economic Analysis*, London: Allen and Unwin.

Schurmann, F. (1967). *Ideology and Organization in Communist China*, Berkeley and Los Angeles: University of California Press.

Scitovsky, T. (1971). *Welfare and Competition*, London: Allen and Unwin.

Seip, J. A. (1958). *Teorien om det Opinionsstyrte Enevelde*, Oslo: Universitetsforlaget.

Sejersted, F. (1975), En Teori om Embedsmannsstaten, Oslo, Historisk Institutt (mimeo).

Selden, M. (1971). *The Yenan Way in Revolutionary China*, Cambridge, Mass.: Harvard University Press.

Sen, A. K. (1967). Isolation, assurance and the social rate of discount, *Quarterly Journal of Economics*, **80**, 112–124.

Sen, A. K. (1970). *Collective Choice and Social Welfare*, San Francisco: Holden-Day.

Sen, A. K. (1973). *On Economic Inequality*, Oxford: Oxford University Press.

Sen, A. K. (1976). Real national income, *Review of Economic Studies*, **42**, 19–39.

Shubik, M. (1970). Game theory, behavior and the paradox of the prisoner's dilemma, *Journal of Conflict Resolution*, **14**, 181–202.

Simensen, J. (1977), Counterfactual arguments in historical analysis. From the debate on the partition of Africa and the effect of colonial rule, Mimeo.

Simmel, G. (1908). *Soziologie*, Berlin: Duncker und Humblot.

Simon, H. (1953). Notes on the observation and measurement of political power, *Journal of Politics*, **15**, 500–516.

Simon, H. (1954a), Bandwagon and underdog effects in election predictions, *Public Opinion Quarterly*, **18**, 245–253.

Simon, H. (1954b), A behavioral theory of rational choice, *Quarterly Journal of Economics*, **69**, 99–118.

Singer, J. E. (1966). Motivation for consistency, in S. Feldman (ed.), *Cognitive Consistency*, New York: Academic Press.

Singer, M. (1963). *Generalization in Ethics*, London: Eyre and Spottiswoode.

Skinner, G. W. and Winckler, E. A. (1969). Compliance succession in rural Communist China: A cyclical theory, in A. Etzioni (ed.), *A Sociological Reader on Complex Organizations*, New York: Holt, Rinehart, and Winston.

Smelser, N. (1959). *Social Change in the Industrial Revolution*, London: Routledge.

Smith, J. (1968). Transportation, in *The International Encyclopedia of the Social Sciences*, New York: Macmillan.

Snyder, D. P. (1971). *Modal Logic and its Applications*, New York: van Nostrand, Reinhold.

Sobel, J. H. (1967). 'Everyone', consequences and generalization arguments, *Inquiry*, **10**, 373–404.

Sosa, E. (1975). Introduction to E. Sosa (ed.), *Causation and Conditionals*, Oxford: Oxford University Press.

Staaf, R. and Tannian, F. (eds.) (1972). *Externalities*, New York: Dunnellen.

Stalnaker, R. (1968). A theory of conditionals in N. Rescher (ed.), *Studies in Logical Theory*, Oxford: Blackwell.

Stampp, K. (1976). Introduction to P. David *et al.*, *Reckoning with Slavery*, New York: Oxford University Press.

Stinchcombe, A. (1968). *Constructing Social Theories*, New York: Harcourt, Brace and World.

Stouffer, S. A. *et al.* (1949). *The American Soldier*, Princeton: Princeton University Press.

Strotz, R. H. (1955–56). Myopia and inconsistency in dynamic utility maximization, *Review of Economic Studies*, **23**, 165–180.

Suttmeier, R. (1974). *Research and Revolution*, Lexington, Mass.: Lexington Books.

Sweezy, P. (1962). *The Theory of Capitalist Development*, London: Dennis Dobson.

Takayama, A. (1974). *Mathematical Economics*, Hinsdale, Ill.: The Dryden Press.

Taylor, A. J. (1960). Progress and poverty in Britain 1750–1850, *History*, **45**, 16–31.

Taylor, C. (1971). Interpretation and the sciences of man, *Review of Metaphysics*, **25**, 3–51.

Taylor, M. (1976). *Anarchy and Cooperation*, London: Wiley.

Taylor, M. (1977). Altruism and cooperation: Their evolution by natural selection and their role in primitive societies, Mimeo.

Thalheimer, A. (1930). Über den Faschismus, in W. Abendroth (ed.), *Fascismus und Kapitalismus*, Frankfurt Vienna: Europäische Verlagsanstalt 1967.

Thernstrom, S. (1970). Working class social mobility in industrial America, in M. H. Richter (ed.), *Essays in Theory and History*, Cambridge, Mass.: Harvard University Press.

232

Thernstrom, S. (1973). *The Other Bostonians*, Cambridge, Mass.: Harvard University Press.

Thomas, R. P. (1965). A quantitative approach to the study of the effects of British imperial policy upon colonial welfare, *Journal of Economic History*, **25**, 615–638.

Thompson, E. P. (1968). *The Making of the English Working Class*, Harmondsworth: Pelican Books.

Thompson, E. P. (1971). The moral economy of the English crowd in the 18th century, *Past and Present*, **50**, 76–136.

Trotsky, L. (1972). *1905*, London: Allen Lane.

Tullock, G. (1974). Does punishment deter crime?, *The Public Interest*, **36**, 103–111.

Ullman-Margalit, E. (1976). The generalization argument, *Journal of Philosophy*, **73**, 511–522.

Vendler, Z. (1967). Any and all, *The Encyclopedia of Philosophy*, New York: Macmillan.

Vernon, R. (1971). *Sovereignty at Bay*, London: Longman.

Vlastos, G. (1967). Zeno of Elea, *The Encyclopedia of Philosophy*, New York: Macmillan.

Walton, G. (1971). The new economic history and the burdens of the Navigation Acts, *Economic History Review*, **24**, 533–542.

Watzlawick, P. H., Beavin, J. and Jackson, D. (1967). *Pragmatics of Human Communication*, New York: Norton.

Weber, M. (1968). Objektive Möglichkeit and adäquate Verursachung in der historischen Kausalbetrachtung, in M. Weber, *Gesammelte Aufsätze zur Wissenschaftlehre*, Tübingen: Mohr.

Weil, E. (1966). *Hegel et l'Etat*, Paris: Vrin.

Weiszäcker, C. C. von (1971a), Notes on endogenous change of tastes, *Journal of Economic Theory*, **3**, 345–372.

Weiszäcker, C. C. von (1971b), *Steady-State Capital Theory*, New York: Springer.

Whitrow, G. (1961). *The Natural Philosophy of Time*, Edinburgh: Nelson.

Wildavsky, A. (1964). *The Politics of the Budgeting Process*, Boston: Little, Brown.

Wilensky, E. and Edwards, H. (1959). The skidder, *American Sociological Review*, **24**, 215–231.

Williams, G. C. (1966), *Adaptation and Natural Selection*, Princeton: Princeton University Press.

Winch, P. (1958). *The Idea of a Social Science*, London: Routledge.

Winckler, E. (1976). Policy oscillations in the People's Republic of China: A reply, *China Quarterly*, **68**, 734–750.

Winter, S. G. (1964). Economic 'Natural selection' and the theory of the firm, *Yale Economic Essays*, **4**, 225–272.

Winter, S. G. (1975). Optimization and evolution, in R. H. Day and T. Groves (eds.), *Adaptive Economic Models*, New York: Academic Press.

Wittgenstein, L. (1953). *Philosophische Untersuchungen*, Oxford: Blackwell.

Yasuba, Y. (1961). The profitability and viability of plantation slavery in the United States, *The Economic Quarterly Studies Review*, **12**, 60–67.

Young, G. (1976). The fundamental contradiction of capitalist production, *Philosophy and Public Affairs*, **5**, 196–234.

INDEX

234

ELSTER